Arabic

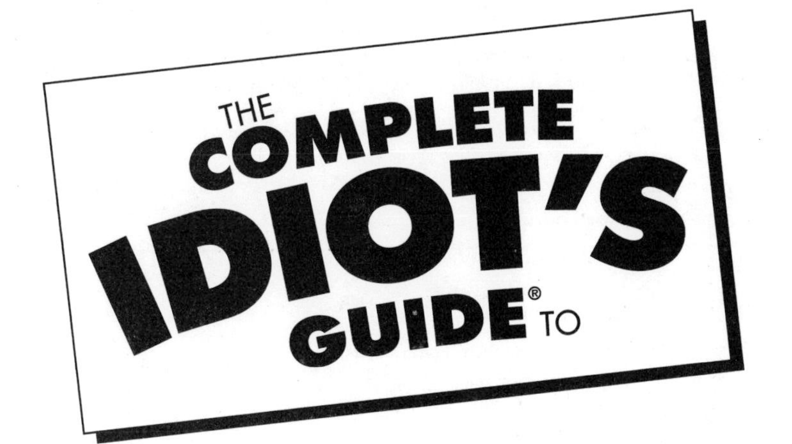

Arabic

by K.F. Habel

A member of Penguin Group (USA) Inc.

For Club M.E.B. I'll see you when I see you.

ALPHA BOOKS

Published by the Penguin Group

Penguin Group (USA) Inc., 375 Hudson Street, New York, New York 10014, U.S.A.

Penguin Group (Canada), 10 Alcorn Avenue, Toronto, Ontario, Canada M4V 3B2 (a division of Pearson Penguin Canada Inc.)

Penguin Books Ltd, 80 Strand, London WC2R 0RL, England

Penguin Ireland, 25 St Stephen's Green, Dublin 2, Ireland (a division of Penguin Books Ltd)

Penguin Group (Australia), 250 Camberwell Road, Camberwell, Victoria 3124, Australia (a division of Pearson Australia Group Pty Ltd)

Penguin Books India Pvt Ltd, 11 Community Centre, Panchsheel Park, New Delhi—110 017, India

Penguin Group (NZ), cnr Airborne and Rosedale Roads, Albany, Auckland 1310, New Zealand (a division of Pearson New Zealand Ltd)

Penguin Books (South Africa) (Pty) Ltd, 24 Sturdee Avenue, Rosebank, Johannesburg 2196, South Africa

Penguin Books Ltd, Registered Offices: 80 Strand, London WC2R 0RL, England

International Standard Book Number: 978-1-59257-703-3

Library of Congress Catalog Card Number: 2007939740

10 09 08 8 7 6 5 4 3 2 1

Interpretation of the printing code: The rightmost number of the first series of numbers is the year of the book's printing; the rightmost number of the second series of numbers is the number of the book's printing. For example, a printing code of 08-1 shows that the first printing occurred in 2008.

Printed in the United States of America

Publisher: *Marie Butler-Knight*
Editorial Director: *Mike Sanders*
Senior Managing Editor: *Billy Fields*
Development Editor: *Ginny Bess Munroe*
Production Editor: *Megan Douglass*
Copy Editor: *Lisanne V. Jensen*
Cartoonist: *Steve Barr*
Cover Designer: *Bill Thomas*
Book Designer: *Trina Wurst*
Indexer: *Johnna Vanhoose Dinse*
Layout: *Chad Dressler*
Proofreader: *John Etchison*

Contents at a Glance

Contents

Introduction

***mar**-Ha-ban*, and welcome to *The Complete Idiot's Guide to Arabic*. In case you haven't noticed, teaching Arabic is becoming more and more popular in schools around the world. And why not? It is a beautiful language.

So what exactly *is* this book? Well, I'll start by telling you what this book is *not*. This book is *not* a complete Arabic course. A truly *complete* Arabic course would require several volumes, and because you are looking for an *Idiot's Guide*, you probably don't have enough time to go through several volumes to learn the language.

This book is also *not* designed for the advanced student of Arabic. Although I would like to think that even advanced students of Arabic could benefit from some of the study tips and information in this book, the odds are that more advanced students have already learned what this book has to offer.

Finally, this book *does not* answer all of the challenges that are involved with presenting Arabic to an English-speaking audience. As far as I can tell from my own research, there is no single book in existence that answers *all* of the challenges presented by teaching Arabic to English speakers. If you know of that book, please inform me so that I may add it to my personal library and begin recommending it to my colleagues.

So that brings us back to what this book *is*. This book is an introduction to the spoken Arabic language, based on Modern Standard Arabic. I chose Modern Standard Arabic as opposed to any of several spoken dialects because Modern Standard is the language that will be understood by the highest number of Arabic speakers (even if the language sometimes sounds a bit too proper for everyday speech).

If you have no experience with Arabic, then this book is a perfect introduction to the language—because you will find a wealth of common phrases from which to build your Arabic vocabulary. If you are concerned with learning a dialect and think that it might be better to study a particular dialect first, I would remind you that many words used in dialect are nothing more than shortened versions of words from standard Arabic. If you learn the proper words first, you will have no problem learning the dialect when your language skills improve.

When writing this book, I kept you—the beginning Arabic student—in mind at all times. Arabic is among the world's most difficult languages for English speakers to learn, and condensing lessons into an *Idiot's Guide* proved to be quite a task. I think you will be happy with the results.

So how does the book work? Well, you read the chapters, listen to the accompanying CD, and learn how to speak some Arabic. It's pretty simple, really. In the beginning, I teach you a bit of geography and culture. Then, we jump straight into the lessons. You start with basic greetings, then move into a (very short) set of grammar lessons. After that, it's full speed ahead. I present you with guidance on how you can use words and phrases (and of course show you those words and phrases), and you are expected to learn.

This book does not contain many long sentences or paragraphs that I expect you to rehearse and memorize. Lessons are generally short, with the expectation that you will return to them several times. My experience in learning Arabic and working with other linguists over the years has shown that if you want to learn to speak, you are going to have to learn to put sentences together for yourself. By filling the pages with sentences I create, you might quickly grow bored and put the book on a shelf. We don't want that to happen. I want you to learn to speak Arabic, and I fully believe you can do it. In fact, I believe you are the type of person who loves to teach yourself—and that is what led you to pick up this book in the first place. So if that sounds like you, then I wish you good luck.

Arabic Sounds and Script

So how does Arabic compare to English? Well, judging by looks alone, I would have to say that Arabic and English don't have much in common—at least, not at first glance. The truth is that any language can be learned (most of us have learned at least one in our lifetime), and if one language can be learned, why not another? Arabic does share some vocabulary with English, and it had a strong influence on the development of Spanish over the past centuries.

I remember my first days learning Arabic. I looked at the printed page and thought to myself, "Bubble … bubble … cloud … dot … dot … I'm *never* going to learn this!" Thankfully, I was wrong. I just had to change my way of thinking.

Arabic presents several problems for the new student. The language is written from right to left, top to bottom. The sounds of the language are created in different parts of the mouth and throat than we English speakers are used to (you'll see what I mean in Chapter 2). Until recently, very few resources were available to Arabic students—and those available were only accessible to students who knew where to look. Only those people who have spent years studying the language can understand many of the guides and texts written so far about Arabic. Few English speakers have had access to Arabic media or people who speak Arabic on a day-to-day basis. Finally, more than 100 years since the first attempts were made to bring Arabic to the English-speaking world, there is still no standardized, accepted method of writing Arabic letters in ways that a normal English speaker can readily understand!

These are the challenges that you as the student and I as the teacher face in this course. These reasons are also why this book focuses on speaking, rather than writing or reading. Trying to include lessons on writing would quickly grow beyond the scope of this book. Hopefully, we will be able to present you soon with an *Idiot's Guide to Written Arabic*. For, now, if you simply must learn some writing, then you can start with Appendix B—an introduction to written Arabic. Between the speaking lessons throughout the book and the writing introduction that can be applied to any vocabulary in the book, you have enough information in this volume to stay busy for a very long time.

The Audio CD

Track 1

This book comes fully equipped for your listening as well as reading enjoyment. There is a CD that comes with the book. On the CD, you will find approximately 45 minutes of pure Arabic sounds. No, I don't mean music—I mean vocabulary and phrases for you to practice. Look for the logo. Wherever you see that logo, you know that you can find those words or phrases on the CD. As advice, I recommend that you repeat the words out loud—speaking them not as an English speaker would but as an Arabic speaker would. You will see what I mean once you've started.

How This Book Is Organized

This book is divided into six primary parts. Each part focuses on a particular aspect of speaking Arabic in everyday situations.

Part 1, "Just Your Basic Language," gives you an introduction to where in the world you can expect to hear Arabic spoken. You will learn how to make all the sounds of the Arabic language, which in some cases may mean "teaching" your voice box some new tricks. After learning how to make all of the sounds in Arabic and learning what sounds you won't find in Arabic, you will move on to putting some sounds together to make your first Arabic words. Before the part ends, you will also learn how to say all of the numbers in Arabic so that you can count the days until you have mastered this wonderful language.

Part 2, "Excavating Grammar," digs into the topic many of us learned to dread from our younger days in grammar school. Luckily, as a beginner in Arabic, you don't need to learn much about grammar to speak successfully. This part starts out with verbs, which are the foundation and most important of all Arabic words. After learning how to use verbs in different situations, we will add other pieces of sentences, one-by-one around the verbs, until you are able to express complete ideas. Before this part is over, you will know how to speak simple phrases and ask questions—which you will quickly see is very important to learning how to speak Arabic correctly.

Part 3, "Express Yourself," covers your first interactions with Arabic speakers. You will start by learning how to politely greet and address new friends and acquaintances. Then, you will learn how to introduce those friends to other friends. The fun will multiply as you learn how to tell others about yourself and your background while asking them questions about themselves. After you are familiar with talking about yourself, you will see how to engage in an everyday conversation about the weather, various entertainment, and your hobbies. Before the part is over, you will even learn how to express yourself to the doctor should the need arise.

Part 4, "Transportation," talks about—you guessed it—getting around in Arab lands. We humans love to get out and see things, and Part 4 will help you do that. This part starts by helping you plan your trip. You will learn when and where you might travel and what the best times might be to go. From your home to the travel agent to the airport customs office, you will find all you need. After arrival, you will learn how to get yourself to all the wonderful Arab sites you wish to visit. At the end of a long day on the bus, in a car, on the train, or on board a boat, you will be happy when the end of Part 4 brings you back to the hotel, where you can relax and get some well-deserved rest. After all, you have to be ready to go out again.

Part 5, "Touring in Arabic," gives you all you need to know about what you may find when you start to explore Arab lands. The first thing you will need to do is find a bank to get some money and figure out the address (if there is one) of the place you are going to visit. After you have figured that much out, you will get a chance to explore all of the famous Arab tourist attractions (and some you may not have heard of, if you are lucky). If you are the shopping type, you will love Chapter 20, which tells you all about the famous Arab markets and how you can enjoy them. Chapter 21 then teaches you how to enjoy dinner in a local restaurant before moving on to Chapter 22, where you see how to replace or find the items you may have used up or left at home.

Part 6, "Getting Things Done," focuses on teaching you how to speak effectively. When I say "speak effectively," I mean that you will learn how to say what you need to say in order to get things done. You will learn how to take charge of situations and put Arabic to your own uses. This part starts by showing you how to get household and personal services. Chapter 24 then shows you how to "get the word out" through the telephone lines or by telling others your opinions. In Chapter 25, you will learn how to speak in business situations and also how to speak about all of the household items you might need if you decide to stay longer. Finally, Chapter 26 shows you how to handle emergencies by giving you phrases that you might be able to use to help improve the situation.

Side Notes

Besides the tips, exercises, and explanations given throughout this text, you will find four side notes to help you get a little more in-depth in your study of speaking Arabic. They are:

Tips

Here, you will find tips on how to memorize words, how to learn new words, and how to save time when studying. Whether tips on pronunciation or grammar, these side notes can save you a lot of time. I wish I would have had them when I was learning Arabic.

Warnings

These side notes are useful to keep you from making cultural or language mistakes. Pay special attention here!

def•i•ni•tion

Here, you will find explanations of unfamiliar or confusing words. You can also find most of these words in the dictionary at the end of the book.

1001 Arabian Notes

These notes are used to give you information about Arab culture, what you might expect to see, and why.

Acknowledgments

This book is the culmination of the efforts of many people over the span of several years. It would be impossible for me to include the names of everyone along the way who has taught me a bit or piece of Arabic or affected my life in some way that directed me toward the creation of this book. That being said, I would like to take the time to thank some of those who have had a direct hand in bringing you the text you are about to read.

First, to Christopher Froehlich, friend and fellow author, thank you for the idea and the e-mail address. To Jacky Sach at Bookends, thank you for keeping the e-mail address for so long and providing your professional encouragement and wisdom throughout this creative process. I owe you a cup of tea and look forward to working with you again soon.

To the publisher, thank you for deciding to go forward with this difficult book; there aren't many others like it, that's for certain. To Mike Sanders, thank you for being receptive of my suggestions and for pushing me when I needed it. To Billy Fields, thank you for figuring out how to get the Arabic text layout correct for the portion on written Arabic (that was not easy work, folks).

To Ginny Bess Munroe, Megan Douglass, and Lisanne Jensen, thank you for your senses of humor while helping me organize my em dashes, ellipses, quotes, and other confusing punctuations. I had a great time working with you all through thousands of edits. To the folks at The Language Lab, thank you for your quick and wonderful work on the CD—well done!

Of course I must thank those who did the illustration, design, indexing, layout, and proofreading. Without all of them, you readers would just see boring pages with boring margins, and that would be a shame. In particular, I wish to express a very special thanks to L. Borealis for coming to our aid with such short notice—and thank you for the hats. Thank you all.

Naturally, I must thank the friends and colleagues who helped make this book a reality—particularly Holmes (for it all), Luera (for the help early on), Mazen (for the expertise), Tobin (for the laughs), and John and Alison (for the advice throughout). To all the members of Club M.E.B., thank you for making learning this difficult language incredibly enjoyable. I never could have done it without you and your "steely reserve." To my family, thank you for all your support. It was a long, long road that led me to this point. Finally, thanks go to my wife, without whose support I never would have attempted this writing. You are the only one who really knows what it was like to write this book. Thank you for forcing me to do what I can, rather than allowing me to do what I will. "Ich liebe dich, Dein K."

Trademarks

Part 1

Just Your Basic Language

So you don't know much about Arabic, eh? Well, don't worry. I didn't either until I found myself studying it for eight hours a day, five days a week. Until that point, I never could have told you that Arabic is the main language in more than 20 countries—much less named all of those countries. But here we are, and these are the things we learn as students of Arabic.

In Part 1, you will get your first taste of Arabic culture as we start with an imaginary trip across the lands where Arabic got its start. Then, barely pausing for a breath, we will get directly into learning all of the sounds you will need to learn an entirely new language. Surprisingly, there aren't too many new ones.

In Chapter 3, you will put together some of the sounds and start with your first and simplest words before moving on to Chapter 4, where you learn all the numbers you could ever wish to use. Be sure to make use of the tips and tricks along the way, write where you need to write, and make notes in the margin of the book if you want to. After all, you paid for it, right?

Chapter 1

A Magical Journey: Arabic Culture and History

In This Chapter

- An imaginary tour of the entire Arab world
- The lands of the *real* Arabia
- From gulf to ocean to sea
- A very brief history of some very old Arab cultures

Fifteen years ago, if someone had asked me what notions the word "Arabia" brought to mind, I probably would have given a simple answer. I might have mentioned Aladdin and his magic lamp. Perhaps I would have said something about Ali Baba or maybe the pyramids and the Sphinx. Writing this book today, however, I realize that there is much more to the word "Arabia" than my childhood movie experiences taught me.

In this chapter, you'll get the chance to find out about the Arab world—particularly which countries are considered Arab, where the Arab world starts and ends, and just how old Arab culture really is. (Psst … it's *really* old.) While you are reading about how all the countries developed and where they are located, you will get your first taste of just how large the

Arab world is. Then, you will see why it is so difficult to determine just who is and who is not an Arab and where in the world you might find Arabs.

Geographic Journey: Where It's At

The Arab world contains about 23 African and Asian countries, ranging from Oman in the east to Mauritania and Morocco in the west. The Mediterranean Sea marks the northern boundary for most of the Arab world, and Sudan and Somalia in Africa mark the southernmost points.

"Arabia" is often used to describe the area occupied by Arabic-speaking people of the Arabian Peninsula in southwestern Asia. This term can lead to confusion when thinking about what it means to be an Arab, however. Arabs are spread out much farther than the Arabian Peninsula. To get a better idea of just how big the Arab world is, we're going to take an imaginary journey from the west to the east, then part way back again.

Way out West: *al Maghrib*

Our first stop on our trip across the Arab world takes us to the western coast of Africa, where we also find—you guessed it—the western edge of the Arab world. The Arab world starts (or ends, depending on your perspective) on the western coast of Africa in the countries of Western Sahara, Mauritania, and Morocco. Not far off to the west of the African coast, in the Atlantic Ocean, are the Canary and Madeira Islands. This western portion of Africa often is referred to as "*al-magh-rib*" or "the West." ***Maghrib*** (often spelled Maghreb) is also the Arabic name for the country Morocco.

Warnings

The main difficulty of writing Arabic words with English letters is remaining true to the original spelling of words. Since Arabic has no equivalent of the English letter *E*, I did not use *E* in spelling out the Arabic words (as in Marrakesh, for example). I understand this may cause some differences in spelling some words that you are used to seeing.

The word "Maghrib" (capitalized) also means "West," or in other words, "the place where the sun goes down."

Morocco's land area and population (33 million people) are both similar to those of Spain. Morocco, an Arab country, is separated from Spain (not an Arab country) by the Strait of Gibraltar, which not only connects the Atlantic Ocean to the Mediterranean Sea but also separates Europe from Africa.

The Strait of Gibraltar gets its name from the Arabic "***jab**-il **Ta**-riq*," which means "Tariq's Mountain." "Tariq" refers to the famous Arab leader Tariq Ibn Ziyad (Tariq, the son of Ziyad). The eastern side of the Strait of Gibraltar is overlooked by the Pillars of Hercules—two mountain islands that are 14 miles apart from one another and "guard" the passage into the Atlantic Ocean. The northern, or European, pillar is the Rock of Gibraltar. The southern, or African, pillar is called "***jab**-il **moo**-sa*," or "The Mountain of Moses."

Morocco's famous open-air markets are always full of sounds from merchants and customers and the fragrances of spices and perfumes. Travelers to Morocco should include the cities Tangier (***Tan**-ja)*, Fez (*faas*), Marrakesh (*mar-**raa**-kash*), and of course Casablanca (***daar** al-bai-**Daa'h***) on their itineraries.

def•i•ni•tion

*Al-**magh**-rib* is the Arabic word for Morocco, but using "***magh-rib***" alone could mean "west" "sunset" or, "the place where the sun goes down." Not only is that a wonderfully poetic way to remember a bit of geographic information about the Arab world, but it also gives you an idea of how versatile Arabic words can be! A person from Morocco would be a ***magh**-rib-ee* if he is a man, or a ***magh**-rib-**ee**-a* if she is a woman.

def•i•ni•tion

"***jab**-il **Ta**-riq*" is Arabic for "Tariq's Mountain." From the Arabic, we get our English word "Gibraltar." Fez, or "***faas***" in Arabic, is both the name of a Moroccan city and the name of the brimless cylindrical hat worn by Arab men in Morocco and other Eastern Mediterranean countries.

Along the Mediterranean

As we continue our journey from left to right across the map, through the Strait of Gibraltar and past the Pillars of Hercules, we find ourselves in the middle of the Mediterranean Sea. Here, all along the northern coast of Africa, Arab cities and countries arose as shipping and trade allowed the wealth of one country to spread to others. The wealth of North Africa continues to fascinate us today. Whether as film crews or tourists, people from around the world flock to the North African countries to witness its amazing landscape and architecture.

The first country we encounter as we move farther into the Mediterranean is Algeria (and its capital, Algiers). With a size four times that of Morocco—its neighbor to the west—Algeria is the second-largest country in Africa. That means Algeria is about as large as all of Western Europe put together. Algeria is also home of the famous fortress, the Kasbah (in Arabic, the ***qaS**-ba*), which has shown up in film and media for more than 60 years.

To the east of Algeria, we find Tunisia with its capital Tunis (***too**-nis*). In Arabic, the capital city and country share the name ***too**-nis*. Like Algeria, Tunisia is overloaded with history. Traders and travelers for more than 3,000 years have at one time or another settled in Tunisia. In Tunisia, you can find everything from the ancient relics of the Phoenicians to Hannibal and his Roman-fighting Carthaginians to the incredible stone dwellings and landscapes featured in modern movies.

1001 Arabian Notes

The Phoenicians were ancient traders from the eastern coast of the Mediterranean who settled along much of the North-African coast, including in what has become modern Tunisia. The Phoenicians may have gotten their name from their use of "phonix," a purple dye they used on linens and wool.

Much of the Tunisian coast runs from north to south. Where the African coastline turns east again, we encounter the western edge of Libya and before long the Libyan capital, Tripoli (Arabic: *Tu-**raab**-lis*). Libya is a little bit bigger than Alaska and has a population of slightly fewer than six million people. In Libya, you can find plenty of ruins left over from the time of the Greeks and Romans. One of the most-visited tourist locations in Libya is the Leptis Magna, the amazing ruins of a Roman city. For those interested in the sweeping reaches of sand in every direction rather than ancient buildings, southern Libya—like Algeria to the west—extends south into the Sahara Desert. One interesting note about the Sahara Desert: it takes its name from the Arabic *Su-**Hraa'h***, which means "desert" in Arabic. So when we say Sahara Desert, we're actually saying "Desert Desert"!

Continuing farther east in the Mediterranean, we pass next into Egypt. Egypt is the land of the Nile, the world's longest river. (Actually, there are several other countries that could make the same claim, so I won't press the issue here.) From ancient to modern cities, Egyptian culture has flourished—thanks largely to the predictable flow and nourishing waters of the Nile. For more than 4,500 years, Egyptian culture has continuously grown and adapted to the world's changes. Today, cities like the Egyptian capital Cairo (*al-**qaa**-hir-a*) and Alexandria (*as-**skan**-dir-ee-a)* stand as living monuments to Egyptian culture through the ages. And next to the modern structures, we can still see pyramids and temples that were built thousands of years ago.

The delta where the Nile flows north into the Mediterranean Sea provides a perfect pausing point before we jump into our next section. You don't need an imaginary life vest for this portion, but it might be a good idea to put on your most comfortable imaginary walking shoes—because we're going to head out overland to see what we can find east of the Mediterranean.

The Syrian Desert and Iraqi Rivers

Are you here already? I guess that means you just can't wait to learn more about the geography of the Arab world. Let's get started! But be ready, we're not in the Mediterranean anymore. We're heading overland across Lebanon, Syria, and Iraq.

Now that we've crossed the Mediterranean Sea from west to east, we can step out of our imaginary boat and onto dry land in the seaport of Beirut, the capital city of Lebanon. In Lebanon, you can still find traces of the Phoenicians and of the imperial Romans in places like Jubail ("Byblos" in scholarly circles) and Baalbek. But Lebanon isn't only for those who are interested in ancient ruins. It is also the birthplace of the artist and poet Khalil Gibran, who wrote many works in both Arabic and English. And if you visit in the winter, you may decide to visit one of the country's many mountain resorts to do some snow skiing. I was surprised when I found out that Arabs ski, too!

Moving farther inland to the east of Lebanon, our journey next takes us to Damascus (*da-**mashq***), the capital of Syria. While there is much to see and do in Damascus, many experts claim that people have been "seeing and doing" things in Damascus longer than anywhere else in the world. What does that mean? Although it is difficult to confirm, many people assert that Damascus is the oldest continuously inhabited city in the world. That is quite a claim, but even if it turned out not to be true, Damascus still has many wonderful temples, mosques, and tombs—and a visit to any of them is time well spent. And remember, Damascus isn't the only city in Syria! There are plenty of other places to visit while you're there.

Warnings

There is a Tripoli, or *Tu-**raab**-lis*, in Lebanon as well as in Libya. If someone talks to you about "*Tu-**raab**-lis*," be sure to find out whether they mean the Lebanese city or the Algerian capital.

1001 Arabian Notes

The Euphrates River, or ***na**-hr al-far-**aat***, and the Tigris River (***na**-hr **dij**-la*) are the two rivers that bordered the ancient land of Mesopotamia. *Mesopotamia* means "land between two rivers." Similarly, Arabs refer to Mesopotamia as "***beyn** al-na-**hreyn***," or "between the two rivers." The exact area of Mesopotamia is difficult to determine but is generally considered to include parts of modern Iraq, Syria, Turkey, and Iran.

Continuing east through Syria, we pass right through the heart of the Syrian Desert—a vast expanse of land that covers part of Syria, Jordan, and Iraq. Thank goodness there are many oases along the way where we can take a break, just as traders have done for thousands of years before us. And now that you've done some walking, it's time to get back on a boat. This time, we're going to ride down the historic Euphrates River (***na**-hr al-far-**aat***).

The Euphrates River, flowing from its headwaters inside Turkey (*not* an Arab country) to the north, takes us southeast out of Syria and into Iraq. Iraq, like so many other Arab countries, is the home of several ancient civilizations. Akkadians, Sumerians, Assyrians, and Babylonians all called this land their home at one point in history. As we float down the Euphrates, the land to the south and west of us—the Syrian Desert—stretches all the way to the tip of the Red Sea. To the north and east of us is the fertile land of Mesopotamia. Along the Tigris River, the eastern boundary of Mesopotamia, you can find many ancient cities. Our own travel down the Euphrates takes us right past the Iraqi city Hilla, which is the modern name for the ancient city Babylon (or "***baa**-bil*"). Modern Hilla is where the Hanging Gardens of Babylon once stood, and it is also where you can find the ruins of the Tower of Babel.

Warnings

I have met many people who use the term "Arabian Gulf" rather than "Persian Gulf" for the body of water between the Arabian Peninsula and Iran. The name is potentially a sensitive topic, so be wary in your conversations. Also, some confusion may arise if you say, "Arabian Gulf," because that term has also been used to describe the Red Sea!

I hope you are ready to change your focus again, because our trip down the Euphrates ends shortly after the river joins with the Tigris in southern Iraq and we float out into the Persian Gulf, which will take us to the Arabian Sea.

Around the Arabian Peninsula

As we float through the marshes that mark the end of the Tigris-Euphrates delta and out into the Persian Gulf, the small but wealthy country of Kuwait and its capital, Kuwait City, lie to the west. The major cities in Kuwait are situated almost entirely along the coast of the Persian Gulf. Though Kuwait is only about the size of New Jersey, Kuwait has approximately 10 percent of the entire world's oil reserves! This wealth of oil helps Kuwait support its tourism industry. Tourists to Kuwait mainly enjoy water activities such as diving for pearls, but there are also a number of islands off the Kuwaiti coast where visitors can see monuments left from almost 5,000 years ago!

Continuing south through the Persian Gulf, we pass along the eastern edge of Saudi Arabia (we'll come back to Saudi Arabia in the next section) until we reach the island country of Bahrain. "Bahrain" literally means "two seas." But the name actually comes from the mixing of freshwater springs on the sea floor with the salty gulf water above. Bahrain only receives about three inches of rainfall per year but has a thriving tourism industry—especially for those who are interested in spending time on the water. In all, Bahrain has 33 separate islands—the largest of which is called, of course, Bahrain. The history of Bahrain extends far back beyond the written word. Many experts believe Bahrain is the location of the ancient city of Dilmun, which is very rich in mythological history.

1001 Arabian Notes

The Arabian Peninsula (also known as *al-ja-**zee**-ra*, or, "the island") is a large area of land between Africa and the Red Sea to the west and Asia and the Persian Gulf to the east. The countries of the Arabian Peninsula include Iraq, Jordan, Saudi Arabia, Bahrain, Qatar, the United Arab Emirates, Oman, and Yemen.

1001 Arabian Notes

Located under the modern Bahrainian capital Manama, Dilmun (sometimes called Telmun) is said to be the true location of the biblical Garden of Eden. Dilmun is also known as the paradise visited by the character Gilgamesh in the epic tale of his adventures. And if Morocco is the place where the sun sets, then Dilmun is the "place where the sun rises" (according to many texts).

Not far south and west of Bahrain, our journey now takes us to the peninsula country Qatar. Qatar juts out into the Persian Gulf, which means that except for the 60-kilometer border linking it to the main portion of the Arabian Peninsula, Qatar is completely surrounded by water. A mostly flat and sandy country with one major airport, Qatar still offers much interest to tourists. People visit Qatar year-round to see its seventeenth-century fortresses, fish and dive off the coast, or view Qatar's rare *oryx* in its natural surroundings.

The next country we pass on our journey through the Persian Gulf is the United Arab Emirates (UAE for short). The UAE was formed in the early 1970s when seven *emirates*, or principalities, joined together under one government. As we pass along the coast of the UAE from west to east, we'll pass the individual emirates one by one. The first emirate we pass is Abu Dhabi, the capital of the UAE. Next comes Dubai, then Sharjah, Ajman, Umm al Quwain, R'as al Khaimah, and finally Fujairah. Since its unification, the UAE has increasingly become a destination for tourists—especially those searching to relax in the sun or on the water.

Now we're going to leave the Persian Gulf and zoom through the Strait of Hormuz, where we'll make a sharp turn south and enter the Gulf of Oman. What country do

def•i•ni•tion

The *oryx* (*ow-**reeks***) is a long-horned antelope with a black-and-white face. There are many different species of oryx, and those in the Arabian Peninsula have long been in danger of extinction.

The word *emirate* comes from the Arabic "***a**-meer,*" which we know as "Amir" or "Emir." In English, "***a**-meer*" means "prince." Thus, we get the word "principality" or "emirate."

you think we'll encounter next? That's right: Oman. Oman covers much of the southern portion of the Arabian Peninsula and has become an incredibly famous tourist destination. If you decide to go to Oman, you can do everything from mountain climbing to camel racing—or you can just lie around on one of the many beautiful beaches, soaking up the sun. Just remember to bring sunscreen. The temperatures in Oman can reach up to 50 degrees Celsius. (That's 120 degrees Fahrenheit!)

As we continue to follow the coastline out of the Gulf of Oman, we will turn south and enter the Arabian Sea. Although we will still head south for a while, we now begin traveling west again. The next country we see—this time, to our north on the right side of our imaginary boat—is Yemen. Created from the unification of North and South Yemen in 1990, Yemen is rich in both modern and ancient attractions. Unlike many other Arab capital cities, however, Sana'a—the capital of Yemen—is located inland at an elevation of 2200 meters. The wonders of Arabic and Roman architecture make the trip up from the port city of Aden to Sana'a well worth the travel, though.

Speaking of Aden, we have now entered the Gulf of Aden, which links us to the Indian Ocean to the south. As we round the corner, so to speak, and head north through "***baab** al-man-dab*," or the Mandab Strait, we will pass the African countries of Somalia, Djibouti, and Eritrea—where the languages of the people have developed through a mixture of cultures over thousands of years. Having passed through the Mandab Strait, we now enter the final portion of our imaginary journey. Prepare yourself to sail north on the Red Sea.

The Red Sea

The Red Sea separates Africa from Asia and has been mentioned in text and verse as long as people have been writing and speaking. As we sail north, Saudi Arabia and its holy cities dominate the landscape to our right (or rather, to the east). Saudi Arabia is of special importance to the Muslim world because it is home to the holy cities of Mecca and Medina.

As we travel north on the Red Sea, we will pass Sudan to the west. With a total area almost twice as large as that of Canada's Northwest Territories, Sudan is the largest country in all of Africa. Much of the Sudan is covered by open land, which leaves room for many wildlife parks and natural preserves. Khartoum, the capital city of the Sudan, lies at the junction of the Blue Nile (which flows out of Ethiopia to the east) and the White Nile (which flows out of Uganda to the south). Looking at a map, we can see that this junction point of the two Niles looks a bit like the trunk of an elephant. And that's what people thought when they named the city at the junction, too. Khartoum is the Arabic word for "trunk of an elephant"!

Warnings

If you are considering visiting an Arab country, remember that political conditions and laws may be different than you are accustomed to. Before booking your travel, be sure to check with the appropriate agency to find out what travel restrictions may apply to you. This will save you difficulty and make your trip more enjoyable.

Continuing north on the Red Sea, we pass beyond the borders of Sudan and find ourselves again on the border of Egypt. This time, though, instead of being south of us, Egypt is to our west. We now can follow the Red Sea between Egypt and Saudi Arabia until the Red Sea splits itself on the Sinai Peninsula into two separate gulfs. To the east is the Gulf of Aqaba, which would take us up to Jordan—where we could visit the Dead Sea, the lowest point on Earth. Or we could take a take a trip to Petra, the amazing city literally carved into the stones of rocky cliffs (and recently voted one of the Seven Wonders of the World).

If we decided to travel up the gulf on the western side of the Sinai Peninsula, then we would be traveling in the Gulf of Suez, which is linked to the Mediterranean Sea by the Suez Canal—one of the most important waterways in the world. Evidence suggests that Egyptians as early as almost 4,000 years ago tried to dig a canal to connect the Red Sea with the Mediterranean Sea. That's a lot of international shipping!

Whatever gulf you choose for yourself, we have now reached the end of our imaginary journey and you've seen quite a bit of the Arab world. Naturally, there are more things to see than could possibly fit into such a short section of a book, but hopefully you've learned a thing or two along the way.

Who Are the Arabs, Anyway?

Now that I've taken you all over the Arab world, it's time for you to learn a bit about the people you're going to meet when you visit. So who exactly are the Arabs? Loosely defined, an Arab is a person who speaks Arabic and lives in an Arabic-speaking country or state. That's a fine definition, but does it mean that if I lived in Kuwait, I would be an Arab? Probably not. Even though I speak Arabic, I would still be seen as a foreigner if I were living in one of the countries we just toured. Actually, when we consider it, answering the question of how to define an Arab is much more difficult than it seems at first glance.

Personal encounters and research have taught me that most Arabs are more likely to consider themselves first and foremost according to their national identity, not according to their identity as an Arab. They would more likely say they are from Syria or Kuwait than say they are Arab. Language is also an important part of identifying an Arab. If a person speaks Arabic as a mother language, he or she may consider himself or herself an Arab.

Warnings

Sometimes a person who we may consider an Arab—based on linguistics or ethnicity—will use the term "Arab" to refer to someone of another country or region. Be careful when applying the term. You don't want to offend anyone.

There are no set rules for determining who is an Arab and who is not. Most times, however, language and ethnicity are the most important factors. So if a person is of Lebanese descent and speaks Arabic, it is probably safe to consider them an Arab.

Arab Populations Around the World

So where in the world can you find Arabs, if not just in the Middle East and Africa? Brazil, for starters. Some estimates say that there are as many as 10 to 15 million Arabs in Brazil—most of them immigrants from the Eastern Mediterranean countries of Lebanon and Syria. In fact, the Lebanese population in Brazil is actually believed to be higher than the Lebanese population in Lebanon! There are about 1.5 million Arabs in the United States.

There are also large Arab populations in Canada (about 200,000), Australia (about 300,000), Argentina (about 400,000), and Mexico (about 250,000). Of course, as the world grows smaller, the Arab populations in many countries will continue to grow. That's good news for you, because it could mean more places where you can practice your Arabic.

A Crash Course in Arabic History

I would be foolish if I thought that I could include enough information in one small section of this book to cover all of the regional, political, geographical, linguistic, and cultural changes that comprise Arab history. I wouldn't even know where to begin my description.

Would I tell you about the ancient cultures of Egypt that reigned for thousands of years B.C.E.? Maybe I would tell you about the times of change in the Arabian Peninsula where the East and West first joined one another. Certainly, I would have to tell you about the trade and shipping thousands of years ago that led to the development of North Africa. But would I then need to include a discussion about the imperial conquests of the Romans about 2,500 years ago or the imperial times of the seventeenth through twentieth centuries that left their marks on the Arab landscape?

No crash course in Arab history would be complete without discussing the expansion of Arab kingdoms from about 632 C.E. until about 711 C.E., when territory under Arab control reached all the way to modern France. And it would also be necessary to include discussion about Saladin, a Kurdish Muslim (but not an Arab) who began the dynasty that reigned over much of what has become today's Arab world.

I am sorry. As I said before, I would be foolish if I thought that I could include enough information in one small section of one chapter of this book to give a decent representation of Arab history. I will include as much information as I can throughout the book, and I recommend you continue to research Arab history on your own. The education you will find is both useful and fascinating.

Practice Makes Perfect

So you've made it through your first chapter and you want to move on. Good for you! But before you go, answer these practice questions to make sure you've got a good grasp of Arab culture.

1. What is the Arabic term for the westernmost Arab countries, where "the sun goes down"?
2. From what Arab country does the Nile flow into the Mediterranean Sea?
3. Which countries are on the Arabian Peninsula?
4. Which sea separates Africa from Asia?

The Least You Need to Know

- The westernmost Arab countries are called by the general term ***al-magh-rib***.
- Today's Arab world emerged slowly from some of the oldest civilizations on the planet.

- The term "Arabia" is used to refer to Saudi Arabia, the Arabian Peninsula, or the entire Arab world.
- Many Arab countries are famous both for their natural resources, such as oil, and their first-rate tourism industries.

Chapter 2

Sound Like a Native

In This Chapter

- Sounds you need to know
- Some things never change
- Speaking from the throat
- Vocalization in your sounds
- Sounds you'll never need

There's an old saying, "You learn something new every day." Well, this chapter has plenty to keep you learning for several days. Your first lesson in Arabic: Arabic text is written from right to left, top to bottom (see Appendix B for examples). Of all the chapters in this book, you will keep referring to this one—checking on your pronunciation of all the Arabic words and phrases you will be using. Learning Arabic sounds probably will be a challenge, but I explain all of the Arabic sounds to you and give you tips to help you feel your way through the sounds in this chapter. As you practice and improve, don't be surprised if not only your Arabic speaking skills improve but also your control over your entire voice range!

Arabic Sounds from A to Y

No matter how difficult they may appear at first glance, all languages contain only a specific number of sounds. The written alphabet of a language is merely a way of using symbols to represent those sounds. You probably know at least one language (I'm guessing you do if you are reading these words), so I'll use letters from the language that we both know (English) to show you how to make all the sounds in Arabic. Be warned, though: for some of the sounds, you will have to use your imagination—and above all, your *throat.*

Let's start with your imagination. Imagine that there is a circle that wraps from the bottom of your chin, around your lower jaw, across your throat, to the top of your spine, around the other side of your throat, and finally across the other side of your lower jaw to the starting point at the bottom of your chin. If you are someone who learns by doing, you can use your hands to feel the points I'm talking about. (Just be careful not to hurt yourself in the process.)

By drawing the imaginary circle around your throat and neck, you have now identified one of the key differences between Arabic and English; that is, you have just circled the area where many Arabic sounds are made. In English and similar languages, almost all sounds that become words occur in the region above the imaginary circle that you drew—more in your mouth than in your throat.

Before we go any further, here are all the sounds you will ever need to know in order to speak Arabic. Don't worry about how to pronounce them yet. We will get to that later in the chapter …

b	*t*	*T*	*th*	*TH*	*j*	*d*	*D*	*dh*	*r*	*z*	*s*	*S*	*sh*	*f*	*k*
q	*l*	*m*	*n*	*h*	*H*	*kh*	*w*	*y*	*'a*	*'u*	*'i*	*gh*	*a*	*aa*	*oo*
ee	*ey*	*ai*	*i*	*u*		*ow*	*'h*								

Now that you've had a brief introduction to the sounds you will hear, let's discuss how they will be written into words. In order to help you learn new words and to help you practice your pronunciation, I use a standard method of writing throughout this entire text. *Arabic words are written in italics, just like this sentence is, and the* ***stressed*** *syllables are marked with* ***bold.*** For example, if the word I wanted to teach you was the Arabic word for "car," I would write *sa-**yaa**-ra.* That's exactly how I would write the word so you know that the second syllable, ***yaa,*** is the syllable that you stress in pronunciation.

Some Sounds Never Change

Since we humans are only capable of producing a limited range of sounds, there are many sounds that overlap between languages. There are actually quite a few sounds that overlap between Arabic and English. You shouldn't have much of a problem remembering these.

The following list shows all the consonant sounds that are the same in English as they are in Arabic. In the columns next to the sounds are examples of the sound in English words (on top) and in Arabic words (underneath, in *italics*). Please note that the definition of each Arabic word is listed in (parentheses) next to the pronunciation.

A	**a**sk	b	**b**ake
***an**-ta* (you, masc. sing.)		***beyt*** (house)	
t	**t**ake	th	**th**ank
bint (girl)		*ith-**neyn*** (two)	
j	**j**est	d	**d**og
***jum**-la* (sentence)		***daar*** (dwelling)	
dh	**th**at	r	**r**ed
***dha**-lik* (that)		*sa-**yaa**-ra* (car)	
z	ja**zz**	s	li**s**t
*zi-**yaa**-ra* (visit)		***sooq*** (market)	
sh	wi**sh**	f	i**f**
***mish**-mish* (apricot)		***fun**-duq* (hotel)	
k	**k**eep	l	**l**earn
kalb (dog)		*sha-**maal*** (north)	
m	**m**oney	n	**n**ew
***mun**-dhu* (since)		***naH**-nu* (we)	
h	**h**er	w	**w**ent
***hee**-a* (she)		***wa**-ra-qa* (paper)	
y	**y**es	*ya-**naa**-yir* (January)	

Tips

When looking at the pronunciation of the words, remember there are different pronunciations for capital and lowercase letters. For example, "H" is pronounced differently than "h", just as "TH" is pronounced differently than "th".

New and Exciting Sounds

You shouldn't be scared of learning to make new sounds when learning Arabic. After all, if all of the Arabic sounds were the same as those we are used to hearing in English, we probably wouldn't consider the two as separate languages. But they *are*. That means you will have to learn to make some sounds you may have never tried before. The biggest difference you will notice between Arabic and English is that Arabic makes use of the back of the mouth and the throat to create sounds. When speaking English, most of the sounds we use take their shape and sound from either the mouth or the nose. In Arabic, though, you will have to get used to making noises from behind your tongue in your throat—and you can forget about sounding "nasal." In addition, you will be relying on your *soft palate* and your *uvula* to make sounds in Arabic.

def•i•ni•tion

The **uvula** is the small piece of flesh that hangs down at the back of the mouth. The sound "kh" is made in Arabic by vibrating the uvula against the back of the tongue. The **soft palate** is the muscular portion at the back of the roof of your mouth. The uvula hangs from the soft palate.

As you get better, you will notice that the differences are most apparent in the sounds that seem to be "harder" versions of sounds that you already know. Don't worry … it really does get easier with practice.

The following table shows all of the Arabic sounds we don't have in English. On the left side of the table, you can see the sound as it is used throughout this book. In the second column, you can see an example Arabic word that uses the sound. The English translation of each word is below the Arabic. Don't get discouraged if you can't hear the differences at first. Your vocal cords and ears will need some training before they start performing at their Arabic best.

New and Exciting Sounds

Sound	Example	Make the Sound
H	***Haal**-a* (situation)	Constrict the windpipe and say "ho" or "ha" from the throat.

kh	*kha-**beer*** (expert)	Like *H*, constrict the windpipe, then use forced air to vibrate the uvula against the back of your tongue—similar to the sound someone makes when snoring.
S	***Suf**-Ha* (page)	Heavier than '*s*' because sound comes from air escaping between the soft palate and the tongue, not the tongue and the teeth (as with the English 's').
D	*i-**Daa**-fa* (addition)	Heavier '*d*'; the sound is made between the back of the tongue and the soft palate instead of between the tongue and the teeth.
T	***Taqs*** (weather)	Heavier '*t*'; the sound is made between the entire tongue and the roof of the mouth instead of between the front of the tongue and the teeth.
TH	***THa**-ha-ra* (to appear)	Heavier '*dh*' sound; constrict the throat and soft palate. The sound comes from the entire mouth.
'a	*mu-**'al**-lim* (teacher)	Constrict the throat and allow only a little air through as if you're at the doctor's office and saying "Ahh." This sound is similar to '*r*' in German and French
'u	*'u-**moom**-ee* (civil)	The same as *'a*; also from the back of the throat, but the "*u*" vowel is spoken.
'i	***jaam**-'i* (mosque)	The same as *'a* and *'u* above but with the vowel sound '*i*.' (*Note: With 'a, 'u, and 'i*, the throat constriction is more important than what vowel sound you use.)
gh	***ghad**-dan* (tomorrow)	Similar to *'a* and *'u* but harder; think of a gargling sound or a purring cat. Constrict your throat and say "ghei." Pretend you are gargling the word. That way, you speak from your throat, not from your mouth.
q	*qi-**Taar*** (train)	Harder than English 'q'; made by closing the back of the tongue to the soft palate and making the '*k*' sound. The *q* is harder than the English *q*. Say "cough," but speak from your throat instead of from your mouth.
'h	***ka**-'his* (cup)	Similar to a light cough; close the airway, then release air out the nose and mouth in the same way as when you say *huh'**uh***.

How Many Vowels Are There, Really?

It's hard to tell how many vowels there *really* are in Arabic. Some people say there are three; some people say there are six. The difference comes from understanding that Arabic is based on consonant sounds, and vowels were spoken but not written. Then, vowels were written—but not all of them. Then, vowel sounds were written but as additions to existing consonants, not as standalone letters.

None of that is too important for you to learn right now. We would just end up in a discussion of what a vowel really is. We'd certainly have to discuss the English cases where *W* and *Y* are considered vowels, and neither one of us would be able to get any sleep tonight. We can have that discussion later. For now, we'll get started with the long vowel sounds.

Some Vowels Are Long

For our purposes, long vowels are those vowel sounds that have an actual corresponding written letter in the Arabic alphabet. Unlike English, which has five vowels—*a*, *e*, *i*, *o*, and *u*—Arabic has just three long vowel sounds: *aa*, *oo*, and *ee*. Yes, just three. Here they are:

> *aa*: Close to the *a* in the word "want" and also close to the "ah" sound you have to make when you go to the doctor and he or she tells you to open your mouth and say "Ahh." ا
>
> *oo:* The same sound as in the word "moon." ـو ـُ
>
> *ee:* The vowel sound *ee* is a special case. Normally, *ee* is the same sound as in the words "keep" and "see." However, depending on what letters surround this vowel, it may also sound like *ey* or *ai.* ي
>
> *ey:* The same sound as in the words "hey," "whey," and "say." Note: sometimes this long vowel may sound like *ey* or *ai.*
>
> *ai:* This sound occurs in two instances. First, it happens when the vowel *ee* comes next to one of the hard consonants (like T or TH). In the other instance, *ai* occurs as a diphthong (which we cover later in this chapter).

So much for the long vowel sounds. There's no point in discussing them more than necessary. Let's keep moving right into the short vowels.

Some Vowels Are Short

There are three long vowels in Arabic and also three short vowel sounds.

> *a*: The short *a* sound is the most common of the Arabic vowel sounds. The *a* sound is the same as the *a* in "about." You will also find this sound at the end of many Spanish words, such as "luna" or "señora." As you'll see later, Spanish and Arabic have many similarities.
>
> *i*: The short *i* sound is the same as in the words "if" and "him."
>
> *u*: The short *u* sound is a bit trickier than the other two short vowels because it is softer and a bit fuller than its English counterpart. The Arabic *u* sounds more like the vowels in the English words "good" and "hood" than in words such as "under" and "but."

If you are worried about whether you will understand the differences between long and short vowels, don't be. And if you're worried that you'll confuse long and short vowels in your pronunciation, don't be concerned. Most people will not even notice a difference in the vowels until they begin writing in Arabic. And with the exception of Appendix A, this book focuses entirely on your ability to *speak* the language, not write it.

So how are you going to recognize short vowels? Easily. They're not as tall as their kinfolk.

Okay, that was a poor joke, I admit—but as you speak more Arabic, you will see that my bad joke actually makes sense. As you familiarize yourself with the language, you'll begin to hear how short vowels really are "shorter" than the long vowels. As soon as you begin to hear the difference, you will be able to start saying Arabic words with more accuracy—which means you will be *using* the language, not just repeating it.

The only other note I will offer about vowels is that when a vowel occurs next to one of the "hard" consonants (*H* or *D* or *TH*, for example), the vowel takes on a slightly different, heavier sound. When your throat is constricted to make the hard consonant sound, the surrounding vowel sounds are also affected. That means you end up saying ***baiD*** for "eggs" instead of ***beed*** or ***beyd*** (these last two aren't words you'll find in this book).

def•i•ni•tion

These Arabic words can be a bit confusing. ***baiD*** means "eggs" while ***beyt*** means "house," and *bai-**Daa'h*** means "white."

Sore Throat? Swallow That Sound

Until you are used to speaking Arabic, your first lessons might leave your throat feeling like you spent too much time singing in the shower. That happens. The more time you spend speaking and practicing, the easier and more natural the sounds will become. Before you know it, your throat and mouth will be singing and dancing (well, maybe not *dancing*) entirely different tunes.

The trick is to forget what you have learned about speaking. For instance, are you one of those people who *enunciate* every letter exactly as it should be? Do you always pronounce things the way they are written? For example, if I told you to say the word "mutton," would I hear the *t* sound? Or would I maybe hear something like "*muddon*" or even "*muh'un*"? These are the types of questions we have to consider when deciding how best to proceed with our lesson in Arabic.

def•i•ni•tion

Enunciate means to pronounce words clearly.

Let's say for argument's sake that you are the type of person who pronounces every letter the way it is written. That's good. It's great, in fact, because it means that you are very aware not only of the way words sound as they come out of your mouth but also of the way they *feel* when you say them. For instance, you know that when you say the phrase, "this thing," the first time you say the letters *th*, your tongue lightly presses against the back of your front teeth. Then, to say "thing," the tongue reaches outside the teeth and presses against them in a bit different motion. It is this motion of the tongue that allows us English speakers to say sentences like, "Thus, there is the thing that we thought was theirs." Practice that sentence a few times before you continue, paying attention to how your tongue moves.

Now that you have a good idea of how the tongue moves when enunciating in English, imagine yourself trying to create the *T, D,* and *TH* sounds without allowing your tongue to touch the back of your teeth. Try saying the name "Todd" a few times in this way. That's probably a strange sensation for you, right? That's what I call "swallowing the sound." While you are working on that, we can move to the next section.

Sound + Sound = Sound Combinations

What is a sound combination, you may ask? A sound combination is just what you think it is: two or more sounds put together. "So," you may ask, "if that's all they are, why do we need to dedicate a section of the book to them?" I'll tell you why. Speaking a language is like baking a cake. Both are based on the mixing of ingredients. The better you understand the combination of sound "ingredients" in Arabic, the better your language "cake" will turn out.

Your Abjad Is Not an Alphabet

Remember when I told you that Arabic uses an abjad and not an alphabet? This is where it becomes important.

In the Arabic abjad, every consonant is paired with a vowel sound. A fine example of this pairing is the verb phrase "he wrote." In Arabic, this phrase is pronounced ***ka-****ta-ba*. We'll get more into the explanation of verbs in another chapter, but for now, just remember that all consonants are paired with vowel sounds in Arabic—even if the vowel sound is silent. I know that sounds strange, but it's good to remember that Arabic uses an abjad, and that letters come in pairs. If this book were focused on writing instead of speaking, I could show you exactly what I mean.

Diphthongs: Vowels That Glide

If you don't recognize the word "diphthong," don't be afraid. It may seem like a scary grammatical lesson that you'll never be able to understand, but diphthongs are nothing to fear. A diphthong is just a pair of vowels put together to make one continuous sound that has the characteristics of both vowels. Still confused? A diphthong starts like one vowel and ends like another.

There are only two diphthongs in the entire Arabic vocabulary: *ai* and *ow*. At the beginning, a diphthong has one vowel sound. At the end it has a different vowel sound. And since you make the transition from the first sound to the second without stopping between sounds, a diphthong is also called a "glide." You *glide* through two different vowel sounds without stopping along the way.

The diphthong *ow* is very close to the exclamation you might make if you dropped a large Arabic dictionary on your toe. I mean, of course, "Ow!" *ow* starts out sounding like "ah," but at some point we barely notice, the sound turns to more of an "oo" before finally ending with "w." And all of this happens in the space of one syllable. But you already know how to make that sound. No need to delay—let's press on.

The other Arabic diphthong is *ai*. This sound rhymes with the words "Thai" and "pie." As you can probably guess, *ai* starts out like "a" but ends like "y."

That's it! Like I told you, there are only two diphthongs in Arabic. Now you can move on to the next section!

"h" or "H" or "kh"... Vocalization

If you looked at the pronunciations listed so far in this chapter and wondered to yourself how you will be able to tell the difference between sounds like *z*, *th*, and *dh* or *h*, *H*, and *kh*, there is no need to worry. *Vocalization* is the key to differentiating between similar sounds.

def•i•ni•tion

Vocalization means using your vocal cords to make a sound. Your **vocal cords** are in your throat and vibrate when air passes through them, allowing you to make different sounds for speech and singing. If the vocal cords are not being used, then the sound is considered **voiceless.**

To give you an example of exactly what vocalization means, let's try an experiment. Try saying the *z* sound without using your *vocal cords*. The odds are that you'll find the task impossible. That's because saying *z* requires you to use your vocal cords.

Now, take what you just learned and apply it to the case of the Arabic sounds *th* and *dh*. The *th* sound is *voiceless*, just as when you say "think thin." But the *dh* sound is vocalized, which gives you sounds like in the words "that there." From these two examples, you can see that even though in English we use the same two letters (th) to represent different sounds ("***th***is" is vocalized while "***th***ing" is not), Arabic uses different letters for the different sounds (*dh* and *th*).

The sounds *h*, *H*, and *kh* are all voiceless, but they still have their differences. The *h*, or "soft h" sound, is soft enough that it can scarcely be heard. In fact, if you don't add a vowel sound to the *h*, then you aren't really doing anything more than breathing out. This is different than the *H* or "hard H" sound.

I've heard the hard *H* compared to a hissing cat, a spitting cobra, and even the air whooshing through an empty fire hose. What all of those examples really show is that the sound is foreign—we English speakers aren't used to it. Whichever analogy you choose to best remember the *H*, just recall that it occurs in the throat, not in the mouth. The mouth just serves as an echo chamber. The *H* sound is made by constricting the muscles around the vocal cords and trying to hiss like a cat. The *kh* sound is also made by constricting the muscles around the vocal cords, but for *kh* you have an added challenge. You need to vibrate the uvula against the back of your tongue. This sound may be difficult to repeat at first, but when you listen to the CD (and you should), you will hear what I mean. The right sound will come with practice.

There is a logical move from the voiceless sounds to vocalized sounds. In particular, if you say *H* by constricting your throat and hissing like a cat, the *'u*, *'i*, and *'a* sounds are the same. You just need to add vocalization. Constrict your throat, breathe out, and add the chime of vibrating vocal cords. It will work. That leaves only one more new sound for you to master!

Everyone I know who learned Arabic after learning English has found the *gh* sound the hardest one in Arabic to make. I was no exception. The good thing for you is that now that I've told you, you don't have to be surprised like I was when I started my classes. I'll share the secret. To make the *gh* sound, all you have to do is put together everything I've told you in this section. You have to constrict the muscles around your vocal cords as if you were going to make the *H*, *'u*, *'a*, or *'i* sound. Then, while vibrating your vocal cords, you breathe out—at the same time bouncing your uvula off the back of your tongue. In short, *gh* is made by vocalizing the *kh* sound.

There you have it—all the new sounds you need to successfully learn how to speak Arabic.

Sounds You Won't Find in Arabic

If you have ever spoken in English with a native Arabic speaker, you may have noticed that he or she might have difficulty pronouncing some of the letters in our English words. That's because there are some English sounds that Arabic doesn't have (and vice-versa). Of course, there are exceptions to every rule—but the English letters you will (almost) never find in Arabic are:

C—Arabic doesn't need a C. It just uses other letters.

G—Sometimes you'll hear *G* (if you travel to Egypt, for example), but a direct equivalent doesn't occur in Arabic. The closest sound is *gh*.

P—Arabic uses *b* in place of our letter *P*.

Q—*q* in Arabic comes close to the English Q, but in Arabic the sound is spoken from the throat, not from the mouth.

V—Arabic uses *f* in place of the English letter V.

X—Arabic uses *k* and *s* to "spell" the English X.

In addition to the consonants you don't hear in Arabic, there are two vowel sounds you (hopefully) never hear because they don't exist. If you do hear them, you can assume the speaker borrowed the sounds from another language or maybe hasn't practiced enough Arabic speaking!

The first vowel sound you won't (or rather, shouldn't) hear in Arabic is the short *e*, as in "pet" or "kept." Don't worry about looking too far for a substitute, though. If the *e* sound finds its way into speech, few people will notice. In fact, the Arabic word for Morocco is often written *al-Maghreb*, and two of Morrocco's most famous cities are Marrakesh and Fez! Don't worry if you use the *e* sound. If your name is "Kevin," for example, no one would expect you to call yourself "*Kafan*." (Don't forget that *v* doesn't exist in Arabic, either.)

The other vowel sound you won't hear in Arabic is the long *o* sound, as in "boast" or "tote." You might notice the missing *o* if your name is "Hope." If that's the case, instead of your name you might hear something like "Howp" or "Hoop." You'll understand the speaker, though, because now you know what to expect.

Practice Makes Perfect

Now that you have introduced yourself to the Arabic sounds, let's see how well you remember them.

1. How might an Arabic speaker pronounce the names "Kevin" and "Hope"?
2. What is the difference between the Arabic *u* and the English *u* sound?
3. What is "wrong" with the English spelling of the Arabic words *Maghreb* and *Marrakesh*?
4. How many vowel sounds does Arabic have?
5. What is the most difficult Arabic sound?

The Least You Need to Know

- Arabic is an abjad, not an alphabet.
- Most Arabic sounds occur in English.
- Some Arabic sounds come from the throat instead of the mouth.
- Some English sounds don't occur in Arabic.

Chapter 3

Words Right out of My Mouth

In This Chapter

- Learning about articles
- Saying "no" in Arabic
- Nouns with gender
- Going plural
- Some easy sentences

In the previous chapter, you learned how to make all the Arabic sounds. The purpose of this chapter is to teach you what to do with them. To keep the lesson as simple as possible, we'll start with the smallest words and work our way toward learning a few basic nouns.

By the time you are done with this chapter, you will be putting together your first Arabic sentences and building your vocabulary in preparation for the upcoming chapters. Have fun!

One or Two Letters, Many Words

In order to get you speaking in Arabic as soon as possible, I decided it would be a good idea to provide you with a small section devoted to some very small words. That way, before this chapter is over you will be able to speak a few simple Arabic sentences without fearing that you will sound like Tarzan.

And the Easiest Word Is ...

"... and the winner of the contest for the easiest Arabic word is ... AND."

That's right. The easiest Arabic word is "and." And how do you say "and"? ***wa***. Simple yet powerful, ***wa*** is the Arabic "and." Let's try a practice phrase.

If you want to say, "John and Jane" in Arabic, the phrase is prounounced "***jaan wa jeyn***." Notice how although the spelling of the names changes, the pronunciation does not. You can also see that the word order doesn't change. That helps you remember. "John and Jane" is still "John and Jane."

The Arabic ***wa*** can be substituted for English "and" wherever you feel the need to add something—or someone—to your sentences.

Warnings

Don't be confused by the way that I talk of "letters" and "sounds" to explain the simplest Arabic words. For example, the word "and" is pronounced with two *sounds* (**w** + **a** = **wa**) although it is written with only one letter.

Two Letters, Three Words

Arabic has three two-letter words that will come in very handy when learning to speak. How do you know they are only two letters long? You don't have the Arabic script in front of you, so you'll have to trust me. But I assure you they only have two letters. And the sounds won't be hard for you to master, either.

yaa- (verily)

This word is the Arabic equivalent of the English "verily," which we don't use much anymore. A more modern example of ***yaa*** would be "hey" or "say." For example, "Say, John ..." In Arabic, you will find yourself using ***yaa*** whenever you want to direct someone's attention to what you are going to say. For example, if you wanted to speak with John and maybe needed to catch his attention, you would say, "***yaa jaan***."

al- (the)

al is one of the most important words you can learn in Arabic. And you can be thankful that ***al*** is so easy to say. ***al*** will become a good friend of yours as you move through this text and through your career as an Arabic speaker. That's because ***al*** is the "the" of the Arabic language. Try to understand this sentence in English: … blue car … one next to … house." Sure, you can probably guess the meaning, but the sentence doesn't make much sense, does it? The same thing could happen in Arabic if you forgot to use ***al***. We'll go into more discussion about using ***al*** later in the chapter. For now, you just need to understand that ***al*** means "the." And here's something you want to keep in mind as you learn to work with ***al:*** the "L" sound might not always be pronounced. We'll also cover why that happens later in this chapter.

1001 Arabian Notes

"***yaa rab***" is a common expression in Arabic, particularly when expressing sympathy. Literally translated, ***yaa rab*** means "Oh Lord" and is used similarly to "my goodness" or "dear heavens."

laa- (no, not)

Just as in English, there are many ways to say "No!" in Arabic—but ***laa*** is the easiest. And you'd better get used to using it. Arabic hospitality is so great that unless you learn to use ***laa***, it won't be long before you find yourself overwhelmed with gifts and offers of food!

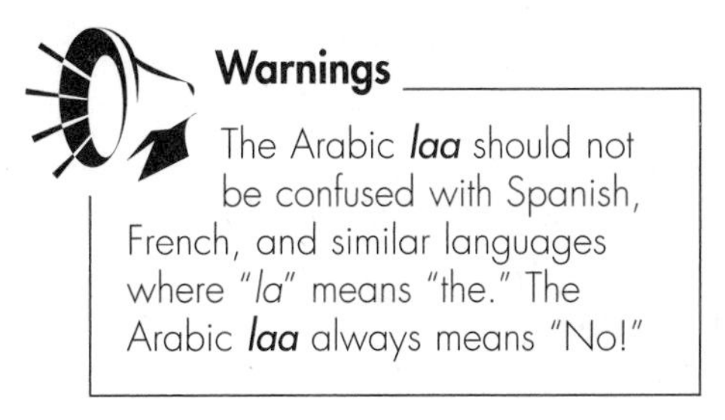

Warnings
The Arabic **laa** should not be confused with Spanish, French, and similar languages where "*la*" means "the." The Arabic **laa** always means "No!"

Some Easy Nouns

Now you have learned about ***al***, ***laa***, ***yaa***, and ***wa***. Do you think you are ready to put them to use? Good. But we're not going to move on quite so quickly. Before we continue, I want to give you some easy *nouns* to build a bit of your vocabulary. We will go into more detail about nouns in Chapter 6, so we'll just cover a few of them here.

Tie That "*taa'h*": Nouns with Gender

One of the grammar rules that makes Arabic different than English is the use of gender. Saying that Arabic uses gender means that the nouns in Arabic are either considered masculine (male) or feminine (female). This is different than English but similar to

def•i•ni•tion

A **noun** is a word that describes a person, place, or thing. Arabic nouns may be either masculine or feminine.

Spanish or French. The gender of a noun determines how the verbs and other words in sentences will be used. So be sure to pay attention to gender in your nouns. The following are some Arabic masculine nouns.

Track 3

beyt
house

kur-*see*
chair

Tif-l
baby boy, child

ki-***taab***
book

sa-***laam***
peace

qam-*ar*
moon

shakhS
person

mas-*jid*
mosque

Hi-***dhaa'h***
shoe

Sun-*dooq*
box

kalb
dog

raj-*al*
man

Hi-***maar***
donkey

mak-*tab*
office

shams
sun

arD
ground/earth

shaa-*r'i*
street

qi-***Taar***
train

Hi-***zaam***
belt

fun-*duq*
hotel

So much for the easy masculine nouns. It's time to take a look at some Arabic feminine nouns. If you look at Appendix A, you will see two letters that are very similar: ***taa'h*** and ***taa'h*** *mar*-***boo***-*Ta*. Literally, "***taa'h*** *mar*-***boo***-*Ta*" means "tied ***taa'h***." With a little bit of imagination, you can see that if you tied the ends of the letters "***taa'h***," you would end up with a small circle underneath two dots. (If you can't imagine what this looks like, you can either ignore this paragraph or sneak a peek at Appendix A.)

Well, that circle with two dots has a few special functions in Arabic. One of those functions is to help you understand that a word is feminine. The ***taa'h*** *mar*-***boo****Ta* is recognized by the final sound *a*. You will often find this *a* sound at the end of feminine nouns. Very often, the *a* sound at the end of a word tells us two things: that the word is a noun and is feminine. Here are some examples of feminine nouns that are easy to recognize because they end with the "a" sound.

Track 3

*im-**ra**-'ha*
woman

*sa-**yaa**-ra*
car

***qiT**-Ta*
cat

***san**-a*
year

***ib**-na*
daughter

***shaq**-qa*
apartment

***ghur**-fa*
room

***maa**-'hi-da*
table

*ma-**dee**-na*
city

*ka-**nees**-a*
church

***jaa**-m'ia*
university

***mad**-ra-sa*
school

***lugh**-a*
language

***dow**-la*
state

***qah**-wa*
coffee

***sha**-ja-ra*
tree

Of course, we all know there are exceptions to every rule. Feminine nouns won't always have the "a" sound at the end. You will have to watch out for such instances as you move along in your studies and increase your vocabulary. "Girl" (***bint***) and "war" (***Harb***) are just two examples of words that don't sound feminine but are.

Pluralizing Your Nouns

When I was first learning German (after struggling with Arabic for a few years), I remember many teachers telling me that the easiest way to learn German nouns was to learn them with their articles: "der," "die," and "das." A similar rule applies to learning Arabic nouns. The best way to learn Arabic nouns is to learn their plurals at the same time. Eventually, you will start to recognize patterns in the way the plurals are made, and you will no longer need books like this one to help you with your studies.

Of course, it's easy for me to say that you should learn the nouns with their plurals. It's something different for you to actually have the opportunity to do so. That's why I've highlighted some basic rules for you to follow.

Words ending with the "a" sound (also remember that they're probably feminine) can be made plural by turning the "a" into *–**aat.*** A couple examples are car/cars (*sa-**yaa**-ra/sa-yaa-**raat***) and library (***mak**-ta-ba/mak-ta-**baat***). Making nouns plural this way can best be understood once you get into reading more Arabic text. When you do, you will see that you create these nouns by changing just one little letter at the end of the word. You also can see that when the ***–aat*** plural is added, the emphasis is shifted to the last syllable.

Tips

Even if it is not correct for a particular word, ***–aat*** is recognized as a plural ending for nouns. So if you are talking to someone and need a plural that you don't know, you can just put ***–aat*** at the end of the word to get the person to understand that you are speaking about more than one of that thing. This may be grammatically incorrect, however, if the plural does not follow this rule, so use the ***–aat*** ending with caution—but it may help you get out of a jam when speaking.

Another way to make nouns plural has to do with nouns that refer to people. I don't want to confuse you by digging into the rules of grammar too much, but another way that words can be made plural is by adding ***–oon*** to the end of the word. Often the ***–oon*** ending is added to masculine nouns. A couple examples of ***–oon*** masculine plurals are *mu-'al-lim-**oon*** (teachers) and *mus-lim-**oon*** (Muslims). We'll discuss proper nouns later in this chapter.

There is a third rule that I'll call the "plural by middle" rule. Can you guess where changes are made to words in this instance? You guessed it … in the middle. The plural by middle rule actually works in two directions. Some nouns with a vowel in the middle, such as *ma-**dee**-na* (city) and *ki-**taab*** (book), actually shrink a little when they become plural. The vowel in the middle is removed, so *ma-**dee**-na* (city) becomes ***mu**-dun* (cities) and *ki-**taab*** (book) becomes ***ku**-tub* (books).

The second part of the plural by middle rule involves masculine nouns that have no "a" sound at the end. These nouns are often made plural by adding **aa** in the middle of the word. This rule is seen in the cases of ***mat**-Haf* (museum), which becomes *ma-**taa**-Hif* (museums) and ***mak**-tab* (office), which becomes *ma-**kaa**-tib* (offices).

Get Definite with the Sun and Moon

I told you earlier in this chapter that I would tell you more about articles later. Well, I suppose it's time for me to live up to my end of the bargain. An *article* is a word used to indicate a noun. In English, we have both *definite* and *indefinite* articles. In Arabic, however, only the definite article (***al***) is used. For example, if you wanted to say "the city," you would say, "*al-ma-**dee**-na*." But if you wanted to say "a city," you would just say "*ma-**dee**-na*." This rule will not change, so keep it in mind as you move along in your studies.

There is one other important rule you need to know regarding the definite article ***al***. Arabic letters are broken into two groups called Sun (or Solar) Letters and Moon (or Lunar) Letters. The group a letter belongs to determines how ***al*** will be pronounced. Specifically, the Sun Letters cause ***al*** to be pronounced ***a***.

def•i•ni•tion

An **article** can be either **definite** (the) or **indefinite** (a, an). Arabic only has a definite article (al).

The Sun Letters are so bright that they cover up the ***l*** sound in the definite article. Okay, maybe they don't cover up the ***l*** sound because they are too bright but because of the way they are formed in the mouth. A common example of how the Sun Letters affect the definite article is in the Arabic greeting *as-sa-**laam** 'a-**ley**-kum* (literally, "the peace upon you"). Another example would be if you wanted to say "the person," you would say, "*as-**shakhS***." There are 14 Sun Letters in all:

T ***t*** ***TH*** ***th*** ***D*** ***d*** ***dh***

S ***s*** ***sh*** ***z*** ***r*** ***n*** ***l***

Any time one of these letters is connected to the definite article ***al***, remember that you don't pronounce the ***l*** sound.

There are also 14 Moon Letters. Because I know you are a sharp reader (why else would you be picking up this book?), you probably guessed that the Moon Letters are the opposite of the Sun Letters. You're right. The Moon Letters do not affect the pronunciation of the definite article, so if you wanted to say, "the moon," you would say *al-**qam**-ar*. If you wanted to say "the paper," you would say *al-**wa**-ra-qa*. You get the idea. The 14 Moon Letters are as follows:

w ***y*** ***a*** ***b*** ***j*** ***H*** ***kh***

'a,'i,'u ***gh*** ***f*** ***q*** ***k*** ***m*** ***h***

Now, you may be wondering why I listed *'a,'i,* and *'u* on the list as the same letter. I did that because they *are* the same letter. The difference is in the vowels that follow. So to stick with your 14 Moon Letters, just remember all three apostrophes ('s) together.

Negate a Noun

Now that you have had a bit of an introduction to nouns, we will take a step back and let you catch your breath. Don't be set back if you did not catch everything on the first reading. It's time to relax and learn to say "No!"

Actually, you already learned to say "no." You learned it when you learned the easy words at the beginning of this chapter. Saying "no" in Arabic is as easy as saying ***laa.*** And ***laa*** is even more powerful than just saying "no." ***laa*** can also be used to say, "not" or "is not." This knowledge will become even more useful when we start working with verbs and longer sentences. But you can learn a couple ways to say "no" right now.

Let's see what we can do with the words you have already learned. Remember John? How do you think you might say he is not a girl? Well, you need to remember what the word for "John" is. That shouldn't be too tough. It's ***jaan.*** Then, you have to remember the word for "girl." That one might be a little more difficult. It's ***bint*** (remember, we saw it as an example of a feminine word that doesn't sound feminine). So now you know how to say "John" and "girl." All you have to do is add the "is not a" to the sentence. Well, since Arabic doesn't use indefinite articles like "a" or "an," the only thing to add to the sentence is "is not." You just learned that "is not" is "***laa,***" so now you have all the parts of the sentence. Let's put them together:

jaan (John) ***laa*** (is not) ***bint*** ([a] girl).

So put together, we get:

jaan laa bint (John is not a girl.)

Tips

There are some words you use all the time in English that rarely are used in Arabic. When speaking Arabic, you never say the words "a" and "an"—and you very rarely will use "is" and "are."

That's all there is to it. I think you have the idea. How would you say that something is "not a house"? Well, if you remember that the word for house is ***beyt***, then all you have to say is "***laa beyt.***" The idea is simple enough, I suppose.

Cognizant of Cognates

Cognates are words in different languages that share a common origin. Since the words have the same origin, they often have the same or similar pronunciations. This knowledge is good for you when you are trying to learn Arabic, because if a word has the same or similar pronunciation in Arabic or English, then there is less for you to learn. This section looks at some of the different Arabic and English cognates and the ways in which you might encounter them.

Cognates Are Foreign to Me

Modern Arabic makes use of many foreign words. In some cases, there is no change to the original words at all—so the words wouldn't technically be considered cognates. But there are a number of cognates that do meet the necessary criteria. If you have any experience in learning Hebrew, Persian, or Spanish, you will find many cognates between those languages and Arabic as you continue your studies.

There are also several English words that haven't changed much since their adaptation from Arabic. This makes them—you guessed it—cognates. The following is a list of modern English words with their Arabic cognates listed in parentheses.

alcohol (*al-ku-**Hool***)

alchemy/chemistry (*al-kee-**mee**-a'h*)

algebra (*al-**jab**-ir*)

tariff (*t'a-**ree**-fa*)

alfalfa (*al-**fuS**-fuS-a*)

lemon (*lee-**moon***)

camel (***jam**-al*)

million (*mil-**yoon***)

Keep Your Cognates Proper

For the sake of making things easier for you, I'm going to include proper nouns as cognates in this section. *Proper nouns* probably wouldn't meet the literal definition of cognates, but I want to be sure you have as much Arabic vocabulary as possible—and I want you to be aware of the changes you will have to make when pronouncing things in Arabic rather than in English.

def•i•ni•tion

A **proper noun** is a noun that identifies the name of a specific person, place, or thing. Proper nouns are capitalized in English.

As far as speaking and listening, people's names will sound pretty much the same as they do in English. Just remember what English sounds do not have an Arabic counterpart and what sound you are likely to hear instead.

*tur-**kee**-a*	***too**-nis*	*di-**mashq***
*Tu-**raab**-lis*	*al-**maa**-ni-yaa*	*af-ghaan-is-taan*

Some of those may be easier to decipher than others. Here are the answers: Turkey, Tunisia, Damascus, Tripoli, Germany (which comes from Allemagne/Alemania, the same as in French and Spanish), and Afghanistan. I could easily provide dozens of such examples, but I think it is enough that you get the idea of how the words may be the same as or similar to those you are used to seeing.

Abbreviated Cogs

Sometimes I think that technology is advancing faster than English can keep up. The faster and faster technology progresses, the less time we have to say all the things we need to say. We don't have time to say "compact disc," so we say "CD." We don't want to waste our time remembering our "Personal Identification Number," so we just memorize our "PIN." Well, some of these abbreviations have found their way into Arabic. I won't try to name them all for you, because by the time this book goes to print, those that I give you will just as likely be out of date and you would be able to come up with your own list as easily as I could provide one. The one thing I will say is that when abbreviated cognates are made plural (this rule goes for many technical terms borrowed from English as well), the plural is often made by adding ***–aat*** to the word. For example, the Arabic plural of CD would be "*see-dee-**aat**.*"

Sentences That Don't Bite

Can you believe that you have almost made it through your third chapter in a book about learning Arabic? Congratulations are almost in order. Okay, I'm just kidding. Congratulations are *already* in order. You have come a long way … now keep going.

Let's take what you have learned so far and put it into some basic sentences.

I mentioned it once before, but want to remind you here. Arabic differs from English in that Arabic (almost) never uses the verb "to be." In English, the present tense (the one that tells us what is going on right now) of the verb "to be" is expressed by using either "is" for one person or thing or "are" for plural people or things. That means that the words "is" and "are" are (almost) never used in Arabic.

Let's look back at the sentence about John from earlier in the chapter: ***jaan laa bint.*** How do you think you would say, "Jane is a girl"? I bet you can figure it out. ***jeyn bint.*** That's it. If you translated the sentence literally, you would get "Jane girl." See what other "is/are" sentences you can create with the vocabulary you have learned so far. Here are a couple to get you started:

*di-**mashq** ma-**dee**-na.*	(Damascus is a city.)
*al-**qiT**-Ta laa **kalb**.*	(The cat is not a dog.)

See what others you can create!

Practice Makes Perfect

Now it is time to review and see how much of all this information you have retained.

1. What are the Arabic words for "and," "the," "verily," and "no"?
2. How would you say, "The man is not a woman" in Arabic?
3. Using the *–**aat*** rule for plurals, how would you say the plural for the Arabic word for "cat"?
4. What is the difference between Sun Letters and Moon Letters?
5. What English word does *al-**fuS**-fuS-a* share an origin with, and why is that important in this chapter?
6. In what country would you find the city of *di-**mashq**?*
7. What English words are rarely, if ever, found in Arabic sentences?

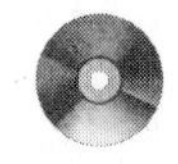

Track 4

The Least You Need to Know

- Arabic nouns have gender.
- There is only one Arabic article: ***al.***
- Arabic doesn't use "is," "are," "a," or "and."
- There is no easy rule for learning Arabic plurals.
- Saying "no" in Arabic is as easy as ***laa.***

Chapter 4

Whose Numbers Are They?

In This Chapter

- Saying any number you want
- Using ordinal numbers
- Telling time in Arabic
- Measuring with the metric system

The numerals we use in the West are actually derivations of numerals that emerged in Hindi culture and made their way west over the course of centuries. The result is that we call the numbers we commonly see "Arabic" numbers, and "Hindi" numbers are the ones that we generally associate with the Arabic language.

I find this evolution of our own numbering system fascinating, but you probably just want to know how to understand all the numbers you will hear and use when you start practicing Arabic. Have no fear. This chapter is all about numbers.

Just Another Number

You might look at Arabic numbers and fear that you will never be able to understand their rules or that you will never be able to memorize all the differences. Actually, you will probably find that just the opposite is true. Some of the number patterns are the same as those in English, and if you have had experience learning another language such as German or Spanish, the numbers you will learn here follow similar patterns as numbers in those languages.

What do I mean? Let's look at the numbers 1 to 10 to find out ….

Breathe and Count to Ten

Forget for a minute that you already learned English. If you were just learning English numbers right now, you might find it interesting that the first group of numbers that have their own words is the group of numbers from 1 to 12. Then, after reaching the number 20, English numbers are broken into groups of 10. Numbers in German are the same way. In Spanish, the numbers 1 to 15 have their own words before being broken into groups of 10, starting with the number 20.

Arabic is much more simple. It breaks numbers into groups of 10 from their beginning at zero and reaching as high as you would like to count.

1001 Arabian Notes

In English, when we want to describe groups of numbers fewer than 100, we use the word "dozens." The Arabic counterpart of this expression is "tens," or *'ash-a-**raat***. For instance, there may be *'ash-a-**raat*** of ways to say "hello" in Arabic.

Okay, let's get started. Here are the numbers 0 through 10:

Track 5

0	***Sif**-r*
1	***waa**-Hid*
2	*ith-**neyn***
3	*tha-**laa**-tha*
4	***ar**-b'a-a*
5	***kham**-sa*
6	***sit**-ta*
7	***sab**-'a-a*

8	*tha-**maan**-ya*
9	***tis**-'a-a*
10	***'ash**-a-ra*

Now that you have seen them, you need a trick or two to remember how to say each of them. Zero (***Sif**-r*) is related to the English word "cipher," which sometimes means "nothing." One and ***waa**-Hid* start with the same sound. *ith-**neyn*** is two and rhymes with "twain," which also means "two."

"Three" and *tha-**laa**-tha* both start with the *th* sound. There is an *r* sound in both "four" and ***ar**-b'a-a*. The Arabic five, ***kham**-sa*, is the only number with the *kh* sound in it. "Six" and ***sit**-ta* both start with the soft *si* sound.

If you had a cold, you might say the English number seven as "sebben." This pronunciation is close to the Arabic ***sab**-'a-a*. *tha-**maan**-ya*, Arabic for "eight," has a double "a" sound in the middle—and "a" rhymes with "eight." Just like our "9" is a reversed version of our "6," the Arabic nine, ***tis**-'a-a*, is pretty much a reversal of ***sit**-ta*. And since you know that *s* comes before *t*, you know that ***sit**-ta* comes before ***tis**-'a-a*.

The only number left is 10, and remembering it is as easy as remembering that ***'ash**-a-ra* is the only number between 0 and 10 that starts with the hard-to-pronounce ***'a*** sound. That's all there is to learning the numbers 1 to 10. Are you ready to move on?

Tips

If you want to learn the numbers 1 through 10 even better, check them out in their written form in Appendix B. Try to come up with a system of remembering them similar to the way that I presented them to you here. It may sound silly, but it works.

The Numbers 11 to 19

If you have read this far, then you are ready to move on to the next phase of numbers. In this section, we cover the numbers 11 through 19. I don't think you need too much practice to learn them, but I will give you one tip.

In some languages, numbers larger than 10 are made by saying, "one-and-ten," "two-and-ten," and so on. That's not quite the rule we use here. To say the Arabic numbers 11 to 19, you speak an abbreviated version, saying "one-ten," "two-ten," and so on. Also, you drop the final ***a*** sound from the "ten" portion, pronouncing it ***'ash**-ar* instead of ***'ash**-a-ra*. Finally, for the numbers 13 to 19, you add a final ***ta*** syllable to the first word (for example: *tha-**laa**-tha-ta **'ash**-ar*). That's all there is to it. Take a look at the numbers 11 to 19.

Track 6

11	*a-**Had**-a **'ash**-ar*
12	*ith-**naa** **'ash**-ar*
13	*tha-**laa**-tha-ta **'ash**-ar*
14	*ar-**b'a-a**-ta **'ash**-ar*
15	***kham**-sa-ta **'ash**-ar*
16	***sit**-ta-ta **'ash**-ar*
17	*sab-**'a-a**-ta **'ash**-ar*
18	*tha-**maan**-ya-ta **'ash**-ar*
19	*tis-**'a**-a-ta **'ash**-ar*

Can you believe you have already made it through all the numbers 0 to 19? I can hardly believe it myself, but here we are. Why not keep going?

20 to 99 Things

For the English numbers 20 through 99, we say the "tens" position first and then the "ones" position. For example, when we say 25, the "twenty" tells us how many tens there are (two) and the "five" tells how many ones (five).

In many other languages, such as in our German example, the numbers 20 to 99 are represented by saying the "ones" position first, saying the word "and," and then saying the "tens" position. The number "four-and-twenty," for example, means 24. This is also the pattern used by the Arabic numbers 20 through 99.

Now, all you have to learn is how to count by tens. Counting by tens is as simple as putting an ***–oon*** ending on the numbers two through nine.

So, counting by tens, here are the numbers 20 through 90:

Warnings

The numbers 20 to 90 actually can be made by adding either ***–oon*** or ***–een*** to the end of the numbers 1 through 9, but the difference depends on the grammar of the sentence. You do not need to worry about the difference. If you want to say "20," you will be understood whether you say *'ish-**roon*** or *'ish-**reen***.

Track 7

20	*'ish-**roon***
30	*tha-laa-**thoon***
40	*ar-b'a-**oon***
50	*kham-**soon***
60	*sit-**toon***
70	*sa-b'a-**oon***
80	*tha-maa-**noon***
90	*tis-'a-**oon***

I suppose I could list the pronunciation of every number between 20 and 99 here, but I trust you feel the same way I do. It would be a waste of space that we could use for other learning. Instead of listing every number between 20 and 99, I decided to just give you a sampling to give you the right idea ....

21	***waa**-Hid wa 'ish-**roon***
29	***tis**-'a-a wa 'ish-**roon***
38	*tha-**maan**-ya wa tha-laa-**thoon***
47	***sab**-'a-a wa ar-b'a-**oon***
56	***sit**-ta wa kham-**soon***
65	***kham**-sa wa sit-**toon***
74	***ar**-b'a-a wa sa-b'a-**oon***
83	*tha-**laa**-tha wa tha-maa-**noon***
92	*ith-**neyn** wa tis-'a-**oon***

That should be enough to get you well on your way. By now, when I ask you to think of a number between 0 and 99, you should be able to give me the answer. Are you ready to take the test? Don't worry. The math quizzes don't come until the end of the chapter.

Hundreds and Thousands and More

Now that you have the basics down, there is not much more for you to learn before counting into the hundreds of thousands. Of course, there are a couple of rules—but this section is set up to get you through the really big numbers.

The Arabic word for hundred is ***mi-'ha***. If you want to say "hundreds" of something, the word for hundreds is *mi-**'haat***. Does that look familiar? It should. To make the plural of hundred, all we do is add the *–**aat*** ending. But do you know what's even easier? You practically never use the plural *mi-**'haat***.

Think back a few pages to when we talked about the tens position and the ones position of a number. Now we add the hundreds position. You already know how to say 100 (***mi-**'ha*). Two hundred is a pair of hundreds, so it is said ***mi-**'ha-**teyn.*** Then, for 300 through 900, the hundreds identifier (***mi-**'ha*) keeps the singular form—and the number telling us how many hundreds drops its final syllable.

That explanation is a bit difficult, so let's take a look:

100	***mi-**'ha*
200	*mi-'ha-**teyn***
300	*tha-**laath mi-**'ha*
400	***ar-**b'a **mi-**'ha*
500	***khams mi-**'ha*
600	***sit mi-**'ha*
700	***sab-**'a **mi-**'ha*
800	***tha-maan mi-**'ha*
900	***tis-**'a **mi-**'ha*

Tips

The numbers 300 to 900 begin with ***mi-**'ha*, the singular form meaning "hundred." The numbers 3,000 to 10,000 begin with *al-**aaf***, the plural form meaning "thousands." Here's a catchy way to remember that rule: thousands are "more," so use the plural form for thousands.

Now, take another look at what I wrote about the numbers and see whether you can tell what I meant. The ***mi-**'ha* only changes with 200, and the other numbers drop their final syllable (***tha**-maan* instead of *tha-**maan**-ya*). I think you are ready to move on.

The Arabic word for 1,000 is ***alf.*** That's pretty easy to remember. In learning the thousands, there is one point we need to focus on. Although the hundreds don't take the plural form, the thousands do. From 3,000 to 10,000, we say the thousands in plural form: *aal-**aaf.*** Then, from 11,000 on up, we switch back to the singular ***alf.*** Why don't we just take a look?

1,000	***alf***
2,000	*alf-**eyn***
3,000	*tha-**laa**-tha aal-**aaf***
10,000	***'ash**-a-ra aal-**aaf***
21,000	***waa**-Hid wa 'ish-**roon alf***
90,000	*tis-'a-**een alf***

You can probably guess that 100,000 is ***mi**-'ha **alf***. So you are getting way up there in your numbers. Why not add the last numbers you likely will ever need.

one million	**two million**	**plural millions**
*mil-**yoon***	*mil-yoon-**eyn***	*mil-aa-**yeen***
one billion	**two billion**	**plural billions**
*mil-**yaar***	*mil-yaar-**eyn***	*mil-yaar-**aat***

Do you think you can remember all of the numbers so far? Let's see. Try this number: 365,438,748,912. Yikes!

Let's look at it written out:

> three hundred sixty-five billion, four hundred thirty-eight million, seven hundred forty-eight thousand, nine hundred and twelve

Goodness gracious. When you are reading through the translation below, try to match the Arabic with the English:

> *tha-**laath mi**-'ha wa **kham**-sa wa sit-**toon** mil-**yaar** wa **ar**-b'a-a **mi**-'ha tha-**maan**-ya wa tha-laa-**theen** mil-**yoon** wa **sab**-'a-a **mi**-'ha tha-**maan**-ya wa ar-b'a-**oon alf** wa **tis**-'a **mi**-'ha wa ith-**naa 'ash**-ar*

You did it! Feel free to take a well-deserved rest before moving on to the next section.

Cardinals, Ordinals ... What's It All Mean?

Simply put, a cardinal number is used for counting. For this reason, cardinal numbers are sometimes called "counting numbers." Cardinal numbers are the numbers you have been learning so far in this chapter.

But what about those other numbers that tell you what you should do first?

As its name suggests, an *ordinal* number suggests *order*. Therefore, ordinal numbers tell us the order in which something occurs. In English, the ordinal numbers often end with the letters "nd," "rd," or "th," as in "second," "third," and "sixth."

In Arabic, there are two ordinal numbers: one masculine and one feminine. The numbers have to be this way because they need to match the gender of the noun they are describing. The following table shows you the difference between the masculine and feminine ordinals.

Ordinal Numbers

English	Arabic Masculine	Arabic Feminine
first	*ow-wal*	***oo**-la*
second	***thaa**-nee*	***thaa**-nee-a*
third	***thaa**-lath*	***thaa**-lath-a*
fourth	***raab**-'i*	***raab**-'i-a*
fifth	***khaa**-mis*	***khaa**-mis-a*
sixth	***saa**-dis*	***saa**-dis-a*
seventh	***saa**-b'i*	***saa**-b'i-a*
eighth	***thaa**-min*	***thaa**-min-a*
ninth	***taa**-s'i*	***taa**-s'i-a*
tenth	***'aaa**-shir*	***'aaa**-shir-a*
eleventh	***Haa**-dee **'aaa**-shir*	*Haa-**dee**-a-ta **'aaa**-shir*
twelfth	***thaa**-nee **'aaa**-shir*	*thaa-**nee**-a **'aaa**-shir*

This information should be enough to really get you going. After twelfth, the ordinal numbers largely repeat themselves. And for the most part, all you have to do to create the ordinal number is add the definite article (your old friend ***al***) to the cardinal number. For example, to say "the fortieth," you would say *al-ar-b'a-**oon**.*

Time After Time

How on Earth could you expect to get anywhere on time if you aren't even able to *tell* time? Hopefully, with all the attention we have given to numbers so far in this chapter, this section will help you overcome some of your problems telling time … or at least guide you toward understanding a bit more when someone is telling you the time.

The first things you need to know when telling time are the words for time. *Time* is ***waq**-t*. But be careful: don't use this word to ask what the time is. To do that, you would ask ***kam** as-**saa'a*** (which literally translates to "How much is the hour?"). This table will help you sort out the words you will need in order to tell time.

Tips

Time (***waq**-t*) can also be used in the philosophical sense. In English, we speak of "difficult times." In Arabic, a similar expression could be made using the plural *times*: *ow-**qaat***.

Words for Time

English	Singular	Dual	Plural
hour	***saa'a***	*saa'a-**teyn***	*saa'a-**aat***
minute	*da-**qee**-qa*	*da-qee-qa-**teyn***	*da-**qaa**-iq*
second	***thaa**-nee-a*	*thaa-nee-a-**teyn***	*tha-**waa**-nee*

Examples:

Five seconds = *kham-**sa** **tha**-waa-**nee***

Three minutes and two seconds = ***tha**-laa-**tha** **da**-qaa-**iq** **wa** da-qee-qa-teyn*

Using the table you just looked at, try to say "three hours" in Arabic. Take a moment … if you said *tha-**laa**-tha saa-**'aaat***, congratulate yourself because you are correct! Try some more on your own.

Warnings

Keep in mind the rule of 10. As you improve, you will need to watch out for a more advanced aspect of using numbers in Arabic. That is, you only use the plural (*da-**qaa**-iq, saa'a-**aat***, and so on) for the numbers 3 through 10. Otherwise, you use the single or dual form. From 11 to infinity, you use the singular noun to go with the number (*da-**qee**-qa, **saa'a***).

When we tell time in Arabic, we always speak of "the hour." That means we say *as-**saa'a***, similar to how you would say, "The time is …" in English.

All you have to do to get the time is add *as-**saa'a*** before the number you are looking for. For example, *as-**saa'a** **kham**-sa* means "five o'clock." Here are some other examples:

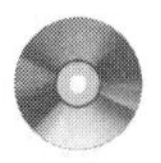

Track 8

> 8:10: *as-**saa'a** tha-**maan**-ya wa **'ash**-a-ra da-**qaa**-iq*.
>
> (The hour is eight and ten minutes.)
>
> 2:05: *as-**saa'a** ith-**neyn** wa **kham**-is da-**qaa**-iq*.

(The hour is two and five minutes.)

3:15: *as-**saa'a** tha-**laa**-tha wa **rub**-'a.*

(The hour is three and one-quarter.)

3:45: *as-**saa'a** **ar**-b'a-a i-la **rub**-'a.*

(The hour is four except one-quarter.)

XX:30: ***niSf saa'a.***

(Half an hour)

7:30: *as-**saa'a** **sab**-'a-a wa **niSf**.*

(The hour is seven and one-half.)

All Things Being Metric

There is not much more for you to learn. Okay, maybe there is, but mastering a language is a lifelong process (and well worth the effort, in my opinion). This section will help you pick up a little more vocabulary before we end the chapter and you have to take your first (and only, I promise!) Arabic math test in the book.

As a general rule, Arabic-speaking countries use the metric system of measurement. It's different than what the United States uses, but Canadians also use it. Although the metric system is used in Arabic, you may at times find it necessary to resort to the United States' system of measurements. For your reference, I have included a bit of each here for you to practice. Remember, you use the singular form and then the dual, then the plural from 3 to 10. When dealing with all numbers 11 and larger, you always use the singular form.

Weights and Measures

English	Singular	Dual	Plural
inch	***booS**-a*	*booS-a-**teyn***	*booS-**aat***
foot	***qad**-am*	*qad-m-**eyn***	*aq-**daam***
yard	***yaard***	*yaard-**eyn***	*yaard-**aat***
mile	***meel***	*meel-**eyn***	*am-**yaal***

meter	***mat**-r*	*mat-**reyn***	*am-**taar***
kilometer	(same)	*keel-o-mee-tar-**eyn***	*keel-o-mee-tar-**aat***
gram	***ghraam***	*ghraam-**eyn***	*ghraam-**aat***
kilogram	(same)	*keel-o-ghraam-**eyn***	*keel-o-ghraam-**aat***
liter	***li**-tir*	*li-tir-**eyn***	*li-tir-**aat***

As a final warning before I end the chapter, the dual form is rarely used in Arabic—so you don't really need to worry about it. In any circumstance, when giving the number and then using the singular form (*ith-**neyn** **qad**-am* instead of *qad-m-**eyn*** or *tha-**laa**-tha **meel*** instead of *tha-**laa**-tha am-**yaal***), you will be understood—so don't worry if you have a hard time learning the numbers at first.

Practice Makes Perfect

If you are not a fan of math and you have been dreading the end of this chapter because I promised you a math test, you are in luck. This quiz is just a review to refresh your knowledge of numbers.

1. How do you say the following numbers?

   194

   283

   56

2. What is an ordinal number?
3. What is the "rule of ten"?
4. How do you say the time, "3:30"?
5. How do you say the time, "6:45"?
6. How do you say "three minutes"?
7. How do you say "eleven seconds"?
8. How do you say "seven meters"?

The Least You Need to Know

- For 21 through 99, you say the ones position first.
- Hundreds don't use the plural form of ***mi***-*'ha.*
- Cardinals are for counting; ordinals are for ordering.
- "***kam*** *as-saa'a?*" means "What time is it?"
- Most often, the metric system is used in Arabic.

Part 2

Excavating Grammar

Grammar rules. Just the thought of them makes me think of younger days when I would rather have been visiting the dentist than learning how to conjugate verbs and do sentence diagrams. Luckily for you, you don't need to know much grammar to go far with Arabic. A few rules will carry you much further in Arabic than in English.

This section serves one purpose: to give you enough of a grammatical foundation to build the sentences you will need to get by as a beginner in Arabic. Part 2 is designed like a drag-racing track—simple, short, and straight-ahead. Here, you will learn the different types of words (yes, there are *types* of words—they're called "parts of speech") and where and when to use them.

Before you are done, you will be able to build your own sentences and ask some easy questions. When practicing, be sure to remember to focus on proper pronunciation—because asking the right question does no good if you pronounce the wrong letters.

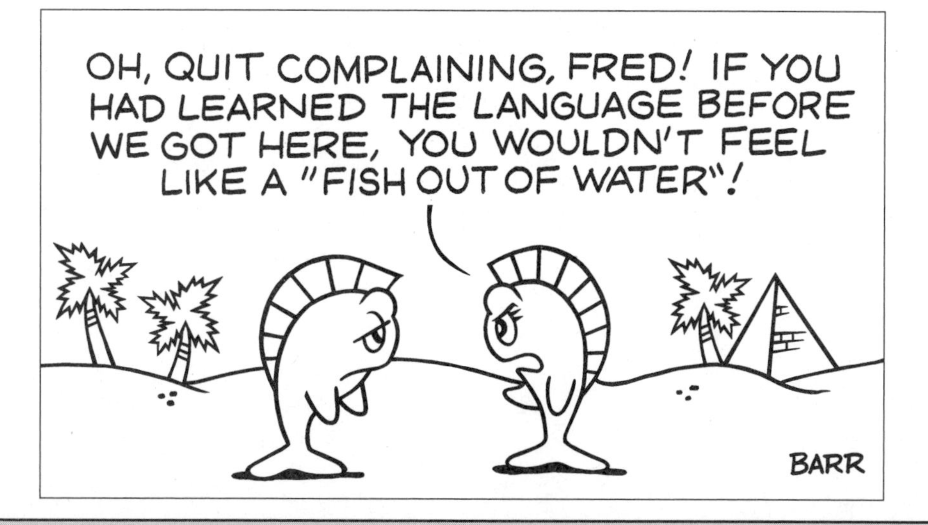

Chapter 5

Conjugation: Use Your Verbs

In This Chapter

- Verb basics
- Changing your verbs for use
- Past, present, and future tenses
- An introduction to hollow verbs
- Building nouns from verb beginnings

Arabic verbs are actually much simpler on a basic level (where we are in this book) than English verbs. Once you learn a few rules about using them, you will be able to twist and turn the verb around any vocal corners you create for yourself.

Basic Verb Structure

Every book I have read about the Arabic language makes one particular point over and over: Arabic is based on the use and construction of *verbs*.

Almost all Arabic verbs are based on a three-letter word stem. The way that we change and use the vowels and syllables attached to that stem determines the meaning of the verb. This construction is a bit different than in English, where a verb has an *infinitive* that we then change in whatever way the sentence requires.

def•i•ni•tion

A **verb** is a word that describes an action, event, or state of being. A verb in its most basic form is called an **infinitive.**

Because Arabic is based on three-letter word stems that may be extended for various meanings, I consider Arabic to be a mathematic language. That is, adding or subtracting letters to or from the word stem results in various meanings.

The most common example I've seen of this type of reasoning is the word ***ka**-ta-ba*, which means "he wrote." Because ***ka**-ta-ba* is also the three-letter word stem, it is as close to an infinitive as Arabic comes. The English infinitive is "to write." In Arabic, the verb word stems always take the third-person male (he) past tense (did, went, wrote).

We go into detail about third person and past tense later in this chapter. ***ka**-ta-ba* is just one of the most common examples of simple Arabic verbs. Following are some other examples. Keep in mind that each of the verbs is in its simplest form (third person, past tense, masculine) and that the other forms are covered later in this chapter:

Track 9

***dha**-ha-ba*
he went

***da**-ra-sa*
he studied

***da**-kha-la*
he entered

***wa**-Sa-la*
he arrived

***ta**-ra-ka …*
he left (a thing)

***laa**-Ha-Tha*
he observed

***THa**-ha-ra*
he appeared

***sa**-qa-Ta*
he fell down

All of the verb examples we've seen so far belong to the simple group of verbs. These verbs are the easiest to understand and work with.

Many verbs also are created by adding one or two letters to the three-letter stem of the word. These types of verbs make up the majority of the verbs we will use in Arabic.

They are identified generally by doubling the middle letter in the word stem (***sal**-la-ma*, or "he protected"), the addition of the ***aa*** sound to the word (***Haa**-wa-la, or* "he tried"), or the addition of the ***t*** sound to the word (*ta-**kal**-la-ma*, or "he talked"). Following are some more common verbs based on these rules.

Track 9

*in-**ta**-THa-ra*
he waited

***waa**-fa-qa*
he agreed

*ta-**bad**-da-la*
he exchanged

***khab**-ba-ra*
he informed

***'aaa**-da*
he returned

*ik-**ta**-sha-fa*
he discovered

***fat**-ta-sha*
he investigated

A third group of verbs—*hollow verbs*—are a bit more difficult to work with. These verbs are more complex because, even though they are built on three simple stem letters just like their counterparts, one of the root letters is both a vowel and a consonant. Two examples of these more complex hollow verbs are ***saa-qa*** ("he drove") and ***qaa-la*** ("he said"). There are plenty of these hollow verbs to check out. You just need to remember that they usually only have two syllables in their basic form and that some funny stuff will happen to them when we start changing their structures.

Put simply, conjugation is the method of changing the way verbs are written and pronounced in order to give the verbs the appropriate meaning. After all, you wouldn't want to say, "He *taked* the pencil," would you? Of course not. So what you do is *conjugate* the infinitive of the verb "to take" in the appropriate way for whatever you want to say. In the above example, you would say, "He *took* the pencil." There you go—Conjugation 101. Now you just have to remember whether it was "he," "she," "they," "I," "we," "us," "them," or "you" who took the pencil.

def•i•ni•tion

A **hollow verb** is a verb in which the second letter of the root is a vowel. Hollow verbs are special cases in Arabic because their structure changes when the verb is conjugated.

From My Point of View

Since you already know some Arabic verbs, let's look at the different *points of view*. In English, we just have three points of view. We have *first person* (the speaker) or the "I" point of view. We have *second person* (the person spoken to) or the "you" point of view. Finally, we have *third person* (anyone who is not the speaker or the one spoken to) or the "he," "she," or "it" point of view.

Arabic has all of these points of view as well, but Arabic also differentiates between male and female or masculine and feminine points of view. Do you remember how I told you in Chapter 3 that nouns have gender? That gender is going to play a bigger part in our studies from here on. And of course, don't forget to consider whether you are dealing with singular or plural (and duals, if you really want to challenge yourself). The following list shows all the possible combinations for points of view for conjugating your Arabic verbs:

def•i•ni•tion

Point of view describes the "grammatical person" in a sentence. In English, there are three points of view: *first person* (I), *second person* (you), and *third person* (he, she, or it).

I	first-person singular
We	first-person plural
You (s/m)	second-person singular masculine
You (s/f)	second-person singular feminine
You (p/m)	second-person plural masculine
You (p/f)	second-person plural feminine
He	third-person singular masculine
She	third-person singular feminine
They (m)	third-person plural masculine
They (f)	third-person plural feminine

Tips

I have intentionally left the conjugations of dual verbs out of this book. I understand that using the dual form is proper in Arabic, but its addition in this text would cause us to lose clarity.

Because the Arabic verbs I have given you so far are all written as third-person masculine singular, you also have learned one of the conjugations of the verb. The next trick is to learn the other conjugations. We have already begun with the past tense, so we continue with that tense.

Verbs Gone Past

Hopefully now you have seen things from another point of view. If you have, then maybe you are ready to move to the next step: working with verbs in the *past tense*.

def•i•ni•tion

There are three tenses in which verbs may occur. The **past tense** is for events that have already happened. The **present tense** is for events that are currently happening. The **future tense is** for events that might or will happen.

All you have to do to create a verb in the past tense is change the ending of the word appropriately for the person who is performing the action (remember that verbs are all about the action).

Table 5.1 shows the person performing the action—in this case, writing. The endings are changed appropriately for each person (or people) who is/are doing the writing.

Table 5.1

Past-Tense Conjugations for "wrote"

Track 10

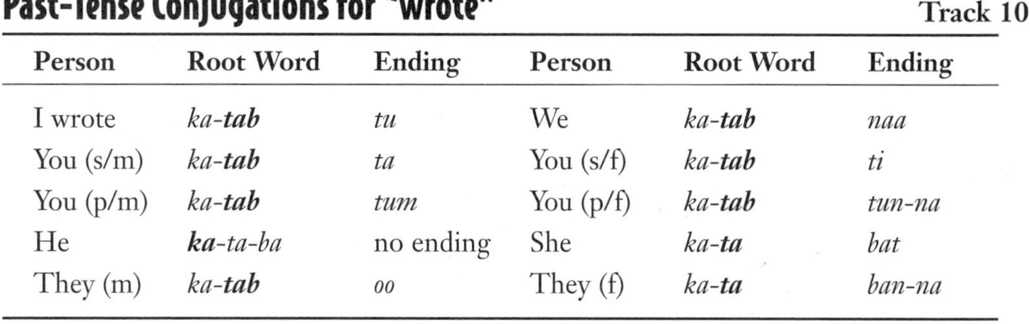

Person	Root Word	Ending	Person	Root Word	Ending
I wrote	*ka-**tab***	*tu*	We	*ka-**tab***	*naa*
You (s/m)	*ka-**tab***	*ta*	You (s/f)	*ka-**tab***	*ti*
You (p/m)	*ka-**tab***	*tum*	You (p/f)	*ka-**tab***	*tun-na*
He	***ka**-ta-ba*	no ending	She	*ka-**ta***	*bat*
They (m)	*ka-**tab***	*oo*	They (f)	*ka-**ta***	*ban-na*

Now that you have taken a look at the chart, see whether you can do a couple verbs on your own. How would you say, "She went"? What about, "I wrote"?

For "She went," the word becomes ***dha**-ha-bat*. For "I wrote," you should say *ka-**tab**-tu*. Let's take a closer look at what happens to the word ***ka**-ta-ba*. Not only did the ending change, but the stress on the sounds also changed. The emphasis switched from the first syllable to the second. Also, we added the "*tu*" sound. That's how you know that you referred to yourself in a verb. And when you hear someone else say "*tu*" in a verb, you will know the speaker is talking about him or herself (even if you may not quite understand everything else he or she is saying).

Do you remember hollow verbs from earlier in the chapter—the ones that had vowels in their roots? I told you they would become a bit more complicated. I also told you we'd get around to explaining them. Well, here's the explanation: hollow verbs have a vowel as their second letter.

Tips

In the past tense for the first- and second-person point of view, most verbs have a sound like a rim shot that one hears after a comedian makes a joke: *ba-**dum**-bum*. Try and remember this to help you pronounce those verbs.

In the examples I gave you before—***saa**-qa* and ***qaa**-la*—you may ask why there are two instead of three letters in the root. Actually, there are three letters in the word stem. It's just that the first two letters run together in pronunciation. I told you that hollow verbs were tricky.

What makes the hollow verbs even more difficult to deal with is the fact that they collapse under the pressure of conjugation. Hollow verbs are not houses made of brick.

When we use hollow verbs in the past tense, they crunch up like aluminum cans. So, where we would expect to say, "I said" by uttering the sounds ***qaal**-tu*, what we actually need to say is ***qul**-tu*. The same thing happens when we say, "I drove." We crunch up the vowel sound and end up saying ***suq**-tu*. Table 5.2 shows the verb ***zaa**-ra*, which means "he visited," conjugated in the past tense.

Table 5.2

Past-Tense Conjugations for "visited"

Track 10

Person	Root Word	Ending	Person	Root Word	Ending
I	***zur***	*tu*	We	***zur***	*naa*
You (s/m)	***zur***	*ta*	You (s/f)	***zur***	*ti*
You (p/m)	***zur***	*tum*	You (p/f)	***zur***	*tun-na*
He	*zaa-**ra***	*no ending*	She	***zaa***	*rat*
They (m)	***zaar***	*oo*	They (f)	***zurn***	*na*

Since there's not much you can do to avoid hollow verbs, it's better to learn to anticipate them. Table 5.3 that follows shows some of the more common hollow verbs, conjugated for "he" and then conjugated for "I" in the past tense. By seeing how the verb is used for "he" and "I" in the following table, you should be able to figure out the other conjugations by looking at the earlier list.

Tips

There are more rules for the conjugation of hollow verbs than would fit into this section. For the most part, the changes among conjugations depend on what vowel is in the middle of the word. The conjugations shown here should get you through most situations.

Table 5.3

Hollow Verbs

Verb	He …	I …
drove	***saa**-qa*	***suq**-tu*
said	***qaa**-la*	***qul**-tu*
won	***faa**-za*	***fuz**-tu*
sold	***baa**-'aa*	*ba-**'aee**-tu*
was	***kaa**-na*	***kun**-tu*

We Verb in the Now

Okay, enough of living and speaking in the past. You already understand what it means to conjugate a verb. You already understand what we mean by point of view.

What you really want to do now is talk about the things that are hip-hop-happening. You want to talk about the *now*. After all, we don't live in the past—we live in the present. And because the present is where you spend all your time, you should be able to explain what you are doing while you are living in it!

When we were working on past-tense verbs, we applied our changes to the end of the word. To conjugate verbs for the present tense, we have to make our changes at both the beginning and the end of the word. Let's take a look.

Using the example verb "study" (***da**-ra-sa*), Table 5.4 shows the different ways verbs are conjugated for the present to include the different points of view.

Table 5.4

Track 11

Present Tense Forms of the Verb "study" (*da-ra-sa*)

Person	Verb Begin	Verb Middle	Verb End
I	***ad*** ...	*ras*	
We	***nad*** ...	*ras*	
You (s/m)	***tad*** ...	*ras*	
You (s/f)	***tad*** ...	*ras* ...	***een***
You (p/m)	***tad*** ...	*ras* ...	***oon***
You (p/f)	***tad*** ...	*ras* ...	***n-na***
He	***yad*** ...	*ras*	
She	***tad*** ...	*ras*	
They (m)	***yad*** ...	*ras* ...	***oon***
They (f)	***yad*** ...	*ras* ...	***n-na***

That may look a little confusing to you, so let's take a look at what we have learned so far. All verbs have a root stem. Usually, that stem is three letters long. When conjugating for the present, you change the stress that occurs on the syllables. So let's take another look—without the verb—and just see what additions we use with the present tense.

Table 5.5

Changes to Verb Beginning and End in Present Tense

Person	Additions	Person	Additions
I	*a …*	We	*na …*
You (s/m)	*ta …*	You (s/f)	*ta … een*
You (p/m)	*ta … oon*	You (p/f)	*ta … n-na*
He	*ya …*	She	*ta …*
They (m)	***ya … oon***	They (f)	***ya … n-na***

All you have to do is insert the verb where the ellipsis (…) appears.

Tips

As a side note, the only time you will use the feminine plural is when there are no masculine items (or people) present in the nouns you are describing. One masculine thing (or person) in the group causes the whole group to be referred to in the masculine form.

Futuristic Verb Usage

You survived the past. You are mastering the present. Do you think that you will endure the future? Of course you will. The future is no problem. In fact, it probably doesn't even deserve an entire section here in the book. I just wanted to keep things balanced.

Arabic future tense is much easier than in English. In English, we have to use the word "will." "I *will* write this book." "You *will* learn Arabic." Arabic speakers do not need to mess with too many words. They just tag another syllable onto the words they already have.

If you can deal with verbs in the present, you can deal with verbs in the future. That's because all you have to do is add the "*ss*" sound, like in the word "hiss," to the beginning of the Arabic verb. To keep things simple, I will use "*si*" to represent the "ss" sound that comes at the beginning of the verbs in the future tense. Table 5.6 shows everything you will need to know in order to use the future tense of Arabic verbs.

Table 5.6

Changes to Verb Beginning and End in Future Tense

Person	Additions	Person	Additions
I	*si-a …*	We	*si-na …*
You (s/m)	*si-ta …*	You (s/f)	*si-ta … een*
You (p/m)	*si-ta … oon*	You (p/f)	*si-ta … n-na*
He	*si-ya …*	She	*si-ta …*
They (m)	*si-**ya … oon***	They (f)	*si-**ya … n-na***

Tips

When thinking about how to conjugate verbs in different tenses, remember that the past has already happened—so the change happens at the end of the word. The present is going on now, so the change happens at both ends of the word. The future has not yet arrived, so the change happens before the beginning of the word.

If you want to talk about things that will happen in the distant future (say, for instance, you are a writer talking about when you will retire), there is another verb you may use for the word "will." The word is ***sow**-fa*. You can use either ***sow**-fa* or *si* … to talk about things that will occur in the distant future, but you should only use *si* … to discuss more immediate activities. Usage varies from person to person and from region to region, so feel free to try out ***sow**-fa* until someone tells you that you are overusing it.

Verb the Noun Builder

Hopefully by now it is too late for you to forget the verb ***ka**-ta-ba*. You remember that this word means "he wrote." Using the root of the word without any vowel sounds, we get *k-t-b*.

Now that we see the word broken down to its absolute basics, we can make some changes and additions to create entirely different words. See if you can find what's in common in the following words:

***kaa**-tib*	***mak**-tab*	*ki-**taab** **mu**-kaa-tib*
***mak**-ta-ba*	*mik-**taab***	*mak-**toob***

You shouldn't have much problem seeing that in every one of those words, the root *k-t-b* stays the same—even in the same order. That's something we don't find in English. So, what do all of the words in this example mean? It wouldn't be fair not to tell you:

***kaa**-tib* writer	***mak**-tab* office	*ki-**taab*** book	*mu-**kaa**-tib* correspondent
***mak**-ta-ba* library or bookstore	*mik-**taab*** typewriter	*mak-**toob*** written	

You can see by looking at the list that the words don't just share their root. They share meanings. All of the words based on the *k-t-b* root have something to do with writing—whether they refer to the person who does it, the place where it occurs, or the *thing* that holds the writing. In Arabic, almost all nouns are built on verbs. You will find out even more about people, places, and things in the next chapter—and when you get there, don't forget to take your verb roots!

Practice Makes Perfect

Another chapter gone by—and another success for you. Now it's time for your test.

1. What are the different "points of view"?
2. How many letters are usually in an Arabic word stem?
3. If the verb ***ra-ka-ba*** means "He rode," how would you say, "I rode?"

Track 12

4. How would you say, "They (m) will ride?"
5. How do you say, "I visited the library?"

The Least You Need to Know

- Verbs are based on three-letter stems.
- Past-tense conjugation happens at the end of the word.
- Present- and future-tense conjugation happens at the beginning of the word.
- Hollow verbs collapse and change when conjugated.

Chapter 6

Pronouns, Nouns, and Even More Verbing

In This Chapter

- All about pronouns
- Pronouns all alone
- Pronouns on the end
- More with nouns and verbs
- Looking for a dual

Whether you know it or not, pronouns are all around you. In fact, I used three of them in the last sentence. Did you find them? Do you think you know what they are? How many of them do you think I have used by now? What on Earth *are* pronouns?

Before you're done with this chapter, you should be able to answer all of those questions. Like so many commercials tell us, "But wait … there's more!" I also added more detail about nouns and verbs in this chapter—along with an introduction to the dual form (even though you can get along just fine without it in most situations).

Pronouns Stick It to 'Em

Here we are again! Welcome to your introduction to pronouns! In simple terms, pronouns are words that take the place of nouns. There are all sorts of pronouns, but for now we will concern ourselves with those pronouns that are strong enough (figuratively) to stand on their own in a sentence. These are known as independent pronouns. They are also called subject pronouns because they act as the *subject* of a sentence or phrase.

def•i•ni•tion

Every sentence can be broken into two main parts: the **subject** and the **predicate.** The **subject** is a noun or pronoun that performs an action or exists. The predicate modifies the subject, telling us how the subject does what it does. In many sentences, the subject has a relationship with an **object.** This **object** is also a noun or a pronoun and is part of the predicate.

In Arabic, personal pronouns are often recognizable in their independent form. That means the pronouns stand alone and are not connected to other words (in another section of this chapter, you will see examples of pronouns that are not separate words—the object and possessive pronouns). Practice the following list of independent personal pronouns until you can recognize and pronounce them without needing a guide. While studying, pay special attention to all the different ways to say "you" in Arabic.

I	***an**-a*	We	***naH**-nu*
You (s/m)	***an**-ta*	You (s/f)	***an**-ti*
You (p/m)	***an**-tum*	You (p/f)	*an-**tun**-na*
He	***hoo**-a*	She	***hee**-a*
They (m)	***hum***	They (f)	***hun**-na*

I told you there wasn't anything to worry about. But before you run off and start throwing together too many patchwork sentences of words you learned before and words you just learned here, there is one other important pronoun to learn: it. And actually, to say "it" in Arabic, you just say either "he" or "she." In other words, you need to figure out whether to use the feminine ***hee**-a* or the masculine ***hoo**-a*. You do that by using the same gender as the noun you are replacing with the pronoun. If "it" is a letter (piece of mail), or *ri-**saa**-la*, then you know that "it" is feminine (it has the feminine ending *–**a***). If "it" is a house (**beyt**), then "it" is masculine.

And that, as they say, is *it*. You have learned all the subject pronouns. Now we can move on to object pronouns. (Or did you want to practice some more? Go ahead. I'll wait for you ….)

Objects of Our Attention

Using pronouns is a great way to communicate. Instead of having to learn a bunch of hard-to-remember nouns (such as "flagellum" and "cornucopia"), we can just say "it." In Arabic, pronouns are just as useful as in English. Learning the Arabic pronouns well will give you a great jump on understanding and using the language.

Since you already learned the subject pronouns, you can now learn the even easier object pronouns. Object pronouns in Arabic get their name because they form the object of the verb in a sentence.

Verbs of action (in other words, verbs that do stuff!) often have an object. I think I can best show you the difference between subject and object pronouns by using an example from English.

In English, we can say the sentence, "He greeted her." This is a simple sentence with both a subject and an object. "He" is the subject; "greeted" is the verb; and "her" is the object. The sentence would be very confusing if we said, "Him greeted she." You already know that "he," "her," "she," and "him" are all pronouns. From earlier in the chapter, you also know that "he" and "she" are subject pronouns. "Him" and "her" are English object pronouns, so you can bet there will be Arabic pronouns to match them.

Tips

In the sentence "He ate it," "it" is the object pronoun that the subject pronoun, "he," is acting upon (ate). Object pronouns are stuck on the end of the verb to which they relate.

Just as English object pronouns are different from subject pronouns, Arabic object pronouns are different from Arabic subject pronouns. There are two big differences. First, object pronouns are not words that stand alone. Second, object pronouns are connected to verbs, not nouns. The following list shows the Arabic object pronouns.

Example verb:

***ta**-ra-ka* (he left); *ta-**rak**-nee* (He left me.)

Track 14

ta-rak …

He left …

Me	***-nee***	Us	***-naa***
You (m/s)	***-ka***	You (f/s)	***-ki***
You (m/p)	***-kum***	You (f/p)	***-kun****-na*
Him	***-hu***	Her	***-haa***
Them (m)	***-hum***	Them (f)	***-hun****-na*

Tips

The pronoun endings ***–hu***, ***–hun***, and ***–hum*** sometimes take the ***i*** sound instead of the ***u*** sound. This happens when they are next to the sounds ***ey***, ***ee***, or ***i***. This rule is based on easier pronunciation and higher-level grammar than we cover in this book, so you don't need to worry about changing your pronunciations.

Use the example verb ***ta****-ra-ka* to practice all of the different object endings before continuing to the next section. Be sure to say them out loud as you go so that you can "feel" how they sound. And notice that the stress comes on the second syllable (-***rak***-).

Possessive Pronouns

To show possession in English words, we use independent (standing alone) pronouns such as "her" or "my," as in the examples "her money" and "my dreams." In Arabic, possessive pronouns are much less complicated because the possessive pronouns are added to the end of the noun. And what's even easier (don't you just love it when things are even easier than you expect?) is that you already know Arabic possessive pronouns. With the exception of one tiny letter, they are the same as the Arabic object endings.

The only difference between the object pronouns and the possessive pronouns has to do with "me." Actually, it has to do with the possessive and object endings for the first-person singular form, which means that the difference has to do with "my" (possessive ending) or "to me" (object ending), rather than actually having to do with "me." The object pronoun for first person singular is *–**nee***, but the possessive pronoun is just *–**ee***.

Examples:	Object Ending	Possessive Ending
	*ta-**rak**-nee*	***qa**-lam-ee*
	He left me	My pen

Because you cannot own a "to run" but can own a "name," Arabic possessive endings are reserved for nouns. Following is a list of the possessive pronoun endings based on ***is**-m*, the Arabic word for "name."

Track 15

My name	***is**-mee*	Our name	*is-mu-**naa***
Your name (m/s)	*is-mu-**ka***	Your name (f/s)	*is-mu-**ki***
Your name (m/p)	*is-mu-**kum***	Your name (f/p)	*is-mu-kun-**na***
His name	*is-mu-**hu***	Her name	*is-mu-**haa***
Their name (m)	*is-mu-**hum***	Their name (f)	*is-mu-**hun**-na*

That wasn't so hard, was it? Since you have the basics down, why don't you try another one on your own? Try telling me all the ways to describe ownership of a house. I've done the first two for you:

My house: ***beyt**-ee*   Our house: *beyt-u-**naa***

Tips

If you work with other Arabic books (and I believe that the more you read, the better your overall learning will be), you may see differences in the spelling of words like ***beyt*** and *beyt-u-**naa***. Some books may write "***beyt**-na*" or "***beyt**-in-a*" for "our house." The truth is that the differences are purely grammatical. Don't worry about which is right—because frankly, the short vowel differences are not important for beginners (and each example can be right). I tried to spell consistently throughout this text so you can see the consonant (important) differences.

Demonstratives: This, That, and the Other

Up to this point, we have covered all the personal pronouns you need to know for Arabic. Personal pronouns have to do with people—but did you know there are other types of pronouns, as well? Remember: a pronoun is a word that takes the place of a noun—any noun, not just nouns relating to people. This section highlights some other pronouns you can use in your conversations.

Demonstrative pronouns are pronouns that demonstrate whether a noun is plural or singular and demonstrate how far the noun is away from the speaker. For example, "this" is a near noun while "that" would be at a distance from the speaker (therefore, a far noun). Demonstratives can be subjects, objects, or objects of a preposition (more about that later). Another way of remembering demonstratives is to picture someone saying "this" to you. When they do, they would demonstrate by showing you the thing to which they are referring. Of course, I'm sure you are getting a bit tired of long explanations by now. You just want to know what they are. Here you go … the Arabic demonstratives:

Table 6.1

Arabic Demonstratives

Close Demonstratives		Far Demonstratives	
this (m)	***ha***-*dhaa*	that (m)	***dha***-*li-ka*
this (f)	***ha***-*dha-hi*	that (f)	*til-**ka***
these (m/f)	*ha-'hu-**laa'h***	those (m/f)	*oo-**laa**-'hi-ka*

Remember: you will only use "these" and "those" when talking about people. Otherwise, you would use the (f) form of "this" or "that."

Another type of pronoun you will find important in Arabic is the prepositional pronoun. As the name suggests, the prepositional pronoun connects to prepositions. I don't want to give away all of Arabic's secrets at once, so … rather than discuss prepositional pronouns here in the middle of an already full chapter, I put the prepositional pronouns with the prepositions in the next chapter. (Psst: you won't have any problem, because you've already learned them ….)

There's one more set of pronouns called relative pronouns. Relative pronouns relate a subordinate clause to the rest of a sentence, and that probably doesn't sound like much fun this early in your learning (it wouldn't be). Relative pronouns also require stronger speaking skills than we've developed so far. For that reason, I have left them out of this book.

Reflexive pronouns are a final type of pronoun that we will discuss in this book. Reflexives only sound difficult. Actually, in Arabic they are not difficult at all—so I put them right here for you to see. Reflexive pronouns are used when the subject and the object of a sentence are the same noun. They are reflexive because they reflect the self.

For example, we say, "He dresses himself," not "He dresses him" or "He dresses he." If we used the second or third sentence, the meaning of the sentence would change. That's why we add the "–self" to "him"—which gives us the sentence, "He dresses himself."

Arabic works the same way. To create a reflexive pronoun, take the Arabic word for "self" and add the appropriate pronoun. We take the pronouns from our list of possessive pronouns because the self belongs to the pronoun ("himself" is "the self that belongs to him").

So … what's the Arabic word for self? ***naf***-*s*.

Let's go through them all.

Track 16

naf-*see* myself	*naf-su-**naa*** ourselves
*naf-su-**ka*** yourself (m)	*naf-su-**ki*** yourself (f)
*naf-su-**kum*** yourselves (m)	*naf-su-**kun**-na* yourselves (f)
*naf-su-**hu*** himself	*naf-su-**haa*** herself
*naf-su-**hum*** themselves (m)	*naf-su-**hun**-na* themselves (f)

You see, it just gets easier and easier. Of course, it is up to you to go back through and practice on your own. I can only do so much here. You'll have to figure out when you want to say "yourself," "himself," "herself," or "themselves" (along with all the other possibilities).

Nouns Need Gender, Too

Think back to the pronoun I gave you for "letter" at the beginning of this chapter (hint: just after the independent pronouns). Do you remember what it was? The pronoun for it (meaning the letter) was actually a "her." We called the letter a "her" because *ri-saa-la* is a feminine noun. Therefore, when it turns into a pronoun, it keeps its gender. This is a bit unusual for an English speaker to consider—but if you have any experience learning other foreign languages, you might already understand the concept of nouns having different genders. In Arabic, the concept of gender is absolutely important.

Warnings

Remember to keep gender in mind for nouns, pronouns, and verbs. Just remember them in order. The noun is the basis. The pronoun takes the place of the noun. And the verb shows how the noun acts. All three must have the same gender.

All the verbs that have to deal with a noun need to follow the rules that apply for the gender of that noun.

Really, it's not too hard—but be sure to watch for pitfalls.

Plural Noun Seeks Plural Verb

We already covered verbs and nouns. In this section, we're going to put them together so you can see how they agree in number as well as in gender.

When I think about my high school English courses, I remember vaguely that my teacher mentioned something about "subject/verb agreement." After a couple hours of digging through dusty memories, I recalled that the verb used in a sentence must agree with the subject of that sentence. In English, we just have to make sure that the subject and verb agree in number (that is, how many things are involved). Therefore, we say "I go," "he goes," and "they go." We don't say "I goes," "he go," and so on.

While Arabic has the added rule that the verbs and nouns must agree in gender, Arabic has the same rules as English for agreement in number. There are some basic guidelines that you can use to help keep your Arabic verbs in agreement with your nouns. These rules will not always apply, but they can help you get started.

Plural human verbs often end in *–**oon*** for masculine.

> Example: *al-**kut**-ub yak-tab-**oon***
>
> The writers write. (masculine plural)

If there is a group of males and females, the masculine plural is used.

Three or more nonhuman things are conjugated in singular feminine form.

> Example: *tadh-**hab** as-sa-yaa-**raat***
>
> The cars go. (third-person singular, feminine, present)

So You Want a Dual

I told you earlier that we wouldn't deal with the dual form of Arabic nouns and verbs, yet … here we are, staring it down. I'm sorry, but there is no getting around it. English is simple. When it comes to numbers and grammar, we have things that occur alone (we call them singular) and things that don't occur alone (we call them plural). Arabic has another case, though: dual.

The dual case in Arabic is reserved for pairs of things; that is, things that happen in twos. For example, in English we say, "One car," but every number more than one gets the plural "cars."

In Arabic, you can say "one car" or *sa-**yaa**-ra*, but before you can say the plural—*sa-yaa-**raat***—you need to say the dual: *sa-yaa-ra-**teyn***. In other words, there is a singular form, a dual form, and also a plural form of Arabic nouns and verbs.

I told you it is an unusual concept to grasp. The dual case is typically created by adding either *–aan* or *–eyn* to the end of a noun or *–aan* or *–aa* to the pronoun end of a verb. So what's the big deal? Why am I making such a fuss?

Most times, Arabic speakers themselves don't bother with the dual—especially not with the dual verb forms. I am just presenting them to you here in this section so you know that the dual form exists. Also, I want to show you those cases where you can expect the dual case so you know what is being said.

Table 6.2

Dual Forms

Pronouns	Independent Pronouns
You (d/m)	*an-tum-**aa***
You (d/f)	*an-tum-**aa***
They (d/m)	*hum-**aa***
They (d/f)	*hum-**aa***

Possessive and Object Pronouns (with example noun *is-m*/name)	
Your name (d/m)	*is-mu-ku-**maa***
Your name (d/f)	*is-mu-ku-**maa***
Their name (d/m)	*is-mu-hu-**maa***
Their name (d/f)	*is-mu-hu-**maa***

Verb Conjugations (with example verb *dha-ha-ba*/he goes)		
	Past	**Present**
(The future tense adds "si" to the beginning.)		
You (d/m)	*dha-hab-tu-**maa***	*tadh-hab-**aan***
They (d/m)	*dha-hab-**aa***	*yadh-hab-**aan***
They (d/f)	*dha-hab-**taa***	*tadh-hab-**aan***

That about covers the dual case … except for one last example: nouns. Generally, you create a noun's dual form by adding the endings ***–aan***, ***–eyn***, or ***–ey***. You are most likely to actually see the dual case in noun form.

Here's an example. Do you remember your numbers? How do you say 200? That's right. Not "two one hundreds," as we see in the forms of the other groups of hundreds (*tha-**laath mi**-'ha* equals 300), but we add the dual form to the noun for 100. If 100 is ***mi**-'ha*, then 200 is ***mi**-'ha-**teyn***. There … you see the formula I just gave you. See what other dual nouns you can think of as we move into the next chapter.

Practice Makes Perfect

We covered a lot in this chapter, but we can't quit. It's time for your practice!

1. What is the independent pronoun for first-person singular?
2. How would you say, "He left it" (masculine)?
3. How would you say, "She leaves it" (feminine)?
4. How would you say, "The cars went"?
5. When are you most likely to see the dual?

The Least You Need to Know

- Independent pronouns stand alone.
- Object and possessive pronouns are almost identical.
- Nouns, pronouns, and verbs must have the same gender.
- You usually see the dual in nouns.

Chapter 7

Other Linguistic Ingredients

In This Chapter

- Educational adjectives
- Garnish your verbs with adverbs
- Prepare for prepositions
- Join words at a conjunction
- Add possession with the idaafa

In this chapter, you'll learn how to add glamour to your sentences by learning the words between the words. We all know that nouns and verbs are the parts of a sentence that get everything done, but adjectives, adverbs, prepositions, and conjunctions give our sentences *style*. When you are done with this chapter, you will be able to use all of these *parts of speech* to give your sentences unique style.

A Dash of Adjectives

An *adjective* is the part of speech used to describe a noun. Adjectives can make nouns big (*ka-**beer***), small (*Sa-**gheer***), long (*Ta-**weel***), or short (*qa-**Seer***)—all without working very hard.

def•i•ni•tion

Parts of speech are the different classes that words are divided into. In English, there are eight parts of speech: nouns, pronouns, adjectives, verbs, adverbs, prepositions, conjunctions, and interjections. **Adjectives** are used to modify nouns.

In English, adjectives come before the noun that they modify. For instance, we read that there is a "big, red, long wagon." Reading along in that phrase, we arrive first at the fact that something is big. Then, reading a bit more, we see that this thing is both big and red. Finally, after reading the descriptive words "big," "red," and "long," we arrive at the "thing"—the wagon.

In Arabic, the noun/adjective order is reversed. First, we say *what* the thing is—then we use adjectives to describe it. "The big, red, long wagon" becomes "*al-'a-ra-**ba** al-ka-**beer**-a al-Ham-**raa'h** alTa-**weel**-a* (literally translated to "the wagon (or "cart") the big the red the long").

Let's get into some practice again:

a big wagon	*'a-ra-**ba** ka-**beer**-a*
the big wagon	*al-'a-ra-**ba** al-ka-**beer**-a*
a huge house	*beyt **Dakhm***
the huge house	*al-beyt al-**Dakhm***

Okay … so why did I just tell you a couple paragraphs ago that the word for "big" is *ka-**beer***, then write "*ka-**beer**-a*" when I talked about the wagon? Easy. The adjectives have to have the same gender as their nouns.

In most cases, you can create the feminine version of Arabic adjectives by adding the *–a* sound to the end of the adjective. Therefore, *ka-**beer*** becomes *ka-**beer**-a.*

Try making the following adjectives agree with the feminine nouns they describe:

*ka-**beer*** big	*Ta-**weel*** tall	*qa-**Seer*** short	***naa**-'im* soft	***Sa**-'ab* hard
***qa**-wee* strong	*Da-**'ieef*** weak	*ja-**deed*** new	*ja-**meel*** handsome	***sah**-l* easy

Did you figure out what the secret was to making all of these adjectives plural? It wasn't very hard, was it? All you had to do was add the ***–a*** sound to the end of each word. Adding ***–a*** is the easiest way to remember how to make Arabic adjectives feminine.

There is another aspect about adjectives that you must remember. Adjectives must match in *number* as well as in gender. In most cases, the number is not a problem.

Anything that is plural and nonhuman is treated like the feminine singular. All you do is add the ***–a*** sound.

When the noun is human, the adjectives become a bit more difficult. When the noun is a word that means plural humans, the adjectives that describe that noun must also be made plural. The problem with this definition is that there are many different ways in which adjectives take the plural. To keep from confusing you, I did not try to include all the adjective plural forms in this portion of the book. They would be difficult to learn, and you would seldom use them in speech.

To get by in most situations, you can use the same plural rules for adjectives that you use for nouns:

–aat for plural feminine

–een or *oon* for plural masculine

–a for singular feminine

Tips

For adjectives, remember that they describe a noun and therefore must "look" like the noun. If the noun is definite (starts with ***al***), the adjective is definite. If the noun is singular or plural, masculine or feminine, the adjective must be the same.

We should cover one other adjective before moving on: the *nisba* adjective. The name is not too important for beginners to know, but what the nisba does is certainly important. The nisba is a way of making an adjective out of a noun by adding the endings ***–ee*** (or ***–ee****-a* for the feminine form).

For example, if I were from Lebanon but did not want to say the words "from Lebanon (***min*** *lub-****naan***)," I could say that I am *lub-****naan****-ee.* Usually the nisba is used to talk about where we are from or about our origins. All we have to do is take the feminine *a* sound off the end of the word (if there is one in the first place), then make the last sounds either ***–ee*** or ***–ee****-a*, depending on the gender of the person you're speaking about.

A final note on the nisba is that usually, the definite article ***al*** is removed. You probably wouldn't want to say, "She is *the* Syrian (***hee****-a as-soo-****ree****-a*)" as often as you would want to say, "She is Syrian (***hee****-a soo-****ree****-a*)."

A Sprinkle of Adverbs

Let's begin with adverbs. An *adverb* is one of the eight parts of speech in English. An adverb is a modifying word, or a word that describes something. What do adverbs describe? Pretty much everything … except nouns. Adverbs can be used to modify verbs, adjectives, other adverbs, entire parts of sentences, and even entire sentences.

Tips

In Arabic, adverbs are used less frequently than in English. Often in Arabic, a prepositional phrase is used in the place of an adverb. Here's an example: "Time passed slowly" in English would be "Time passed with slowness" in Arabic. Prepositional phrases are covered later in this chapter.

In English, we generally associate adverbs with the ending *–ly*, as in words such as "generally," "really," "quickly," "undoubtedly," and "naturally." How many other *–ly* words can you come up with?

Adverbs are used to indicate how much, what, how, where, when, or to what extent something occurs. As one example, in the sentence, "The man went quickly," the adverb "quickly" is used to tell us how fast (and to what extent) the man went.

The best way to remember how to change English adverbs into Arabic adverbs is to assume there will be a preposition involved. In English, we would use one word with the *–ly* ending—while Arabic often creates a prepositional phrase to describe what, how, where, when, or to what extent something occurs. We will go over such examples later in this chapter and throughout the remainder of this book.

If a rule can be made for Arabic adverbs, it would be that adverbs are the words that end with an ***–an*** sound. Still, there are several adverbs we can learn in this section.

Following are some Arabic adverbs that describe *place*:

Track 17

*hu-**naa***	*hu-**naa**-ka*	*b'a-**eed**-an*	*qa-**reeb**-an*
here	there	far	nearby (also "soon")

Next are some adverbs that describe *time*:

*a-**kheer**-an*	***a**-ba-da*	*aH-**Hyaa**-nan*	***daa**-'hi-man*
recently	never	sometimes	always
***baa**-kir-an*	*Haa-**lee**-yan*	*ka-**theer**-an*	*qa-**reeb**-an*
early	currently	often	soon
*al-**aan***	*yoo-**mee**-an*	*us-boo-**'aee**-yan*	*shah-**ree**-yan*
now	daily	weekly	monthly
*san-aw-**wee**-yan*	***ghad**-dan*		
yearly	tomorrow		

Here are some adverbs that describe manner, or *how:*

***jid**-dan*	*ta-**maa**-man*	*a-saas-**see**-an*
very	precisely	basically

*fi-'**al**-an* really	***ha**-ka-dha* so (thus)	***Ha**-san-nan* exceptionally
*sa-**wee**-an* together (1)	*taq-**reeb**-an* almost	***m'a**-an* together (2)
*wa-**Heed**-an* alone	***ai**-Daan* also	

Note: for "together" (1) and (2), the words are identical in meaning and usage depends largely on the speaker's preference. For me, *sa-**wee**-an* was easier to pronounce when I began learning Arabic.

Warnings

Be careful when using words like *daily* and *weekly,* because they may not always be adverbs. If they describe a verb ("He visited ***yearly,***" for example), they are adverbs. If they modify a noun (a ***weekly*** newspaper), they are adjectives.

A Smidge of Prepositions

If prepositions are important in English, they are *very* important in Arabic. So … what is a *preposition*?

Prepositions are used to link nouns or pronouns to other parts of a sentence. An object follows them and clarifies the function of the preposition. In Arabic, prepositions can be either a single letter added to the beginning of an Arabic noun or pronoun—or they may stand alone as independent words. If the preposition is connected to the beginning of another word, it cannot be disconnected from that word and is therefore called an *inseparable* preposition. If the preposition stands alone, it is called a *separable* preposition.

def•i•ni•tion

A **preposition** is a word that links a noun or pronoun to another word or phrase in a sentence. If we break it down, we see *"pre-position." Pre* means "before" and *position* means "place," so prepositions are words that come at the "before place"—or before their objects.

In either case, the preposition will have an object. This object can be conjugated just like the direct object pronouns we discussed in the last chapter.

There are actually four inseparable prepositions. Of those, only three are shown here. I did that because you will rarely need to use the inseparable prepositions *wa* and *ta*. They are reserved for exclamations of prayer and praise.

Preposition	Meaning	Example
bi-	in/at/near/by/with *bi-**sur**-'aa* (quickly)	*bi-sa-**yaa**-ra* (by car)
li-	for/to/on account of *li-**la**-'ib* (for play)	*lil-mak-tab* (for the office)

The prepositions use their pronouns exactly the same way that verbs use possessive pronouns.

Look at how we put the prepositions with their pronoun endings on the word "with" to see what I mean:

Track 18

m'a …

With …

… me	***m'a**-ee*	us	***m'a**-naa*
you (m/s)	***m'a**-ka*	you (f/s)	***m'a**-ki*
you (m/p)	***m'a**-kum*	you (f/p)	***m'a**-kun*
him	***m'a**-hu*	her	***m'a**-haa*
them (m)	***m'a**-hum*	them (f)	***m'a**-hun*

A Touch of Conjunctions

Just a couple more sections and you'll be finished with this chapter. You've learned quite a lot already, and hopefully you are excited about learning even more. In this section, you will learn Arabic conjunctions. There are actually several ways to define a conjunction, but all you really need to know is that conjunctions are joining words—joining two or more words in a sentence. Those other words can be parts of clauses or words all by themselves.

You already know the most common Arabic conjunction: ***wa***. We covered it in the beginning of the book when you had just learned how to make the sounds. Do you remember what it means? ***wa*** means "and."

Now, can you picture the word "and" coming somewhere other than between two words in a sentence? Most often, it lies between other words—just like other conjunctions.

Here are some other common Arabic conjunctions:

fa
therefore

***in**-na*
when/since

***am**-ma fa*
regarding

an
that/in order that

*ka-'**han**-na*
as it were

*li-'**han**-na*
because

***il**-la an*
except that

***wa**-'hin*
although

ow
or

***thu**-ma*
then

*wa-**laak**-in*
but/yet

***lam**-ma*
after/when

low
if

*low **laa***
if not

The Idaafa

The idaafa is something that looks like a noun/adjective phrase with one glaring exception: only the first word in the idaafa has the definite article. Idaafa means "addition." And the idaafa is actually used to show possession. But what the idaafa *really* looks like is two or more nouns with nothing between them but the definite article or the occasional demonstrative. Yuck. That still sounds pretty difficult. Let's take a look.

If we wanted to say, "The man's dog," we would say ***kalb** al-**raj**-al*. Let's look at it from another English direction. Instead of saying, "The man's dog," we can just as easily say, "The dog of the man." This second example better highlights the idaafa.

The Arabic ***kalb** al-**raj**-al* would literally be translated as "dog the man." Can you see what's missing? Take "the" out from before "dog," and take "of" out from between "dog" and the second "the." If you do those two things, you have the same phrase in Arabic and in English. That's the idaafa!

The easiest idaafas will have two nouns or pronouns separated by our buddy ***al*** or by one of the demonstratives (such as *this*, or ***ha**-dhaa*). Let's take another look to clarify:

Tips

If the definite article ***al*** comes right after a vowel sound (such as ***a*** or ***ee***), you can run the sounds together. In fact, you will hear them run together more than you will hear them separated. I left them separate in this text (example: ***beyt ha**-dhaa ar-**raj**-al*) so you can see the different words. Also, the words will still be *written* separately.

The house of the man: ***beyt** ar-**raj**-al*

The house of this man: ***beyt ha**-dhaa ar-**raj**-al*

Some final notes on idaafas:

- They do not have to have the definite article at all.
- Only the last word of the idaafa has the definite article.
- They can be several words long, such as:
  "The car of the teacher of the school"
  *Sa-**yaa**-ra (of the) mu-**dar**-ris (of) al-mad-**ra**-sa*
- The last word determines whether the idaafa is definite or indefinite.

Whew! I think you've got it! What do you think? Continue to the practice section to make sure.

Practice Makes Perfect

Well, you have reached another chapter end. How many does this make so far? Seven? It's hard to believe. Just a few more questions and you will be through—well, on your way to success. Actually, you have already learned enough Arabic to get yourself started in some conversations. Why not go out and share what you have learned?

But first, let's practice:

Track 19

1. If ***beyt mu**-tas-sikh* means "a dirty house," how would you say "a dirty car"?
2. If Iraq is pronounced *'i-**raaq***, how would you say, "She is Iraqi"?
3. What is the most common sign that an Arabic word is an adverb?
4. What does Arabic often use instead of adverbs?
5. How would you say, "It (feminine) is in the house"?
6. What do the conjunctions *–**an***, ***wa***, ***fa***, *li-'**han**-na*, and *wa-**laak**-in* mean?
7. What does the phrase *sa-**yaa**-rat **jaan*** mean?

The Least You Need to Know

- Adjectives describe nouns or pronouns.
- Adverbs describe just about everything else.
- Prepositions give us useful phrases.
- The idaafa is another way to show possession.

Chapter 8

Work Those Interrogatives

In This Chapter

- Your first questions
- Asking more than the "five Ws"
- Questions at different times
- Answers you might get
- Don't let them speak too quickly

In this chapter, you learn how to ask "is" and "are" questions. Then, we get into some real interrogation—at least, some real interrogatives. You learn how to ask any of the (seven) "five Ws." You also learn how to answer these questions. Naturally, you also learn how to defend yourself from too many questions by learning how to say things like, "I don't understand" and "Please speak more slowly."

Are You as I Am?

If you are looking to start asking questions to spur your Arabic education, is/are questions are the easiest to ask. "Hal" is the key here. Some of you may think I'm referring to a robot from some science-fiction movie. Actually, I am referring to the Arabic interrogative ***hal***. The job of an interrogative is to ask questions. In Arabic, ***hal*** tells you there is a question coming—specifically, an is/are question.

hal comes at the beginning of a sentence, introducing the question, so there is no doubt you will be asking a question. It doesn't matter whether the question is singular, plural, masculine, or feminine. ***hal*** is your friend. Take a look at a couple examples.

*hal **an**-ta **tadh**-hab?*
Are you (masculine) going?

*hal **an**-ti tadh-hab-**een?***
Are you (feminine) going?

*hal **ta**-ra-ka?*
Did he leave?

*hal **ta**-ra-kat?*
Did she leave?

*hal **ta**-ra-kat al **beyt**?*
Did she leave the house?

Tips

The thing to remember about *hal* is—just like all of the other interrogatives—it will always come at the beginning of the sentence. When you hear an interrogative at the beginning, you know that a question is coming.

If you care for a little less action in your sentence (when no one needs to *go* somewhere), you can also use ***hal*** for questions such as the following:

Is that your dog? *hal **ha**-dhaa **kalb**-u-ka?*

Or, if someone just had a child, you could say:

Is it (he) a boy? *hal **hoo**-a **wa**-lad?*

At Least Five Ws

Many of you have heard about journalism's "five Ws": who, what, when, where, and why. There is also another one that we often overlook: "how." Of course, it doesn't start with "w" like the other ones, but that doesn't matter. It ends with "w," and that's close enough. All of them are interrogatives. (While you are making sure to ask all the proper questions, don't forget to ask "which" and "how much," either.)

In English, if you say, "When I get back …", you are probably not asking a question. This is an important example to keep in mind as we go through the interrogatives. In Arabic, interrogatives are only used for questions. We are not concerned with any other possible uses of the five Ws. If they aren't used to ask a question, then they aren't interrogatives. Besides … in Arabic, you would use another word in those situations, anyway.

Here are the Arabic interrogatives. Learn them well. They are the keys to getting your questions answered.

who	***man***	what	***maa**-dha/**maa***
where	***ai**-na*	when	***mat**-a*

why	*li-**maa**-dha*	how	***keyf**-a*
how much/many	***kam***	which	***ai***

Now that you have seen the interrogatives, why not run a practice round before we go to the next section?

Track 20

Who is your (masculine) friend (feminine)? *man Sa-**dee**-qa-tu-ka?*

What are you (masculine) doing? ***maa**-dha **ta-f'al**?*

Where are you (feminine) going? ***ai**-na **tadh**-hab-een?*

When are you (masculine) leaving? ***mat**-a **tat**-ru-ka?*

Why did she say that? *li-**maa**-dha **qaa**-lit **dha**-lik?*

How is your (masculine) health? ***keyf**-a **SuH**-tu-ka?*

How much did we pay? *kam **daf**-'a-naa?*

Which man did you (masculine) see? *ai ar-**raj**-al raa-'hey-ta-hu?*

Warnings

*li-**maa**-dha*, Arabic for "why," actually means "for what." Think of "why" as another way of asking, "For what reason?".

You may have the tendency to pronounce ***keyf**-a* like the English word "key." Remember from our pronunciation guide, however, that *–**ey*** rhymes with "hey" or "they," so ***keyf**-a* rhymes with ***theyf**-a*.

Ask Some Questions

Let's continue with our question words. This time, you get the chance to ask some basic questions and practice your vocabulary. Most of this will be a review for you, but I will try to keep things fresh.

Notice how the interrogative comes first in the sentence. Also, pay attention to how the verbs change for the past, present, and future tenses—even though the interrogatives stay the same.

*hal **dha**-ha-ba?*	*hal **tadh**-hab?*	*hal si-**nadh**-hab?*
Did he go?	Is she going?	Will we go?

That covers the question words *is* and *are*. What about the other questions? Let's see …

If we want to take a look at asking questions about *who* (***man***), the questions may look something like the following:

> *man* ***ta****-ra-ka al-****man****-zil?*
> Who left the home?

Tips

Notice in the question, "Who left the home?" we use the verb for "he left" (*ta-ra-ka*). That is because we are not sure whether the person who left the house is male or female or whether it was one person or several people. The "he left" form is safe for us to use in such unknown cases.

> *man* ***yadh****-hab bil-****khaa****-rij?*
> Who goes outside? (Literally: "Who goes in the outside?")

> *man si-yu-****zoor****-naa?*
> Who will visit us?

There, you have three separate questions that begin with the interrogative "who." Now, let's look at the interrogative *what (****maa****-dha):*

> ***maa****-dha sa-'****hal****-ta?*
> What did you ask?

> ***maa****-dha ya-f'al-oon?*
> What are they doing?

> ***maa****-dha si-****ta****-qool?*
> What will she say?

Again, we have the question word—this time, ***maa****-dha*—coming first in the sentence. When you hear the interrogatives at the beginning of a sentence, you can be sure that you are hearing a question—so be prepared to answer! Also, just so you know, there is another word sometimes used to ask the question "what." That word is just a shortening of ***maa****-dha;* it is ***maa. maa*** is used for asking questions like, "What is your name?" (***maa*** *is-mu-ka/ki*). We will cover it more in later sections and chapters, so I didn't include more examples of ***maa*** here.

In case you haven't noticed by now, for each interrogative I present one question in the past tense, one in the present tense, and one in the future tense. I do this both so you can repeat the questions a few times to yourself and also so that you can see the ways verbs change forms for the different tenses. Now, let's look at questions that use the word *where (****ai****-na).*

> ***ai****-na ta-waq-****qaf****-naa?*
> Where did we stop?

> ***ai****-na* ***yadh****-hab-an-na?*
> Where are they (feminine) going?

***ai**-na si-na-**'ha**-kal?*
Where will we eat?

Warnings

When asking where someone comes from, we start with the preposition "from." In English, we say, "Where are you from?" But Arabic grammar (and proper English, according to most) causes us to say, "*min **ai**-na **an**-ta?*" or "From where are you?" Did you guess that you might say, "***ai**-na **an**-ta **min**?*" If you asked the question that way, a native speaker would think that you were asking, "Where *you are* from?"

If we are able to ask all those other questions and discover so much information just by asking a few simple questions, of course we will want to know when (***mat**-a*) something is to take place. Why not take a look at a few questions that take advantage of asking,"when"?

***mat**-a **wa**-Sa-lat?*
When did she arrive?

***mat**-a tu-**ghaa**-dir-oon?*
When are you departing?

***mat**-a si-nu-**saa**-fir?*
When will we travel?

And then, there is the question so many children have been asking adults around the world since time began: "Why?" (*li-**maa**-dha*).

*li-**maa**-dha **'ab**-ir-a ad-da-**jaaj** aT-Ta-**reeq**?*
Why did the chicken cross the road?

*li-**maa**-dha as-si-**ma'h** zar-**qaa'h**?*
Why is the sky blue?

*li-**maa**-dha si-**na**-ta-**kal**-lam fee-**maa** b'ad?*
Why will we talk later?

So there you have the so-called "five Ws" of English. But there are a couple more "Ws" that can be just as important if you are really trying to get information. Why not continue? The "sixth W"—if there can be such a thing—is most certainly *how* (***keyf**-a*).

***keyf**-a 'a-**raf**-ta **dha**-lik?*
How did you know that?

***keyf**-a **an**-ta al-**yoom**?*
How are you today?

***keyf**-a si-na-**qar**-rar?*
How will we decide?

1001 Arabian Notes

In Arabic, you will encounter verbs in their masculine form more often than in their feminine form. This has nothing to do with a competition between men and women. It is just the way the language works. For that reason, from this point in the text, please assume I am talking about masculine verbs unless indicated otherwise with a feminine (f) marking.

We're still not to the end yet. But as they say, "We can see it from here." Another important question we sometimes have to ask—especially when we're looking for clarification—is *which* (***ai***), as in which thing someone is talking about.

***ai** sa-**yaa**-ra faD-**Dal**-ti-**haa**?*
Which car did you (f) prefer?

***ai feelm tu'u-raD**?*
Which films are showing?

***ai** aj-**juz**-ur si-yu-**zoo**-roo-haa?*
Which islands will they visit?

Tips

In the "which" questions, two of the questions have the feminine ending ***haa***. This ***haa*** is a *reflexive pronoun* that *reflects* back on the object being indicated; that is, in the first sentence, *–**haa*** at the end "reflects" back to the car, because "car" is the object being "preferred" and is therefore the object of the sentence. In the second sentence, the word "islands" is the object of the sentence, so *–**haa*** "reflects" back to that word.

Last but not least, we need to know how to ask *how much* and *how many (**kam**)*. Knowing this word will come in especially handy when you start haggling for better prices in the market.

***kam** sa-**yaa**-raat?*
How many cars (are there)?

***kam** as-**s'ir**?*
How much does it cost (literally translated to "How much is the price?")

Now you know how to ask questions. Naturally, the next step is for you to get some answers. Keep reading, and maybe you will find the perfect answer to your questions!

Get Some Answers

You have asked some questions, so why not focus a little bit on some of the answers you may get? I cannot count the number of times when first learning Arabic that I asked for directions in perfect Arabic tones, only to have someone—excited that I spoke the language—answer me so quickly that I had no idea what was being said.

I don't want that to happen to you, so I am going to equip you with some answers that match the questions in the last section. Naturally, I can't offer all the possible answers—but I can provide some of them. To keep things consistent, below I have given you one answer to each of the questions we asked before. I haven't made things too easy for you, though. I have only given you the Arabic version of the questions. It is up to you to figure out what each question means.

*hal **ta**-ra-ka?* — *n'am, **ta**-ra-ka.*
Yes, he left.

*hal **ta**-ra-kat?* — *n'am, **ta**-ra-kat.*
Yes, she left.

*hal **ta**-ra-kat al-**beyt?*** — *n'am, **ta**-ra-kat al **beyt.***
Yes, she left the house.

Of course, you want to see the answers to the questions you asked in the last section. Here they are:

*hal **dha**-ha-ba?* — *n'am, **dha**-ha-ba.*
Yes, he went.

*hal **tadh**-hab?* — *n'am **tadh**-hab.*
Yes, she is going.

*hal si-**nadh**-hab?* — *n'am si-**nadh**-hab.*
Yes, we will go.

Track 21

*man **ta**-ra-ka al **man**-zil?* — ***ta**-ra-ka fa-**reed** al **man**-zil.*
Fareed left the house.

*man **yadh**-hab bil **khaa**-rij?* — ***yadh**-hab **ab**-ee bil **khaa**-rij.*
My father went outside.

*man si-ya-**zoor**-na?* — *si-ya-**zoor**-na a-qaa-**rib**-na.*
Our relatives will visit us

***maa**-dha sa-'**bal**-ta?* — *sa-'**bal**-tu, "**maa hoo**-a is-mu-**ka?**"*
I asked, "what is your name?"

***maa**-dha ya-**f'al**-oon?* — ***hum** ya-**ghan**-noon.*
They are singing.

***maa**-dha si-**ta**-qool?* — *si-ta-**qool is**-mu-haa.*
She will say her name.

Tips

When you want to ask someone his or her name—*sa-'**hal**-tu* ***maa hoo**-a is-mu-**ka***—you are actually saying, "What is it your name?" You can shorten this sentence to ***maa** is-mu-**ka*** or *is-mu-**ki*** (f), if you want to. But you would *not* say, ***maa** hee-a is-mu-ki*. The ***hoo**-a* is a pronoun based on the word ***is**-m*, which is masculine (therefore, ***hoo**-a*).

***ai**-na ta-waq-**qaf**-na?*	*ta-waq-**qaf**-na fee al **maT**-'am.* We stopped in the restaurant.
***ai**-na yadh-**hab**-an-**na**?*	*yadh-**hab**-an-**na il**-a al-**maq**-ha.* They (f) are going to the coffee shop.
***ai**-na si-**na**-'ha-kal?*	*si-na-**'ha**-kal fee al-**maT**-'am.* We will eat in the restaurant.
***mat**-a **wa**-Sa-lat?*	***wa**-Sa-lat fee aS-Sa-**baaH.*** She arrived in the morning.
*mat-a tu-**ghaa**-dir-oon?*	*nu-**ghaa**-dir b'ad al-THu-hur.* We are leaving in the afternoon.
***mat**-a si-nu-**saa**-fir?*	*si-nu-**saa**-fir fee aS-**Saif.*** We will travel in the summer.
*li-**maa**-dha **'ab**-ir-a **lil** wa-**Sool** **i**-la ad-da-**jaaj** aT-Ta-**reeq?***	*al-**jaa**-nib al-**'ha**-khar.* To get to the other side.
*li-**maa**-dha as-si-**ma'h** **zar-qaa'h?***	*li-**'han**-na as-**su**-Hub bai-**Daa'h.*** Because the clouds are white.
*li-**maa**-dha si-**na**-ta- li-**'han**-na **ley**-sa **kal**-lam fee-**maa** b'ad?*	*la-**dey**-na al-**waq**-t al-**aan.*** Because we don't have the time now.
***keyf**-a 'aa-**raf**-ta **dha**-lik?*	*ta'al-**lam**-tu-hu fee al-mad-**ra**-sa.* I learned it in school.
keyf**-a **an**-ta al-**yoom?	*shu-**kraan**, an-a bi-**kheyr.*** Thank you, I am fine.
***keyf**-a si-nu-**qar**-rir?*	***yum**-kin an-nu-**qal**-lib **'um**-la **m'ad**-i-**nee**-a.* Maybe we could flip a coin.

***ai** sa-**yaa**-ra faD-**Dal**-ti-**haa**?*	*faD-**Dal**-tu as-sa-**yaa**-ra al-Ham-**raa'h**.* I preferred the red car.
ai feelm tu'u-raD	***Tu'u-raD sab**-'aa af-**laam**.* Seven films are showing.
***ai** aj-**juz**-ur si-ya-**zoo**-roo-haa?*	*si-ya-**zoo**-roon **Siq**-qil-**lee**-a **fuq**-T.* They will only visit Sicily.
***kam** sa-**yaa**-raat?*	***kham**-sa sa-yaa-**raat**.* Five cars.
***kam** as-**s'ir**?*	*as-**s'ir** mi-'ha-**taan** doo-**laar**.* The price is $200.

Easy Responses to Easy Questions

Sometimes you don't need an entire paragraph to answer questions. Sometimes you do not need more than just a word or two to get your point across. Here's why: in English, every question that starts with the word "is" or "are" is a yes-or-no question. In other words, no matter what answer someone expects, you can give that person a simple "Yes" or "No." This is a perfect system if you are not the talkative type.

n'am Yes	***ru**-bim-aa* Perhaps	***laa*** No	*min al-**mum**-kin* Possibly
*aH-**Hyaa**-nan* Sometimes	***daa**-'hi-man* Always	*a-ba-dan* Never	***kal**-laa* No way
***Tab**-'aan* Of course	***li**-maa **laa*** Why not	*laa mush-kil-a* No problem	*mus-ta-**heel*** Impossible

There likely will be times when you might not be asked a question but *will* have to chime in with a word or two to keep the conversation on a level you can follow. These are the "*Whoa!*" words you need. People tend to speak quickly, and especially when you are first learning a new language, it takes some time to listen, translate, and understand what is being said. Don't be embarrassed to ask someone to slow down. It is better to ask than to answer a question with a response that doesn't make any sense because you didn't understand what was being said. When you find yourself in one of these situations, use one of the following phrases:

*'**af**-waan, laa **af**-ham …*
Excuse me, I don't understand …

***laa af**-ham **shey**-'han*
I don't understand a thing …

***af**-ham qa-**leel**-an*
I understand a little …

*a-ta-**kal**-lam qa-**leel**-an **fuq**-T bil-'**ar**-ra-**bee**-a*
I speak only a little Arabic …

***an**-a a-**t'al**-lim al-'**ar**-ra-**bee**-a*
I am learning Arabic …

*al-'**ar**-ra-**bee**-a ja-**deed**-a **lee***
Arabic is new to me …

*raj-**jaa**-'han at-ta-**kal**-lam bi-**buT**-Ta'h?*
Please speak slowly …

***yum**-kin an ta-**qool dha**-lik **mur**-at **ukh**-ra*
Can you say that again?

***af**-ham **juz**-'han min **dha**-lik*
I understand part of that …

As you may expect by now, there are several new words in these phrases for you to learn. Don't be put off by them, however. You will have them down after a couple practice rounds.

1001 Arabian Notes

My experience has shown that you will never offend someone by politely asking him or her to speak more slowly or repeat what was said. More likely, the person will be impressed by your desire to learn—and he or she will happily oblige your request.

Whew! That was quite a lot for this chapter. I hope you don't feel overwhelmed. Just remember, this is not the type of book you read through once and then put on your shelf (at least, I hope not!). For many of these sections and chapters, it will take several readings to grasp all the information. If you are one of the lucky few who can pick up all the knowledge the first time around, then good for you! Maybe you will be teaching your friends before too long.

Practice Makes Perfect

One more chapter down. After this quiz, you have only one chapter left before you move into Part 3: "Express Yourself." Keep up the good work!

1. What is the Arabic word used to introduce questions that start with "Is" or "Are"?

2. How would you say, "Are you going?" to a group of women, men, boys, and girls?
3. What are the "five Ws" in Arabic?
4. How would you say, "Which woman went?"
5. If someone says to you, "*ta-waq-**quf**-na fee al-**muT**-T'aam,*" what have they said?
6. How would you say, "I am learning Arabic. Please speak slowly."?

The Least You Need to Know

- ***hal*** at the beginning of a sentence means a question is being asked.
- ***man, maa**-dha/**maa**, **ai**-na, **mat**-a*, and *li-**maa**-dha* mean "who, what, where, when, and why."
- Repeating questions asked of you is a good way to remember new vocabulary.
- *'**af**-waan, laa **af**-ham* means "Excuse me, I don't understand."

Chapter 9

Snap-In Sentence Construction

In This Chapter

- How to order your sentences
- Verbs first
- Comparing this to that
- Only the best for you

Up to this point in the book, you have been learning Arabic one piece of a sentence at a time. I have given you words or phrases to look at with the expectation that you will practice them as you prepare for bigger and better things to come. So when do we finally get to the "bigger and better" things? Is *right now* soon enough?

This chapter is called "Snap-In Sentence Construction" because in the coming pages, we take the pieces we have learned so far and start to connect them with one another in ways you never thought possible. Okay, maybe you did think of some of the ways these sentences can be put together. That could even be why you are still reading this text. You not only thought of the possible ways to put these sentences together, but you also want to get going on them *right away!* Fine, then. Let's get started with our "snap-in sentences."

Word Order or Word Jumble?

In English, we have things pretty easy. For the most part, sentences occur in a familiar order. I mean, if we make a statement, we start with the subject and then move on to the verb—and then if there is an object, that comes in the last part of the sentence.

Look at this sentence: *I went to the store*. In this case, "I" is the subject, then we have the verb, "went," followed by the phrase "to the store," a prepositional phrase that tells where "I went."

Arabic uses a different pattern for its sentences. Often in an Arabic statement, the verb comes first. Therefore, if we take the same example we used for English, *I went to the store*, the Arabic becomes *dha-**hab**-tu **an**-a **il**-a ad-duk-**kaan***, or "went I to the store." More often, because the verb *dha-**hab**-tu* already tells us who went to the store (*-tu* indicates *I*), you would just say, "*dha-**hab**-tu **il**-a ad-duk-**kaan***." You can take the ***an**-a* out of the sentence. This is the Arabic sentence pattern of *verbal statements*.

def•i•ni•tion

In English, we are used to seeing sentences in the order subject-verb-object. Arabic uses **verbal statements,** which means that the verb comes first in the sentence. The subject then follows the verb, and the object is the last part of the sentence.

Another peculiarity of Arabic is that it rarely uses the present tense of the infinitive "to be." This is quite different than in English, where we say "is" and "are" quite often. Actually, I think it would be difficult for me to get through a day without using "is" and "are." Somehow, though, Arabic does just fine without those two words.

Tips

Although ***hal*** is used to ask a question that in English would start with *is* or *are*, ***hal*** is still not the Arabic word for *is* and *are*. In questions involving ***hal***, you still need to have an action verb, such as ***hal tadh**-hab* ("Are you going?"). If you use ***hal*** in a question like ***hal jaan raj**-al*, you are saying, "Is John is a man?", but you don't see the second "is."

Nouns Go Verbing

As I described in the last section, there are three common types of Arabic sentences: the noun statement that uses no verb; the verbal statement that puts an action verb first, followed by the subject, then by the object (if there is one); and of course there is the question, which begins with an interrogative.

Let's take a look at a verbal statement that has an object: ***a'a**-Taa* ("He gave"); *a'a-**Tey**-tu* ("I gave"):

> *a'a-**Tey**-tu-**hu** sa-**yaa**-ra*
> I gave him a car.

In this case, you can tell by the last *two* syllables who did the giving (*–tu* means "I") and to whom I gave the thing (***–hu*** translates to "him"). All that is left to see is what is being given. In this case, a car is being given. (How nice of me!)

Tips

Although I stress the order of words in the verbal sentence structure, don't worry if you don't always put the verb first in your statements. This is a common mistake that I believe comes from being so used to saying things in our familiar English pattern. Although some native speakers may correct you, they will still understand you.

Now, say for instance you want to talk about something that can't quite be explained in two or three words. Perhaps one friend of yours, Henry, *saw* another friend of yours, Ahmed. Now, let's say you want to tell a third friend, Noor, about who Henry saw. But how? Easy. (***raa**-'ha* means "He saw"; *ra-'**bey**-tu* means "I saw"; and ***ra**-'hit* translates to "She saw.")

> ***raa**-'ha **bin**-ree **aH**-mad*
> Henry saw Ahmed.

Okay, but let's say Noor is the one who saw Ahmed. That's easy, too.

> ***ra**-'hit **noor** **aH**-mad*
> Noor saw Ahmed.

Of course, you could add phrases to either of these sentences showing exactly where Ahmed was seen:

*... **fee** al-**beyt***	*... bil-**khaa**-rij*
... in the house	... outside

The important thing to take away from these examples is that the verb comes first, the subject (the one doing the action) comes second, and the object (if there is one) comes last in the sentence.

That Was, or Will Be, a Negatory

If you think back to the easiest words we covered in this book, you will remember that we learned ***laa***. ***laa*** means *no*. You can use ***laa*** as a one-word response to questions that are asked of you. You can also use ***laa*** to *negate* entire sentences.

def•i•ni•tion

To **negate** a sentence means to put "no" or "not" into the sentence. If I negate the following sentence, "He went to the bank," then I change the sentence to "He did ***not*** go to the bank." In Arabic, the verbs ***laa***, ***ley**-sa*, and ***maa*** are used as negating verbs. Of these, ***laa*** is the most commonly used.

laa is the word we use to negate a sentence in the present tense. If I want to say, "I do not go," then I say "I go"—but I put the negating verb ***laa*** at the front of the sentence. The result is the sentence ***laa adh**-hab*, or "not I go." This sentence structure may seem a bit out of order, so let's change the place of "not" in English to "I go ***not.***" There. Now you see an English verbal statement with the negating word at the end.

So what do you say if you *did not* do something, as in the *past* tense? Since you already know how to negate sentences in the present tense, you also know how to negate verbs in the past and in the future. How do I know this? Because whether we're negating in the past, present, or future tense, only one word changes.

We start with the future. If we want to say "no" in the future, we say "will not" plus the verb that we are negating. In Arabic, "will not" is combined into one word: ***lan.*** Does ***lan*** look familiar? It should, because it is almost the same as the present tense's ***laa.*** In our ***lan*** sentences, ***lan*** takes the place of two words: "will" and "not." So because this ***lan*** already says "will not," we use the present tense of the verb we are negating. That makes sense. In English, we wouldn't want to say, "I will not will go." Arabic is the same way. The ***lan*** says "will not," and the present tense "go" gives us the complete phrase "will not go." Have a look.

***laa adh**-hab*	***lan adh**-hab*
I do not go.	I will not go.

Tips

I am a big fan of memory tricks, so here is one you can use to remember the negating verbs. The ***lam**b* has a ***laa**t* of ***lan**d*. If you remember this silly statement, you can remember that ***lam*** negates the past, ***laa*** negates the present, and ***lan*** negates the future.

Practical, isn't it? Now, if you can believe it, negating action verbs is just as easy in the past tense as it is in the present and future tense. What do you think we need to do to negate a past-tense sentence?

If you answered, "Build a skyrocket out of toothpicks and paper straws," then you obviously have other things on your mind and should probably take a break before continuing with the lessons! If, however, you answered, "Change one letter," then you are absolutely right. Negating past-tense sentences is as easy as saying ***lam.*** As in the future tense, ***lam*** takes the place of two words—this time, "did" and "not." So we are able to continue using the present tense of the verb. Now we have:

lam yat-rak	*laa yat-rak*	*lan yat-rak*
He did not leave.	He does not leave.	He will not leave.

Comparatively Speaking

So how would you compare apples and oranges in Arabic? The answer, of course, is "Easily." There are two Arabic words we can use for comparisons when both items being compared are equal (we'll get to nonequal comparisons in just a moment).

The first word is ***mith**-la*. ***mith**-la* literally means "like," so it is perfect for comparison. Here's how our orange/apple comparison would look:

> *al-**bur**-tu-**qaan** **mith**-la at-tu-**faaH***
> (The) oranges (are) like (the) apples.

Sure, the translation "The oranges are like the apples" doesn't have the same ring to it, but the meaning of the statement stays the same.

You can use ***mith**-la* for pretty much any comparison that would use the English word "like." There is another comparison word as well, though. In English, the word "as" is used for comparisons when both objects are of equal value. "As" is a shorter word than "like"—and for that reason, maybe we sometimes prefer to use "as." Similarly, Arabic has a comparison word that is shorter than ***mith**-la*. That word is ***ka**-*.

***ka**-* is actually not a word but a prefix ("*pre*" meaning before; "*fix*" meaning attached, thus "attached to the front") that we can stick on our Arabic words to give them comparisons. Sticking ***ka**-* on the front of our words works the same way as when we change our verbs from "he did" to "I did" or "she does." We just plug that syllable onto the beginning of the word. Look at the following examples:

def•i•ni•tion

bur**-tu-**qaal means "orange" (with the plural ***bur**-tu-**qaan***) in Arabic. It also means the color "orange." But that's not what's surprising. ***bur**-tu-**ghaal*** is the Arabic name for the country Portugal—which, as you can see by looking at the spelling, is very close to the word we use in English and to the Arabic for "orange."

***mith**-la* means "like" in Arabic, but ***mith**-lan* means "for example."

1001 Arabian Notes

If you have studied Egyptian spirituality or mythology, you may recognize ***ka*** as the name of a particular spiritual life force. This is not the ***ka*** I am talking about in this text, although I do recommend you research more about this other, fascinating side of ***ka*** with its own ties to the Arabic world.

*ib-raa-**heem** **qa**-Seer **ka-fa-reed***
Ibrahim is as short as Fareed.

Piece of cake, right? Well, then just keep right on going …

Getting Better Than

If you feel comfortable making comparisons when one side is no better than the other (because both sides are equally great, right?), then maybe you want to move on to something a little bit more challenging. That could easily be situations where one side of a comparison is a little bit more "something" than the other.

The easiest way (and therefore not always the best way) to express that one object is more *something* than another object is to say it in just that way:

(insert object name here) (is) **more** (insert adjective) than (insert other object name here).

The Arabic will turn out a bit choppy, but you will be understood. Let me show you what I mean. We'll go back to our two houses, with one being better than the other.

(This house) (is) more (good) than (that house).
(***ha**-dhaa al-**beyt***) ( ) ***ak**-thar* (***Ha**-san*) *min* (***dha**-lik al-beyt*).

Note: there is an empty set of parentheses in the Arabic translation, because we don't use the verb "to be" in the present tense.

Now, if you were to say something is "more good" in English, you would be understood, but that isn't really the best or most grammatically correct way to make your feelings known. More likely, you would say:

This house is better than that house.

In Arabic, this way sounds better, too:

***hadh**-a al-**beyt** **aH**-san min **dha**-lik al-beyt.*
This house is better than that house.

All you have to do is take the quality, change the first sound to ***a**-*, squish the middle and end sounds together with an ***a*** sound between them, then add the preposition ***min.*** There is no need to bother using *ak-thar*. Therefore, for "better than," we take "good" (***Ha**-san*) and put it into the recipe I just gave you:

Ha**-san* becomes ***aH**-san **min
good becomes better than

The great part about these comparative phrases is that you can use the formulas for virtually any adjective.

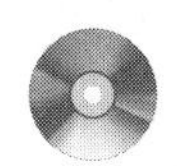

***ja**-meel-a (pretty; f)*	***ka**-beer (big)*
***aj**-mal-a **min** (prettier than)*	***ak**-bar **min** (bigger than)*
*Ta-**weel** (long)*	*Sa-**gheer** (small)*
***aT**-wal **min** (longer than)*	***aS**-ghar **min** (smaller than)*

If you don't want to say "than" (because you just want to say "bigger," for example), all you have to do is leave the ***min*** off. For instance, "bigger" would then become simply ***ak**-bar.* See whether you can think of a few more examples to practice on your own before you move on.

Warnings

Although the formula for creating comparative words works in most cases, there are always exceptions to the rules. In such cases, I'm sorry—but you will just have to learn those comparative words one at a time.

Simply the Best

The *superlatives* are words of the highest order. They are the words with the highest degrees. (No, I don't mean in terms of temperature.) Superlatives are simply the *best.* They are also the *most*, the *longest*, and also the *worst.* Do you see a pattern here? I hope so. I'll give you a hint … good, better, and *best.* "Best" is the superlative, or the word with the highest degree of goodness. Maybe you're wondering how "worst" could be considered to have the highest degree of anything? That's also easy. "Worst" has the highest degree of badness (bad, worse, and worst).

All we need to do to create superlatives in Arabic is use the comparative forms we just learned (the ones that sound more proper; the ones that add ***–a*** and scrunch the rest of the word). To create the superlative, we just add one of our favorite buddies—the definite article ***al***—to the front of the comparative form and take the ***min*** out of the phrase.

***aH**-san min* better than	***aS**-ghar min* smaller than
*al-**aH**-san* the best	*al-**aS**-ghar* the smallest

That's really all it takes to make superlative forms. Have fun with them, but remember … there are always exceptions.

Did You Read That Article?

One of the surest ways to see what is going on in a sentence is to look for ***al.*** The definite article ***al*** is somewhere to be seen in most Arabic sentences, and where ***al*** is located can tell you a lot about that sentence. For example, consider the comparative and superlative phrases we have learned in this chapter.

If we are talking about the comparative forms, ***al*** isn't involved. But if we talk about the superlative forms, ***al*** is right there next to the descriptive word—telling us exactly how superlative the thing being described really *is* (example: ***al aH**-san*).

Warnings

"***min*** *al*" means "among the." I know I told you before that we remove the *min* from the comparative form to create the superlative, but there is a pitfall to watch out for: ***min*** *al-**aS**-ghar* means "among the smallest," and the same formula can be used to create other "among the …" phrases.

Another clue the definite article ***al*** will give you is when an idaafa is present. You remember the idaafa, right? That's the phrase used to show possession when two nouns come in order and only the second noun has the definite article (example: ***beyt*** *al-**raj**-al*, or "the house of the man").

And of course, you cannot forget that if a noun has the definite article (*al-**beyt***), then the adjectives that describe the noun also will have the definite article (*al-**beyt** al-ka-**beer** al-**akh**-Dar*, which means "the big green house").

It Is Imperative That You …

I still think you have it in you to squeeze a little more knowledge into your brain before the end of this chapter. What do you think? What's that? You're all for it? Okay, then here we go. Let's talk about *imperatives!*

def•i•ni•tion

An **imperative** is a word or phrase that is used to give a command or make a request. The subject of an imperative is **inferred,** which means it is not spoken (because the subject is already understood). Here's an example: "Take heed!" really means "You take heed.") Arabic imperatives start most often with the sound *i-*, and the endings match the gender of the person to whom you are speaking.

If you have ever told someone "Stop!" or "Wait," then you have dealt with imperatives. Imperatives are unique in grammar because they do not need a spoken subject; the subject is *inferred*. You probably don't say, "You Stop!" or "You please hold the elevator!" Imperatives are spoken directly at a person (or other object) and are always spoken in the present tense. (If you don't believe me, try making an imperative request in the third-person past or future tense.)

Let's take a look at the typical syllables you add to make the imperative listed by person or group you want to "command":

> ***i***- … (no ending) = masculine singular
>
> ***i***-(verb)-***ee*** = feminine singular
>
> ***i***-(verb)-***oo*** = masculine plural
>
> ***i***-(verb)-***ann*** = feminine plural

Warnings

The guidelines given for the imperatives will not always work as outlined here. They may change depending on the word stem from which they are made. For example, the stem for "Stop!" is ***wa***-*qa-fa*, which becomes "***qif!***" in the imperative form.

So let's take a look at some one-word imperatives. Note: to make the feminine and plurals of the imperatives in the following list, you just need to add the appropriate endings.

Stop!	***qif!***	Drink!	***ish***-*rab!*
Eat!	***kul!***	Go!	***idh***-*hab!*
Quiet!	***is***-*kut!*	Sit!	***ij***-*lis!*
Stand!	***qoom!***	Listen!	***is***-*m'a!*
Walk!	***im***-*shee!*	Look!	***in***-*thur!*

Track 23

I'm sure you wouldn't always say, "Walk!" with a tone that needs an exclamation mark, but I put the exclamation marks there so you remember that these are imperatives.

There are also some imperatives that can be used in more complete sentences:

Shut the door.	***igh***-*liq al-**baab***
Turn to the left.	***door il***-*a al-ya-**saar***
Ask about the way (directions).	***is***-*'hal 'an aT-Ta-**reeq***
Tell me your name.	***qool lee is***-*mu-ka/ki*

Track 23

That's it! You made it though another chapter! Congratulations are in order, because … from here on out, things will just get easier!

Practice Makes Perfect

Okay, maybe things won't get easier right away. There is a quiz at the end of every chapter. Don't worry—you'll do fine. (Psst: if you are worried about not doing well on the quiz, you can always sneak a peek at the back of the book for answers. Of course, then you won't learn from the questions.)

1. What is meant by the phrase "verbal statement"?
2. If "***da**-ra-sa*" means "he studied," how would you say "She will not study"?
3. If "*al-**ak**-mal*" means "the most complete," how would you say "among the most complete"?
4. What does "***door**-ee **il**-a al-ya-**saar***" mean?
5. How would you tell a group of men and women to stand up?
6. If "*qa-**reeb***" means "close," how do you say "closer" and "closest"?

The Least You Need to Know

- Verbal statements begin with a verb and are the most common statement in Arabic.
- ***min*** is the difference between comparatives and superlatives.
- ***al*** can help you identify what words do.
- Imperatives start directions with ***i***-.

Part 3

Express Yourself

Whenever I watch media advertisements these days, I cannot help but think how the world is becoming increasingly "me"-centric. Whether customizing our phones, cars, homes, or online personalities, we all try to "express ourselves."

There is nothing wrong with it, either. In fact, I support the idea of self-expression 100 percent—particularly when it comes to speaking Arabic. In that light, it is good for us that we have Part 3. In this part, you learn all about expressing yourself—from introductions to explanations. Before you are finished, you will be able to talk about yourself, your family, your likes, and your dislikes—and you will even be able to explain your symptoms to the doctor if you end up needing medical services while traveling in Arab lands.

Chapter 10

Your Everyday "Meet-and-Greet"

In This Chapter

- Getting to know you
- Over-the-top greetings
- The best manners of speaking
- In the blue corner, introducing …

Most likely, to prepare for your first conversations in Arabic, you are not just going to walk up to someone on the street and start rattling off sentences about who you are and how "***jaan fee*** *al-****beyt.***" If you did that—even if he or she did understand you—the person you spoke to would probably think you were either crazy or that you mistook him or her for someone else.

This chapter is designed to prevent such potentially uncomfortable situations. We focus on the basic greetings and conversation starters you can use to spark a new friendship and open a new outlet for all of your pent-up Arabic phrases. (Just make sure to use the greetings first!)

Greetings, Salutations, and Hello

Imagine you and I were to pass one another on the street and I came up to you and said, "John isn't going to the doctor today, so he's still in the house; but at least the car's out of the shop. Hi! I'm glad to hear that. How are you? You just missed him." You probably would look at me like I'm crazy and continue walking. This wording doesn't follow the normal progression of conversations.

Polite conversation etiquette recommends that when you see a person for the first time or are preparing to open a conversation, you should offer a greeting before continuing with other details. Conversations should have some sort of beginning-to-end order; otherwise, they would just sort of swirl around until one person or the other ran out of time or patience (a very difficult way to meet new friends).

Arabic is creative and colorful, and you could probably get *very* creative and colorful when coming up with interesting greetings to use for friends and family (when you are able to read at a more advanced level, be sure to check out some of the beautiful prose that Arabic has to offer). For now, though, we will stick to a few basic ways to say hello in Arabic. You've probably even heard one or two of the following already:

Track 24

***ah**-lan*	hello
***ah**-lan wa **sah**-lan*	hello and welcome
***mar**-Ha-ban*	welcome
*nur-**Hib**-u-kum*	we welcome you

There are also some wonderful Arabic greetings that require special responses. This Islamic greeting can be used to greet someone at any time of the day:

*as-sa-**laam** 'al-**ey**-kum*
(greeting; "The peace upon you")

… *wa 'al-**ey**-kum as-sa-**laam***
(response; "… and the peace upon you"

Here is a greeting and response that is used in the morning:

*Sa-**baaH** al-**kheyr*** ("Good morning"; a greeting that literally translates to, "morning goodness")

*Sa-**baaH** an-**noor*** ("Good morning"; a response that literally translates to, "morning light")

This greeting and response is used at night:

> *ma-**saa'h** al-**kheyr*** ("Good evening"; a greeting that literally translates to, "evening of goodness")
>
> *ma-saa'h an-**noor*** ("Good evening"; a response that literally translates to, "evening of light")

So why go to the trouble of using these code word-sounding greetings and responses? Because these greetings are polite and show not only that you care about the person with whom you are speaking but also that you care about learning his or her language.

Above all, it is important to remember that Arabic greetings are given with respect. They are peaceful, even ("Peace upon you" and "Upon you, peace"). Even if you are among friends and are about to jump into a conversation about racing cars and watching movies, you should greet them with respect. The respect you earn from them will be your true key to learning Arabic when you've moved beyond this book.

Warnings

*as-sa-**laam** 'al-**ey**-kum* is a greeting typically associated with Islam. If the person you are speaking with is not Muslim (one who adheres to Islamic beliefs), you may want to use another greeting, such as ***mar**-Ha-ban*, which is a polite way of saying "hello" or "you are welcome." You will have to determine what is best in your situation.

Warnings

The right hand is most often used for gestures, particularly among Muslims, as the right hand is used for prayer. It is unlikely someone would be offended if you used your left hand to wave, but remember to be sensitive to your audience. There are a number of books and Internet sources dedicated to helping you understand such cultural issues.

Make Friends Easily: Exaggerate!

When I say that in order to make friends easily you should exaggerate during your Arabic greetings, I don't mean that I think you should say things you don't believe. I'm talking about exaggerating your body movements. Compared to English, Arabic is an active language. The Arabic language has even developed some signs you can make with your hands (and face) to help get your point across. (Language isn't *all* about speaking.)

To help you put some more power into your greetings, here are some movements you can make to help accentuate your words and help you fit in with native speakers and make friends more easily.

- **Shaking hands:** Hopefully you know what this gesture is by now. You'd better get used to it when meeting new Arabic friends, because they will shake your hand when they meet you, shake your hand when you say goodbye, and sometimes shake your hand when they want to give you their assurance (if they promise you something, for example). Depending on the excitement level, the handshake can range from soft and slow to squeezing your hand between both of theirs.

> **1001 Arabian Notes**
>
> Putting motions into your language will help you make friends more easily because the atmosphere of the conversation will turn away from the formal and toward the familiar. It's doubtful anyone would be offended by your gestures, but if you are in doubt as to whether you should use a gesture at a particular moment, it's best not to use it.

- **Pulling you close:** If you are walking with an Arabic speaker and he or she suddenly reaches over, grabs you by the elbow, and pulls you closer, don't be alarmed. He or she may just want to share a secret with you or speak frankly. The average "personal space" among Arabs may be much closer than you are used to. Try to get over it—or if you are uncomfortable, try to find a polite way to express your feelings.
- **Come over here:** If an Arab puts his or her right hand toward you, palm down, fingers extended, then claps his or her fingers to the palm a few times, he or she is not waving at you. This person is saying, "Come here." Most likely, he or she will actually tell you to come as well, but you may encounter this gesture nonetheless.
- **Just a moment:** Stick your right hand out, palm up, and put the tips of all your fingers together. Now, bend your hand at the wrist a few times. You have just said, "Slow down" or "Just a moment." I find this gesture—combined with the word ***la**-Ha-THa* (moment)—to be an effective way of slowing down conversations that are moving too quickly.

So just how many questions can you expect when you first see an Arabic-speaking friend? Lots. Here are some more common greetings you may encounter and use throughout your Arabic day:

Track 25

***keyf**-al-**Haal** al-**yoom**?*	How are you today? (literally translates to, "How is the situation today?")
***keyf**-a an-ta/ti?*	How are you? (m/f)
***keyf**-Haal-ki/ka?*	How is your health? (f/m)
***keyf**-kum/kun-na?*	How are you all? (m/f)

Every country and area will have its own greetings, as well. Be sure to add those to your lists as you learn them from friends, the Internet, and your travel.

Here are some of the answers you might give when asked how you are doing:

laa baa-*'his*	"Not bad."
Taa-*yib*	"Okay."
jeyd	"Good."
'a-***THeem***	"Great!"
jeyd jid-*dan*	"Very good."
ta-***maa***-*man*	"Perfect!"
ta'a-***baan***	"Tired."
kul shey 'al-*a* ***maa*** *yu*-***raam***	"Everything is fine."
an-*a bi*-***kheyr***	"I am fine."
shu-***kraan***	"Thank You!"

By the way, if you are visiting someone in his or her home, it is common to bring a small gift as a token of appreciation. And be prepared for that person to offer you gifts in return.

1001 Arabian Notes

If you accept a gift from an Arabic-speaking person, you should have something to offer him or her in return. That way, neither side feels that it has contributed more or less than the other. I do believe many Arabs would give you everything they had if you let them, but if you took everything they had and did not offer the same to them, they might just as likely be offended. Be careful!

While it is fine to accept gifts from friends, you must beware: Arabs may offer you something as a gift just because you say you like that thing. For instance, commenting on a nice painting hanging in someone's home could result in that person offering you the painting as a gift. Try to avoid situations such as these whenever possible. You can comment on the lovely things a person has, but you should be prepared with a polite refusal should your friend subsequently offer you the item you admired.

As a final note, there are a couple of words you can add to your greetings—depending on whom you are addressing. If you are greeting a man or woman who is more than

1001 Arabian Notes

The Hajj is the religious journey made by a Muslim to Mecca, in Saudi Arabia. This journey is one of the Five Pillars of Islam and is a central portion of Islamic belief. The Hajj occurs during the twelfth month of the Islamic calendar and is undertaken by millions of Muslims each year.

about 60 years of age (this is not an exact age), you may address him or her as "***hajj***" or "***hajj-a***." This term refers to a Muslim who has made the pilgrimage (you can also use the terms for someone of any age who has made the religious journey to Mecca) but can also be used for someone who has lived long enough to see a lot in his or her lifetime.

If you want to refer to someone respectfully, you may always address him or her as "my sir" or "my lady." The word for "my sir" is *sa-**eed**-ee*; the word for "my lady" is *sa-**eed**-a-**tee***.

Up Close and Personal

You may be surprised how quickly your Arabic-speaking friends will open up to you if you invite them. Of course, one of the best ways to develop a good relationship is by showing them that you speak (at least a little of) their language. Even the smallest phrases can help you increase your circle of friends in the Arabic-speaking world.

In fact, why don't we take a look at some of the common Arabic words for "friend" right now?

***qalb**-ee*	my heart
*Sa-**dee**-qee/Sa-**dee**-qa-tee*	my friend (m/f)
*Ha-**bee**-bee/Ha-**bee**-ba-tee*	my darling (m/f)
*'a-**zee**-zee/'a-**zee**-za-tee*	my dear (m/f)
***'aee**-nee*	my dear (literally, "my eye")
***akh**-ee*	my brother
***'am**-ee*	my uncle
***ukht**-ee*	my sister

Another tip on these words: you can see that each word has the possessive ending ***–ee***, meaning "my." If you drop the ***–ee*** and the ***–tee*** endings (except in the case of ***ukht**-ee*, where you just drop the ***–ee***), you form the root word. For example, ***qalb**-ee* minus the ***–ee*** becomes ***qalb*** or "heart." And be careful how you say ***qalb***, because although it means "heart," the similar-sounding word ***kalb*** means "dog." There is quite a difference in how those two words might be interpreted by someone!

Now we can put a few of the phrases together. If you are greeting a man who is a bit older than you, you can say to him, "***keyf**-al **Haal yaa 'am**-ee?*" (which means, "How are you, dear uncle?").But if you want to get really up close and personal, then you want to talk about the family. More importantly, you would ask the person about *his or her* family. Here are some great ways to ask about family.

1001 Arabian Notes

'aee**-nee* literally means "my eye," but the same word is used for "spring" and also for "fountain." So, if you think of those terms when calling someone "'aee**-nee,*" consider that you are calling them the wellspring of your existence. Really, it's quite a lovely term.

***keyf**-a* …	How is/are …
*az-**zow**-ja*	the wife
*az-**zowj***	the husband
*al-**us**-ra*	the family
*al-**a**-hil*	the family
*al-'**aaa**-'hil-a*	the family
*al-**mur**-ra*	the wife (also, "woman")
*al-ow-**laad***	the boys
*al-bi-**naat***	the girls
*al-aT-**faal***	the children
*aS-**SuH**-Ha*	the health

Note: there are several words for family listed here because you will hear all of them used in Arabic greetings. When you exchange greetings, you can try to use as many of them as possible.

I Am and Is Me?

Sure, you can tell your Arab friends who you are … or can you? You are more than just a name. Let's use a little fill-in-the-blank exercise for you to practice talking about who you are:

an**-a* ____________ ***an**-a **min ___________

This section is all about you and who *you* are. If someone thanks you, you should respond appropriately. The following list has some words you will find very useful as you begin to express yourself with others.

Track 26

***ah**-lan wa **sah**-lan*	"Hello, and welcome" (literally: "You are very welcome")
*laa **shu**-kir **'al**-a al-**waa**-jib*	"No thanks necessary"
***'af**-waan*	"Excuse me"/"Please"
*aT-Ta-**faD**-Dal(-ee)*	"If you please" ("After you")
***shu**-kraan*	"Thank you"
***alf shu**-kir*	"1,000 thanks"
***shu**-kraan ja-**zeel**-an*	"Thank you very much"
***alf as**-if*	"1,000 apologies"
***as**-if/**as**-if-a*	"Sorry" (m/f)
***m'a** sa-**laam**-a*	"Goodbye" (literally: "Go with peace")

Think for a moment about the favorite people in your life. Think about why they are your favorite people. Maybe they are polite. Maybe they are understanding. Maybe they are creative. Whatever characteristics they have that you like, those are probably characteristics you would like to display to others. Here is a list of characteristics I hope you can use to help gain and keep friendships with your Arabic-speaking friends.

Track 26

***an**-a*	I am …
ka**-rim/**ka**-rim-**a	honored (m/f)
*sa'a-**eed**/sa'a-**eed**-a*	happy (m/f)
*mus-**roor**/mus-**roor**-a*	pleasured (m/f)
*mush-**koor**/mush-**koor**-a*	thankful (m/f)

Another way in which Arabic speakers often express gratitude is to speak of themselves in the plural form. For example, instead of saying, "I am thankful," an Arabic speaker might say, "We are thankful" or ***naH**-nu mush-**koor**-oon*. This is an extremely polite way of speaking. Think of it as a way of telling someone that their actions are greater than those of one person could ever possibly be—and therefore, you must refer to yourself and to the speaker in the plural form.

So what does it take to be a good person?

> ***shukh**-san **jeyd**-an, **boo**-a ow **bee**-a …*
> A good person, he or she is …

Track 26

***dha**-kee/dha-**kee**-a*	smart (m/f)
*moo-**thooq**/moo-**thooq**-a*	dependable (m/f)
*mub-**di'a**/mub-**di'a**-a*	creative (m/f)
***muD**-hiq/**muD**-hiq-a*	funny (m/f)
*mu-**'bad**-dab/mu-**'bad**-dab-a*	polite (m/f)
*Sa-boor/Sa-**boor**-a*	patient (m/f)
***haa**-di'h/haa-di'h-a*	quiet (m/f)
*sha-reef/sha-**reef**-a*	honest (m/f)
***qaa**-wee/**qaa**-wee-a*	strong (m/f)

These words are just a miniscule sampling of all the things a good person can be. Hopefully you will be able to express at least a couple of these qualities in your first conversations. And remember, when at a loss for a way to describe a good person, you can always say ***jeyd jid**-dan*. He or she will understand that you mean "very good." Actually, you will find literally hundreds of ways to use ***jeyd jid**-dan* in your first conversations.

Practice Makes Perfect

Once again, we find ourselves at the end of a chapter. Maybe this chapter was a bit easier for you. Maybe you think there was not enough information in it. If that is the case, don't worry. You will have plenty of opportunity to be overwhelmed in the coming chapters as I heap more and more vocabulary (but hopefully not more rules) on you. Let's practice!

1. If I say to you, *ma-**saa'h** al-**kheyr***, what have I said? And what is the proper response?
2. How would you say, "How is your health, my dear brother?"
3. Why must you be careful if you call someone "***qalb**-ee*"?
4. How could you say, "Excuse me, ma'am (lady)?"

5. What useful term means "very good"?
6. How would you say, "My brother is a very smart man"?

The Least You Need to Know

- Politeness will get you far.
- Flattery will get you further.
- Close friends can be called as family.
- Asking about others opens others' hearts.
- Everything will turn out ***jeyd jid**-dan.*

Chapter 11

Glad to Meet You

In This Chapter

- Who *is* this cat?
- Living all over this world
- Family tree or family maze?
- Straight to the questions

You will probably notice as you move through this chapter that the pace of learning will pick up speed. Don't worry, though. There are plenty of rest stops along the way where you can catch your breath. You will probably also notice that there are words and questions taken from earlier chapters that find their way into the current pages. No, those aren't accidents. I just recall them every once in a while to keep things fresh in your memory.

Speaking of fresh in your memory … this chapter is all about introductions and getting to know your new Arabic friends. Here, you can find out what to say (or maybe sometimes what *not* to say). You learn how to introduce family members and talk a little bit about them. You also learn to ask some questions of new acquaintances to help get things started on the right foot. All these wonderful bits of language are waiting for you. Enjoy.

Let Me Introduce My Noun

In this section, we talk about introductions. When making an introduction, we *indicate* one person or object to another person or object. Most likely, you will be indicating things to another person. Otherwise, you would probably just be talking to yourself.

If I wanted to introduce you to my brother, I would say, "*This* is my brother." If I wanted to introduce you to my cat, I would *indicate* the cat by saying, "*This* is my cat." See how the word *this* doesn't change, regardless of what we are introducing? Practical, eh?

Because you already know that the word for "brother" is ***ukh***—and maybe you know that the word for "cat" is ***qiTT*** (feminine form: ***qiT**-Ta*)—all you have to do is add the word "this" and the possessive ending to the noun, and you have your introduction sentence. Take a look:

***ha**-dhaa **akh**-ee*	This is my brother
wa	and
***ha**-dha-hi **qiT**-Ta-tee.*	this is my (f) cat.

Notice in the sentence that I say ***ha**-dhaa* for my brother but ***ha**-dha-hi* for my cat. I do that because "brother" is a masculine word. Since I don't have a male cat, I used the feminine form of "cat," therefore ***ha**-dha-hi* (feminine for "this"), in the second part of the sentence.

Tips

If you are dealing with a feminine noun that ends with the *–a* sound and you want to say that someone owns that noun, then the *–a* sound becomes a *–t*. The letter that indicates the feminine form (*taa'a mar-boo-Ta*) changes shape. For example, ***qiT**-Ta* (cat) becomes ***qiT**-Ta-tee* (my cat) or ***qiT**-Ta-tu-hu* (his cat).

When you are using ***ha**-dhaa* and ***ha**-dha-hi* to introduce or indicate items, the ending of the words will help you out. If you want to say, "This is my dog" (***kalb***), then you put the *first-person singular possessive* ending on the word for dog. "First-person singular possessive" is just a fancy way of saying you add *–ee* to the word. So "my dog" becomes ***kalb**-ee*. Then you just add ***ha**-dhaa* to complete the sentence.

If you don't have a dog—or if you don't feel like talking about your dog and would rather say, "This is a dog"—then you don't add the possessive ending. So "This is a dog" becomes ***ha**-dhaa **kalb.*** That's it. Remember these rules about possessive endings when moving through introductions.

Later in the chapter, we will get to introducing all the different members of your family. But before we do that, let's focus a little on the family itself. There are several Arabic words for "family"—more than we have in English. Take a look:

All of these mean "family" and are followed by their plural form:

*'aaa-'hi-la/'a-**waa**-'hil*
a**-hil/a-hil-**oon
***us**-ra/**us**-ar*

The following means "relative" and is followed by the plural:

*a-**qaa**-rib/aq-ri-**baa'h***

Now I'll add a couple possessive forms so you may see the difference:

'aaa-'hi-la-tee my family	*a-hil-u-ki* your (f/s) family
***us**-ar-ee* my families	*aq-ri-**baa'h**-u-ka* your (m/s) relatives

I could continue for hours listing words related to family and friends, but I don't think we need to do that. If you are looking for a great drill to practice your possessive endings, go through the words for family using all of the possible endings ("my," "your," "your" [f], "his," "her," "our," "your" [pl], "your" [f/pl], "their," and "their" [f]). That will give you a workout.

If you are introducing your family, you will likely be asked a few questions about them. I won't try to guess all the possible questions you may receive, but I can give a couple suggestions. Maybe someone will ask where you live. That's a reasonable request. They might use a couple of verbs to ask this question:

***sa**-ka-na* he resided	***yas**-kun* he resides	*as-kun* I reside
tas-kun she resides	*sa-ka-nat* she resided	*sa-kun-tu* I resided
***'aaa**-sha* he lived	***y'a**-eesh* he lives	*'aaash-tu* I lived
'aaa-shat she lived	*t'a-eesh* she lives	*'aa-eesh* I live

Note: tas-kun and t'a-eesh also mean "you reside" (m/s) and "you live" (m/s)

By now, you should know that if I give you the verb ***sa**-ka-na* for "he resided," you should be able to figure out that "We reside" would be ***nas**-kun*. Being able to put the beginnings and endings on verbs is probably the most important factor in your being able to take off with Arabic speech. That's why I am not going to give you all the forms of the verbs. I *want* you to have to work to figure out what the verbs are. That way, you will have to remember what I wrote before (it's just fine to jump back and look at the verb charts), and you will be able to use the language without feeling the need to dive into this book whenever you encounter new words you want to use.

Tips

I understand it is difficult to flip pages to find the correct conjugation of verbs, but it really is worth the effort. It would take a lot of book space to list all the conjugations of the verbs we use. And because once you learn the verbs you don't need to refer to the charts any longer, we save space for other language lessons.

So if someone asks you "***ai**-na **tas**-kun?*" he or she has just asked where you live (or reside). If you are a woman, then the person would (most likely) ask you "***ai**-na **tas**-kun-ee?*"

Say you just introduced an Arab friend to another friend, Bob. This other friend doesn't speak Arabic. Now you have to be the translator. Yikes! Actually, there are a few things you already know and will be able to answer. For instance, the first thing you would say might be:

> ***Ha**-dhaa Sa-**deeq**-ee; **is**-mu-hu **bub.***
> This is my friend; his name is Bob.

If your Arabic-speaking friend then asked "***ai**-na **y'a**-eesh?*" you would know that he or she is asking where Bob lives. That's easy enough. With the vocabulary you have so far, there are plenty of answers you can give … provided you understand that the person just asked where Bob lives. (Note: the key is the beginning of the verb ***y'a**-eesh*. The "y" sound means third person.)

> ***y'a**-eesh …* … ***fee** bi-**naa**-ya **ukh**-ra*
> He lives … … in a different building
>
> … ***m'a**-naa **fee beyt**-u-**naa***
> … with us in our house
>
> … ***m'a** us-**ra**-tu-hu fee ma-**dee**-na Sa-**gheer**-aa*
> … with his family in a small city

That's all it takes to introduce one of your friends to another and to say a sentence or two about him or her. See what else you can come up with about Bob. Feel free to flip back in the book to get some more vocabulary words to fit into your sentences. I'll wait for you.

A Family Affair

Are you done talking about Bob (or ***bub***, or ***baab***, or whatever you decided to call him)? Maybe we should find someone else to talk about.

> ***ha**-dha-hi **b'aD** af-**raad** al-**us**-ra.*
> These are some members of the family.

***jad**-da* grandmother	***jadd*** grandfather	***umm*** mother	***ab*** father
ukht sister	***akh*** brother	***ib**-n* son	***ib**-na* daughter
***Ha**-feed* grandson	***Ha**-feed-a* granddaughter	***'am**-ma* paternal aunt	***'am*** paternal uncle
***khaal**-a* maternal aunt	***khaal*** maternal uncle	***waa**-lad* parent	***Tif**-l* child

> ***ha**-dhaa/**ha**-dha-hi …*
> This is my …

Note: For those ending with the feminine *–a*, use ***–tee*** instead of ***–ee.***

"Cousin" is a word you may have noticed is missing from the list of family members. It's not that I forgot; the truth is, the words for "cousin" are already in the list. Arabic doesn't use a special word for "cousin." Instead, in Arabic you would just say, "son of …" or "daughter of …" Think about it this way: my father's brother's son would be ***ib**-n '**am**-ee.* My mother's sister's daughter would be ***ib**-na **khaal**-a-tee.*

def•i•ni•tion

The **paternal** aunt and uncle are those on the father's side; that is, the father's sisters and brothers. The **maternal** aunts and uncles are those on the mother's side. Arabic makes this distinction in names (although we do not in English). Your mother's sister would be ***khaal**-a* to you. Your father's brother is your ***'am***.

Here is the same list you just looked at—this time, in plural form.

*jad-**daat*** grandmothers	*aj-**daad*** grandfathers	*um-mu-**haat*** mothers	*aab-**aa'h*** fathers
*ukh-a-**waat*** sisters	*ikh-**waan*** brothers	*ib-**naa'h*** sons	*ib-**naat*** daughters

*aH-**faad*** grandsons	*Ha-feed-**aat*** granddaughters	*'am-**maat*** paternal aunts	*i'am-**aam*** paternal uncles
*khaal-**aat*** maternal aunts	*ukh-**waal*** maternal uncles	*waa-lad-**dey**** parents	*aT-**faal*** children

1001 Arabian Notes

Arabic culture is built around the family and family relationships. It is common in Arabic for close friends to refer to one another as "uncle," "aunt," "cousin," "brother," or "sister," depending on their relationship. If one of your Arabic friends refers to you in this way, do not be alarmed. Be honored.

Introducing Friends and Relatives

There are plenty of ways to get more out of your Arabic, but the best way is to add more action. And what's the best way to do that? Add more verbs. The more verbs we add, the more options we have to get thoughts out of our minds and into the real world.

So who are we going to put into action? Who else—our friends and family, of course. Let's take a look at how adding just a few verbs (or maybe a few dozen, we'll see) can add an entirely new level to the Arabic we've learned so far—and take us quite a distance in our conversations.

Table 11.1

Family Action Verbs

Past-Tense Verb	Present-Tense Verb	Noun Form
***da**-ra-sa* He studied	***yad**-rus* He studies	*di-**raa**-sa* studies
*ish-**ta**-gha-la* He operated	*yash-**ta**-ghil* He operates	*ish-ti-**ghaal*** operation
***'aa**-mi-la* He worked	***ya'a**-mil* He works	***'am**-l* work (noun)
*is-**taq**-ba-la* He met/received	*yis-**taq**-bil* He meets/receives	*is-tiq-**baal*** reception
***'ar**-ra-fa* He introduced	*yu-**'ar**-rif* He introduces	*t'a-**reef*** introduction

*t'**ar**-ra-fa* He became acquainted	*ya-**t'ar**-raf* He becomes acquainted	***t'aa**-ruf* acquaintance
***qaa**-bi-la* He greeted	*yu-**qaa**-bil* He greets	*qa-**bool*** greeting
*al-**ta**-qa* He met	*yal-**taq**-ey* He meets	*li-**qaa'h*** meeting

Of course, there is more to an introduction than just saying, "This is So-and-So." First of all, I don't know anyone named "So-and-So." Second, if you want the people you have introduced to get along as friends on their own accord, you should offer a statement about each to the other.

> *t'**ar**-raf-tu-hu bil-mad-**ras**-a.*
> I became acquainted with him in (the) school.

Maybe one of your friends works in a coffee shop. Then, you would say:

> *yash-**ta**-ghil/**ya'a**-mil bil-**maq**-ha.*
> He works in a café.

One other way you may spark a friendship between two people you know is to say where each is from. You already know how to say, "He is from …" or "She is from …" (***hoo**-a min/**hee**-a min*). There is another way to say where someone is from, though: by using the *nisba adjective*.

Tips

As you advance more, you will notice that certain verbs *always* require certain prepositions to follow them. The verbs *t'**ar**-ra-fa* and *al-**ta**-qa* always use prepositions. For example, most often the preposition is ***bi-*** (with/at).

You may be thinking, "Oh great … more grammar." No, I promise you this will be short—as will all the lessons from here on out—as you see them stuck into other sections with the vocabulary that is now more important than stuffy rules. The *nisba adjective* is an adjective that is made from a noun. It is usually used to describe where a person comes from, his or her nationality, or the person's heritage. All you have to do to create a nisba adjective is remove any definite articles that may be on the noun and take off any long vowels. Then, you add ***–ee*** to the end of the word for males and ***–ee**-a* to the end for females.

For instance, if you are from America (***an**-a min am-**ree**-ka*), then you would say, "I am an American" (***an**-a am-ree-**kee***). Women would say ***an**-a am-ree-**kee**-ya* (unless of course they are not American). Then, they would say whatever is appropriate.

The nisba is a great tool for both introducing friends and improving your ability to explain things in Arabic. There are actually only a few examples of nisba-like adjectives in English compared to Arabic, but I have selected some for your reference. As you are looking through them, think of the nisba adjectives as another way of saying "of *someplace*" or "of *some type*." ***bee**-a bree-Taa-**nee**-ya* could be translated in that way as "She is of Britain."

*bree-**Taa**-nee* British	*bal-**jee**-kee* Belgian	*fa-**ran**-see* French
*as-**baa**-nee* Spanish	*'i-**raa**-qee* Iraqi	*lub-**naa**-nee* Lebanese
*mak-**see**-kee* Mexican	*al-**maa**-nee* German	*magh-**rib**-ee* Moroccan
*ka-**na**-dee* Canadian	*am-**ree**-kee* American	*hoo-**lan**-dee* Dutch (of Holland)
***roo**-see* Russian	*yaa-**baa**-nee* Japanese	***See**-nee* Chinese

Note: to make feminine versions of the nisba adjectives, add "*-ya*" to the end of the word because the "ee" is doubled.

That list should give you a little better idea of how you can create and use adjectives to declare a little bit more about your friends. And maybe the introductions you give will spark another new friendship.

Asking About Family Members

You may remember one very important question from Chapter 8. See if you can remember how to say, "What is your name?" Can you think of it? Wait a minute … and take the time to recall. Don't look ahead. Should I tell you? Okay, here's the answer:

> ***maa** is-mu-ka/ki?*

This question is very important. If you have trouble remembering it, try saying it out loud a few times. (Don't worry if someone gives you a strange look. Just pretend you don't see them.)

So you've gotten the person's name. Good job. Now … what are you going to do with it?

Warnings

When you're learning someone's name, make sure you get it right. Arabic names can be very difficult for those who are unfamiliar with the language. Some men's names are very similar, for example. Ahmad, Hamad, and Muhammad are all based on the same three letters: H, m, and d. You may want to have the person spell his or her name as well, because vowels may change and consonants may double.

In Arabic, there are two ways to ask someone about the things they have. (For the examples, I will use the second-person feminine singular form; be sure to use whatever form you need for your situation.)

***hal 'and**-u-ki …*	Do you have …
*la-**dey**-ki …*	Do you have …

Those two forms are all you need to ask some great questions. For example:

***hal 'and**-u-ki aT-**faal**?*	Do you have children?
***kam** aT-**faal** la-**dey**-ki?*	How many children do you have?

If you wanted to ask someone's age (or their children's ages), you would ask the question "How much age?" *'**um**-r* is the Arabic word for "age."

***kam 'um**-ru-ka?*	What is your age?

(This is the masculine form. I learned not to ask women their ages.)

***kam 'um**-r aT-**faal**-u-ki?*	What are your children's ages?

You also could use *'**um**-ru-hu* to ask about a specific son or *'**um**-ru-haa* for a specific daughter. You just need to make sure you use the correct ending for the person you are asking about.

Before you go, you should review any vocabulary in this chapter that you are not certain of—and you should go through the final section. You know what it is.

Practice Makes Perfect

There certainly was a large amount of information in this chapter. I bet you never knew there was so much to say about your family, did you? Before you leave, be sure to answer the following questions:

1. How would you say, "This is my mother"?
2. If someone says "***keyf**-a **Haal**-u-ka al-**yoom**?*" what has he or she asked?
3. If you are a woman from Spain and you wanted to say, "I am of Spain and my husband is American," what would you say (in Arabic, of course)?
4. How would you ask a woman how old she is?
5. If someone tells you *tis-taq-**bil**-nee **fee** al-ma-**Taar**,* what has he or she told you?

The Least You Need to Know

- There are many names for family members.
- Asking about family wins Arabic hearts.
- The nisba adjective helps you tell about yourself.
- You can use ***'and*** and *la-**dey*** to ask someone what they "have."

Chapter 12

Tell Me About Yourself

In This Chapter

- The city and life outside
- What do you do where you come from?
- Students are people, too
- A hobby for every personality
- Up close, but not *too* personal

If I were in your position—beginning to learn a new language—I think this would be one of my favorite chapters in this book. That's because this chapter is all about *talking*. And not only do you get to talk, but you also learn to talk about *yourself*. "Myself" has always been one of my favorite conversational pieces.

Before you are done with this chapter, you will be able to talk about your hometown. You will learn how to say what things go on there, what the people do on a daily basis, and how they spend their time. Then, toward the end of the chapter, you will get to talk about your hobbies—sharing even more of your personality. Finally, you will learn to ask a couple (but not too many) personal questions of your Arabic friends. So sit back, turn on the reading lamp, and enjoy.

Where Are You From?

So where have you been?

*ma-**dee**-na* city	*wa-**laa**-ya* state	***bal**-ad* country (nation)
*qa-**ree**-a* town/village	*mun-**Tuq**-a ree-**fee**-a* rural area	*mu-**qaa**-T'aa* province

def•i•ni•tion

*wa-**laa**-ya* is only used for a state, such as Rhode Island. For a "state" in a larger governmental meaning, such as in the term "Western states," you would use the term ***dow**-la*.

*mun-**Tuq**-a ree-**fee**-a* could mean "country area," "rural area," or "provincial area," depending on the context of the sentence.

***an**-a min qa-**ree**-a Sa-**gheer**-a fee wa-**laa**-ya kaa-lee-**foorn**-yaa.*

I am from a small town (village) in the state of California.

Notice how in this sentence I use the word for village instead of saying a "small city." I do that just to give the person I'm speaking to a better idea of how small my hometown really is. You could just as easily say *ma-**dee**-na Sa-**gheer**-a* if you wanted.

But maybe you're not from a small town. Maybe you're from a big city. That's easy, too. You could say something like the following:

***an**-a min ma-**dee**-na **ad**-moon-**toon** fee mu-**qaa**-T'aa al-**bir**-taa.*

I am from the city of Edmonton in the province of Alberta.

*ka-**theer** min an-**naas***	many people
*qa-**leel** min an-**naas***	few people

If you want to say the complete sentence, then you would want to say, "There are many/few people." The most common word for "there" is *hu-**naa**-ka*. *hu-**naa**-ka* is a very useful word because you can use it in an abstract sense that doesn't refer to a specific place, such as, "There are many people." You can also use *hu-**naa**-ka* to indicate a specific location. For example, "She is there" would be ***hee**-a hu-**naa**-ka*. So putting everything together, we would get something like the following:

*fee **ad**-moon-**toon** hu-**naa**-ka ka-**theer** min an-**naas**.*

In Edmonton, there are many people.

*hu-**naa**-ka qa-**leel jid**-din min an-**naas** fee qa-**ree**-a-**tee**.*

There are very few people in my town (village).

Now, so far in this chapter we've added quite a bit of vocabulary—most recently, the words for "people" (***naas***) and "there" (*hu-**naa**-ka*). As both a practice for these new words and as a review of the numbers you've learned, why don't you see whether you can tell me how many people are in your hometown?

*hu-**naa**-ka? min an-**naas** fee _______-**tee**.*

Where Do You Work?

Just like your life history is based largely on the places you've been, your life story would not be complete without discussing all the things that you've done. (Well, maybe not *all* of the things that you've done. I'm not too sure your new Arabic friends will want to hear how many times in your life you've stopped to tie your shoelaces. Then again, if you have kept track, why not tell them?)

Track 30

*hal **ta'a**-mal fee aS-Si-**naa'aa***
Do you work in industry?

*hal **ta'a**-mal ka-**theer***
Do you work a lot?

***kam** min an-**naas ta'a**-mal **m'a**-hum*
How many people do you work with?

*hal **an**-ti al-ra-**'hees**-a fil-**'am**-l*
Are you (f/s) the boss at work?

*hal an-ta mu-**waTH**-THif*
Are you an employee?

*hal ta-**sooq** sa-**yaa**-ra*
Do you drive a car?

***maa**-dha **ta**-f'al fee **yoom** al-**'am**-l al-**'aaa**-dee*
What do you do on a normal workday?
(literally translates to: "What you do in day of the work the normal?")

*yum-**kin**-u-kum al-**mash**-ee **il**-a al-**'am**-l*
Can you walk to work?
(literally translates to: "Possible for you [m/pl] the walking to the work?")

Tips

I included literal translations of two of the questions so you may see how some more complex sentences are formed. Notice the way the words jump around in order. Also note the way *idaafas* are used (workday translates to ***yoom** al-'**am**-l*).

Reading the literal translations gives a better understanding of why someone who speaks Arabic might leave out words such as "is" or "are"—and also why they might jumble their word order—when speaking English.

***ai**-na tash-**ta**-ghil-**ee**?*
Where do you (f) work (operate)?

*hal 'aa-**mil**-ta hu-**naa**-ka li-**waq**-t Ta-**weel**?*
Have you worked there a long time?

Of course, if you are going to ask these questions of other people, you should be prepared to answer them when they are asked of you. A good method for answering is to repeat the question. For example, if someone asks me:

*hal 'aa-mal-ta hu-**naa**-ka **mun**-dhu **wuq**-t Ta-**weel**?*
(Literally translates to: "Did you work there since time long?")

I could say:

*n'am, **a'aa**-mal hu-**naa**-ka **mun**-dhu **wuq**-t Ta-**weel**.*
(Literally translates to: "Yes, I work there since time long.")

The only difference between their question and my answer is that I added "yes" at the beginning, changed the verb to "I," and made it present. And instead of using "for," I used "since." This may not be the perfect Arabic answer your friends expect, but it will get you by.

So what are all the professions? What exactly could you be?

*mu-**dar**-ris fee **mad**-ra-sa*
a teacher in a school

*ma-**zaa**-r'a fee al-Ha-**qool***
a farmer in the fields

*mu-**Haa**-sib fee **mak**-tab*
an accountant in an office

*Ta-**baakh** fee **maT**-'am*
a cook in a restaurant

*Sar-**raaf** fee al-**bank***
a cashier at the bank

*us-**taadh** fee **jaa**-m'ia*
a professor at a university

*khab-**baaz** fee **mukh**-baz*
a baker in a bakery

***Daa**-biT **shur**-Ta fee Ma-**HaT**-Ta*
a police officer in a station

saa-'hiq 'al-aT-Tu-ruq
a driver on the roads

mu-math-thil fil-mus-raH
an actor in the theater

Tee-yaar 'al-a mat-n Taa-'hi-ra
a pilot aboard a plane

Ta-beeb fee mus-tash-fa
a doctor in a hospital

That is quite a lot to be. Remember, if the occupation listed has more than one word, the word order could be different than you are used to saying. For example, ***Daa**-biT* means "officer" and ***shur**-Ta* means "police," but a ***Daa**-biT **shur**-Ta* is a "police officer." This is because "police" and "officer" are both nouns, so we use the idaafa.

I think you have a lot going for you now. Why don't we move on to the next section?

def•i•ni•tion

Remember that ***'al**-a* means "on." When you are talking about "on" as in, "on a plane/ship/train," a better word would be "aboard." In Arabic, "aboard" is ***'al**-a **mat**-n*.

If you don't want to say "police officer," you could say use the nisba adjective ***shur**-tee* for "policeman" or *shur-**tee**-ya* for "policewoman" instead.

What Do You Study?

So what if you haven't quite gotten to the "work" part of your life yet? What if you are still a student and don't know what you will become? Well, first of all, many people have been working jobs for many years and still have no idea what they want to do when they "grow up." Second, if you are a student, why not just talk about that?

'al**-m al-a-**Hyaa'h	biology
*ar-ri-**yaa**-Dee-**aat***	math
*al-'**al**-m*	science
*at-taa-**reekh***	history
*al-**fann***	art
*al-Ha-**koo**-ma*	government

def•i•ni•tion

You may know that **biology** and **psychology** are both sciences (***'al**-m*), so when we translate to Arabic, we just use what sciences they are. Biology is the "science of life" (***'al**-m al-a-**Hyaa'h***), and psychology is the "science of the self" (***'al**-m an-**nafs***).

Don't confuse your **math** with your **sports,** however. Remember this little phrase: "Math adds an extra syllable." (*ar-ri-**yaa**-Da* means "sports"; *ar-ri-**yaa**-Dee-**aat*** means "math.")

*ar-ri-**yaaD**-a*	sports
'al**-m an-**nafs	psychology
*al-**an**-klee-**zee**-a*	English
*al-**'ar**-ra-**bee**-a*	Arabic
*al-**as**-baa-**nee**-a*	Spanish
*al-lugh-**aat***	languages

Here are some useful words to describe your level of education.

***row**-Da*	kindergarten
***mad**-ra-sa ib-ti-da-'**bee**-a*	elementary school
***mad-ra**-sa mu-ta-**wa**-siT-a*	middle school
***mad-ra**-sa thaa-na-**wee**-a*	secondary school
*kil-**lee**-a*	college
*ma-**dras**-a tak-nee-**kee**-a*	technical school
***jaa**-m'ia*	university
*mad-**ra**-sa ma-ha-**nee**-a*	vocational school

So what would you say about all these wonderful places of education? I hope you would speak of learning! If you were studying to become a teacher, that might be exactly what you would say:

__an__-a a-__t'al__-lam 'an at-t'al-__leem.__
I am learning about education.

at-taf-__keer juz'h mu__-him min ad-di-__raa__-sa.
Thinking is an important part of studying.

u-__fak__-kir __'an__ di-__raa__-sa __'al__-m an-__nafs__ fee al-__jaa__-m'ia.
I am thinking about studying psychology in the university.

Tips

To help remember groups of vocabulary words, try removing all of the vowels and just keeping the three-letter word stems. For example, the stem ***d-r-s*** gives us all the words ***da**-ra-sa* (he studied), ***mad**-ra-sa* (school), *di-**raa**-sa* (studies), and *mu-**dar**-ris* (teacher)—all of which have to do with education.

Arabic for the ninth-year level of education would be ***Suf** at-**taa**-s'i*. ***Suf*** is the Arabic word for "grade" (meaning educational year). You just combine ***Suf*** with whatever level you need from your list of ordinal (meaning "ordered") numbers.

What Are Your Hobbies?

If you are a person who enjoys many hobbies (and I suspect you might be, judging from the fact that you decided to learn such a challenging language), then you know that there are many (*ka-**theer***) ways to enjoy your free time. Maybe you like to read. Maybe you like to write (I know I do). Maybe you prefer the outdoors and exercise. Whatever your hobbies, you should enjoy them—and you should proudly tell your Arabic-speaking friends about them.

Track 31

***maa hee**-a hi-waa-**yaat**-u-ki?*
What are (they) your (f/s) hobbies?

*la-**dey**-ya ka-**theer** min al-hi-waa-**yaat**.*
I have many hobbies.

***maa hee**-a al-ash-**yaa'h** al-**lat**-ee tas-ta-**ma**-t'a-**een** bi-**haa**?*
What are the things that you (f/s) enjoy?

Hobbies are certainly things that someone must enjoy. Otherwise, I don't think they would be called hobbies. They would just be called "things I do." So, what are they? No list could include them all, but here are some popular hobbies:

*qi-**raa'h***	reading
*ki-**taa**-ba*	writing
*mu-**shaa**-had-a at-**tal**-li-fiz-**yoon***	watching television
*as-si-**baa**-Ha*	swimming
*aS-**Said***	hunting
la**-'ib ow-**raaq** al-**l'ab	playing (at) cards
***kur**-a **tan**-is*	tennis
*al-**mash**-ee*	walking
'iaa**-zif al-ghee-**taar	playing guitar
***kur**-a al-**qad**-am*	soccer
*ar-ra-**koob***	riding
*aS-**Said** as-**sam**-ak*	fishing (literally translates to "hunting fish")

Tips

Both **tennis** and **soccer** start with ***kur**-a*. ***kur**-a* is the Arabic word for "ball." Almost any sport that involves a ball uses ***kur**-a* in its name. If you have a hard time remembering the name of your game (volleyball is called ***kur**-a aT-**Taa**-'hi-ra*, or "airplane ball," for example), just say ***kur**-a*—then use your imagination and act out the game for your friends.

If you have hobbies, I hope you do get to spend some time enjoying them between your normal days and reading this book. And how do you *prefer* to do your hobbies?

> ***u**-Hib la-**dey**-ha al-**waq**-t li-**nafs**-ee.*
> I like having (the) time to myself.
>
> *u-**faD**-Dal al-**waq**-t m'a aS-di-**qaa'h**-ee.*
> I prefer (the) time with my friends.
>
> *mu-**'aTH**-im al-**waq**-t an-a bi-**nafs**-ee.*
> Most of the time, I am by myself.
>
> *u-**faD**-Dal jum-**hoor**.*
> I prefer a crowd.
>
> *an-a **daa**-'hi-**man** s'a-**eed**-a.*
> I (f) am always happy.

Pronunciation is difficult in a foreign language. This might become all too apparent if you try to say a word from the book several times, only to have your Arabic-speaking friend say, "Oh, you mean …"—then repeat the word exactly as you were certain you said it. That happens. See whether you can find out what part of the word you misspoke, and keep trying until you get it right.

A Little More Detail, Please

Say you have already gone through the basics of a conversation. You have said who you are. You've told your new friends about your family. You have even introduced a few of them to one another. What remains to be said? Well, if you must know, there are plenty of details you can cover without having to work too hard.

> ***maa**-dha **ta**-f'al(-een) …*
> What do you do (Add –een for [f]) …

*fil-**waq**-t al-**faa**-'hi-Dee* in your spare (extra) time	***b'ad** al-'**am**-l* after work

> *hal hu-**naa**-ka ________________ **qa**-reeb min **hu**-naa?*
> Is there a ________________ near here?

***naa**-dee ley-**lee**-a*	night club
mar**-kaz ash-sha-**baab	youth center

***see**-na-maa*	cinema
*kaa-**zee**-noo*	casino
*Ha-**dee**-qa*	park
*Ha-**dee**-qa al-**Hai**-waan*	zoo
***mal**-'aab*	playground
***Haf**-la*	party

Warnings

Some Arabic cultures have standards of conduct that may be unfamiliar to you. This situation is especially true regarding relationships between men and women. If you are a man, it may be inappropriate for you to speak with a woman who is not your wife. Be certain that you know how people will react to the things you say before you begin asking them questions that deal with these potentially sensitive issues.

Those questions may get you going in the direction you want to head, but maybe you want to get a bit more personal. Remember, in Arabic culture it is utterly important to remain polite under all circumstances. That means never asking a question that should not be asked—and never asking someone to go against his or her personal or cultural beliefs.

That being said, you may sometimes find it appropriate to ask questions that are a little more personal. Here are some typical questions you might come across:

*hal **an**-ta/ti …*	Are you … (*–ta* = masc/*–ti* = fem)
***a'a**-zib(-a)*	single (add –a for feminine)
*mu-ta-**zow**-waj(-a)*	married (add –a for feminine)
*bi-**nafs**-u-ka/ki*	by yourself (*–ka* = masc/*–ki* = fem)
***m'a waa**-Hid*	with someone
m'a** Sa-**dee**-qa-tu-**ka	with your girlfriend
***m'a** Sa-**dee**-qu-ki*	with your boyfriend
***m'a zowj**-u-ki*	with your husband
***m'a** zow-jat-u-ka*	with your wife

m'a *'a-**roos**-u-ka*	with your bride
m'a *'a-**rees**-u-ki*	with your groom

And then, there is one question that you never know when you may need:

***m'a hoo**-a **raq**-m ta-li-**foon**-u-ka/ki?*
What is your telephone number?

def•i•ni•tion

The proper Arabic word for telephone is ***haa**-tif*, but it is rarely used outside formal conversation, such as you might hear on the radio or television. More likely, you would hear and use *ta-li-**foon***.

There are no doubt many other important questions you might think of that should be added under this section, but we have to keep moving—because there are many other important sections left in the book. Don't worry, though. I'll keep adding vocabulary words as we go along. Enjoy your quiz!

Practice Makes Perfect

We can't end a chapter where you learn to tell about yourself without actually testing your ability to talk about yourself. With that in mind, here are your practice questions:

1. How would you say, "I am from a very small town (village)"?
2. Translate the following into simple English: *hal 'aa-**mil**-ta hu-**naa**-ka **mun**-dhu **waq**-t Ta-**weel**?*
3. How would you ask a man what he is doing after work?
4. What does *hal hu-**naa**-ka **mul**-l'ab **qa**-reeb min **hu**-naa* mean?
5. How would you ask a woman for her telephone number?

The Least You Need to Know

- Your home is always worth talking about.
- Asking questions about work gains friends.
- Asking questions about school gains friends, too.
- Hobbies help you enjoy your spare time.
- ***m'a hoo**-a ar-**raq**-m?* means "What is the number?"

Chapter 13

Bring the Sunscreen

In This Chapter

- In the heat of it all
- Do thermometers go that high?
- Sandstorm or snowstorm?
- I prefer something a little cooler

Quick! What are the first three words that pop into your head when I say, "Arab world"? I'll give you time to answer. Just a few more seconds and … what did you come up with?

I guess you can't really tell me what you came up with for this exercise, but I *can* tell you what *I* thought of. My answers were "desert," "sand," and "hot." I suppose that if I extended my list a little bit, I would end up with magic lamps and pyramids—but they can take a backseat to a true force in the Arabic-speaking world. Pretty much wherever you go in the Arabic world, you will have to pay attention to the weather.

Lucky for you, you are reading a book that includes an entire chapter devoted to the weather, temperatures, and finding ways to keep cool (I'm talking about *this* book). What's that? You're not convinced? Keep reading and you'll find out.

Hot Enough for You?

If you were listening to the weather report for al-Azizia, Libya, on September 13, 1922, you would have had the chance to hear a one-of-a-kind weather report. On that day, you could have heard a world-record temperature of 57.7777777778 degrees Celsius. That's *136 degrees Fahrenheit!* That's hot weather, and it's right in the middle of the Arabic-speaking world.

I'm not trying to scare you. I'm just warning you that the temperatures in the Arabic world can get hot. Now that I've gotten you thinking in large degrees of warmth, why not look at some "hot" vocabulary.

shams	sun
***ram**-l*	sand
*kuth-**baan** ar-ra-**maal***	sand dunes
*Ha-**raar**-a*	heat
*Ha-**raar**-a sha-**deed**-a*	extreme heat
***da**-ra-ja al-Ha-**raar**-a*	temperature
Sa-Hraa'h	desert
*bur-**kaan***	volcano
*mey-**zaan** al-Ha-**raar**-a*	thermometer
jaaf	dry/arid
***'ar**-iq*	sweat
*Ha-**rooq** ash-**shams***	sunburn

Tips

If you do decide to visit one of the Arabic-speaking countries with a hot climate, you may want to visit during the winter months when temperatures are milder. The hottest months are generally June through September, and temperatures become more comfortable from the end of September through October and November.

If you are going to visit any country, it is a good idea to know what sort of weather to expect. In Arab-world countries, this is especially true because there is a good chance the climate may be significantly different than anything you have experienced before. You could, of course, check the forecast on the Internet (if you have access)—but before you do, why not ask some of your new Arab friends about the climate where they are from?

> ***maa hee**-a **da**-ra-ja al-Ha-**raar**-a al-**'aaa**-dee-a fee **bal**-ad-u-**ka/ki?***
> What is the average temperature in your country?
>
> *hal **hoo**-a aj-**jow jaaf** ow **ruT**-bee?*
> Is the climate arid or humid?
>
> ***mat**-a **aH**-san **waq**-t lil-**saf**-r?*
> When is the best time to travel?
>
> *hal **hoo**-a a-**Harr** fee **soo**-ree-a ow lub-**naan?***
> Is it warmer (hotter) in Syria or Lebanon?
>
> *hal **yak**-fee al-Ha-**raar**-a li-**ka/ki?***
> Is it hot enough for you?

Of course, I don't expect you to spend all of your time in conversations asking questions. I'm sure once you have experienced the true warmth of Arab climates, you will have plenty of things to say. Here are a few conversation pieces you might be able to use to take your mind off the heat.

Track 32

> *hu-**naa**-ka **'a**-raq fee **'aee**-nee.*
> There is sweat in my eye.
>
> ***aH**-taaj an-na-**THaa**-raat ash-**shams**-ee-a.*
> I need sunglasses.
>
> ***laa** u-**reed Darb**-at ash-**shams.***
> I don't want sunstroke.
>
> *a'a-**ta**-qid an as-sa-**khaan** mu-**'aT**-Tal-a!*
> I think the heater is broken!
>
> ***ha**-dhaa **ley**-sa **mum**-ti'a.*
> This is not pleasant.
>
> ***ha**-dhaa ley-sa **sey**-'han **jid**-dan.*
> This is not very bad.

With all of those new sentences to practice, it is only fair to give you a quick review of some new words and also a few (gulp) grammar points you can start working into your conversations. The vocabulary will help you deal with the heat. The grammar will help you sound more like a native.

Here are the new words we added:

Darb**-at ash-**shams	sunstroke

*al-'**aaa**-dee*	the average/normal
jow	climate
***sa**-fa-ra*	he traveled
*a-**Harr***	warmer/hotter
***yak**-fee*	it suffices
***yaH**-taaj*	he needs
***a'a**-shur bi-Ha-**raar**-a.*	I feel warm. (I'm too hot.)
*mu-'**aT**-Tal*	broken

Tips

You probably noticed that I didn't use the exact words in the review that I did in the text. I did that on purpose so that you can see a couple different uses of the same word root and hopefully recognize the words more easily.

Now for the grammar.

ow: ***ow*** means "or," as in:

*hal tu-**Hib** al-Ha-**raar**-a **ow** al-bu-**roo**-da?*

Do you prefer heat or cold?

an: ***an*** means "that." You already know that "that" is a popular word that has many uses. ***an*** is a bit different. In Arabic, you use ***an*** between two verbs of action. For example, in the sentence "I want to travel," you use two different verbs. The first is "want," and the second is the infinitive "to travel." Well, you remember that Arabic doesn't use infinitives, right? So the way you solve this problem is by sticking ***an*** in between the two verbs. Then, you just conjugate both verbs the same way. The sentence "I want to travel" becomes:

*u-**reed an** u-**saa**-fir.*

I want *that* I travel.

Whether *tu-**reed an** tu-**saa**-fir ow **laa*** (you want to travel or not), here we go!

How Hot Is It?

How hot can it get in Arab countries? I think you know by now that it can get pretty hot. But still, when it comes to knowing *exactly* how hot it is, you should expect to use the *centigrade* temperature scale. If you are not used to keeping track of temperatures in degrees *centigrade*, you'll soon see that it isn't very hard at all.

***fah**-ran-**haa**-yit*	Fahrenheit
*mi-'ha-**wee**-a*	Celsius
***fowq** aS-**Sif**-r*	above zero
***taHt** aS-**Sif**-r*	below zero

See whether you can unscramble the following phrase:

*ad-**da**-ra-ja Ha-**raar**-a aj-**jis**-m aT-**Tub**-ee-'**iee**-a*

the temperature the body the natural

The answer is: The natural (normal) body temperature …

So what *is* the normal body temperature? For humans, it's about 98 degrees Fahrenheit. So, you would say:

*ad-**da**-ra-ja Ha-**raar**-a tha-**maan**-ya wa **tis**-'a-een.*
The temperature is "eight and ninety" (98).

But because you are learning the centigrade system, you would probably want to use the correct numbers.

Normal body temperature is about 37 degrees centigrade.
*ad-**da**-ra-ja Ha-**raar**-a **sab**-'a-a wa tha-laa-**thoon**.*

The temperature is "seven and thirty" (37).

def•i•ni•tion

The **centigrade** temperature scale is the scale based on the freezing and boiling temperatures of water. The freezing point (0° centigrade) is 32° Fahrenheit. The boiling point of water (100° centigrade) is 212° Fahrenheit. A quick way to change from Fahrenheit to centigrade is: subtract 32 from your Fahrenheit number; divide the result by nine; multiply that number by 5. This won't be exact, but should be close enough for most purposes.

Tips

It is easy to confuse the centigrade temperature system with Celsius, which is almost identical. If you want to, you could make a cognate out of "Celsius" and say, "***sal**-see-yoos*"—but it sounds more Arabic to use *mi-'ha-**wee**-a*, which means "based on hundreds." The English "centigrade" also means "based on divisions of one hundred."

Sometimes temperatures can reach higher than 50 degrees centigrade (or *Celsius*, if you prefer), and daytime temperatures across the summer months are often between 45 and 50 degrees centigrade. That's 115 to 125 degrees Fahrenheit.

You Change Like the Weather

If you are going to travel, you will need to find out what sort of weather to expect in any land you visit. When you are visiting the Arab world, you really need to be prepared for anything.

Probably the best source of useful information about the weather will be your new group of Arabic-speaking friends. They may have been where you are going—and besides just telling you about what great tourist locations to visit, they also can tell you what to expect from the weather when you get there.

So you might want to ask:

> ***keyf**-a aT-**Taqs** fee bal-**ad-u-ka/ki?***
> How is the weather in your country?

There are plenty of ways for the weather to be. If you visit Tunisia during the summer, your friends might tell you the weather is ***Haar jid**-dan* (very hot). If you plan on visiting the mountains of Lebanon in the winter, your friends might say it is ***ba**-rid wa mu-**thal**-laj* (cold and icy). Here are some of the other words you might find useful when asking about the weather:

*hal hu-**naa**-ka*	is/are there
*hu-**naa**-ka*	there is/are
thalj	snow/ice
*am-**Taar***	rains
*ri-**yaaH** ram-**lee**-a*	sandstorms (sandy winds)
Taqs** ja-**meel	nice weather
***ghaa**-'him*	clouds
*'a-**waa**-Sif*	storms
*Da-**baab***	fog
*ru-**Too**-ba*	humidity
*ri-**yaaH***	winds (that blow)

Maybe you would like to ask about the weather forecast. There are plenty of ways to ask, but I suggest that you say:

> ***maa hoo**-a aT-**Taqs** al-mu-ta-**waq**-qa'a?*
>
> What (it) (the weather) (the expected)
>
> What is the expected weather?

You could easily add to this question whatever date or time period you wanted. You could say the specific date (we'll cover all the dates in Chapter 15), or you could say "for tomorrow" (which is *li-**ghad**-dan)*.

> **Tips**
>
> All of the vocabulary should be available in the dictionaries at the back of the book.

Pretend you are talking with your friend Muhammad, who is from Lebanon, and you want to ask him about the weather there:

> You: ***keyf**-a aT-**Taqs** fee lub-**naan**?*
>
> Muhammad: *aT-**Taqs** ja-**meel jid**-dan fee aS-**Saif**, wa-**laa**-kin fee ash-shi-**taa'h** **hoo**-a **ba**-rid wa mu-**thal**-laj.*
>
> You: ?

If you have ever tried to communicate in a foreign language, you might have a similar experience to the one in the short dialogue above. You know what you asked ("How is the weather in Lebanon?"), but do you know what Muhammad told you?

Have a closer look:

*aT-**Taqs** ja-**meel jid**-dan*	the weather is very lovely
*fee aS-**Saif***	in the summer
*wa-**laa**-kin fee ash-shi-**taa'h***	but in the winter
***hoo**-a **ba**-rid wa mu-**thal**-laj*	it is cold and snowy (icy)

Where Can I Go to Cool Off?

There is a flip side to the temperature coin, though: the cold. If you don't believe it can truly get cold in Arab countries, then you've probably never heard that Ifrane, Morocco, holds the record low temperature for the entire continent of Africa. In 1935, the temperature dropped to –11 degrees Fahrenheit (or about –24 centigrade).

Yes, I know. Many of you are now saying, "Heck, that's nothing!" Just remember … that temperature is the coldest on record for the entire *continent*, and I'm certain the people in Ifrane on that chilly evening weren't thinking, "This is *nothing*." They were probably cold—and you would be, too.

The reason why it's easy to feel cold in desert climates is because when the sun goes down, it feels as if someone turned a heater off. Temperatures that were higher than 120 degrees Fahrenheit may drop to 60 or 70 degrees. That's a 60-degree temperature drop! Your body feels this change.

But I'm not going to use this entire section to argue about the weather. I'm going to tell you what you can do to stay cool!

Warnings

If you visit a foreign country and decide to go swimming or otherwise enjoy yourself in the open water, remember that there may not be a lifeguard on duty or any postings about where it is safe to swim or enter the water. Please be very careful. Inform yourself about any dangerous conditions at your location. Be careful not to take on something you aren't ready for. There are always lessons available.

Track 32

*hal hu-**naa**-ka qa-**reeb** min **hu**-na?*

Is there a ________near here?

***mas**-baH*	swimming pool
*bu-**Hey**-ra*	lake
***shaa**-Ti'h*	beach/shore
***na**-hr*	river
bir**-ka al-ku-**baar	adult pool
bir**-ka al-aS-Si-**Ghaar	children's pool
***ba**-Hr*	sea
*sha-**laal***	waterfall
***jad**-wal*	stream

Of course, you don't have to jump into the water to cool off. Maybe you just want to get out of the heat.

*'af-**waan** yaa sa-**eed**-ee/sa-**eed**-a-**tee**.*

Excuse me, Sir/Ma'am.

*hal **t'a**-rif(**-een**) **ai**-na **aq**-dar an **aj**-jid ...*

Do you know where I am able to find ...

*math-looj-**aat***	ice cream
thalj	ice
*mu-**keyf** al-ha-**waa'h***	air conditioner
*ma-**kaan** maa **ba**-rid*	someplace cool
***maa'h ba**-rid*	cold water
shey**-'han lil-sha-**raab	something to drink
keys** ath-**thalj	bag of ice
***mar**-wa-Ha*	fan
*thal-**laaj**-a*	refrigerator
THul** min ash-**shams	shade from the sun
*ji-**haaz** at-tah-**wee**-a*	ventilator ("blowing device")
maa'h lil** sha-**raab	drinking water

And of course, maybe you have your own ideas of what you want to do to cool off.

*u-**reed an** ...*	I want to ...
***as**-baH **fee** al-bu-**Hey**-ra*	(I) swim in the lake
al**-'aab **fee** al-**maa'h	(I) play in the water
is**-tir-**khaa'h fee** al-**birka	relaxing in the pond

With so many ways to cool off, you might not even notice how hot it really is. Just be sure to drink lots of water and wear sunscreen if you spend time in the sun. And ... congratulations! You've made it through another chapter.

def•i•ni•tion

I told you before that many words can be similar. *sa-**ba**-Ha* means, "He swam." *si-**baa**-Ha* means "a swim" or "swimming" but ***sub**-Ha* means "glory" or "majesty." But then, if you change the **s** to the hard ***S*** sound accidentally, the entire word changes. *Sa-**baaH**,* as you already know, means "morning."

Practice Makes Perfect

I don't need to explain what's coming. By now, you have seen enough to know ….

1. What is meant by this weather report: "… *aT-**Taqs** al-**yoom** **boo**-a **Haar** jid-dan.*"?
2. How do you say, "The temperature today is 43 degrees centigrade."?
3. How would you ask the following question of a woman or girl: "Do you prefer the heat more than the cold?"?
4. How might you describe the weather if the winds were blowing so hard that clouds of sand blew across the ground?
5. How would you say, "I want to swim in the lake."?

The Least You Need to Know

- In Arab lands, you need to be prepared for the weather.
- June through September are usually the hottest months.
- Winters in Arab lands can be cold as well.
- Swimming is one of the most popular ways to cool off.

Chapter 14

I Don't Feel So Hot

In This Chapter

- All the pieces of you
- Is there a doctor in the house?
- It hurts when I press … *ouch!*
- I've had this feeling before
- What can you give me for it?

I'm going to go out on a limb here and say that by this point in our lives, most of us had had at least one interaction with a doctor at one time or another. I don't think that is too far of a stretch. I'm also going to go out on a limb and say that many of us have *not* had the experience of dealing with a doctor or a hospital visit in *the Arab world*. If you have had such an experience, though, I hope that everything went smoothly for you.

If you have *not* dealt with medical issues in Arabic, I bet that I know the reason why: you don't know how to speak very much Arabic. That's why you bought this book (and I hope by now you are feeling more and more confident in your speaking ability). The more time you spend using Arabic, the more likely you will find yourself wanting to describe health issues—either with friends or with a professional. This chapter is here to help. Have fun learning, and try to stay healthy.

Head Bone Connected to the …

Somewhere in my mind's file labeled "Distant Memories," I remember a song that I learned in childhood. The song was about all the different parts of the body and how they are connected. I don't remember the verses of the song, and I certainly don't remember the tune. I *do* remember that I used to mix the words up, though, and most times I would end up with my "chin bone connected to my waist bone."

Years later, I did learn that the chin is *not* connected to the pelvis—at least, not directly. I also learned that anatomy professors do not appreciate singing during final exams. Well, I won't try to teach you a song in this chapter—but I do think I can teach you some body parts without too much trouble. But I'll warn you: you're going to have to figure out for yourself how they all fit together.

ra-*'his*
head

'aeen/'u-yoon
eye/eyes

unf
nose

fam
mouth

sinn/*is*-***naan***
tooth/teeth

li-***saan***
tongue

dhi-***raa'a***
arm

mir-*faq*
elbow

rusgh
wrist

yad/ai-*da*
hand

iS-*b'a*
finger

Sud-*r*
chest

THah-*ra*
back

kha-*Sir*
waist

rij-*l/ir*-***jaal***
leg

ruk-*ba/ru*-***kab***
knee

qad-*am/aq*-***daam***
foot/feet

iS-*b'a al*-***qad***-*am*
toe

udh-*n/aa*-***dhaan***
ear/ears

sh'ar
hair

'u-*nuq*
neck

kat-*if/ak*-***taaf***
shoulder/shoulders

jild
skin

Tips

To ask someone how to say a specific word, you can say, "***keyf***-*a ta*-***qool***-*(-een)* ***ha***-*dhaa bil*-***'ar***-*a*-***bee***-*a?*" (In other words, "How do you say X in Arabic?") While you ask, you can point at the thing you are asking to learn. An even better way to ask is to say, "***maa ma'a***-*na X bil*-***'ar***-*a*-***bee***-*a?*" In other words, "What is the meaning of X in Arabic?"

So what are some of the things you can do with your new words? Let's take a look. In Arabic, you can:

*if-**taH**(-ee) **fam**-ka/ki*	open your mouth
***ir**-f'a(-ee) dhi-**raa'a**-ka/ki*	raise your arm
*is-**tal**-qa(-ee) **'al**-a **THah**-ra-ka/ki*	lie on your back
*is-ti-maa'a m'a al-aa-**dhaan***	listen with the ears

If I remember correctly from my (admittedly) limited experience in biology and anatomy classes, there are more than 200 bones in the human body, countless types of infections and illnesses one could have or get, and way too many organs for me to keep track of. Therefore, I have limited the selection in this book to those that I think will be the most useful for you.

So you've had the chance to learn a few parts of the body (*aj-**jis**-m*) and have tried the words out on friends. But if you are ill or need to see a doctor, you will need to know how to say more than the names of a few parts of the body. First and foremost, you will need to know how to get the appropriate treatment. That means you are going to need to know *which type* of doctor you need to see.

You might want to ask,

*hal **an**-ta/ti tas-ta-**Tey**-'u **an** tu-**sheer**(-een) 'al-**ey** ...*

Are you able to recommend ...

*Ta-**beeb***	doctor
*Ta-**beeb** 'u-**yoon***	eye doctor
*Ta-**beeb** am-**raaD** in-nis-**saa'h***	gynecologist
*Ta-**beeb 'aam***	general practitioner
*Ta-**beeb** aT-**faal***	pediatrician
*Ta-**beeb** a'a-**Saab***	neurologist
*Ta-**beeb** am-**raaD** jil-**dee**-a*	dermatologist
*Ta-**beeb** al-is-**naan***	dentist
*mus-**tash**-fa*	hospital
*'i-**yaa**-da*	clinic
*mu-**mar**-riD-a*	nurse (f)

*jar-**raaH***	surgeon
*sa-**yaa**-ra is-**'aaaf***	ambulance
***daar** at-**tow**-leed*	birthing clinic

Tips

While you will learn much from this book, you should always have someone who speaks both English and Arabic with you if you need medical attention in an Arabic-speaking land. You should also make sure to find out how payments are handled. Not all insurance policies will work when you are traveling, and sometimes you may be expected to pay cash for treatment you receive.

To tell your friends why you are asking for recommendations, you may want to say:

***an**-a mu-**reeD**(-a).*	I am sick.
***laa** a'a-**shurr** **jeyd**-an.*	I don't feel well.

If you want to make it known that you prefer a female doctor, you just have to change one word. You change the word for "doctor" to the feminine form, just like you do for most other nouns. Instead of saying *Ta-**beeb**,* you just say, *Ta-**beeb**-a.*

Symptoms All over Me

No one knows better than you how you are feeling. If you don't feel well, there are symptoms that will either appear or that you will feel. Being able to indicate these will help ensure that you get the proper treatment.

Listed here are some of the more common symptoms you may encounter.

Track 34

***'and**-ee …*	I have …
al**-am al-**Halq	sore throat
*Su-**daa'a***	headache
*gha-sha-**yaan***	nausea
***Hak**-ka jil-**dee**-a*	itching
*su-**'aaal***	cough
war**-ram/in-ti-**faakh	swelling
***al**-am*	aching

*'**aT**-sa*	sneezing
*is-**baal***	diarrhea
*im-**saak***	constipation
***ar**-aq*	insomnia
***Hum**-ma*	fever
***dow**-kha*	dizziness

*'**and**-ee **ha**-dha-hi al-u'u-**raaD** li-**waq-t** Ta-**weel.***
I have (had) these (the) symptoms for a long time.

*hal **ha**-dha-hi al-u'u-**raaD** **Ta**-bee-'**iee**-a?*
Are these (the) symptoms normal?

***Maa**-dha ta-**THun** 'an **ha**-dhaa?*
What do you think about this?

*hal tu-**fak**-kir **an**-na-nee bi-**Haaj**-a ad-da-**waa'h?***
Do you think I need (the) medicine?

I am not a doctor of any sort of medicine, so I am in no way qualified to make any claims about how to take care of yourself. I do know that I have read in several sources that we can prevent many illnesses by eating healthy foods, drinking plenty of fluids, and getting enough rest. Every body is different, and I am sure you know best what your body needs.

> **1001 Arabian Notes**
>
> If you hear someone sneeze, there are several polite phrases that you could say—but I recommend the easiest. All you have to do when someone sneezes is offer him or her "health" by saying, "***SuH**-Ha*." If you sneeze and someone "blesses" you, you can just say "*shu-**kraan***" ("Thank you").

My personal opinion is that many times, sicknesses can be avoided by decreasing one important feature of all the planning and organizing: the stress. I believe that if we conduct thorough preparations—and with enough time to get everything done—we will have a lot less stress. And when we have less stress, we are less likely to become ill on vacations.

Here are a couple other tips to avoid making yourself sick once you have begun your journey: don't try to do too much, and take care in your selection of food. Wherever you eat, be sure the food is clean and fresh.

It Is Paining

The Arabic word ***al**-la-ma* (it hurts/pains) will be very useful to you when you are speaking about medical and health issues that you may have. The practical thing about ***al**-la-ma* is that it is used as both a verb and a noun. That means you can use the same word to say that something "hurts" you or that you "have pain." Here are a couple examples.

> *yu-'al-**lim**-nee **ha**-dha-**hi** al aH-**dhee**-a.*
> These shoes hurt me.
>
> ***'and**-ee **al**-am bil-**kat**-if.*
> I have shoulder pain.

Let's say that now you are at the hospital or clinic—or you're just speaking to a friend about a specific medical condition.

The doctor (or whomever you are speaking with) will want to know what is going on. He or she might say something like:

Tips

You can always indicate an injury or where something hurts by pointing to the sore spot and saying *yu-**al**-lim **hu**-naa* ("It hurts here") or *al-mush-**kil**-a **hu**-naa* ("The problem is here").

> ***qul lee 'an** u'u-**raaD**-u-ka/ki.*
> Tell me about your symptoms.
>
> *kha-**bar**-nee **'an** mush-kil-**at**-u-**ka/ki**.*
> Inform (tell) me about your problem.
>
> *ta-**bey**-yin **lee Hai**-thu yu-**al**-lim.*
> Show me where it hurts.

Sharp or Soft, It Hurts

If you have ever experienced physical pain (and again, I'm assuming that you have), then you know that not all pains are the same. Some appear suddenly, then disappear just as quickly. Some pains develop over a period of time, eventually reaching a degree we can no longer bear. Some pains are with us all the time, like shadows or taxes. Some pains are spread all over, and some are concentrated in one place. Some pains hurt more when you press down; some when you let off (I know from experience that appendicitis, the swelling of the appendix, hurts more when you let off the pressure quickly).

However the pain comes to you, more than anything you just want to make it disappear. Well, if someone is going to help you get rid of the pain, he or she will probably need to know some more specific details about it. So here you go:

*ikh-**ta**-fa al-**al**-am* the pain went away	***THa**-ha-ra al -**al**-am* the pain appeared
fee kul** ma-**kaan all over (everywhere)	*yu-**al**-limm **hu**-naa fu**q-T*** it hurts here only
al**-am sha-**deed severe pain	***al**-am **'aaa**-mee* generalized pain
*aa-**laam** mu-**faa**-ji-**'ha*** sudden pains	*yakh-**taf**-ee **faj**-'ha-tan* disappears suddenly
*yu-**al**-lim aH-H**yaa**-nan* hurts sometimes	*yu-**al**-lim **daa**-'hi-man* always hurts
*yu-**al**-lim m'a **Daght*** hurts with pressure	*yu-**al**-lim **idh aT**-laq aD-**Daght*** hurts if I release pressure

Sometimes things hurt on the inside, and you might know exactly which part of your inside is bothering you. In those cases, you would just need to say that you "have a problem with …" (*'and-ee mush-**ki**-la **m'a** …*).

*di-**maagh***	brain
Halq	throat
ri**-ha/ri-'ha-**taan	lung/lungs (dual)
qalb	heart
***ma**-'i-da*	stomach
***baT**-n*	belly
'a**-Da-la/**'a**-Da-**laat	muscle/muscles
'aTH**-m/'i-**THaam	bone/bones
***ka**-bid*	liver
***kul**-ee-a* (or) ***kul**-wa*	kidney
dam	blood
***zaa**-'hi-da doo-**dee**-a*	appendix

def•i•ni•tion

You probably wouldn't say that you "have a problem with your brain" (*'and-ee mush-**kil**-a **m'a** ad-di-**maagh***) because of what jokes others might make. Don't worry about the others. Explain yourself. To describe the actual mass of tissue inside your skull, you can also use the word ***mukh***.

The Usual Suspects

Again, I don't mean to presume—but chances are that there are some illnesses you may have had at least once in your life.

Track 35

***kaa**-na **'and**-ee **ha**-dhaa **fee** al-**maa**-Dee ...*	I have had this in the past ...
***ha**-dhaa ja-**deed lee** ...*	This is new to me ...
*a'a-**ta**-qid an-a-**nee** ...*	I think I have ...
*zu-**kaam***	a cold
*inf-**loo**-in-**zaa***	influenza
***'ad**-wa*	infection
*il-ti-**haab***	inflammation
*dow-a-**raan***	circulation
Dur**-bat ash-**shams	sunstroke
*taj-**feef***	dehydration
*Has-**saas**-ee*	allergic
***'ad**-wa al-**udh**-n*	ear infection
***rab**-boo*	asthma
*ghey-**boob**-a*	fainting
kas**-r adh-dhi-**raa'a	a broken arm
*il-ti-**haab** al-qa-Sa-**baat***	bronchitis
*tas-**meem** al-gha-**dhaa**-'hee*	food poisoning

Tell It to Me Straight

If you have spoken to a doctor or other medical care specialist about your medical needs, you are probably hoping to get a diagnosis.

an**-ti/ta fee **Haa**-ja ikh-ti-**Saas-i.
You need a specialist.

*'and-ki/ka iH-ti-yaaj-**aat khaa**-Sa.*
You have special needs (requirements).

Warnings

In many Arab lands, the water delivered to people's homes does not go through as strict controls as those that exist in some countries (like the United States and Canada). For that reason, you should take note of the water you are drinking. Bottled water is advisable in most situations, and a carbon filter is probably a good idea.

Hopefully you won't end up with any illnesses during your trip. If you do have to deal with an issue, however, you will want to get as much information as you can from the person telling you what's wrong.

hab**-ba/ha-**boob	pill/pills
*da-**waa'h***	medicine
***waS**-fa*	prescription
*as-pir-**een***	aspirin
*ta-**Has**-san*	improved/it improves
*ta-**Haq**-qaq/ya-ta-**Haq**-qaq*	checked/he checks
*tash-**kheeS***	diagnosis
*ha-**boob** ma-**sak**-an-a*	painkillers
***had**-da-da/yu-**had**-did*	scheduled/he schedules
***yaH**-wee*	it contains
***raa**-ja'aa/yu-raa-ji'u*	consulted/he consults
***yash**-fee*	it heals
*Da-**maa**-da*	bandage
***'aaa**-ya-na/yu-**'aaa**-yi-nu*	examined/he examines
*'a-ma-**lee**-a*	operation
*ji-**raa**-Ha*	surgery
*'a-**laaj** Ta-bee-'iee*	physical therapy

Finally, there are a couple of phrases you will want to know for certain situations in the doctor's office—just to make things go a little more smoothly.

***maa**-dha yum-**kin-a-nee** an a-f'al Didd-haa/li-haa?*
What can I do against/for it?

***khudh**-haa tha-**laath** mur-**aat** yoo-**mee**-yan.*
Take it three times daily.

*Ha-**Sool 'al**-a ka-**theer** min ar-**raa**-Ha.*
Get plenty of rest.

*ta-**taS**-Sul **bee**-ya **fee** as-Sa-**baaH.***
Call me in the morning.

Once again, you did it! Congratulations! No doubt there are plenty more phrases that could have snuck into this chapter, and I left the sentences and phrases pretty blank for you. Maybe you don't like it that way, but I wanted to get as much vocabulary into the chapter as possible.

Have fun with the this chapter's practice questions. They are the most challenging yet!

Practice Makes Perfect

Track 36

No one wants to practice talking about visits to the hospital and dealing with doctors. But just to make sure you know what to say should the need arise, why not practice here?

1. How would you say, "I have a severe headache, and it always hurts."?
2. How would you say, "I think I have a tooth infection" (remember: infection of the tooth)?
3. What would you do if the doctor told you to "*is-**tal**-qa **'al**-a **THah**-rak wa if-**taH** al-**fam***"?
4. What does the statement, "***raa**-ja'aat ikh-ti-**Saasi***" mean?
5. What does the statement, "***an**-ti/ta fee **Haa**-ja 'a-ma-**lee**-a ji-**raa**-Hee-a wa 'a-**laaj** Ta-bee-'iee*" mean?
6. If the doctor tells you, "***khudh**-ee ith-**neyn min ha**-dha wa ta-**taS**-Sul-ee **bee fee** as-Sa-**baaH**,*" what has he or she told you?

The Least You Need to Know

- Medical treatment may be different than what you are used to at home.
- *Ta-**beeb*** means "doctor."
- Take someone with you who knows both languages.
- Only drink and swim in safe water.

Part 4

Transportation

Many of us come from lands of wide-open spaces. We like room to roam, even if we don't always get as much of it as we would like. Arab lands are designed perfectly for us. There is one problem, though. How are we going to get around?

For every problem, there is a solution (although some solutions may remain in the realm of theory). To the problem of transportation in the wide, wide Arab world, there is the solution of Part 4. You will learn all about getting around in Arabic. You may end up pointing, jumping, and waving to get your point across—but you are determined, so you will succeed.

Whether you're talking about planes, ships, autos, or motorcycles—you name it—where there is a will, there is a way for you to get to your destination. And what should wait for you at the end but a nice, relaxing evening in your hotel room.

Chapter 15

Almost Time to Go

In This Chapter

- Deciding where to go
- The big, wide Arab world
- A calendar or three
- Your first questions
- Asking for help at the airport

No matter where in the Arab world you decide to visit, you will be pleasantly surprised. From the new tastes, sounds, smells, and customs to the jovial conversation, Arab lands are full of more historical and modern wonders than one person could expect to see in a lifetime.

Of course, there are plenty of things you will need to prepare before you go. Most importantly, you will have to decide *where* you will travel. After that, you will have to decide among the hundreds if not thousands of different ways to enjoy yourself while you're there. I'm not trying to limit your possibilities, but the more preparations you can make before you leave, the more free time you will have when you arrive at your destination. (And the less stress you will experience.)

In this chapter, you get a taste of just how many different places there are to visit. Then, after you've whetted your appetite for travel, you are introduced to airport conversations on your way to your own personal adventure.

Surf or Safari?

Are you looking for beaches and underwater exploration? Do you want to scuba dive in "*al-**ba**-Hr al-**aH**-mar*" (the Red Sea)? Maybe you would prefer a journey along the Nile (*an-**neel***), or perhaps you want to visit ancient ruins. Whatever you prefer, the Arab world presents plenty of opportunities to suit your tastes. All you have to do is decide what it is you're looking for.

> **1001 Arabian Notes**
>
> There is much debate regarding how the Red Sea, or *al-**ba**-Hr al-**aH**-mar*, got its name. One thing for certain is that the water itself is not red, although the bacteria growing near the Red Sea's surface may give that illusion (because the bacteria themselves can be red).

Then, you just say, "*u-**reed** an **a**-ra* …" (which means "I want to see …").

*ah-**raam***	pyramids
*sad as-**waan***	Aswan Dam
*kha-**raa**-'hib*	ruins
ab**-oo al-ha-**lool	the Sphinx
*an-**neel***	the Nile
*al-**ba**-Hr al-**meyt***	the Dead Sea
*al **ba**-Hr al **aH**-mar*	the Red Sea
daar** al bai-**Daa'h	Casablanca
*ma-**'aaa**-bid*	temples
*Hi-**yaa** bu-**ree**-a*	wildlife
*ma-**Daiq jab**-il **Taa**-riq*	the Strait of Gibraltar
qab**-r Sa-**laaH** ad-**deen	the tomb of Saladin

Where in the Arab World?

Many people get confused when trying to understand where exactly the Arab world is. That's because the mixing of different cultures and peoples over time has left us with vaguely drawn boundaries.

def•i•ni•tion

The verb *u-**reed*** means "I want." Use it to make your desires known. The verb *aH-**taaj*** means "I need." Use *that* phrase to make your point more clear.

Another difficulty is that many people assume there is no difference between the *Muslim* world and the *Arab* world. There is, however. A good rule to remember is that the Arab world consists of those places where Arabic is the standard language—approximately 20 countries. The *Muslim* world, however, consists of those locations where Islam is the primary religion.

Following is a list of commonly recognized countries in the Arab world. Should you want to visit one or more of them, you just need to say, "*u-**reed** an u-**zoor** **bal**-ad aj-nab-**ee***" (which means "I want to visit a foreign land"). Or, if you are speaking with a friend, he or she might ask you: ***ai**-na tu-**reed** **tadh**-hab fee al-**'aaa**-lam al-**'ar**-a-bee*. In other words, "Where in the Arab world would you like to go?"

*al-ja-**zaa**-'hir*	Algeria
*al-ba-**Hreyn***	Bahrain
***maS**-r*	Egypt
*al-'ir-**aaq***	Iraq
*al-**ur**-dun*	Jordan
*al-ku-**weyt***	Kuwait
*lub-**naan***	Lebanon
***leeb**-yaa*	Libya
*moo-ree-**taan**-yaa*	Mauritania
*al-**magh**-rib*	Morocco
*'um-**aan***	Oman
***qaT**-ar*	Qatar
*as-s'aoo-**dee**-a*	Saudi Arabia
*as-soo-**daan***	Sudan
***soo**-ree-a*	Syria
***too**-nis*	Tunisia

> **1001 Arabian Notes**
>
> If you decide to go on a *safari*, you already know the word for that. *"Safari"* comes from the Arabic word ***saf**-ar*, which means "journey." If you think of a safari as a hunting expedition, you would say ***raH**-la aS-**Said***—which literally means, "hunting trip."

*al am-aar-**aat*** *al 'ar-ra-**bee**-a* *al mu-**ta**-Hid-a*	United Arab Emirates (U.A.E.)
*al-**ya**-man*	Yemen

If you're looking at that list and thinking that some of the country names are missing, you may be right. There remains much contention over establishing an official list of Arab countries. Also, there are parts of the Arab world that are states or provinces but not countries.

What Month and Season?

No matter when you are traveling, you will need to be prepared for the weather. When packing for your trip, be sure to check the weather forecasts for your destination—because while some places in the Arab world can become extremely hot (even in the winter), others may be extremely cold. You'll want to know what it's like where you're going so that you don't end up swimming in a snowsuit!

*rab-**bee**-i'*	spring
Saif	summer
*kha-**reef***	autumn
*shi-**taa'h***	winter

There are three common ways you will hear Arabs express the months of the year. They may use the same months you already know, with a bit of change to the word. Arabs may also use the month's number (***'ash**-a-ra* would be used to indicate the tenth month, or October). The third way you might encounter months is according to their *Syriac calendar* names. Syriac names are most often used in the *Levant*. Use the following table to learn the Arabic months.

***ai sha**-hr tu-**reed** as-**saf**-r?*
Which month do you want to travel?

***mat**-a tu-**reed** as-**saf**-r?*	When do you want to travel?
***ha**-dhaa ash-**sha**-hr*	This month
*fee **sha**-hr …*	In the month of …

*fee **faS**-l …*	In the season of …
*fee ash-**sha**-hr al-**qaa**-dim*	In the coming (next) month

def•i•ni•tion

The **Levant** includes Syria, Jordan, Lebanon, the Palestinian states, and parts of Israel. In these places, you may find the **Syriac calendar,** which uses names from **Syriac**—a language of the region that is even older than Arabic.

Table 15.1

Arabic Months

English Month	Arabic Pronunciation	Syriac Name
January	*ya-**naa**-yir*	*kaa-**noon** ath-**thaa**-nee*
February	*fib-**raa**-yir*	*sh-**baaT***
March	***maa**-ris*	*aa-**thaar***
April	*ab-**reel***	*nee-**saan***
May	***maa**-yoo*	*a-**yaar***
June	***yun**-yoo*	*Hu-zey-**raan***
July	***yul**-yoo*	*tam-**mooz***
August	*a-**ghus**-Toos*	***ab***
September	*sib-**tim**-bir*	*ay-**lool***
October	*uk-**too**-bir*	***tash**-rin al-**ow**-wal*
November	*noo-**fim**-bir*	***tash**-rin ath-**thaa**-nee*
December	*di-**seem**-bir*	*kaa-**noon** al-**ow**-wal*

def•i•ni•tion

The **Gregorian** calendar takes its name from Pope Gregory XIII and is the most-used calendar in the world. A **lunar** calendar is based on cycles of the moon. A **solar** calendar is based on cycles of the sun.

By Which Calendar?

In some instances, you may notice that Arabic dates are expressed according to the *Islamic* or *Hijri* calendar (*al* ***taq****-weem al* ***hij****-ree*). This calendar is significantly different than the *Gregorian* calendar we are used to, because the Hijri calendar is *lunar* and the Gregorian calendar is *solar*.

Although during your travels you will most likely find dates listed according to the Gregorian calendar, it is a good idea to learn the Islamic calendar as well. The following list shows the common names for the months of the Islamic calendar:

First month	*mu-**har**-ram*
Second month	*Sa-**far***
Third month	*rab-**bee**-'i al-**ow**-wal*
Fourth month	*rab-**bee**-'i ath-**thaa**-nee*
Fifth month	*ju-**maa**-da al-**ow**-wal*
Sixth month	*ju-**maa**-da ath-**thaa**-nee*
Seventh month	***raj**-ab*
Eighth month	*sha'a-**baan***
Ninth month	*ra-ma-**Daan***
Tenth month	*shaw-**waal***
Eleventh month	***dhoo** al-**qi**-'a-da*
Twelfth month	***dhoo** al **Hij**-ja*

Report to the Airport

The chances are that before you actually land at your Arabic destination, almost everyone you encounter will speak English. But if you want to try out your Arabic, look around. Are the other passengers speaking Arabic? Do the service personnel at the counters speak Arabic? If they do, talk to them! Try using as many words as you can from the following list of airport vocabulary:

Track 37

*hal **t'a**-rif(-een)*	Do you know …
***ai**-na yum-**kin** an **aj**-jid*	Where can I find …
*khu-**TooT** joo-**wee**-a*	airlines
*ba-**waa**-ba*	gate
Saal**-at al-ma-**Taar	airport lounge
*Ha-**qaa**-'hib yad-a-**wee**-a*	hand luggage
*ma-**Taar***	airport
*mif-**taaH***	key
***ma**-mar*	aisle
***quf**-l*	lock
*ru-**kaab***	passengers
***mak**-tab at-**tadh**-kir*	ticket desk (counter)
*ta'h-**kheer***	delay
***maq**-'ad*	seat
*iq-**laa'a***	departure
*Ha-**qee**-ba*	suitcase
***da**-ra-ja al-**oo**-la*	first class
*b-**Taa**-qat/**tadh**-kir-a*	ticket
*Tai-**raan***	flight
*tar-**qee**-a*	upgrade
***Taa**-'hi-ra*	airplane
waq**-t al-wu-**Sool	arrival time
Saal**-at wu-**Sool	arrival terminal
*Tai-**yaar***	pilot
sha**-ri-kat Tai-**raan	airline company
khuT**-Ta aT-Tai-**raan	flight plan
***raq**-m ar-**riH**-la*	flight number
***da**-ra-ja iq-ti-**Saa**-dee-a*	economy class

Ai-na Adh-hab? (Where Do I Go?)

All of the signs look the same, and everyone except you seems to know where they're going. How will you be able to get to your gate? Easy. You just have to ask someone, "***Ai**-na **adh**-hab?*" (In other words, "Where do I go?") They will be more than happy to help you.

In the following example, you want to know how to get to gate number two:

> ***an**-ta: "'**af**-waan, **ai**-na **hee**-a al-ba-**waa**-ba **raq**-m ith-**neyn?**"*
>
> You: "Excuse me … where is gate number two?"
>
> *al-maj-**hool:** "**qu**-du-man, **thu**-ma **il**-a al-ya-**saar**."*
>
> Stranger: "Straight ahead, then to the left."
>
> ***an**-ta: "**qu**-du-man, **thu**-ma **il**-a al-ya-**saar?**"*
>
> You: "Straight ahead, then to the left?"
>
> *al-maj-**hool:** "n'am, bi-**jaa**-nib **Saal**-at al ma-**Taar**."*
>
> Stranger: "Yes, beside the airport lounge."
>
> ***an**-ta: "**Saal**-at alma-**Taar**, **Taa**-yib. shu-**kraan!**"*
>
> You: "The airport lounge. Okay. Thank you!"

You probably noticed in the example conversation that I have you repeat the directions the stranger gives you on how to get to gate number two. There are two reasons why I did that. First, by repeating the instructions you make certain that you understand the instructions. Second, repeating the stranger's words will help you improve your own pronunciation and better understand others when they're talking to you. Believe me, this practice helps.

At What Time of What Day?

Traveling to the Arab world probably means you will be flying at some point during the night. I remember the first time I flew over the Nile at night. With blackness to the east and west as far as I could see, a narrow strip of lights along the river stretched to the north and south out into the haze. I will never forget that view.

If you don't want to miss the view and you really want to impress the service personnel and the new friends you're bound to make on your trip, you can find ways to discuss the different parts of the day. For example, maybe you would like to travel during specific hours. If that is the case, then all you need to say is, "***u-reed** as-saf-r* ..." and add the appropriate words from the following list of parts of the day:

***b'ad** aTH-THuh-r*	afternoon
*fee an-na-**haar***	in the daytime
*fee aS-Sa-**baaH** al-**baa**-kir*	in the early morning
*ma-**saa**-'han/fee al-ma-**saa'h***	in the evening
*Sa-**baa**-Han/fee aS-Sa-**baaH***	in the morning
***fee** al-ma-**saa'h** al-mu-ta-**'ha**-khir*	in the late evening
***qab**-l aTH-THuh-r*	before noon
*fee al-**leyl***	at night

How Did You Say ...

Unless you are one of the very lucky few who understand all the Arabic they hear the first time around, you will probably be surprised during your first conversations in Arabic. If you are like me, you will have prepared your first statement exactly as you want to say it. You'll say what you want, and then the person you spoke to will rattle off a response so quickly that you won't understand a word.

Don't be scared if something like this happens to you. The Arab world is full of different dialects, and each individual speaks at his or her own speed. If you don't understand something, all you have to do is ask the person to say it again, or *mar-ra-**teyn*** (which literally means "two times").

def•i•ni•tion

*mar-ra-**teyn*** means "a second time" or "again." Depending on the situation, you could also say ***mar**-ra **ukh**-ra*, which means "another time," or ***mar**-ra **thaa**-nee-a*, which also means "a second time."

Here are some more ways you can ask someone to repeat what he or she said:

*hal **yum**-kin an ta-**qool dha**-lik **mar**-ra **ukh**-ra?*
Could you say that one more time?

*hal **yum**-kin an tow-DeeH?*
Could you clarify that?

*ra-**jaa**-'han, ta-ta-**kal**-lam bi-**buT**-Ta'h.*
Please speak more slowly.

And of course, you may use the ultimate bail-out statement:

> *hal ta-ta-**kal**-lam(-een) al-**an**-klee-**zee**-a?*
> Do you speak English?

Final Call Before Departure

You're at the gate. You are almost ready to take off. But before you go, I want to remind you of something my grandfather used to tell me: "Don't rush to failure." I would never let that happen to you, so I've included this last section of the chapter to make sure you are more than prepared for taking off on your adventures in the world of Arabic.

Don't forget that the words used for airlines take the nisba form (*khu-**TooT** aj-joo-wee-a*).

1001 Arabian Notes

One of the first things you may notice about Arabs is that they are highly unlikely to rush toward failure because they approach situations slowly and deliberately. Take a lesson from them, and learn to relax. After all, it should be fun!

Useful Airport Statements

Sometimes you just need a quick reference to get your point across. Use the following table of essential airport phrases to assist you. Don't worry if some of the vocabulary is new. We will cover it in upcoming chapters.

***aH**-taaj …*	I need …
*mu-**saa**-'id-a **Ham**-il Ha-**qaa**-'bib-ee.*	help carrying my bags.
***kur**-see al-mu-ta-**Har**-rak.*	a wheelchair.
*mu-**q'a**-id i-**Daa**-fee **'al**-a al-**Taa**-'hi-ra.*	an extra seat on the plane.
***yum**-kin ta-**bey**-yan **lee ai**-na an-**ta**-THar?*	Can you show me where to wait?
*maa **hee**-a al khid-**maat 'al**-a aT-Tai-**raan**?*	What services are on the flight?
***ai**-na **yum**-kin at-tad-**kheen**?*	Where can I smoke?

Show Me Your Passport

Many people may be concerned about the searches they have to undergo when they walk through airport security. Usually, the searches aren't too "personal"—and most times, male security officers search male passengers and female officers search female passengers. If you *do* have concerns, be sure to bring them up to security personnel—preferably *before* they start searching you. This will save you trouble and save time for those in line behind you.

Finally, here are some of the words and phrases you might need when going through security checks and customs:

Track 38

*ja-**maa**-rik*	customs
***mak**-tab al-**m'a**-loo-maat*	information desk/office
***mak**-tab aj-ja-**maa**-rik*	customs office
*ja-**waaz** as-**saf**-r*	passport (travel pass)
*bi-**Taa**-qa as-**saf**-r*	(travel) ticket
*am-**ti'aa***	baggage
*mun-**doob** aj-ja-**maa**-rik*	customs officer
***mak**-tab at-**tadh**-kir*	ticket office/desk
***faHs am**-an-nee*	security screening
***if**-ta-Ha al-Ha-**qaa**-'hib*	open the bags (luggage)
***b'aD as**-'hi-la*	some questions
*ow-**raaq***	papers
*ash-**yaa'h** shakh-**See**-ya*	personal things
***ley**-sa la-**dey**-naa **shey**-'han*	we have nothing

Whew! I would say you have pretty much all of the incidentals covered. Have fun on your journey … you're on your way!

Practice Makes Perfect

You've come a long way already. There was quite a load of information in this chapter for you to take in, so I'll make it a little easy on you in the practice quiz. Climb aboard!

Translate the following sentences into Arabic:

1. I want to see pyramids.
2. I want to visit Morocco.

Answer these questions:

3. What is the ninth month of the Hijri calendar?
4. How do you say the Syriac name for the month of June?
5. How do you say, "I would like to travel"?
6. How do you say, "Where do I go?"
7. What are the basic interrogatives in Arabic?
8. How do you ask, "When is departure?"

The Least You Need to Know

- No matter what your travel interests may be, the Arab world offers everything to suit your tastes.
- There are three ways to say each month in Arabic.
- You will probably fly at night.
- When lost in the airport, ask new friends for help.
- ***mak**-tab al-**m'a**-loo-**maat*** means "information office."

Chapter 16

You're Getting There How?

In This Chapter

- Get things cheap without *being* cheap
- Blue yonder or deep blue?
- I'll take something with wheels
- Your ticket to traffic
- Oops … we'd better repair that!

There's more to travel in the Arab world than just *getting* there. However you arrive, once you are there, you will find many wonders to see: you can spend days getting lost (on purpose) in the street markets, relaxing as you sit on the beach, or wandering in the desert and seeing more stars than you ever imagined existed. But to do any of this, you are going to have to move around.

Within the Arab world, there will be as many short journey travel opportunities as you may find anywhere. Why not take the time for a cruise along the Mediterranean coast or a flight above the Nile at night? This chapter is all about the many ways you can move around. What are you waiting for? Get *going*!

By Air or By Sea

However you decide to move around, you can gain a lot of useful language (hopefully all of it appropriate and none offensive!) from fellow travelers.

As you know by now, I expect you to use the words and phrases from the rest of the book as well—but here are some cruise- and flight-specific vocabulary words you might find helpful along your way.

***Taa**-'hir*	flying
*ib-**Haar***	sailing
***'al**-a **mat**-n*	onboard (aboard)
*sa-**fee**-na*	a ship
***zow**-raq*	boat
yakht	yacht
*sha-raa-**'iee**-a*	sailboat
***Taa**-qim*	crew
*mu-**Deyf**(-a)*	attendant/steward
***jow**-la ba-Har-**ree**-a*	cruise
*mad-**dar**-aj*	runway
*mee-**naa'h***	port
*al-**ba**-Hr al-'a-**meeq***	the deep sea
***qam**-ra **khaa**-Sa*	private cabin
*Ta-**beeb 'al**-a **mat**-n*	doctor on board
***THa**-hr as-sa-**fee**-na*	deck of the ship
*tas-**lee**-a*	entertainment
qaa**-'hi-ma ar-ruk-**kaab	passenger list

There are endless ways you can end up in a conversation and countless conversations you might have. If this is your first trip to a foreign land, you might want to talk about that. If you are making a business trip, maybe you will want to talk about the sort of business you do. Look at this sample conversation for some ideas.

Track 39

*hal a-**khadh**-ta **ha**-dha-hi ar-**riH**-la min **qab**-l?*
Have you taken this trip before?

***n'am** saa-**fr**-tu **il**-a **maS**-r **'ad**-at mar-**raat**.*
Yes, I've traveled to Egypt several times.

*hal **an**-ta tu-**saaf**-fir **daa**-'hi'man **'al**-a **mat**-n **Taa**-'hi-ra?*
Do you always travel on a plane?

***laa**, a-**khadh**-tu sa-**fee**-na fee al-**maa**-Dee, wa-**laa**-kin fee **ha**-dha-hi ar-**riH**-la, **las**-tu **'and**-ee al-**waq-t** li-**jow**-la ba-Har-**ree**-a.*
No, I have taken a ship in the past, but on this trip I do not have the time for a cruise.

Tips

When learning a new language, don't try to memorize conversations or phrases in one complete sentence as you expect to say it. This limits your creative ability with the language, and if someone doesn't understand your sentence, you'll be out of luck. Focus instead on different uses of the words.

Public Transportation

Public transportation (usually buses and trains) can be a great way to get around … sometimes. Depending on where you are, you may have the best of luck or may spend hours waiting for a bus to arrive to take you to your destination. It would be impossible for me to try to predict what you can expect from public transportation in the Arab world. There are too many different factors to consider, such as distance between locations and technology.

That doesn't mean you can't learn a thing or two about public transportation from this book. The reality is that you can do just as much talking about public transportation in the Arab world with your Arabic-speaking friends at home as you can on vacation. In fact, talking about differences between public transportation in different places is a great way to practice your conversational ability.

***maa hee**-a al-fu-**rooq beyn** an-**naq-l** al-**'aam hu**-naa wa an-**naq-l** al-**'aam fee** …?*

What are the differences between public transportation here and public transportation in …?

***ai**-na al … mow-**jood(-a)**?*	Where is the … located?
***maa hoo**-a al-**mow**-q'i …?*	What is the location of …?

And what sorts of things might you be looking for or asking about? Hopefully the following list will get you going in the right direction.

Haa**-fil-a/**baaS	bus
***tha**-man*	fare/cost
***mow**-qif*	stop (as in bus stop)
*ruk-**kaab***	passengers
***jow**-la*	tour
***Haa**-fil-a see-yaa-**Hee**-a*	tour bus
*qi-**Taar***	train
*mu-**han**-dis*	engineer
*ma-**HaT**-Ta al-qi-Taar-**aat***	train station
***'ad**-ad mu-**waa**-qif*	number of stops
*ra-**Seef***	platform (sidewalk)
***qaa**-T'i at-ta-**dhaa**-kir*	conductor (for tickets)
***maq**-Sid*	destination
*dhi-**haab fuq**-T*	one-way
tadh**-kir-a lil-**yoom	ticket for the day
*sa-**ree**-a*	nonstop (fast)
***sik**-ka Ha-**deed**-a*	railways
***yash**-mal aj-jam-**ee**-'a*	all-inclusive
*ma-**HaT**-Ta*	station
*see-**yaa**-Ha*	tourism
***saa**-'hiq*	driver

If you are looking for a bus in an Arab country and you expect to find yourself on a 40-foot liner, you may be in for quite a surprise. In some places, "buses" are what I grew up knowing as "vans." Drivers wait on crowded street corners with these vehicles that hold 8 or 10 people and occasionally yell out their destination. When enough people have gathered for the journey, the fun really begins. In such cases, the "buses" are given their name more for their function than for their size.

It's Always a Negotiation

No matter how you decide to get where you are going, there is a good chance you will end up in some sort of negotiation. Whether seeking a better price for your vacation or looking for the most convenience in travel, you will find that discussion and negotiations will be part of normal conversations when you are talking with native Arabic speakers. You might as well prepare yourself from the beginning for these types of conversations.

Here is a good way to understand how negotiating, or bartering, works according to Arabic customs. If you wish to purchase something, the seller states a (sometimes very) high price. This price would probably be too ***ghaa**-lee* or "expensive" for you. You should not take this as an insult but rather the seller's way of saying he or she believes you are wealthy enough to pay so much. You reply with a (sometimes very) low price. This is your way of saying you are humbled by the suggestion but are unable to pay the price stated. This process goes round and round a couple times until (hopefully) you and the seller agree on a price that makes both of you happy. The seller might call this a "special sale" or a ***rukh**-Sa **khaaS**-a*.

What does all this negotiation have to do with moving around in the Arabic-speaking world? You might need to do a bit of negotiating to figure out the best way to get around. There is another type of negotiation you will need to deal with in the Arab world, as well: negotiating distances, or getting around. In the following sentences, the word *Ta-**reeq**-a* means "method" or "means"—but the word *Ta-**reeq***, without the final ***a***, is used for "path" (as in a linking point between two distances). *Ta-**reeq*** and *Ta-**reeq**-a* are largely interchangeable (they both mean "way"), but if you can remember the difference I indicate in the following sentences, you will be ahead of the game.

Tips

Do not feel guilty if you don't want to pay the first price offered by someone selling you goods in a negotiation-style setting (like in a market or for a ride to the airport). Pay what you feel comfortable with, even if it means having to ask around before you make a decision.

***maa hee**-a al-Ta-**reeq**-a al-**as**-r'aa?*

What is the fastest method?

***maa hoo**-a al-Ta-**reeq** al-**aq**-Sar?*

What is the shortest path?

> ***maa hee**-a al-Ta-**reeq**-a al-**ar**-khis?*
>
> What is the cheapest method?
>
> ***maa hee**-a al-Ta-**reeq**-a al-**af**-Dal?*
>
> What is the most preferable path?

You also can see that for *Ta-**reeq*** we use the masculine pronoun ***boo**-a*—and for *Ta-**reeq**-a*, we use the feminine pronoun ***hee**-a*. The pronouns are also an indicator that you are learning your Arabic exceptionally well.

So you have your questions prepared—but if you are going to get into a discussion (and probably a negotiation), you will have to go somewhere. That's easy enough. You can just add *lil-**saf**-r* (for travel), ***min***, and ***il**-a* to what you are saying:

> ***maa hoo**-a al-Ta-**reeq** al-**aq**-Sir lil-**saf**-r **min** … **il**-a …?*
>
> What is the shortest way to travel from … to …?

Add those few words, and you can get yourself involved in many different conversations. And don't forget to say something if the price (*si'r*) is too expensive (***ghaa**-lee*).

Note: you may notice that the "'" in "*si'r*" comes *after* the ***i***. That is not an error. There is no vowel sound paired with the '. Usually it would be written with a following vowel such as ***'u***.

Depending on what questions you ask, you may get a variety of responses. Here are some of the more common answers you might receive.

***sah**-l*	easy
Sa'ab	difficult
***laa** mush-**kil**-a*	no problem
***ta'h**-tee **m'a**-ee*	come with me
***ha**-dhaa **b'a**-eed*	that's far
***ley**-sat **b'a**-ee-da*	it's not far
***Tab**-'aan*	of course
*li-**maa laa***	why not
*mus-ta-**Heel***	impossible

If you are not interested in getting into too much of a discussion—or if you have asked someone for help and are already involved in a discussion—there are a couple more ways to state your needs clearly.

*in-na Da-**roo**-ree al-wu-**Sool il**-a …*
It is necessary to get to …

***kam** as-**si'r** as-**saf**-r **il**-a …*
What is the price to travel to …

***ha**-dhaa **ghaa**-lee **jid**-dan.*
That is very expensive.

*u-**waa**-fiq **'al**-a as-**si'r**.*
I agree to the price.

Between all of these statements and those you have learned so far in the book, you should be able to find a sentence or two that will advance your discussion in the right direction. Now, you just need to decide where you want to go.

Warnings

Be wary if you ask someone for a ride and he or she tells you, ***laa** mush-**kil**-a* or ***ley**-sat mush-**kil**-a*. This person may be telling you, "No problem," or "not a problem," but this is not a guarantee that he or she knows how to get where you need to go (at least, directly). The person may mean it is no problem to take you because he or she knows what area you mean—or that person may know who to ask for better directions. Or, perhaps that person knows that if he or she drives around long enough, eventually you will reach the destination. Be selective when choosing drivers.

Renting Cars or Cars for Hire

Maybe you don't want to take a bus. Maybe taking the train doesn't allow you to get out and see the things you want to see. Maybe you want to *rent* a car. If that's what you want to do, then I say, "Congratulations!" I would also say that most likely, you are in for an experience you will never forget. I know I'll never forget my Arab-land driving experiences.

Following are some of the vocabulary words you will probably need for renting a car in the Arab world.

*ee-**jaar**-ee*	rental
*wa-**keel***	agent

*sa-**yaa**-ra Sa-**gheer**-a*	small car
***si'r kaa**-mil*	total price
***'a**-ra-ba*	vehicle
*ru-**soom** i-**Daa**-fee-a*	additional fees
*sa-**yaa-ra** ee-**jaar**-a*	rental car
***'aq**-d*	contract
***rukh**-Sa si-**yaa**-qa*	driver's license
saa**-qa/ya-**sooq	drove/he drives
Ha**-ra-kat mu-**roor	traffic
*ha-**wee**-a **akh**-ra*	other identification
*Ta-**reeq** al-**'aam***	public road
*Ta-**reeq** as-sa-**ree**-a'a*	highway
*ma-**saaf**-a maH-**dood**-a*	limited distance
***ban**-zeen*	gasoline (benzene)
***taa'h**-meen*	insurance
***Haa**-dith sa-**yaa**-ra*	car accident
*kam am-**yaal mum**-kin u-**sooq**-haa?*	How many miles can I drive it?

Warnings

When renting a car, be sure not to give away pieces of identification to people you do not know. Keep your passport and other identifications with you at all times, and do not let someone keep these documents as insurance that you will return the car. If they say they need to keep your items, you may want to seek another location to rent your car.

When you are driving, you may notice other drivers hanging their arms out their car windows and waving. If the person's palm is skyward with fingers and thumb together—and his or her arm is moving straight up and down—that driver is saying, "just a moment." And that probably means either "Slow down!" or "I'm coming over."

Of course, if you think this is all too much for you to handle on your own but you don't want to rely on a bus or train to get around, you may want to take a taxi. Taxis in Arab lands also can be quite an experience. While it may be the quickest way to get somewhere, it could also turn out to be one of the greatest adventures of your life.

Taking a taxi (*sa-**yaa**-ra tak-**see***) in an Arab land can be quite interesting because you get to experience how driving is *really* done. If you are driving in the desert—say, from a city to a remote set of ruins—you might find yourself being driven *off* the road to get around livestock or wildlife (but without the driver slowing down). If you are riding in a city, you might find that cars pass uncomfortably close to people or to one another in the streets. This experience can be harrowing, but if you are out for adventure, it can also be exciting.

Here are some questions and phrases you might want to use:

> *hal **ha**-dhaa sa-**yaa**-ra **aa**-man-a lil **saf**-r?*
> Is this car safe to travel in?
>
> ***mun**-dhu **mat**-a ta-sooqq sa-yaa-**raat**?*
> How long have you been driving cars?
>
> *ra-**jaa**-'hin, al-**Ha**-dhir.*
> Careful, please.
>
> ***ley**-sat hu-**naa**-ka is-t'i-**jaal**.*
> There is no hurry.

Warnings

It is very important that you remain safe when traveling. While riding in a taxi can be fast, it can also be dangerous. If you expect to use a taxi, make arrangements through a trusted source beforehand—and if possible, always travel with a native Arabic speaker whom you trust. Be aware of and adhere to any government restrictions on travel, as well. And don't forget to buckle your seatbelt!

One final note about taxis: there are not necessarily any defining marks on cars that are used as taxis. The car could be painted with its original paint job, and the driver might set his or her own rates. In some places, taxis can be identified by a distinctive orange color on the panels above the wheels (quarter panels) with the rest of the vehicle being painted white. Prices are probably not set, and there may not be a meter in the car.

Go Get Things Fixed

If you are traveling by car in desert heat, wind, and sand, you are putting that car under a lot of stress. And knowing that the vehicle is a rental, it has probably been exposed to plenty of stress.

Overheating, broken hoses, flat tires, and malfunctioning air conditioners are fairly common problems that may be caused by no regular maintenance over the course of the car's existence. You can't do anything about the way a car was treated before you got it, but you can use the old adage "better safe than sorry" to make sure you don't end up renting a car that's going to leave you stranded on the side of the road, waiting for service to come from who knows how far away.

When renting a car, make sure you check its condition before you take off (another reason to only rent from a trusted source). Check the tires for wear and security and all hoses and cables for rust or wear. Make sure that all seatbelts and mirrors are present and that they function correctly; check all fluid levels (if you plan on traveling long distances with a rental car, take extra fluids the car may need); and be sure that all applicable licenses and registrations are in order. You'll want those in case the police stop you for some reason.

Here is some vocabulary to help start you out.

Track 40

*ra-**jaa**-'hin tu-**bey**-yin **lee** al …*

Please show (indicate for) me the …

*'aj-**laat***	tires
*mu-**keyf** al-ha-**waa'h***	air conditioner
mus**-ta-wa an-**nafT	oil level
*ji-**haaz** tad-fi-**'ha***	heater
*mu-**rash**-shiH al-ha-**waa'h***	air filter
***aH**-zim-a al-**mir**-wa-Ha*	fan belts
***mir**-wa-Ha al-mu-**har**-rik*	engine fan
*ma-**raa**-ya*	mirrors
***aH**-zim-a ma-**qaa**-'id*	seatbelts
*ma-**qaa**-'id*	seats
*i-shaa-**raat***	signals
*mas-**saa**-Ha az-zu-**jaaj***	windshield wipers
*aq-**faal** al-ba-**waab***	door locks
***'aj**-la iH-tee-yaa-**Tee**-a*	spare (reserve) tire
*mif-**taaH rab**-T lil-'aj-**laat***	tire wrench
***maa'h zaa**'hid-a*	extra water
***loo**-Ha as-sa-**yaa**-ra*	license plate

*tab-**reed** al-mu-**har**-rik*	radiator (engine cooler)
*raa-**f'i**-a as-sa-yaa-**raat***	jack (car lifter)
***ban**-zeen i-**Daa**-fee*	extra gasoline (petrol)

If you do end up going to the service shop, you will want to discuss prices *before* repairs begin. You don't want to end up paying for a number of repairs you didn't cause or need. You also don't want to end up spending a long portion of your vacation waiting for your rental car to get out of the shop so you can get back to touring. These are just a couple more reasons you will want to make arrangements before you travel, including what type of insurance is available for rentals.

Tips

If the car begins to overheat, you sometimes can cool the engine off enough to reach a service station by turning on the *heater* instead of the air conditioner. This will be uncomfortable, of course, but it could keep you from having to spend an even more uncomfortable afternoon in the desert sun.

Before we close the chapter, here are some final phrases that could come in handy if you find yourself in the repair shop.

*al-**Haa**-dith **ley**-sat kha-**Taa'h** min-**nee**.*
The accident was not my fault.

*la-**qad** at-taa'h-**meen** 'an **kul** al-iD-**raar** **'al**-a as-saa-**yaa**-ra.*
There is insurance for all damages on the car.

*as-sa-**yaa**-ra hee-a mu-**'aT**-tal-a.*
This car is broken (something is wrong with it).

*an-a **las**-tu mas-**'hool**-an **'an** al-**aS**-laa-**Haat**.*
I am not responsible for (paying for) the repairs.

***kam** min al-**waq**-t **an**-ta bi-**Haaj**-a **il**-a **j'al** al-**aS**-laa-**Haat**?*
How much time do you need to conduct the repairs?

*aH-**taaj** **'aj**-la ja-**deed**-a.*
I need a new tire.

*a'a-**ta**-qid is-Ta-**Dam**-tu bi-**shey**-'han **m'a** as-sa-**yaa**-ra.*
I think I hit something with the car.

Hopefully you won't need these sentences unless you are telling an old story to new friends. There are plenty more phrases we could put together, but hopefully you are getting into the habit of piecing your own sentences together to fit your needs. I hope you are ready for this chapter's quiz!

Practice Makes Perfect

If you haven't been doing it for the quizzes so far, I suggest you take out a piece of paper and something to write with—then answer the following questions *before* you turn to the back of the book to check your answers. Be sure to answer *all* the questions, even if you feel you don't know the answer. Force yourself to learn.

1. Translate the following from Arabic into English: *mu-**keyf** al-ha-**waa'h***; *'aj-**laat***; *ma-**raa**-ya*; *mus-ta-**Heel***.
2. How would you ask a woman if she has "taken this trip before"?
3. Translate: ***maa hoo**-a al-**mow**-q'i al **mow**-qif al-**ow**-wal.*
4. Translate: *hal hu-**naa**-ka ru-**soom** i-**Daa**-fee-a **ow** hal **ha**-dhaa as-**si'r** al-**kaa**-mil?*
5. Translate: "The accident was not my fault, and I want a new rental car."

I hope those weren't too much for you. Congratulations on yet another chapter completed! Now that you know all about getting around in the Arabic-speaking world, I think you've earned a break. Coming up next … relaxing in the hotel.

The Least You Need to Know

- When driving yourself around Arab lands, drive defensively and be prepared.
- You will have to negotiate for almost everything in the Arab world.
- Desert conditions are hard on vehicles.
- Public transportation may be different than you expect.
- ***ley**-sat mush-**kil**-a* doesn't always mean "No problem."

Chapter 17

Hotel Hospitality

In This Chapter

- Reserve some things for yourself
- Just the way you like it
- The best services ever
- Make your stay even better

If Arab hospitality is world famous, what better place to experience it than in a marvelous hotel packed with a staff brimming with pride and ready to take care of your every need? If you have any doubt about the hospitality of Arab hotels, you might want to search the Internet for "luxury hotels." The odds are you will find several pages of listings for extravagant lodgings in many places where Arabic is the native language.

Of course, if you are *not* one of the richest people in the world, you may want to try to learn some Arabic skills that could help you get a room and some basic services in a more economical hotel. I'm sure you will find the service staff just as friendly. To help you, a little ability to speak the language goes a long way toward winning friends—and this chapter is full of just the language you need.

Have No Fear of Reservations

Thanks to the Internet and electronic bank transfers, it is now possible to make reservations for almost any destination in the world in a matter of minutes (or even seconds)—without even having to speak with customer service personnel. While this may be perfectly fine with some readers, others may prefer to pick up the phone and make hotel reservations through a live interaction with a real person.

Warnings

Be sure not to confuse *fun-duq* (hotel) with *Sun-**dooq*** (box). Although the two words sound similar, you probably would not make a very good impression if you called a hotel and told them you would like to make a ***Haj**-z* (reservation) for a room in their *Sun-**dooq**!*

If you are calling a hotel, there is a good chance that when someone picks up the phone, he or she will say, "Thank you" (*shu-**kraan***) or state the name of the hotel (***fun**-duq*) that you reached. The person will probably also give his or her own name and ask whether he or she can help you. For the most part, you don't need to worry about understanding exactly what the person says. You can continue by offering him or her a greeting (*Sa-**baaH** al-**kheyr***), saying your name (***is**-mee …*), and saying that you have a question (***'and**-ee soo-**'hal***). Then, you can get right into the conversation. Here are some phrases that will help you make a hotel reservation for your Arab vacation.

Track 41

*mu-**waTH**-THif-a is-tiq-**baal:** Sa-**baaH** al-**kheyr**, **fun**-duq an-nu-**joom**, **is**-mee sa-**meer**-a, **keyf**-a na-saa-**'id**-kum?*

Receptionist (f): Good morning, Stars Hotel, my name is Samira, how may I (we) help you?

***an**-ta: Sa-**baaH** an-**noor**. **is**-mee mar-**waan** wa **'and**-ee soo-**'hal** la-**kum** …*

You: Good morning. My name is Marwan, and I have a question for you …

*mu-**waTH**-THif-a is-tiq-**baal: n'am?***

Receptionist: Yes?

***an**-ta: u-reed an **a'a**-rif **'an** …*

You: I would like to know about …

Remember, this is just sample dialogue to help you get going. You can begin the conversation however you want. I doubt most of you are really named "Marwan" and you are probably more likely to use your last name than your first name when making hotel reservations, anyway. And speaking of making reservations, Here are some other ways to say what you need:

*u-**reed** **Haj**-z li-**ghur**-fa.*
I would like a reservation for a room.

*u-**reed** **ghur**-fa fee fun-**duq**-kum.*
I would like a room in your hotel.

The receptionist will need to ask you some questions to complete your reservation. Some of the questions may include:

*li-**kam** li-**yaal**?*	For how many nights?
*li-**kam** min an-**naas**?*	For how many people?
***mat**-a ta-ta-**waq**-q'aa al-wu-**Sool**?*	When do you expect to arrive?
*bi-**ai** taa-**reekh**?*	On what date?

And of course, there are plenty of new words you will need to know to make your conversation go as smoothly as possible.

***ghur**-fa*	room
***Haj**-z*	reservation
*li-tad-**kheen***	smoking
gheyr** tad-**kheen	nonsmoking
*sa-**reer***	bed
***m'a man**-THar*	with a view
*sa-**reer** ka-beer*	king-sized bed
*sa-**reer**-taan*	two beds
*ja-**naaH***	suite
*il-**ghaa'h***	cancellation
*mu-ta-**waf**-fir(-a)*	available
*takh-**feeD***	discount
*mu-**saa**-fir*	traveler
*li-**yaal***	nights
*us-**boo**-'a*	week
*nu-**joom***	stars
*fu-**Toor***	breakfast

*sa-**reer** i-**Daa**-fee*	extra bed
*mu-**Dam**-man*	included
***ghur**-fa **muTH**-lim-a*	a dark room
*Ham-**maam***	bathroom/water closet/bath
doosh	shower
***baan**-yoo*	bathtub
*twaa-**leet***	toilet
*taa-**reekh** al-wu-**Sool***	date of arrival
*is-tiq-**baal***	reception
*mu-**ghaa**-dar-a*	check-out
*sa-**reer** **Tif**-l*	child's bed (crib)

def•i•ni•tion

If you are familiar with another language—particularly Spanish, French, or German—you will probably recognize the words for **shower** (*doosh*), **bathtub** (*baan-yoo*), and **toilet** (*twaa-**leet***). These words share pronunciation and meaning (they are cognates) across several languages. And be sure to avoid confusing *Ham-**maam*** (water closet, or WC) with *Ha-**maam*** (doves/pigeons).

Between what you have learned so far in the book and in this chapter, you should be able to get through most hotel bookings. But what can you do once you've made the reservation? Well, it is probably a good start to ask where the hotel is and how to get there. You also will want to make sure that someone will be available at the front desk when you arrive. Here are just a few more phrases to help everything go smoothly:

> ***maa hoo**-al-'an-**waan fun**-dooq-kum?*
> What is the address of your hotel?
>
> ***Hat**-ta **ai saa'a** fee al-ma-**saa'h mum**-kin al-wu-**Sool**?*
> Until what hour in the evening is arrival possible?
>
> *hal shakhS **da**-'hi-man **'and mak**-tab al-is-tiq-**baal?***
> Is there always a person at the reception desk?
>
> ***maa hoo**-a **waq**-t al-qu-**doom?***
> What is check-in time?

If you really get stuck, you can always ask whether the person speaks English (most likely they will), or you can just ask how to say specific words by saying ***maa m'a**-na … ("What does X mean?")*.

To the Room, Porter

In many hotels, there are people called porters and concièrges whose main task is to do everything they can to help you enjoy your stay. The porter is the one who carries your baggage to and from your room and may also deliver requested items to your room. In my experience, the concièrge is the person who remains in the lobby/reception area of the hotel and orchestrates the behind-the-scenes portion of your stay.

So what are you going to ask? All of the basic questions, of course. How long have they worked for the hotel? (*__mun__-dhu __mat__-a __an__-ti/ta __ta'a__-mil[-een] hu-__naa?__*) How long have they lived in the area? (*__mun__-dhu __mat__-a ta'a-eesh[-een] __fee__ al min-__Taq__-a?*) And the list goes on. But there are other questions you may have that you won't think of until you are actually in your hotel room looking at your surroundings. Here are some more vocabulary words you might be able to use for such situations:

Ham-__maal__	porter
am-ti-__'a__	baggage
__'a__-ra-ba	cart
__sa__-'ha-la/__yas__-'hal	asked/he asks
boo-__waab__	doorman/concièrge
__khaz__-na al-__Hif__-iTH	security box
mif-__taaH__	key (for unlocking)
__Saal__-a lil-in-ti-__THaar__	lobby (waiting hall)
is-__tey__-qa-THa/yas-__tey__-qaTH	woke/he wakes
a-ta-__waq__-q'aa mu-__kaa__-lim-a	I am expecting a call
__mud__-a al-i-__qaa__-ma	duration of the stay
__maa hee__-a as-saa-__'aaat__ li	what are the hours for
'a-__shaa'h__	dinner
gha-__daa'h__	lunch
__ghur__-fa ri-yaa-__Dee__-a	exercise room
__mas__-baH	swimming pool
__mal__-'ab	playground
__ghur__-fa li-__mu'h__-tam-ar-__aat__	conference room

muq**-ha al-**in**-tir-**nat	Internet café
***Haa**-na*	pub
raq**-m at-ta'h-**keed	confirmation number
***ad**-ad al-**ghu**-raf*	number of rooms
***ghur**-fa-teyn mu-taS-Sal-a*	adjoining room

1001 Arabian Notes

The English use of the word **baksheesh** (Arabic: ***baq**-sheesh/bakh-**sheesh***) refers to a small amount of money that is given as a gratuity for services, although many English speakers believe the term refers to a specific denomination of money or money from a specific country. Although these small tips are common for services, there is no overall standard for how much should be given.

Now you have a few more words to add to your conversations. You should also know that if you want an item from one of the local shops, it is often a good idea to ask the concièrge. He or she will be able to get it for you.

Often, the concièrge will send someone to get the items you requested. In such situations, it may be appropriate to give ***baq**-sheesh* (a tip) to whoever retrieved the items you requested. Rather than giving the money directly to the deliverer, however, you may be expected to give the ***baq**-sheesh* to the concièrge.

Here are just a few more words you might want to use to support your conversation before you even get to your room.

*baq-**sheesh***	tip (gratuity)
*khid-**maat** mu-ta-**waf**-fir-a*	available services
*a-**maa**-kin al-**aH**-san*	the best places
***Ha**-ma-la/**yaH**-mil*	carried/he carries
***qaa**-ba-la/yu-**qaa**-bil*	greeted/he greets
*in-ta-THa-ra/yan-**ta**-THar*	waited/he waits

It probably won't take much to break the ice with the concièrge or the porter. A simple statement or two could put the person in a talking mood—and through interactions with him or her, in a few days you will be able to learn more than this book could ever teach you. (This book is a great place to start, but it should not be the end of your education in Arabic.)

Some questions and statements you might want to use to get a conversation started with the concièrge or porter are as follows:

***ai** ma-**shaa**-had ta-**koon** **Da**-roo-**ree**-a li-**nar**-a **ow**-wal-an?*
Which sights are necessary for us to see first?

***fee raa'h**-yu-ka/ki*
in your opinion

***ai**-na **hoo**-a al-ma-**kaan** al-**af**-Dal lil-**ak**-al?*
Where is the best place to eat?

*hal hu-**naa**-ka qa-**waa**-'id **khaaS**-a?*
Are there special rules?

***an**-a u-Haa-wil an a-ta'**al**-lim al-'**ar**-ra-**bee**-a.*
I am trying to learn (the) Arabic.

*ta'a-lee-**maat khaaS**-a*
special instructions/directions

Go to the Third Floor

One thing you do not want to happen, particularly if you are carrying a heavy load of luggage by yourself up the stairs, is to hopelessly wander around looking for a room that isn't there. And this situation could happen quite easily if you are not prepared. That's because the "first" floor may not mean the same thing to you that it does to your hotel staff. What you know as the first floor probably means the ground floor to the staff, and the "second floor" to you probably means the first floor to them.

The best way to get to your room without any problems is to get directions (unless you just want to follow the porter). Of course, to get directions you need to know what you are being told. So here are some words you might encounter when you receive instructions:

Track 42

***ma**-mar*	hallway/corridor
***miS**-'ad*	elevator
*sul-**lam***	staircase
aa**-la ath-**thalj	ice machine
*mu-**qad**-dim-a*	forward
***mash**-a/**yam**-shee*	walked/he walks
daa**-ra/ya-**dowr	turned/he turns
door!	Turn!

***makh**-raaj*	exit
***Taa**-biq*	floor/story
***im**-shee!*	Walk!
*ya-**saar***	left (direction)
*ya-**meen***	right (direction)
***da**-ra-ja*	stairway
***magh**-sal*	laundry

Tips

To help yourself learn the vocabulary words, it is a good idea to write them on a separate piece of paper in sentences that you create on your own. Then, you should repeat the sentences out loud—trying to develop a conversational flow with the words. This way, your mind has to work to produce the sentences, which helps you remember them.

If you are looking for something you have never seen before (like a hotel room in a foreign country), it is probably a good idea to get as much information about the location as possible. It doesn't help much if you can find the right hallway but not the right corner—or the right floor but the incorrect hallway. Therefore, even after you have received your instructions, you will want to repeat them and make sure you know exactly where you are going.

***ai**-na **ha**-dhaa bil-**Dab**-T?*
Where is this, exactly?

***yum**-kin tu-**bey**-yin **lee 'al**-a al-kha-**reeT**-a?*
Can you show (indicate for) me on the map?

Track 42

And if you ask these questions, they will probably get you more precise instructions. In that case, you'd better be prepared.

*ta'a-lee-**maat** da-qee-**qee**-a*	precise (minute) instructions
*maD-**booT***	exact
il**-a al-wa-**raa'h	backward
*al-a-**kheer***	the last one (final)
***qab**-la al …*	before the …
***b'ad** al …*	after the …
*bi-**jaa**-nib al …*	beside the …
***'ab**-ra min al …*	across from the …

*wa-**raa'h** al …*	behind the …
***ruk**-n*	corner

I'm sure that on the one hand, you don't want your search for your room to turn into an interrogation—but on the other hand, you probably don't want to waste time looking for something that should be easy to find. So, to end this section, I'll give you some phrases that you will find useful not only for moving around the hotel but wherever you find yourself in need of movement.

Track 42

***kam** mar-**raat**?*	How many times?
*hal hu-**naa**-ka ar-**qaam** '**al**-a al-ab-**waab**?*	Are there numbers on the doors?
***kam** ar-**kaan**?*	How many corners?
***il**-a al-ya-**meen** **ow** al-ya-**saar**?*	To the right or to the left?

Hopefully this section gives you more than enough language to get yourself to your hotel room without any problem. The next section covers many of the common issues you might have once you get into your hotel room.

Get Some Service!

Once again, I am going to make a large generalization and say that you have probably forgotten something during your existence. (And if you have never forgotten a single thing, please tell me your secret!) While traveling, maybe you forgot a comb, your wallet, or are just a forgetful person like I am (it's not a crime; we just have to be better at organizing). Whatever you may have forgotten, don't let it ruin your vacation.

The good thing about being in a hotel is that if you forget something, you don't always have to go without that item for the duration of your stay. For many small items, you can call the front desk and see whether they have the item. If they do not have it, there is a good chance they can get the item for you—either through the concièrge, the porters, or just through someone they know.

Warnings

Remember, if you are traveling to a foreign land, your electrical appliances may not work. The voltage on the appliances may be stronger than you are used to—and the plugs may be shaped differently. If you plug the wrong instrument into an outlet, you could damage or destroy the device. Be sure you have any adapters you might need.

*na-**sey**-naa*	we forgot
*hal min al **mum**-kin al-Ha-**Sool 'al**-a …*	is it possible to get …
***moo**-sa al-Hi-**laaq**-a*	razor
***min**-sha-fa*	towel
*fur-**shaa** al-is-**naan***	toothbrush
*fur-**shaa sha'a**-ra*	hair brush
*m'a-**joon** al-is-**naan***	toothpaste
*wi-**saa**-da*	pillow
***shar**-shaf*	bed linens
*baT-Taa-**nee**-ya*	blanket
*mik-**waaa***	iron (clothing press)
*mu-**jaf**-faf ash-**sh'ar***	hair dryer
***Saa**-boon*	soap
***shaam**-boo*	shampoo
mushT	comb
***Taa**-wil-a li-**keey** al-ma-**laa**-bis*	ironing board

But the things you need in your room aren't always going to be things that you forgot. You might walk into your hotel room and find out that there are problems with some of the items there—or you just may have some questions about the hotel's services.

*hu-**naa**-ka mush-**kil**-a.*	There is a problem.
*naH-**taaj***	we need
*mu-**keyf** al ha-**waa'h***	the air conditioner
*mu-**'aT**-Tal*	broken
***khid**-ma al-**ghur**-fa*	room service
*tan-**Theef jaaf***	dry cleaning
***magh**-sal*	laundry
***qaa**-'hi-ma al-**aT**-T'im-a*	menu (list of the foods)
***khuT khaa**-rij-**ee**-a*	outside line
*af-**laam***	films (movies)

Now, you have several more ways to get things arranged just the way you want them to be in your room.

Here are a few polite ways you might want to begin your request:

> ***ley**-sa la-**dey**-naa …*
> We don't have a …
>
> *yum-**kin**-kum ir-**saal shakhS m'a** …?*
> Can you send someone with …?
>
> ***naH**-nu bi-**Haaj**-a **ak**-thar min al …*
> We need some more …
>
> ***keyf**-a **yum**-kin al-Ha-**Sool 'al**-a ak-**thar min** al …?*
> How can I get more …?

You're almost through the chapter. But before we end, I'd like to give you a bit more vocabulary, focused on *some* things you might need to say when getting ready to go into the city.

Some Final Tips Before the City

To help you get the most out of your preparations, it's time to add to your Arabic language arsenal by focusing on the word ***maa***.

You already know that ***maa*** means "what." If you have any experience with different Arabic dialects (local versions of Arabic spoken differently in different regions), you may have heard ***maa*** used in place of ***laa*** (no/not). Well, here I am going to show you another way to use ***maa***—this time to add *some*.

In this short section, you will learn a few sample sentences that show you how you might use ***maa*** to speak with a bit of uncertainty.

Take a look at what I mean:

> *ta-**rak**-tu al-mif-**taaH** li-**ghur**-fa-tee **fee** ma-**kaan maa**.*
>
> I left the key to my room someplace/somewhere.

In this sentence, the phrase ***fee** ma-**kaan maa*** literally means "in place unknown." This usage is what I mean by "uncertainty." Using ***maa*** after nouns can be helpful in your conversations, because when we use ***maa*** with a word, we say that we just aren't quite *sure*. I'll explain.

If I say, "I left my socks in a place," I probably know where I left my socks. However, if I say, "I left my socks *some*place," then I probably don't know where I left my socks. (It's a good thing I have another pair.) "Someplace" becomes a pronoun that tries (but doesn't really succeed) in telling us where I left my socks.

There are many pronouns that use ***maa,*** and if you can learn to use them, you will have a better grip on Arabic—and you will be able to have more creative conversations with the people you're going to meet very soon when we go to the city. Take a look at some more ***maa*** pronouns:

> *si-u-**saa**-fir **il**-a al-**qaa**-hir-a **yoom**-an **maa.***
> I will travel to Cairo someday.
>
> ***shakhS**-an **maa a**-kha-dha **min**-sha-fa-tee.*
> Somebody took my towel.
>
> *fa-**qad**-tu Ta-**reeq**-ee bi-Ta-**reeq**-a-**tin maa.***
> I lost my way somehow.
>
> ***an**-a **ab**-Hath **'an shey**-'han **maa.***
> I am searching for something.
>
> ***fee waq**-t-an **maa** si-**naH**-taaj sa-**yaa**-rat ee-**jaar**-a.*
> Sometime (at some point), we will need a rental car.
>
> *li-**sab**-bab **maa**, na-**sey**-tu **is**-mu-ka.*
> For some reason, I forgot your name.
>
> *ghad-dan, si-nu-**Haa**-wil an **na**-ra ma-**kaan maa** ja-**deed.***
> Tomorrow, we will try to see someplace new.

Strange as it may sound, you can definitely impress the hotel staff by using *maa* and expressing yourself with some "uncertainty"!

1001 Arabian Notes

If you want to confirm something (or confirm it as much as possible) in Arabic, you want to know the phrase *in **shaa'h** al-**lah** (Allah)*. That means "God willing." This phrase is used by Arabic speakers to say they want something to be done or that they will try to do it. Figuratively, this phrase means "Things will be done if God wants them to be done." Although the phrase comes from Islam, you may hear non-Muslims use the phrase, as well.

Because we are dealing with ***maa*** words, I might as well give you a few more just to help you along your path toward fluency.

> *ta-'**ha**-kha-dha al-i-**jaa**-za **kul**-la-**maa** tu-**reed**.*
> Take the vacation whenever you want to.
>
> *ik-**ta**-shaf sa-**laam** **bey**-thu-**maa** **ta**-jid **nafs**-u-ka.*
> Find peace wherever you find yourself.
>
> *wa **bey**-na-**maa** **an**-ta **fee** i-**jaa**-za …*
> And while you are on vacation …
>
> *mah-**maa** **Ha**-da-tha, **laa** tir-**t'ab**.*
> Whatever happens, don't panic.

I think those four sentences should be ones we carry with us at *all* times (***fee kul al waq**-t*), not just when we are on vacation. If you can remember them in Arabic, though, you will have your own "vacation mantra" to follow ***kul**-la-**maa*** (whenever) you begin to feel stress creeping into your mind.

Practice Makes Perfect

Now comes your first chance to practice all the new words you need for the hotel. And you don't even have to make a phone call to practice. All you have to do is take the quiz.

1. Translate: "I would like to reserve a room in your hotel."
2. Translate: "a nonsmoking room with two beds and a nice view".
3. Translate: "Someday, I will take my wife to try and see someplace new."
4. Translate: "*fur-**shaa** al-is-**naan** wa m'a-**joon** al-is-**naan** **mu**-him-a **jid**-dan.*" (Note: ***mu**-him-a* translates to "important.")
5. Whom in the hotel might you ask about the local highlights? a) *mu-**waTH**-THif-a is-tiq-**baal***; b) ***khuT** **khaa**-rij-**ee**-a*; c) *mu-**jaf**-faf ash-**sh'ar***

The Least You Need to Know

- *baq-**sheesh*** is a gratuity for services.
- Your electronic devices may not work in your hotel room, so bring an adapter.

- *hu-**naa**-ka mush-**kil**-a* means "There is a problem."
- In Arab hotels, the third floor could be your fourth floor.
- Those at the front desk can handle most issues.

Part 5

Touring in Arabic

Have you ever been on a tour? If so, you probably know that regardless of how much time you spent preparing, you still were not ready for one or two little surprises that popped up along the way. If you are touring in Arabic, you may be in for even more surprises.

Hopefully, Part 5 will help you prevent any unwanted surprises and leave you with lifelong memories of only pleasant surprises. Touring in Arabic can be quite a shock to the unsuspecting traveler, but if done properly it can be among the most rewarding experiences of your life.

So … get ready to go to market; get ready to go to the restaurant; get ready for the city; get ready, get ready, get ready … because here we go!

Chapter 18

Preparing for the City

In This Chapter

- Cold, hard green
- Banking at the exchange
- Discovering hidden fees
- Learning better ways to say "No!"
- Finding yourself along your way

Traveling to a foreign country can be incredibly exciting. But it can be incredibly frightening, as well—especially if you run out of money and don't know how to get more. Don't worry, though. This chapter was written with you, the traveler, in mind.

I suppose the odds of you realistically going to a foreign country and running out of money and not knowing what to do about it are probably pretty slim. Modern technology and electronic money transfers have created a financial world small enough to fit on small plastic cards that we carry in our wallets.

But credit and debit cards might not be useful to you if you are going to be spending most of your time checking out markets and attractions where computers are nowhere to be seen and prices are largely determined by your willingness to negotiate. For situations like that, it is best you know as much as possible about money.

Money, Money, Money

Cash, green, bucks, dough, bread, cheese… no matter what you call it, money makes the world go 'round. At least, it allows you to get around the world—and around the world may be how far you have to go to get to the Arab land of your choice.

> **1001 Arabian Notes**
>
> Depending on where you visit, you may hear the English word "pound" used to refer to money that in Arabic is called ***jun**-ya* or ***gheen**-ya*. Of course, you might recognize this type of money as "guinea" or "guineas." The British pound, for example, is called the ***jun**-ya bree-Taa-**nee**-ya*.

There are many different currencies found in the Arab world. Depending on where you go, you may use dirham, rial, riyal, pounds, lira, or even U.S. dollars. Let's jump into some vocabulary.

*doo-**laar***	dollar
sheek	check
*bi-**Taa**-qa 'i-ti-**maad***	credit card
***ka**-sa-ba/**yak**-sib*	he earned/he earns
*dee-**naar***	dinar
***jun**-ya*	guinea
***lee**-ra*	lira
*mu-**baa**-da-la*	exchange (act of exchanging)
maal**/nu-**qood**/fu-**loos	money
***jun**-ya bree-Taa-**nee**-ya*	British pound
***da**-fa-'a/**yad**-f'aa*	paid/he pays
*dir-**haam**/di-**raa**-him*	dirham/dirhams
***'um**-la **m'a**-din-**nee**-a*	coins (small change)
***Sa**-ra-fa/**yaS**-rif*	spent/he spends (money)
*al-**baa**-qee*	change (the remainder)
*fu-**loos** **wa**-ra-qee*	paper money (bills)
***Suk** see-**yaa**-Hee*	traveler's checks
*ra-**Seed***	fund/balance
***tha**-man*	value

*ma-**kaa**-sib*	earnings
***'um**-la*	currency
***naq**-dee*	monetary

Here is another tip. You may not feel comfortable talking about some financial matters with your new Arabic friends. That is understandable, but you should be prepared for them to ask how much money you earn. You shouldn't see this as an insult. It is probably just because they are curious to know more about you. If they do ask, you might feel yourself caught between the discomfort of avoiding their question and the discomfort of divulging such private information about yourself.

If this situation were to happen to me, I would probably say something like:

> ***us**-ra-tee **qaa**-dir-a **'al**-a al-**ak**-l wa **an**-a s'a-**eed.***
>
> My family is able to eat, and I am happy.

or:

> *laa Haaj-a **il**-a al-Ha-**deeth** 'an al-**maal beyn** aS-di-**qaa'h.***
>
> There is no need for talk of money among friends.

Either of the two previous sentences should help you steer the conversation away from money you earn and toward things you feel more comfortable discussing.

But enough talk about all the issues that may or may not be uncomfortable for you. You probably want to focus on something more useful in conversation, like how to put your money to use. One thing I'm sure we all know is that money isn't much good if you aren't able to use it. There are two common Arabic words for "use" when you want to say, "make use of."

*is-**ta'am**-al/yas-**ta'a**-mil*	used/he uses
*is-ti'i-**maal (or)** is-tikh-**daam***	the using/use
*is-**takh**-da-ma/yas-**takh**-dim*	used/he uses

Can you think of how you might put "use" to work for you? How would you say, "I would like to use the money"? Any ideas? There are two ways I would break the sentence down.

First, "I would like" translates to "*u-**reed.***" Then we have to figure out what it is that we would like. We would like to "use." Because "would like" and "use" are both verbs, we have to throw ***an*** in between them to keep them from running over one another.

We also have to make sure that we conjugate "use" for our own purposes (first-person singular). Finally, we add the word for money (*an-nu-**qood***).

Now, we have:

> *u-**reed an** as-**takh**-dim/as-**ta'a**-mil an-nu-**qood**.*
>
> I would like (that) I use the money.

Now, there is another way to say basically the same thing you've just said—except this time, you are only using *one* verb. Instead of saying, "I would like to use the money" or, "I would like that I use the money," you could say, "I would like the use of the money."

Look at the sentence again. "I would like (verb) use (noun) of the money (second noun)." What we have in this case is a nisba adjective instead of two verbs. In a sense, the "use" *belongs to* "the money." We could also say, "I would like the money's use."

Tips

The Arabic word for "used to" (as in, I "used to" do something—a repeated behavior) is ***kaa**-na*. The use of ***kaa**-na* is a bit more complicated and therefore will be covered in a later chapter. You have enough to worry about at the moment with the other uses of "use."

So how would we say that in Arabic? Again, the answer is simple:

> *u-**reed** is-ti'i-**maal**/is-tikh-**daam** an-nu-**qood**.*
>
> I would like the use (of) the money.

You can see in this second example that we don't need to worry about conjugating two verbs or putting ***an*** in the correct place. We just have to make sure that the definite article is only at the beginning of the second noun. (With *an-nu-**qood**,* you just don't hear the ***l*** sound of our buddy ***al***.)

At the Bank

When you travel to the Arabic-speaking world, you will find most banking services available at most locations. But you should always make sure what services will be available *before* you travel. You also will want to familiarize yourself with all the applicable rules for both your bank and the bank you will be using when you arrive.

When you are choosing a bank, make sure to ask a couple of key questions regarding any applicable fees. Doing this will probably save you a little money and make your transaction, and trip, in the Arab world a lot smoother. If transferring money to a bank in the Arab world, you should expect delays of days or more before you will have access to the money. In most cases, however, banking will be similar to what you are used to (the tellers at most international bank branches will probably know English, as well.)

The reality of banking in most tourist destinations is that you should have little difficulty finding the banking services you need. In locations where banking is limited or branches are too small to handle your needs, you may be able to get help from your hotel. You will, of course, have to have your account information and appropriate identification available (but you should have that anyway).

Warnings

Unfortunately (and often unnecessarily), many travelers fall victim to scams or robbery by making mistakes such as providing personal and/or account information to people who they do not know or carrying obvious large amounts of money or valuables. Please learn how to keep yourself safe on your trip. Your government travel authority can provide you the information you need.

Now, let's take a look at some of the words you might need when you interact with the local bank.

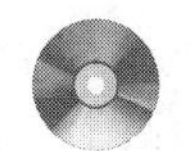

Track 43

***maS**-rif*	bank
*ta-**gheyr***	change (switch)
*taH-**weel***	an exchange
*Sar-**raaf***	cashier
***sa**-Ha-ba/**yas**-Hab*	withdrew/he withdraws
***ow**-da-'a/ya-**wad**-'a*	deposited/he deposits
***Haw**-wa-la/ya-**Haw**-wal*	transferred/he transfers
*Hi-**Saab***	account
*bi-**Taa**-qa i'i-ti-**maad***	debit/credit card
*ta-ka-**leef***	charges
*mun-**Sar**-af*	expenditures
farD	loan
*taH-**weel** i-lak-troo-**nee**-ya*	electronic transfer
*ra-**Seed** al-Hi-**Saab***	account balance
***mab**-lagh*	amount
***'um**-la maH-**lee**-ya*	local currency
s'ir** aS-**Sarf	exchange rate
***faa**-'hi-da*	interest

*mun*S-***roof** al-**jeeb***	pocket change
raq**-m al-Hi-**Saab	account number
*Hi-**Saab jaa**-ree*	checking account
*Hi-**Saab** too-**feer***	savings account
***mad**-fu'u*	payment
*ji-**haaz** li-**Sarf** al-**aa**-lee*	Automatic Teller Machine (ATM)

With this vocabulary, you should be able to ask pretty much any question that might arise when trying to accomplish your monetary tasks. Still, it never hurts to have a few useful phrases prepared.

*hal **t'a**-rif **ai**-na al* ___________________ *mow-**jood?***
Do you know where the ___________ is located?

***keyf**-a **aj**-'al* ___________________?
How do I make a/an___________________?

***maa**-dha **yum**-kin-ka ta-**qool lee 'an** …?*
What can you tell me about …?

hal ___________________ *min al **mum**-kin hu-**naa**?*
Is ___________________ possible here?

***an**-a bi-**Haaj**-a **il**-a* ___________________.
I am in need of ___________________.

*hal **taq**-bal* ___________________ *hu-**naa?***
Do you accept ___________________ here?

In English, we sometimes say (or wish we could say) that "money is no object." More and more, that is really becoming the case because many of us tend to rely more and more on the ability to conduct transactions electronically. Still, there always remains the chance that you will need to go to some sort of bank when you are on vacation. Don't let it be a hassle. Just make sure you know what to expect before you arrive.

If you do find yourself in a bank in a foreign country, be sure to be polite. Remember, the local population will still be there when the next one of us non-natives arrives. Try to leave them happy that you visited. In the bank, that probably doesn't mean much more than saying, "Excuse me/please" (*'af-**waan***), "if you please" (*Ta-**faD**-Dal*), and "thank you" (*shu-**kraan***). And if a bank visit is necessary, you will definitely have to pay attention to their hours of operation.

What Do You Mean, "Closed"?

This is probably not a statement you want to be making at 2:30 on a Friday afternoon while you stand in front of the bank or money exchange, minutes before you were expecting to climb onto a tour bus for a weekend of travel, photos, and shopping. But if you are not aware of the business hours, you could end up facing similar circumstances.

"Sure," some of you are saying, "then I would just use an ATM." That's fine. But there are plenty of us who prefer actual financial service representatives to ATMs—and some of us don't even have the proper cards for an ATM.

The banking hours and days will likely be different than you are used to when you visit your Arab destination. This is not difficult to adjust to but could turn out to be an unpleasant surprise if you are expecting services but can find none. In regions where Islam is a large part of government, you will also want to be aware of prayer times so that you do not wander the streets in search of services only to find that all stores are closed. In some instances, you could even find yourself in trouble with the authorities if you are out during times designated for prayer—so be sure to know before you go.

1001 Arabian Notes

In many Arabic-speaking areas, the workweek is based upon the Islamic principle of Friday being the holy day. Therefore, weekends are Friday and Saturday. Sunday is the first day of the workweek. Arabic language reflects this, as Sunday is ***yoom*** *al-**aH**-Had* (the first day) and Saturday is ***yoom*** *as-**sab**-t* (the seventh day).

That means you need some more vocabulary (the more the better, right?):

*Da-**reeb**-a*	tax
*at-**'aaab** kha-**fee**-ya*	hidden fee
***tak**-lif-a i-Daa-**fee**-a*	extra cost
***magh**-laq*	closed
*mash-**ghool***	busy
*ta-**faa**-wa-Da*	negotiate
*mu-**naa**-Sa-ra*	support (backing)
*mu-ta-**kal**-lif*	sponsor
*um-**waal** shi-ree-**kee**-a*	company funds

*Da-**reeb** as-sa-yaa-**raat***	motor vehicle tax
*Da-**reeb**-a 'a-**qaa**-ree-a*	real estate tax
*Da-**reeb**-a ad-**dakh**-l*	income tax
*maf-**tooH***	open (not closed)
***Ta**-lab*	(a) request
*is-tith-**naa'h***	exception
***Haal**-a Ta-**waa**-ri'h*	emergency situation
***far**-'a*	branch
***mak**-tab ra-**'hee**-see*	main office
*mu-**kaa**-faa-'ha **Saf**-qa*	transaction fee
*'u-**qoo**-ba maa-**lee**-a*	monetary penalty
*mu-**deer***	director
***m'u**-fee min aD-Da-**raa**-'hib*	tax-free (free of taxes)
*i-**daa**-ra*	administration
*Sar-fee-**yaat***	payments/disbursements
*Ha-**waal**-a maa-**lee**-a*	money order (transfer)
s'ir	price

You probably already know what I'm going to throw at you next: useful phrases. I will, but first I want to explain that I put the phrases into the chapters the way I have with a goal in mind: you should learn the *art* of Arabic, not the *science*. A coworker and world-class linguist often reminds me that language is an art, not a science. Results will not be exactly repeated across many trials or various populations. With that in mind, I hope you are able to take the short sentences, phrases, and terms I have provided you in these chapters and bend and meld them into Arabic verbiage as you need it. We will save the more advanced lessons (hopefully) for a subsequent book.

So what phrases might you need to discover the details of your banking transactions? I'm glad you asked.

*min **faD**-la-**ki takh**-bar-**een**-nee **'an** …*
If you (f/s) please, inform (f/s) me about …

ai**-na **yum**-kin **an aj**-id **m'a**-loo-**maat 'an…?
Where is it possible for me to find information about …?

***maa hee**-a as-saa-**'aaat** al-**'am**-al?*
What are the hours of operation?

***mat**-a an-**tum** …*
When are you (pl/m) …

Finally, before we move out of the bank and get you on your way into the world of sightseeing and tourism, there is one more very important term you should know. "***s'ir** aS-**Sarf***" literally means "price of the exchange" and translates more properly into "exchange rate." Exchange rates can vary widely (from currency to currency, location to location, and financial institution to financial institution).

If you are traveling to several locations during your vacation, you want to know the exchange rates to expect at each location *before* you go. If you leave the rate up to the person you are dealing with, you may cause yourself to pay more money than necessary.

1001 Arabian Notes

In some locations, there is a method of money transfer called the **hawala** (*Ha-**waa**-la*). This type of transaction is based on social networks and does not involve government regulation. Opinions vary on the use of hawalas, with governments generally opposing them for lack of regulation. Those who support hawalas favor their speed (transactions are as fast as a phone call) and their accessibility (knowing the "right" people). The hawala is not connected to banking, and I do not advocate its use—but as a cultural point, it is worth noting.

Street Full of Addresses

You've survived the bank. You've gotten past all of the hidden fees. You have checked and double-checked all of your visas, passports, and identifications. In short, you are prepared to go out into the Arabic world. Or are you?

How are you going to get there? Sure, maybe you decided to take a taxi (gulp) or rent a car (gulp, gulp). If you have a tour bus, you probably don't have to worry about getting downtown—but what happens when you get off the bus? How are you going to know what to see and how to get there? More importantly—and I say this from personal experiences that have tested my own creativity with the language—how are you going to find your way *back* once you've wandered off the beaten path? What do you do when you get lost?

Okay, fine. You won't get lost. You have a navigation system or GPS or whatever you want to call it. You have a map, and you know how to read it. You may even have a compass or maybe a string that stretches all the way back to where you started. Good for you. I still think it is a good idea for you to learn some "get there" words to use … just in case you do have problems getting there.

Track 44

shaa-*r'i*/*sha*-***waa***-*r'i*	street/streets
bi-***naa***-*ya*/*bi-naa*-***yaat***	building/buildings
mow-*qif as-sa-yaa*-***raat***	car park/parking lot
'un-***waan***	address
ta'a-lee-***maat***	directions/instructions
raq-*m al*-***beyt***	house number
ra-***Seef***	sidewalk
ji-***haaz*** *al-mi*-***laa***-*Ha*	navigation system
zu-***qaaq***	alley/side street
muf-***ta***-*raq aT-Ta*-***reeq***	intersection/crossroad
dar-***raa***-*ja*	motorcycle
mis-***baaH*** *ash*-***shaa***-*r'i*	street lamp
i-***shaa***-*ra al-mu*-***roor***	traffic light
laa-***fi***-*ta at-taw*-***waq***-*qif*	stop sign
burj	tower
shur-*Ta al-mu*-***roor***	traffic police
muz-***da***-*Him*	crowded
zi-***Haam***	traffic jam
Ha-*ra-kat al-mu*-***roor***	traffic
kee-***loo***-*mit-r* (***kee***-*loo*)	kilometer
meel/*am*-***yaal***	mile/miles
ta-***tab***-*b'a*/***ya***-*ta*-***tab***-*b'a*	followed/he follows
qu-*du-man*	straight ahead
naa-*ti-Hat sa*-***Haab***	skyscraper
da-***waar***	traffic circle/roundabout
'and-*a*-***maa***	when (statement)

And while I'm sure you don't need them, I'm going to include some phrases here at the end of the list. Many of you will probably want to skip right over this section. That's fine. You can come back to it later if necessary.

In a situation where you are lost, you can usually get by with a simple interrogative and the correct noun. For example, you might say:

***ai**-na al- …______?*		***keyf**-a **yum**-kin al-wu-**Sool il**-a …?*
Where is the … ______?	or	How is it possible to arrive at …?

Those are just a couple of ideas, though. By this point in the book, you probably know enough vocabulary to be even more creative with your phrasing. See whether you can think of seven different ways to get somewhere using the question words you know already and the vocabulary from the previous list. It shouldn't be too hard. I've given you two ways already. I'll even throw in one more for good measure.

***hee**-a qa-**reeb** min al …*

It is near the …

I'm sure you understand by now. But here's a final note before I close this chapter. When you get lost (which I'm certain will *never* happen to you) and someone is kind enough to give you directions to get where you are going (which they will be; it's human nature), you probably should repeat what that person says, using words you understand but different than what he or she gave you. For example, if someone tells you:

"Walk to that building" (***im**-shee **il**-a **til**-ka al-bi-**naa**-ya*)

you might respond:

"The second one, there on the corner?" (*al-**thaa**-nee-a, hu-**naa**-ka **'al**-a ar-**ruk**-n?*)

If you change what they say into your own words, you tell them that you understand and you force yourself to pay attention to what they are saying. Don't just ask someone for instructions, then nod your head, clueless, while they detail your route for you. I've tried getting places that way. I always ended up stopping again to ask for directions before too long.

Practice Makes Perfect

There was a lot of vocabulary in this chapter, and I believe you deserve a rest for a little bit before you jump into Chapter 19, which will have even *more* vocabulary. So I tried to keep things easy for you here. Note: there may be multiple answers to the following questions. Pay attention to how the statements are formed more than to the specific words used.

1. Translate: "I need money for my daughter."
2. Translate: "She needs to get money for her dog."
3. Translate: "***kam*** *i-shaa-**raat** al-mu-**roor** hu-**naa**-ka **qab**-l al-**burj**?*"
4. Translate: "***'and**-ee **Haal**-a Ta-**waa**-ri'h. hal is-tith-**naa'h** min al-**mum**-kin?*"

The Least You Need to Know

- Banking, including fees, might be slightly different.
- Friday and Saturday, not Saturday and Sunday, are considered the weekend in most Arab countries.
- Don't be too proud to ask for directions.
- When receiving directions, make sure to repeat them back to the person who gave them to you.

Chapter 19

What a Sight!

In This Chapter

- So much to see, so few pages
- Get out and dance
- Sit down for a while
- You ***kaa-na*** do it

The pace of learning is picking up, and with the increased pace comes the pressure of adding new vocabulary to what you already know. You have now reached Chapter 19, where you actually get the chance (if you haven't already) to have some *fun* with Arabic.

You've made your trip, gotten through customs, decided how to get around, and found your way to your hotel. All that remains is for you to go out and experience Arab culture! And there are many ways to do that. With so many "sights" to see and "sites" to visit (there is a difference between those two words; read the chapter to find out!), you won't even notice how much you are learning as you make your way through this chapter. That's just the way it should be, too.

This chapter starts out with the different places, sights, and ways to "see" before moving on to a brand-new verb that will give you an even better grasp of all the things you ***kaa-na*** say in Arabic. But I don't want to give too much away in the beginning. You'll just have to keep reading.

The Sights to Be Seen

Quick: how many things are there to "see" in the world? I'll give you five seconds to respond. Did you come up with the answer? Here's mine: lots.

There are simply lots of things to see, and whether you knew it or not, virtually all of the things that can be seen also can be *described* in Arabic. If books were foot races, then it would take a 200-kilometer ultra marathon-length dictionary to include all of the different things to see in the Arab world. As it is, this book is more like a four- or five-kilometer afternoon jog through the park. As with jogs through the park, though, if you keep working at the lessons in this book, you will get the results you want. And now … let's go brain-jogging.

Tips

To help yourself remember new words without forgetting those you have learned earlier in this book, create your own practice lessons. I suggest using as much vocabulary as possible with variations in verb conjugation. Using different contexts helps you work in the *art* of Arabic, rather than the *science* of memorization.

Many, Many Things

If you are going to visit the Arab world, then of course you will want to be able to describe the things you want or plan to see and the things you have already seen. But I must make an admission at this point. Not all of you are going to travel to Arab lands. Some of you are studying the language because you have friends who speak Arabic, because you are interested in Arab culture, because you just want to learn this lovely way to speak—or even because you took a test and now someone has told you that you *will* learn Arabic.

Whether you are traveling to the Arab world or not, you will want to be able to talk about different aspects of society—either in your own culture or as part of the Arab lifestyle. If you can imagine yourself trying to explain what interests you have or what sorts of things you would like to see, you can probably also find a good use for the following list. As you study these words (maybe by writing and practicing some sentences or even entire paragraphs), think of the various social situations in which they might be useful.

***ra**-'ha/**ya**-ra/ra-'**bey**-tu*	he saw/he sees/I saw
***na**-THa-ra/**yan**-THar*	he viewed/he views
***THa**-ha-ra/**yaTH**-har*	he appeared/he appears

__shaa__-hi-da/__yash__-hid	he witnessed/he witnesses
__shey__/ash-__yaa'h__	thing/things
__sooq__/as-__waaq__	market/markets
__naas__	people
__mow__-q'i	site (location)
__maTH__-har/__mash__-had	sight (spectacle)
si-__yaa__-Ha	tourism
si-__yaa__-Hee/Hee-a	tourist/(m/f)
Hai-__waan__/Hai-__waan__-aat	animal/animals
ri-__yaaD__-a/ri-__yaaD__-aat	sport/sports
tas-__lee__-a	pleasure/fun/enjoyment
__maq__-ba-ra/ma-__qaa__-bir	cemetery/cemeteries
__qab__-r/Da-__reeH__	grave/tomb
__ghaa__-ba	forest
__sam__-ak	fish
jum-__boor__/ja-__maa__-heer	crowd/crowds
si-__baaq__/si-baaq-__aat__	race/races
zi-__faaf__	wedding
__Haf__-la	party (celebration)
duk-__kaan__/da-kaa-__keen__	store (shop)/stores
__mar__-kaz at-ta-__saw__-wuq	shopping center
__HiS__-n/Hu-__Soon__	fortress
__qaS__-r/qu-__Soor__	castle (palace)/castles
ma-__waa__-qi'i __taa__-ree-__khee__-ya	historical sites*
aH-__daath__ tha-qaa-__fee__-ya	cultural events

**Note: keep in mind as you travel that there may be locations where you are not allowed to go either because you are a tourist or because you are not a Muslim. Certain cemeteries and mosques, as well as holy sites, may have such regulations. Non-Muslims are not allowed into the Saudi Arabian cities of Mecca and Medina, for example. Mind these cultural points when you are planning your vacation.*

Never Too Much

In Arabic, there is just no way to say "too much." If you have ever heard a native Arabic speaker talk in English, you might have puzzled over a statement he or she made that should have involved the word "very" but instead substituted "too." For example, if a native Arabic speaker wanted to say, "We saw *very* many children," he or she might actually say, "We saw *too* many children." While in some cases this may be correct (I will not try to determine how many children are actually *too* many), the speaker may have actually meant to say, "We saw *very* many children."

This is actually a fairly common mistake, and you will notice it more as you have more interactions with native Arabic speakers. The problem stems from the fact that there is no way to say "too," meaning "an excessive amount," in Arabic. You just can't say "too much." For us English speakers, it is difficult to understand how a word could simply be absent from a language—leaving no satisfactory way to explain a concept. (In Chapter 20, you'll see how in Arabic you can "gift" an item, which is a verb we don't have in English.)

Not being able to say "too much" in Arabic gives you an interesting insight into Arab culture. In a culture known for its profuse generosity, people can never give or have "too much."

If you really need to say "too much" in Arabic, perhaps in a restaurant or while visiting friends who are trying to send you home with a store's worth of gifts, the closest you can come would be something like the following:

***laa**, **an**-a mu-ta-**shak**-kir(-a), wa-**laa**-kin **ha**-dhaa **ak**-thar min al-**laa**-zim.*

No, I am grateful (thankful), but this is more than necessary.

Obviously, saying, "This is more than necessary" doesn't have the same power as saying, "This is too much." After all my years speaking Arabic and working daily with native Arabic speakers, I still have not found a better way to say "too." And so far, no native Arabic speakers have been able to explain a good way to make that statement, either.

1001 Arabian Notes

Many phrases that cannot be stated in Modern Standard Arabic (the basis of this book) can be stated in the various dialects. Asking a native speaker about a specific phrase may help. Be careful, though, because what is understood in one dialect may be misunderstood in another dialect.

Grab Your Cleats and Trunks

If you are looking for things to see and do in the Arab world, you won't have to go far. With an abundance of pleasant weather and company, you could spend your entire vacation just meeting new people and learning new habits. Hobbies and sports are two of the best ways to get to know new friends. If you are touring and are interested in sticking to things you know, tourist spots will have an abundance of entertainment to keep you occupied.

If you're traveling with children, you may want to include a waterslide, theme park, or zoo on your trip. If you do, just be certain that you consider the safety of the attractions—because regulations governing safety may be different than you are used to.

If you feel more like losing yourself in the local customs, you won't have to look far to find someone willing to show you things off the beaten path. Maybe your new friends will take you out and show you a bit of falconry. Maybe they will take you out for a day on the boat or just an afternoon on the beach. It may even be that you aren't going anywhere but just want to be able to talk about the things you enjoy back home. Whatever the case, you should find the following words helpful.

Track 45

***boo**-leengh*	bowling
***lu'u**-ba **bees**-bool*	baseball
*ar-ri-**yaa**-Da*	sports
***lu'u**-ba **kur**-a **qa**-dam*	football (soccer)
***la**-'ib-ba/**yal**-'aab*	played/he plays
***la**'ib*	playing
Said** bil-bu-**'booz	falconry
***kur**-a al-**maD**-rib*	tennis
*ad-dar-**raj**-a*	bicycling
***Said** as-**sam**-ak*	fishing
Said	hunting
*ru-**koob** al-**far**-as*	riding horses
*si-**baak** al-ki-**laab***	dog racing
***fir**-qa*	team
***lu'u**-ba*	game

*mu-**laa**-ka-ma*	boxing
*mu-**baa**-raa*	tournament
ghowS	diving (sport diving)

So Much to See and Do

You've gotten there. Now … what are you going to do? Are you going to tour? Are you going to spend your time lying on the beach? Are you looking for parties that last long into the night? Maybe you want to discover ancient architecture that you once thought you would only see on television. Whatever your desire, you can find the activities to match.

Do a Little Dance

If you are traveling a long distance to the Arab world, probably for the first time, you most likely will have a hard time getting to sleep on your first few nights. You will be so excited about the things you are going to see. (And there is the possibility you might have a hard time sleeping because you are used to being awake in a different time zone.)

If you are up anyway, you might want to check out the nightlife in one of the bustling Arab cities. Each has its own attractions and its own personality. It would be impossible for me to describe all the variations, so you will have to see for yourself.

If you aren't interested in the nightlife but still want to fill your time with activities, there are plenty of daytime options available. With so much sun, sand, and surf in the Arab world, recreation extends far beyond dry land. Even the sky is within your reach if you want to spend an afternoon jumping out of planes (with parachutes, of course). If water is more in line with your tastes, then you can find plenty of opportunities to cool off. Nearly every place where Arabic is the major language (some might go all out and say "everywhere"), there is a major body of water accessible for water sports.

You just need to decide what you are looking for:

*u-**reed** an …*	I want to …
***nuz**-ha*	recreation
***khey**-yam*	camping

***naa**-dee ley-**lee**-a*	night club
***ra**-qa-Sa/**yar**-qaS*	danced/he dances
***Haf**-la*	party
*tad-**reeb***	training (practice)
*tam-**reen***	exercise
***ra**-ka-da/**yar**-kuD*	ran/he runs
***khab**-ba*	jogging (trotting)
*ghi-**naa'h***	singing
*mu-**ghaa**-mir-a*	adventure
***Ha**-ra-ka/yaH-**Har**-rak*	moved/he moves
*ta-**zal**-laj **'al**-a al-**thalj***	snow skiing
*tas-**sal**-laq aS-Su-**khoor***	rock climbing
***qa**-fa-za/**yaq**-faz*	jumped/he jumps
*ha-**booT** bil-ma-THa-**laat***	parachuting (skydiving)

To get a little more practice, take a look at the following imaginary dialog and then practice it a few times on your own. You can insert vocabulary from throughout the book for more practice. As you are going through the drill, imagine yourself actually having a conversation—not just repeating phrases you have memorized. Think of what other questions someone might ask you and what responses they might give to your questions.

Tips

If a verb is given in a list as "[past tense]/he [present tense]," you can use that verb for yourself or anyone you choose. Just change the form to match your needs. You can use the verb charts in the verb chapter to see what changes you need to make.

"***maa hee**-a al-ash-**yaa'h** al-**lat**-ee ta-ta-**waq**-q'aa min **ha**-dha-hi ar-**raH**-la?*"

"What are the things that you expect from this trip (vacation)?"

"*a-ta-**waq**-q'aa al-**fur**-Sa li …*"

"I expect the chance to …"

Enough Exercise! I Want to Relax!

Let's face it. Maybe you're not as young as you once were. Maybe you aren't really that interested in going to parties all night. Maybe you have passed the age of adventure (or you've just learned to keep adventure in your mind without putting your body through too much stress).

Maybe you're thinking, "What is he talking about? I'm as fit as ever!"

Fine … I take it back. The only point I'm trying to make is that maybe, just maybe, you'll want to spend at least part of your vacation doing something that doesn't involve too much stress. I'm talking about *relaxing*. If that is your case, you will find plenty of opportunities—even if you just want to get out of the heat for a while so you have the energy to go out again later—when nighttime arrives.

Track 46

***keyf**-a tu-**faD**-Dil al-**tam**-ti'a la-**dey**-kum?*	How do you prefer your enjoyment?
*u-**faD**-Dil al …*	I prefer the …
*mas-ra-**Hee**-ya*	theater
***Haf**-la moo-see-**qee**-ya*	concert
***Haa**-dith-a*	event
Haf**-la/Haf-**laat	party/parties (event)
*mas-ra-**Hee**-ya ghi-**naa**-'hee-ya*	opera
*raqS tam-**thee**-lee* (also *baa-**lee**-a*)	ballet
*is-**taq**-la*	lying (lounging)
*ju-**loos***	sitting
*qi-**raa'h***	reading
*ki-**taa**-ba*	writing
Haf**-la ash-shi-**waa'h	barbecue (grill party)
***maq**-ha*	café
*is-ti-**Haam***	bathing
nowm	sleeping
***Halm** al-ya-qa-THa*	daydream
***fak**-ka-ra/yu-**fak**-kir*	thought/he thinks

***na**-si-ya/**yan**-sa*	forgot/he forgets
*ta-**'ham**-mal/ya-ta-**'ham**-mal*	meditated/he meditates
*ka-**nees**-a/ka-**naa**-'his*	church/churches
***mas**-jid/ma-**saa**-jid*	mosque/mosques
*Sa-**laaa**/Sa-la-**waat***	prayer/prayers
***ra**-sa-ma/**yar**-sum*	drew/he draws (to sketch)
***ras**-m*	drawing (a sketch)
***low**-wa-na/ya-**low**-wan*	painted/he paints
***Sal**-la/yu-**Sal**-lee*	prayed/he prays
*ta-**waq**-qa-fa/ya-ta-**waq**-qaf*	he paused/he pauses

However you choose to enjoy yourself, you should try to take in as much as possible. Some chances present themselves only once in life. Make the most of them. Try to fill your vacation with as many activities as possible, but don't overdo it. I know from experience that if you are tired, you can have just as much enjoyment from a day of lounging around talking to the locals as you could if you spent the entire time traveling around to the local *sights*.

def•i•ni•tion

I promised you definitions of the words **site** and **sight.** Here you go. A **site** is a location. A **sight,** such as the Sphinx, is a spectacle or something worth seeing. So the Sphinx could be a ***sight*** worth seeing, although its ***site*** may not be optimal.

The Best Ways "to Be"

If you can remember way back to Chapter 3, I told you that in Arabic we rarely use the verb "to be." Well, you are far enough along in the book that I have to let you in on a little secret: there really *is* a verb "to be." What's more, you will actually use it quite a bit as you improve.

At this point, some readers may say, "Well, why did you wait so long to tell us this?" I waited so long because Arabic, once you really start digging into it, is a complex language. Actually, it is complex enough that despite the extended history of English books being written about the language (well more than 100 years), there still exists no standard method of writing Arabic in English. The more complex lessons can wait for a more complex book.

You have reached a point, though, where you can use a bit of a push into some new speaking skills. Imagine this. You know that the word ***Taa**-lib* means "student," and you are visiting the Arab world to study. If someone were to ask you why you are visiting, you probably would say something such as, "***an**-a **Taa**-lib.*"

I would congratulate you. My work will have been a success. But now imagine it is 15 years after your time as a student in the Arab world. You have just met a new Arab friend (because you never gave up on learning the language), and you say to him or her, "I traveled to Egypt (*saa-**fir**-tu **il**-a al-**maS**-r*)." Naturally, he or she will want to know why.

What would you say?

I'm sure you could think of something. Maybe *da-**ras**-tu hu-**naa**-ka* ("I studied there"). Why not make it much simpler? Just say, "I was a student."

Aha! You don't know how. I think it's time we remedy that. The following table outlines all the different uses of the verb ***kaa**-na*, which means "to be."

Table 19.1

The Verb *kaa-na*

	Past	Present	Future
	was/were ...	**am/are/is ...**	**will be ...**
I	***kun**-tu*	*a-**koon***	*si-'ha-**koon***
You (m/s)	***kun**-ta*	*ta-**koon***	*si-ta-**koon***
You (f/s)	***kun**-ti*	*ta-koo-**neen***	*si-ta-koo-**neen***
He	***kaa**-na*	*ya-**koon***	*si-ya-**koon***
She	***kaa**-nat*	*ta-**koon***	*si-ta-**koon***
We	*kun-**naa***	*na-**koon***	*si-na-**koon***
You (m/pl)	*kun-**tum***	*ta-koo-**noon***	*si-ta-koo-**noon***
You (f/pl)	*kun-**tun**-na*	*ta-**kun**-na*	*si-ta-**kun**-na*
They (m)	*kaa-**noo***	*ya-koo-**noon***	*si-ya-koo-**noon***
They (f)	***kun**-na*	*ya-**kun**-na*	*si-ya-**kun**-na*

When looking to use ***kaa**-na*, you need some notes to help you along. ***kaa**-na* is used the least in the present tense. When speaking, you will find yourself most often using variations of ***kaa**-na* to simplify your description of past events. For example:

kaa**-na **jaan** fee al-**beyt.

(he was) John in the house. (John was in the house.)

Remember, the verbs come first in most statements. If you want to make the sentence simpler, you can just say ***kaa**-na fee al-**beyt.*** (He was in the house.)

Compare that to:

*si-ta-**koon** fee al-**beyt.*** (You (m) will be in the house.)

(Also: She will be in the house.)

Note: the same verb conjugation is used for second-person m/s and third-person f/s. This conjugation rule applies to all verbs.

Those of you who already have some experience with Arabic may know that the future tense of ***kaa**-na* often uses ***sow**-fa* instead of *si-* in combination with the verb. I congratulate you on your knowledge and encourage you to use the verbs as you know them to be appropriate. I left *si-* on ***kaa**-na* in this book to keep things as simple as possible for beginners.

Why don't we take a look at some other common uses of ***kaa**-na*? Practice them well, because the better you know them the easier it will be for you to slide from topic to topic in your conversations. Keep in mind as well that ***kaa**-na* is used when the words "am," "are," "is," "was," "were," "be," and "will be" are used in English.

If there is no other verb in the sentence, ***kaa**-na* is used by itself.

***kun**-tu **Taa**-lib.* (I was a student.)

***kaa**-nat ja-**meel**-a.* (It was lovely.)

*si-ya-**koon** aT-**Taqs** ja-**meel.*** (The weather will be pleasant.)

However, if there is more than one verb in the sentence, you use the correct form of ***kaa**-na* plus the present tense of the second verb.

*'**and**-a-maa **kun**-tu **adh**-hab **il**-a as-**sooq** …*

When I was going (second verb) to the market …

***hee**-a **kaa**-nat **tad**-ras …*

She was studying …

Practice Makes Perfect

There are only two questions in this chapter's practice section. All you have to do is write a paragraph of your own, then translate mine. Sounds pretty simple, doesn't it? I assume that because you are serious enough to get this far in the book, you are serious enough to do a little extra work on your own.

So … here goes. Have fun!

1. Describe yourself, your history, your hobbies, your family, your likes, and your reasons for learning Arabic in 10 sentences or more. (Note: the consonants are more important than the vowels, especially when speaking. Don't worry if you make spelling errors.)
2. Translate the following:

   ***ah**-lan wa **sah**-lan, is-mee **key wa an**-a **ak**-thar min tha-laa-**theen san**-na. u-**Hib** al-**lugh**-at al-'ar-a-**bee**-a li-'**han**-na-haa **lugh**-a ja-**meel**-a jid-dan. '**and**-ee **us**-ra ka-**beer**-a wa **hee**-a mu-**him**-a **jid**-dan **lee**.*

I know I didn't write 10 sentences, but then, you don't need to know everything about me.

The Least You Need to Know

- There is more than enough to see in Arab lands.
- You can witness a sight at a site.
- You just can't find "too much" to say in Arabic.
- You can practice your Arabic by writing what you know about yourself.
- ***kaa**-na* means "to be" and will take you further with your abilities.

Chapter 20

Ready, Set, Market!

In This Chapter

- Streets paved with gold and markets
- Color me twice
- Find clothes and fit in
- The cultural insider

It used to be that when I heard the word "market" I would picture my mother driving us to a large store in the "big" city, where we would stock up on a shopping cart or two full of groceries that lasted our family almost a month. That image forever changed the first time I saw a real-life Arab market.

If you have never been to an Arab market, you are missing one of the most interesting, unforgettable cultural experiences you might ever witness. The noise, different smells, crowds, perfumes, and spices all combine together to form memories that you will not easily let go.

In fact, it is quite overwhelming if you are not prepared. No worries, though. This chapter is all about preparing you for the market. Whether you have visited them or not, when you are done with your lessons here you will be able to talk like you have been there.

What Will You Have?

If you are going to a market, the first thing you need to decide is what you're looking for. Most likely, depending on where you are, there is a market (***sooq***) for everything. What's more, markets for certain items won't necessarily be in the same part of town as markets for other items. You might have a gold ***sooq*** in one location, but to buy a brass tea set you might have to make your way to an entirely different section of town. If the city is big enough, this could mean planning multiple days of going to the market just to get your souvenir shopping done. But the efforts will be worth it.

Warnings

Be careful to watch your belongings when shopping at the market. The crowds, noise, unfamiliar surroundings, and number of escape routes make markets prime territory for pickpockets. Don't carry more money than you need, and avoid wearing expensive jewelry.

Another thing you should be aware of is that when you hear ***sooq*** (or the plural, ***as-waaq***), you probably shouldn't expect to spend your time shopping indoors. Rather, you should expect narrow streets with row after row of merchants—each in his or her own small, tented stall, selling items.

Gold in the Streets

Ooh, the gold market. Travelers to the Arab world have been talking about the luxury and experience of visiting the gold ***as-waaq*** as long as they have been visiting there. As long as I live, I doubt I will forget the sight of row after row of tents, each full of jewelry all made entirely from gold. There was so much gold that the street seemed to be made of it.

Wherever you are traveling in the Arab world, you will want to try to take a trip to the local gold market. They are in most tourist cities, and the locals love to have tourist business (that's how they make the most money).

First, if you are planning to purchase gold in the ***sooq dha-hab-ee*** (gold market), then you should know what reasonable prices for gold are. Most prices should reflect the international rates that you can find from your local jeweler, the Internet, or other sources of information. You don't want to fall victim to that tourist impulse to pay the asking price for everything you see. Until you are confident in your ability to haggle for prices (or to resist sudden impulses to buy), you will probably want a native Arabic speaker to help you with your purchases.

You should also be prepared to deal with crowds. If you are in a large city like Dubai, the crowds and traffic can cause long delays (and discomfort, if it's hot outside), so you should plan accordingly.

But there are more markets than just those for gold. With its love for precious jewelry and long history of trading with foreign lands, the Arab world offers markets that sell some of the most beautiful jewelry you may ever see.

If you don't know what you are looking for, you probably will need some phrases to get going on your search:

*u-**faD**-Dil **shey**-'han ...*	I prefer something ...
***an**-a **ab**-Hath **'an** ha-**dee**-a.*	I am looking for a gift.
***ai**-na **kul** al ...*	Where is/are all the ...
***dha**-hab*	gold
***fiD**-Da*	silver
***lu'h**-lu'h*	pearl
*mu-**jow**-ha-**raat***	jewelry (gems)
*'**iq**-d/'u-**qood***	necklace/necklaces
*si-**waar**/a-**saa**-wir*	bracelet/bracelets
Ha**-laq/Ha-laq-**aan	earring/earrings
***khaa**-tim*	ring
saa'aa	watch (timepiece)
zur kum** al-qa-**mees	cuff links
saa'aa** lil-**jeyb	pocketwatch
***maa**-sa*	diamond
*ish-**ta**-ra/yash-**ta**-rey*	bought/he buys
*takh-**feeD***	reduction (in price)
*Sa-**HeeH***	genuine
*qee-**raat***	carat
*qee-**yaas***	measurement
***khaS**-m*	rebate
***waz**-n*	weight
***Haj**-m*	size

Ha**-jar as-sa-**feer	sapphire
*fey-**rooz***	turquoise
*zu-**mur**-rud*	emerald
*yaa-**qoot aH**-man*	ruby
*kah-ra-**maan***	amber
Ha**-jar ka-**reem	precious stone
*blaa-**teen***	platinum
***ja**-ra-za/**ja**-raz*	bead/beads
***baa**-'aa/ya-**bee**-'u*	sell
***rukh**-Sa*	sale (reduced price)
***jow**-ha-ra/ja-**waa**-hir*	jewel/jewels
*Hu-**lee***	jewelry (trinket)

You will have a great time if you know what you are looking for and know what to expect. Of course, you have to remember that the gold and jewelry markets are just a sample of all there really is to see.

Tips

You probably won't have much luck negotiating in the market if you simply ask for the price (***kam** as-**si**'r*). You should expect to ask the price, hear a number, then say something along the lines of, "***ha**-dhaa ka-**theer,** a'a-**Tey**-tu-ka/ki* …" (in other words, "That is a lot; I will give you …" It won't be easy, but I wish you good luck.

Two Colors for Every Occasion

Even if you don't know Spanish, you might know that "Casablanca" means "white house." You might also know that Casablanca is a city in Morocco. What you might not know is that in Arabic, Casablanca is called ***daar** al-bai-**Daa'h**,* which means, naturally, "white house."

That is an easy enough concept to follow. ***daar*** means "house" and *bai-**Daa'h*** means "white." Simple, right? So what would you call "The White House," meaning the place where the president of the United States lives? Can you guess?

If you said, "***daar*** *al-bai-****Daa'h***," I'm sorry to tell you that you're wrong. Actually, "The White House" in Arabic is called ***beyt*** *al-****ab****-yaD*. *Yikes!* What just happened?

Just like adjectives and nouns, the colors in Arabic have gender. Depending on the thing they are describing, Arabic colors will either be masculine or feminine.

Looking at the previous examples of white houses, you can see that we have two different words for "house." ***beyt*** is masculine and therefore requires the masculine ***ab****-yaD* for "white." ***daar*** is … well, I suppose you can figure that out on your own. As for why one "white house" is different than another, as my Dad used to tell me, "That's just the way things are."

In order to figure out just how you can color your life, look at the following table.

Table 20.1

Two Colors for Every Occasion

English	Arabic Masculine	Arabic Feminine
white	***ab****-yaD*	*bai-****Daa'h***
red	***aH****-mar*	*Ham-****raa'h***
black	***as****-wad*	*sow-****daa'h***
green	***akh****-Dar*	*khaD-****raa'h***
brown	***bu****-nee*	*bu-****nee****-ya*
orange	*bur-tu-****qaa****-lee*	*bur-tu-qaa-****lee****-ya*
yellow	***aS****-far*	*Saf-****raa'h***
gray	*ra-****Saa****-See*	*ra-Saa-****See****-ya*
blue	***az****-raq*	*zar-****qaa'h***
purple	*ur-ju-****waa****-nee*	*ur-ju-waa-****nee****-ya*
gold	***dha****-ha-bee*	*dha-ha-****bee****-ya*
silver	***fiD****-Dee*	*fiD-****Dee****-ya*
pink	***war****-dee*	*war-****dee****-ya*

Track 47

Try to learn the colors well because they will help you out as we move into the next section, when you get to look for something other than gold in the market.

All Haggled Out

Negotiating prices is hard work. There is no doubt about that. But it is also an adventure, and adventure is what many of us want when we are exploring new locations. Of course, adventure isn't *all* we want. If you go somewhere, you usually want to *have* something from that place.

Now, before you throw your arms up and tell me you aren't interested in collecting a roomful of trinkets, let me explain. I know that the things that will last the longest after your trips are those memories that cost nothing but remain priceless. However, I also know that many people want to have at least one thing to be able to hold and show others when they get back home—even if it may not be for them.

If gold and precious jewelry aren't in your budget, I understand how you feel. But don't dismay. There are still plenty of other ways to fulfill your shopping cravings.

Clothes-Minded

I've been told that clothes say a lot about our personalities. In my case, I suppose that means my personality is a few years old and wearing out along the seams. Oh well—some things will never change. Other things will.

One thing I would like to change your opinion about (unless you know this already), is that people in the Arab world do not *all* wear traditional costumes or clothing, not any more than Germans all wear *Lederhosen* and *Dirndls* or than tourists from the United States wear Hawaiian shirts and white socks with their sandals.

1001 Arabian Notes

Even if you do see locals on your vacation wearing traditional robes, dresses, and other clothing, they are often wearing the latest fashions in Western-style clothing underneath their traditional dress.

Every culture has its own style, but the world has grown very small. Walking the streets of any city in the Arab world today, you will find an amazing mix of fashion—including all of the latest trends. So if you are looking for something to take home with you—either for yourself or for a friend—you may want to consider clothes.

__mum__-kin tu-__bey__-yin __lee__ ______________ *ja-__deed__(-a)*?

Can you show me a new ______________?

u-__reed__ ha-__dee__-a li-Sa-__deeq__-ee/Sa-__deeq__-a-__tee__.

I want a gift for my boyfriend/girlfriend.

*min-__faD__-la-*__kum__ u-__reed__ ______________ *__jeyd__(-a)*.

Please, I would like a good-quality ________.

shaal**/shaal-**aat	shawl
*min-**deel***	handkerchief
*Hi-**dhaa'h**/aH-**dhee**-a*	shoe/shoes
*sa-raa-**weel***	trousers
qa-meeS/qum-Saan	shirt/shirts
*ban-Ta-**loon jeenz***	jeans (pants)
jow**-rab qa-**Seer	socks
*ma-**laa**-bis daakh-**lee**-ya*	underwear
***blooz**-a*	blouse
***kan**-za*	sweater
*Hi-**zaam/aH**-zi-ma*	belt/belts
***qub**-ba'aa*	hat
*na-Thaa-**raat** sham-**see**-ya*	sunglasses
*jaa-**keet***	jacket
*tan-**noor**-a*	skirt
*fus-**taan***	dress
kees** an-nu-**qood	purse (money tote)
***thowb** as-si-**baa**-Ha*	bathing suit
***badh**-la*	suit
*ma-**laa**-bis*	clothing
*ban-Ta-**loon** qa-**Seer***	shorts (short pants)
na'al**/ni-**'aaal	sandal/sandals
***mi'i**-Taf*	coat (clothing)
*mi-**THal**-la*	umbrella
***badh**-la tad-ree-**bee**-ya*	training (jogging) suit
*az-**yaa'h taq**-lee-**dee**-ya*	traditional costumes
*mu-**laa**-bis is-laa-**mee**-ya*	Islamic clothing

The Everything Market

Several years ago, I witnessed what I believe to be one of the shortest negotiations in open-air market history. Purchasing several grocery items for lunch one hot afternoon, I watched one man walk up to the merchant, describe what he wanted, and ask about the price. "Twelve," came the quick reply.

"No, that is far too much." The buyer placed three U.S. dollars on the counter and walked away. Bewildered for a moment, the merchant looked from the buyer to me and then back to the buyer before putting the money away and turning to one of the many other customers standing at his kiosk.

Warnings

I do not recommend you try to make purchases by demanding a bottom-level price, leaving your money, and walking away. The interaction I observed was between two locals who knew one another. Remember that when you are traveling, you are an ambassador for your country. The things you do will reflect positively or negatively on your country and attitudes of locals toward future tourists from your country.

Observing this interaction taught me two things. First, the price on everything—including lunch—is probably negotiable. Second, no matter how often I shop in an Arab market, I could never get away with an act like that. I just don't have it in me.

You will have to find the way you feel most comfortable when making your purchases, but you should never allow yourself to feel like you are being cheated. If you do, it is probably because you allowed yourself to buy something for a price you knew to be too high (no one is forcing you to buy things).

Once you do find your purchasing comfort zone, you will find many unusual or hard-to-find items that make perfect souvenirs (if you want them) to take home with you when your trip comes to an end. What sorts of things? Take a look:

*Taq-m ash-**shaai***	tea set (tea service)
Soof**/aS-**waaf	wool/wools
*qu-**maash***	cloth
***tuH**-fa*	antiques
*a-**thaath***	furniture
*ta-**zey**-yan*	decoration
zah**-ra/zu-**hoor	flower/flowers
*taj-**heez**-a*	equipment

*tam-**ween***	supplies
***Soo**-ra/**Sa**-war*	picture/pictures
*ad-**aaa**/ad-a-**waat***	instrument/instruments
*mis-**baaH**/ma-**saa**-biH*	lamp/lamps
*mi-**raaa**/ma-**raa**-yaa*	mirror/mirrors
*ad-a-**waat** aT-**Tabkh***	cooking utensils
***haa**-tif **kha**-la-wee*	cellular phone
*maz-ha-**ree**-ya*	vases
*a-**waan** fiD-**Dee**-ya*	silverware
sal**-la/si-**laal	basket/baskets
*ba-**Daa**-'hi'i jil-**dee**-ya*	leather goods
lu'u**-ba/lu'u-**baat	toy/toys
*fin-**jaan shaai***	teacup
*ib-**reeq** ash-**shaai***	teapot (kettle)
***ba**-Ha-tha/**yab**-Hath (with **'an**)**	searched/he searches
*tadh-**kaar***	souvenir
'iT**-r/'u-**Toor	perfume/perfumes
***taa**-bil/ta-**waa**-bil*	spice/spices
*yaas-**meen***	jasmine
shaai	tea
*nu-**Haas aS**-far*	brass
'aaaj	ivory

Note:** the verb ***ba**-Ha-tha/**yab**-Hath* needs to be used with the word ***'an (for). Otherwise, it won't make sense. Look at a few examples.

> ***nab**-Hath 'an 'u-**Toor wa** ta-**waa**-bil li-ukh-**waat**-u-na.*
>
> We are searching for perfumes and spices for our sisters.

Tu-Hib ***umm****-ee ba-****Daa****-'hi'i jil-****dee****-ya* ***wa tab****-Hath 'an-haa* ***daa****-'hi-man* ***fee*** *al-as-****waaq****.*

My mother loves leather goods and always looks for them in the markets.

This Way or That Way?

Once you get moving in the markets, you will discover an amazing ability to customize your purchases. Sometimes I feel this is something we could use more of in our own shops and stores—the ability to make changes or get alterations *before* you lay down your hard-earned money for a product.

In virtually all of my shopping experiences, anything that could be modified was. And I was not expected to pay for the items until I was completely satisfied with how things looked. While you probably won't be able to get a television customized to different sizes or shapes, many things—especially jewelry, clothing, and accessories—can be personalized to your every desire. Because that's the case, why not get things set up the way you want them?

Tips

Arab markets are great places to buy inexpensive, handmade crafts you will not easily find outside the local area. If you are looking for souvenirs, handmade items are often cheaper and possess a charm that is not easy to come by. Just make sure the products are not forbidden by any laws—either where you are visiting or where the item is going.

Shape It Up

Let's face it. People are not all the same shape—nor do they all prefer things that are shaped the same. Look at one item of fashion—a woman's handbag—and you can get an idea of what I mean.

Sometimes they are round; sometimes they are square. Sometimes they look like little cylindrical thermoses. Other times they are so small they look as if they could scarcely hold a stick of gum. Still other times they look like a small car could fit into the pockets with room left over on the sides.

Yes, we all have the shapes we prefer. Because we are in a market where we can get things shaped just the way we want to match our personalities, why not take advantage?

*u-**reed** an-hu/haa **ak**-thar qa-**lee**-lan min ...*

I would like it a little more ...

***taq**-l qa-**lee**-lan **min** ...*	A little less ...
***hal** ta-**koon** **ak**-thar min ...*	Are there more ...?
shak**-l/ash-**kaal	shape/shapes
*mu-**rab**-b'a*	square
*daa-**'bir**-ee*	round
*mu-**thal**-lath*	triangle
***qiT**-'aa/**qiT**-'a*	piece/pieces
***naa**-'im*	soft
***shak**-l*	form
***aq**-Sar*	shorter
***aT**-wal*	longer
***qa**-Ta-'aa/**yaq**-Ta'a*	cut/he cuts
***kab**-ba-ra/ya-**kab**-ba-ra*	enlarged/he enlarges
***na**-Ha-ta/**yan**-Hat*	engraved/he engraves
***ak**-bar*	bigger
***aS**-ghar*	smaller
***ath**-khan*	thicker
***ar**-qaq*	thinner
***akh**-faf*	lighter (weight)
***muTH**-lim*	dark
***af**-taH*	paler
khaa**-Ta/ya-**kheet	sewed/he sews

"As" You "Like" It

With all this negotiation and shopping, you really should have the chance to get things just the way you want them. And just in case you feel a little nervous about making adjustments, always remember you can just use your fingers and point out what you are interested in—and start asking questions.

The following words and phrases should help you get through even more situations that need clarification.

Track 48

*ka-**maa***	as (before a verb)
***mith**-l*	like (such as)
*fee **ha**-dhaa aT-Ta-**reeq***	in this way
***ha**-ka-dha*	so (thus)
*ka-**dha**-lik*	that way
***ley**-sa ka-**dha**-lik**	not so (not that way)
*ta'a-**deel***	adjustment
*al-ma-**qaas***	the fit (the size)
***bad**-da-la/yu-**bad**-dil*	changed/he changes
*ta-**ghey**-ya-ra/ya-ta-**ghey**-yar*	altered/he alters
***ghaT**-Ta/**yigh**-Tee*	covered/he covers
***na**-za-'aa/**yan**-za'a*	removed/he removes
*a-**Daaf**/yu-**Deef***	added/he adds
***aS**-la-Ha/**yuS**-liH*	repaired/he repairs
***wa**-ja-da/**ya**-jid*	found/he finds
*ik-**tash**-a-fa/yak-**ta**-shif*	discovered/he discovers
khaaS	special
***shakh**-See*	personal
*mum-**taaz***	excellent
*bil-**Dab**-T*	exactly

*hal ta'a-**deel** min al-**mum**-kin?*

Is an adjustment possible?

*ik-ta-**shif**-tu an **ha**-dhaa bi-**Haaj**-at taS-**leeH**.*

I discovered that this is in need of repairs.

***ai**-na wa-**jad**-ta **dha**-lik?*

Where did you find that?

Gifting It All Away

For me, one of the most fascinating words in the entire Arabic language is ***wa-ha-ba**/ya-**hib*** (he gifted/he gifts). ***wa-ha-ba*** means "to give as a gift." Sometimes I wish we had a great word like that in English. Those of you who speak German know that *schenken* is the German word with the same definition. So why don't we have "to gift" in English?

Of course, I can't answer that. I could say that maybe our verb "present"—somewhere in its history—used to have a definition that meant "to give as a gift," but I can't be certain. Now we have to say, "He presented her with a present" or, "He presented her the ring." But in the second example, we don't know that he made a gift of the ring. Maybe she just dropped it and he returned it to her.

> **1001 Arabian Notes**
>
> If you meet someone multiple times and they always bring you a small gift, you may want to ask them to stop. Explain your gratitude, but it can quickly become too ***ghaa**-lee* (expensive) for them. Also, if they are bringing you gifts, you should have gifts for them.

Arabic doesn't have these problems, because the verb "to gift" is still in common use. And speaking of gifts, you have to be careful of what gifts you accept when visiting Arab friends. If you aren't, they might try to give you everything they own. So what can you do?

If you've had any experience with Arabic speakers, you may have heard by now that it is impolite to turn down anything that is offered. I'll tell you a secret. That is a myth. There are polite ways to refuse. If you don't believe me, put yourself in this situation: you don't smoke, but your Arab friend does. He doesn't want to be impolite, so he offers you a cigarette. What do you do?

I've heard many different answers to this question. Some friends even told me they just accepted the cigarette and kept it to give to a smoker later. I think there is a better way. You could say:

*shu-**kraan** laa u-**dakh**-khin.*

Thank you; I don't smoke.

Or even simpler, put your hand over your heart, shake your head, and say, "***laa**, shu-**kraan**.*"

If you do this, you can expect them to offer again—maybe waving the offered item in front of you. If you still don't want it, you just have to repeat yourself again. They might offer a third time. Decline again. If they stop offering, a bit of an Arab custom has just occurred. They have offered an item to you enough times to show that they are gracious (and you have declined enough times to show that you really don't want it). This should work in most situations and is an important lesson, because you need to keep it in mind for times you offer items as well.

1001 Arabian Notes

"*in **shaa'h** al-**lah***": This Arabic phrase literally means "If God wills it," and you will encounter it often when speaking Arabic with friends—especially if they are Muslim. You should note, though, if you are asking someone to do something for you, the most definite answer you receive may be "*in **shaa'h** al-**lah**.*" Do not let this bother you. The speaker is only confirming that he or she is not in control of all events in the world.

Whenever you take something for yourself and have Arabic-speaking friends around you, you should offer the item to them first—starting with the oldest friend. If they decline, offer the item again. You may be surprised to see that they accept it. If they do decline again, offer a third time just to make sure. This way, you have shown that you are a gracious host. To some of us, this may seem a bit unnecessary and frustrating ("Why don't they just say what they mean from the beginning?"). If you begin to feel this way, try to remember that you are learning new customs, not trying to force your own on others.

Before we end the chapter, there are some phrases you may want to know that will help you get through some potentially difficult cultural situations.

> ***ha**-dhaa **mu**-him **jid**-dan **lee.***
>
> This is very important to me.
>
> ***maa**-dha **taq**-Sid bi "**an**-a u-**Haa**-wil"?*
>
> What do you mean by "I will try"?
>
> *fee **raa'h**-yu-ka hal ta-**koon** **mush**-kil-a?*
>
> In your opinion, is there a problem?
>
> ***ha**-dhaa ha-**dee**-a **a**-hib-hu li-**kum.***
>
> This is a gift. I "gift" it to you.
>
> ***an**-a **mu**-ta-**shar**-rif wa-**laa**-kin **laa** **yum**-kin **an** aq-**bil** **ha**-dhaa.*

I am honored, but it is not possible to accept this.

*shu-**kraan** wa-**laa**-kin-na-**nee** Has-**saa**-see(-a) …*

Thank you, but I am allergic …

*la-**kum sha**-raf **lee yak**-fee min **qab**-l.*

You honor me enough already.

Practice Makes Perfect

Before you go out to the crowded street markets, you will want to practice your "market language" here:

1. Translate the following: ***an**-a **zur**-tu us-**taadh** fee **jaa**-m'ia **'and**-ma **kun**-tu **fee** al **qaa**-hir-a. **qaa**-la **hoo**-a **lee** an **hoo**-a **mu**-him-a **jid**-dan al-zi-**yaa**-ra **il**-a al-as-**waaq fee** al-ma-**dee**-na. dha-**hab**-naa sa-**wee**-an **wa kaa**-na mum-**taaz.** ash-ta-**rey**-tu ka-**theer min al**-ma-**laa**-bis wa **ai**-Daan ash-**yaa'h li-us**-ra-tee.*

That's it! Good Luck!

The Least You Need to Know

- A ***sooq*** is the place to go to find what you need or want; just be sure to go to the right one.
- You can find the latest of all fashions in the clothing market.
- Have a local help with your negotiations.
- Treat the market vendors with respect during your negotiations.
- You can politely refuse a gift. It just might take some time.

Chapter 21

"More Couscous, Please!"

In This Chapter

- Going out for takeout
- What's on the menu?
- "Special order coming through!"
- "I want dessert, not a desert!"
- Something to quench my thirst

If you have had little contact with the Arab world and were surprised by all of the indulgences available in the markets of Chapter 20, this chapter is going to leave you absolutely speechless as we talk about food in the Arab world. (Actually, it probably wouldn't be good for you to end up speechless, because this book is designed to teach you how to speak in Arabic.)

Do you remember earlier in the book when I explained to you that there is no way to say "too much" in Arabic? When it comes to mealtime, you will probably find out just how large a difference the words "too" and "much" might make. But you don't need to worry. You will be too busy enjoying your meals to worry about how much you eat.

Are You Hungry Yet?

If you are going to be spending your days out and about, shopping and taking in all of the sights, you won't want to try and get by on an empty stomach. The chances of you not getting enough to eat in the Arab world are very slim. If you take a vacation to the Arab world, it probably wouldn't be the best time to start a diet. Between being polite and trying new foods, you may find yourself eating much more than expected.

A Time to Eat

Mealtimes in the Arab world may be flexible compared to what you are used to. Also, the amount of food eaten at meals may differ greatly depending on where you are visiting and the traditions of the locale or of your hosts. For instance, if you are visiting people who are quite traditional, you can expect to be served much more food than you can consume at any meal.

Tips

Although this chapter focuses on going out to eat in the Arab world, many of the customs described here will apply just as well to meals you may share with Arabic-speaking friends in your own home, town, or city. The more tips on culture and etiquette you can learn, the more likely you are to impress your hosts and guests.

You should also be aware that during the month of Ramadan, Muslims may not eat or drink between sunrise and sunset. You should be aware of this fact when planning your travel, and if you are traveling during Ramadan, inform yourself of local customs so that you avoid any unintentional inconveniences. (You wouldn't want to ask someone to cook for you at 2 P.M. if they can't eat with you, right?)

If you are staying at a hotel, you most likely can get the same foods you are used to eating pretty much any time of the day. But if you want the "true" Arabic experience, you may choose to seek out more local, regional, or customary cuisine.

The following short lists are broken down by meal so you can see what you might expect at any time of day, but the reality is that you will want to familiarize yourself with local specialties when you arrive. There is no overall definition for "Arabian" food.

Breakfast:

Track 49

khubz	bread
***jub**-na*	cheese
*zey-**too**-na*	olives

Track 49

*mu-'aj-jan-**aat***	pastry
'uj**-ja **beyD	omelet
bai**-Da/**baiD	egg/eggs
***shoor**-ba*	soup
*fu-**Toor***	breakfast
***zub**-d*	butter
*mi-**rab**-ba/mi-rab-ba-**yaat***	jam/jams (noun)
*'a-**sal***	honey
***lab**-an*	yogurt
*'a-**See**-da*	porridge
***dibs** as-**suk**-kar*	molasses

When eating breakfast, don't be surprised if you find that you are expected to just dig in by tearing off a piece of bread and using it to choose from the available fillings—eating the delicious combinations piece by piece. Breakfast is generally informal and can be enjoyed as such. During Ramadan, you may find that breakfasts consist of heavier or larger portions as the food must sustain until the evening meal, after sunset.

Lunch:

*fa-**laa**-fal*	falafel
*san-**dweesh***	sandwich
*ka-**baab***	kebab
*su-**juq***	sausage
*gha-**daa'h***	lunch
*sa-**la**-Ta*	salad
ruzz	rice
***ba**-Taa-Ta*	potatoes
***m'a**-ka-**roo**-na*	noodles
*sha-**waar**-ma*	shawarma

def•i•ni•tion

A **shawarma** is a sandwich consisting of shaved meat (goat, lamb, chicken, turkey, and so on) grilled on a skewer and served on bread with vegetables and dressing. **Falafel** means "peppers" but as a meal is created from fried balls of fava beans or chickpeas that are wrapped in bread. **Kebabs** come in many variations, but originally the word meant "fried" and not "grilled" (***mash**-wee*).

Generally, larger meals are taken at the end of the day, when the temperature has dropped. Depending on the location and customs, lunch may be served promptly at noon or an hour or two afterward. Lunch may consist of a sandwich, such as a *shawarma*, or some sort of soup or stew. Most times, the goal of lunch is to keep hunger away until dinner arrives.

Dinner (supper):

Track 49

***koos**-koos*	couscous
*kha-**roof***	lamb
***mash**-wee*	grilled
laH**-m/lu-**Hoom	meat/meats
*'a-**shaa'h***	dinner (supper)
*da-**jaaj** makh-**booz***	baked chicken
***deek roo**-mee*	turkey
*maq-**lee***	fried
*makh-**booz***	baked
*mun-**sha**-wee*	broiled
***yakh**-na*	stew
***mas**-looq*	boiled
***laH**-m **baq**-ar*	beef
***laH**-m **khin**-zeer*	pork*

*Note: pork is forbidden in Islam, so remember that it may not be available in many locations.

Because dinner/supper is most often the largest meal of the day, it is at this time that you can expect to find the largest menu. There is no way I could fit enough vocabulary into this chapter. Fortunately, most restaurants and hotels will have menus available in English. And as always, you can practice your Arabic by asking for descriptions of the items on the menu.

Restaurant Manners

When dining out, it is always important to remember your restaurant manners. Depending on where you are, there may be sections of the restaurant that only men are allowed into—with other sections allowed for couples, groups, or families. (So it is probably a better idea to let someone seat you than to choose a seat for yourself.) You should also know that Muslims may not consume pork or alcohol, so those items may not be on the menu.

> ***mum**-kin **na**-ra al-**qaa**-'hi-ma?*
>
> May we see the menu?
>
> *hal **yum-kin-naa** sha-**raa'h** aT-**Ta'aaam** hu-naa?*
>
> Can we buy food here?

If you sit down to eat and notice that there are no utensils, you may ask for them. If you are eating in a group and notice that no one has utensils, it could be that the food being served is designed to be eaten with your hands. If that is the case, you should eat with your right hand (as eating with the left hand can be considered inappropriate). If you are ever in doubt as to the proper etiquette, you can ask one of the locals. (Warning: although someone who goes to dinner with you may claim to know "all the Arab customs" because they have been out so many times, it may still be better to ask a local. Just because someone has gone out several times doesn't mean he or she is following proper etiquette.)

My first Arab dining experience in someone's home turned out to be quite a surprise. To start with, dinner was at 11 P.M.—something I really should have expected, given the long, hot days. Women and men ate in separate rooms, so our group actually got split up. Then, as we sat down to eat, I noticed our host had not set a place for himself. Also, although I did have a plate, I had no utensils. All of the food was set in the center of the table, and we served ourselves with our hands. Finally, although it was the middle of the summer, we were given nothing to drink.

The meal turned out fine and was delicious. I learned a little about traditions while we ate, too. As it turns out, the host did not set a table for himself because he wanted to make sure that we were properly served first. We were. There was at least twice as much food as we grown men could eat. I noticed the host sneaking off later to grab his own food between conversational pauses. The women ate in a separate room so they could dress more casually and speak more freely than they could have if both groups were kept together. We weren't given water because the host (and many others) believed drinks during meals are unhealthy. Eating by hand was different but not at all unpleasant. If you ever get the chance to be a guest at an Arab dinner, I recommend you take the opportunity.

Of course, you will want to know some useful phrases so that your hosts can see you are interested in learning about their culture. The following words and phrases should help you get through most meal and social situations:

*mu-**Daif***	host
Daif	guest
***maa'h**-du-ba*	banquet
***da'a**-wa*	invitation
*li-**baas***	attire
***ras**-mee*	formal
***'a**-ra-Dee*	casual
*mu-**naa**-sib*	proper
***a**-ka-la/ya-**'ha**-kal*	ate/he eats
*'aT-**shaan***	thirsty
*jow-**'aaan***	hungry
***sha**-ra-ba/**yash**-rab*	drank/he drinks

***ai**-na **naj**-las?*

Where do we sit?

ai**-na ya-**'ha**-ka-**loon** al-**aa**-kha-**roon?

Where will the others eat?

ya**-jab an nan-**ta**-THar lil-**aa**-kha-**reen?

Should we wait for the others?

***maa hee**-a aT-Ta-**reeq**-a aS-Sa-**HeeH**-a lil …?*

What is the proper way to …?

When you are done with your meal (and I mean *really* done—after food has been offered several times and you have had two or three plates more than you usually eat), you can signal that you really won't accept more by saying ***al-Ham**-du lil-**laah***, which means "praise be to God." You will hear it not only at the end of meals but also when someone wants to express his or her gratitude in general. Actually, ***al-Ham**-du lil-**laah*** is one of the most common Arabic phrases you probably will hear, right along with ***in-shaa'h** al-**lah*** ("God willing"). Finally, as you leave the table, you can express your gratitude to your host by saying ***daa**-'hi-man* (always).

Tips

The easiest way to impress your Arab hosts is to simply "mind your manners." Be sure to sit up straight, keep your hands on the table where others can see them, dress appropriately, keep your elbows off the table, keep your napkin on your lap, don't lean on objects, and don't draw unnecessary attention to yourself. When in doubt, just watch those around you and then do as they do.

What Can You Bring Me?

The world is smaller than it was even just a few years ago. When we consider food, it wasn't long ago that most fruits and vegetables were only available in specific regions at specific times of the year. Now, companies are able to get perishable goods delivered around the world literally overnight. The result is that there really is no longer a limit on what types of food you might be able to find in an Arab location. The question is, what type of food do you *want?*

These days, if you were to sit in an Arabic restaurant and ask a waiter, "What can you bring me?", the answer would most likely be, "Whatever you want." That's not too surprising, given the natural Arab pride in hosting and the actual ability to transport products so rapidly around the world. So before you decide to ask, "What can you bring me?", you should probably ask yourself the question, "What do I want?"

*maa **yum**-kin **an taH**-Dar **lee?***

What can you bring me?

*maa **hee**-a al-**khas**-See-a hu-**naa?***

What is the specialty here?

***maa**-dha ta-**waS**-see?*

What do you recommend?

*u-**reed** **shey**-'han taq-lee-**dee**-ya.*

I would like something traditional.

*maa **hee**-a **ak**-la al-mash-**hoo**-ra al-**aq**-lee-**mee**?*

What is the most famous regional dish?

Easy on the Saffron

With a history of use that dates back thousands of years, saffron is widely considered the most expensive spice in the world. Famous for both its golden-yellow color (the feminine Arabic word for "yellow" is *Saf-**raa'h***) and its unique taste, saffron continues to flavor Arabic food to this day in the Near East, Middle East, and southwest Asia.

There are, of course, other seasonings (many, in fact). Which ones you prefer is merely a matter of personal taste. Personal taste is just as important when it comes to determining the ingredients of your food. You will have to decide what spices you wish to have on your food when visiting the Arab world. Keep in mind that while something may sound tantalizing on the menu, your digestive system might react differently than you expect if you introduce too many new foods and spices all at once.

*hal **ha**-dhaa aT-**Ta'aaam** **yaH**-twee ...?*	Does this food contain ...?
***maa hee**-a al-ma-koo-**naat**?*	What are the ingredients?
qamH	wheat
***tee**-na*	fig
***nakh**-la*	dates (fruit)
*Ham-dee-**yaat***	citrus
***ba**-Sa-la*	onion
*Ta-**maa**-Ta*	tomato
*ba-**Taa**-Ta*	potato
***qir**-fa*	cinnamon
***jaaow**-daar*	rye
*sha-**'ieer***	barley
ruzz	rice
*Ta-**Heen***	flour

heyl	cardamom
*na'a-**naa'a***	mint
***za'a**-tar*	thyme
*ik-**leel***	rosemary
milH	salt
***fal**-fal*	pepper
thoom	garlic
***sim**-sim*	sesame
*jowz aT-**Teen***	nutmeg
*za'af-**raan***	saffron
***suk**-kar*	sugar

If you are concerned about what you eat but do not want to risk offending your host or restaurant staff, you should remember that a host is less likely to feel offended or upset if you ask for something different than if you *didn't* tell him or her that you wanted something different—then became sick from something you ate. Whatever you think you want or are skeptical of, you should make your concerns known. And when in doubt, *ask*.

Watch What I Eat

Let's face it. Many of us *like* to eat. Sometimes we like to eat just a little too much. We can't help it. When things taste good, we want to have more. When we aren't sure whether things taste good, we want to try them again just to make sure we *really* don't like them. There is nothing wrong with this behavior, provided we don't take it too far.

If I had followed my first Arab dining experience with identical behavior for the dining experiences that followed, I might have doubled my weight in the span of one vacation. Thankfully, I learned to cut back a bit on my portions (despite the constant urging of my host). I also discovered that while the lamb, chicken, and beef were delicious, so were the many "healthier" foods available.

If you are going to be spending your days out and about on the town, fruits and vegetables make great snacks to eat between the larger meals of the day. They also can be combined with your lunch or dinner or even served as a meal by themselves, so I have added a list here to help you.

***ai**-na ta-**koon** ____________ **Taa**-za-ja?*

Where are there fresh ____________?

***ai**-na **hoo**-a **ha**-dhaa maq-**Too**-'a?*

Where is this harvested?

*baT-**Teekh***	melon
***faa**-ki-ha/fa-**waa**-kih*	fruit
*khud-ru-**waat***	vegetables
***baam**-yaa*	okra
***mish**-mish*	apricot
*bur-tu-**qaal***	orange
*tu-**faaH***	apple
mowz	banana
*sa-**la**-ta*	salad
*fa-**raaow**-la*	strawberry

1001 Arabian Notes

Tabouli (*tab-**boo**-la*) is a famous Lebanese salad that consists primarily of tomatoes, parsley, bulgar (burghul) wheat, mint leaves, lemon juice, and olive oil. This healthy and delicious salad makes a great addition to any meal, particularly if you are concerned about watching your calories.

Some of us have to watch what we eat because we just can't eat certain foods. Our bodies don't allow us. This is no reason to enjoy ourselves less when visiting the Arab world, though. We just have to be more careful about the things we choose. If this is the situation for you (or someone traveling with you), you may find the following sentences useful.

***'and**-na Ta-la-**bee**-a **khaaS**-a.*

We have a special order.

*maa **hee**-a al-**agh**-dhee-a la-**dey**-kum li mur-**Dee** as-**suk**-ree?*

What foods do you have for a diabetic?

***an**-a Has-**saas**-see min …*

I am allergic to …

*aH-**taaj shey**-'han bi-**doon** …*

I need something without …

Room for a Little More

Whether you are looking for dessert after a large meal or a refreshing drink to help you cool off, there is always room for more. If you liked what you got for dinner, you are going to love what you can find for dessert. Like main dishes, desserts in the Arab world have flavors that belong in a class all by themselves. Until I got the chance to try the desserts, I had no idea what I had been missing all my life.

Naturally, between dinner and dessert you will probably want to get yourself a nice drink to wash everything down. You shouldn't have any problem there. Arabian coffee and tea have been famous for centuries, and more familiar drinks will be available in virtually all hotels. You can even find soda pop and more popular "Western" drinks being sold in small kiosks on the corners of most city streets.

A Drink to Cool Off

Some things aren't that different in the Arab world than they are in the world you are used to. Drinks are one of those things—with one exception. Adhering to religious doctrine, Muslims do not drink alcohol. You need to be aware of this, lest you try and order something that may not even be available in a restaurant you visit.

After most meals and during social visits to friends' homes, many Arabs offer coffee or tea. Coffee is generally taken without cream or sugar (or they are added before being served). Tea is usually sweetened beforehand as well (and may be sweetened more than you are used to). If you have difficulty falling asleep after consuming caffeine, you probably don't want to drink Arabic coffee or tea (they might call it "Turkish tea") too soon before you go to bed. If you want to impress your Arab friends as they are filling your cup, you can jiggle the cup to show that it is full enough. That should surprise them.

Otherwise, there is little you need to know about drinks … other than what they are called.

*qah-**hwa***	coffee
shaai	tea
***Soo**-daa*	soda
*'a-**Seer***	juice
maa'h	water
*'a-**Seer** tu-**faaH***	apple juice
*'a-**Seer** bur-tu-**qaal***	orange juice
*mash-roo-**baat** ar-roo-**Hee**-ya*	alcoholic drinks (spirits)
*sha-**raab**/mash-roo-**baat***	drink/drinks
***sha**-ra-ba/**yash**-rab*	drank/he drinks
***shoo**-koo-**laa**-ta **saa**-khi-na*	hot chocolate
*Ha-**leeb***	milk
*sha-**raab** al-lee-**moon***	lemonade
*na-**beedh***	wine
***beer**-a*	beer
*mi-**yaah** ma'a-da-**nee**-ya*	mineral water

Desserts from Heaven

So, you haven't had enough. You want some dessert. That's fine, but do you have room for more food in your stomach? No matter. Desserts in the Arab world don't need to be served directly after meals. Most times, you can purchase desserts and sweets in shops and snack on them whenever you choose.

Of course, you will have to decide which desserts you want to sample. There are too many to list here. Also, the same item may be called by different names in different locations. That means you may have to do a bit of research (asking people) to find out what you prefer, but if you have to do research, why not explore something as enjoyable as tasting sweets?

Most desserts you find in the Arab world will have Arabic names that don't translate well into English. It wouldn't make sense to list them, so instead I created the following list of common terms to help your sweet tooth research:

*Hal-wa-**yaat***	candy/sweets
*taH-**lee**-a*	dessert
***shoo**-koo-**laa**-ta*	chocolate
boo**-za Ha-**leeb	ice cream (frozen cream)
*bak-**laa**-wa*	baklava (baklawa)
*ka-ra-**mil**-laa*	caramel
*Hal-wee-**yaat***	pudding
***kree**-ma makh-**fooq**-a*	whipped cream

I could list 100 different desserts, and none of them might be of any use to you because regional variations create different names for the different foods. What you really need to know is how to ask for the right kind of dessert.

*maa-**dha** ta-**waS**-See al-Hal-wa-**yaat**?*

What do you recommend for dessert?

Warnings

Beware that you don't consume more sweets than your body can handle. Many desserts in the Arab world have a high amount of sugar, which causes them to taste great—but can easily create stomachaches if you eat too much.

Eating for My Tastes

Before we close the chapter, there are a few more notes that you will want to know about going out to eat in an Arabic restaurant. These are the sorts of cultural notes that may not help you *too* much with the language (but I hope they will). Overall, they *should* help you make more informed decisions about how you want to conduct yourself in various culinary (food-related) situations.

Regardless of whether you are at a restaurant, visiting a friend, or ordering service to your hotel room, there is ***daa**-'hi-man* (always) someone whose opinion you can ask about the food. Because Arabs are always happy to give their opinions and you are trying to learn Arabic, why not put the pieces together and see what someone else thinks about the local cuisine?

***maa hoo**-a al-**af**-Dal **maT**-'am fee al-min-**Ta**-qa?*

What is the best restaurant in the area?

*hal **hee**-a mu-**naa**-sib-a li-**us**-ra-**tee** an ta-'**hak**-al hu-**naa?***

Is it appropriate for my family to eat there?

"Hot" means different things to different people. When we are talking about food, "hot" can mean "served at a high temperature" or "spicy." While it is reasonable to expect the food you order to be "hot" in temperature, you might be surprised to discover that Arabic food is not usually too "spicy hot." Certainly, it all depends on you and how you want your food prepared. Anything can be made to order.

*hal la-**dey**-haa ka-**theer min at**-ta-**waa**-bil?*

Is this spicy?

ai now**-'a min al-**fal**-fal **tas**-takh-**dam**-u-**haa?

What sort of peppers do you use?

Warnings

Be careful when ordering "spicy" Arabic food, particularly if you are used to things being "spicy" the way a jalapeño pepper is spicy. Hot spices in the Arab world might not burn your tongue, but they can get hot *after* you have swallowed your food—which can be quite unsettling to those who don't know what to expect.

Finally, when the meal is over, you have pushed yourself away from the table, and you are ready to end the evening, you are probably going to need to understand a few things. First, if you were invited to dinner, it is not likely you will be expected to pay. You may make a gesture toward paying, but your host will most likely say they will pay the bill. To fulfill the social obligation, you can pretend to offer to pay a couple more times, but in the end, let your host pay. You can repay him or her later.

If there is a group of people and each wants to pay on his or her own, one person should probably pay for the group and then the others can pay him or her back in a more discreet location. Also, when it comes to tipping, the customs are different in different locations. In some places, tipping is not part of a meal or service. In others, a small percentage of the meal cost may be given to the server. You should ask (maybe your concièrge) about tipping before you go out to dinner.

And last but not least, here are some sentences to help you close out your dining experience.

***kaa**-nat la-**dheedh** faa-**too**-ra.*	It was delicious.
*ra-**jaa**-'han ta-**jeeb**-nee al-faa-**too**-ra.*	Please bring me the bill.

*ad-**fa'a** '**an** kul **shey**.*	I am paying for everything.
***an**-a ad-f'aa fee mar-ra al-**qaa**-dim.*	I will pay next time.
*si-**nu-'aa**-id qa-**reeb**-an.*	We will return soon.
*shu-kraan li-**kul shey**.*	Thank you for everything.
***Hat**-a **fee mur**-a al-**qaa**-di-ma …*	Until the next time …

Practice Makes Perfect

It feels to me as if this chapter passed a little too quickly. I suppose that in a way, it did. But that's only because there is so much information that could go into these pages and only so much room available. I hope you paid attention to the readings, though, because you will need your memory to get all the practice questions right. Translate the following phrases:

1. I am looking for candy for my children.
2. ***maa hoo**-a al-**af**-Dal **maT**-'am fee al-min-**Ta**-qa?*
3. One water and one wine, please.
4. ***maa hee**-a al-ma-koo-**naat fee** al-fa-**laa**-fal?*

The Least You Need to Know

- Be prepared for several courses of food.
- You may not receive utensils.
- Be mindful of where you order pork or alcohol.
- Ask the locals about proper dining etiquette for the region.
- Always express your gratitude before leaving.

Chapter 22

Something Is Missing Here

In This Chapter

- Let no thing be forgotten
- When you don't know the word, describe it
- Common items to remember
- Recalling events to others
- Thinking of where else it may be

I'm going to make an admission to you. It may come as a bit of a surprise for some—perhaps not to others. It is a revealing admission; you will learn a weakness of mine when I tell you. But it is important … I lose things. No matter how hard I try to remember to always place my possessions in locations so I always know where they are, I manage again and again to forget where I've put them by the time I need them once again.

If you are someone who occasionally loses items, if you sometimes forget to pack items you invariably need for your vacation, or even if you never forget your own things but you may have to speak for someone else who has forgotten an item, you will find some great conversation tips in this chapter. We cover many different ways you can get yourself the new item you need—or another version of the items you already have.

What Did You Forget?

The worst part about forgetting an item is that you will never know you forgot it until it's too late. You don't think to yourself, "Oh, I will forget this tomorrow, so I had best take care of it today."

If we forget something, it stays missing until we find it, forget about it, or replace it. On vacation, forgetfulness can cause us even more problems because we don't always know where we need to look for a replacement. Forgetting something in a place where we don't speak the language—that makes things even more difficult.

I may not be able to help you remember everything for your trip to the Arab world, but I can certainly help you learn how to try to find those things that need replacing. We start with a look at some of the verbs you might need if you are going to explain yourself.

Track 50

*na-**sey**-tu*	I forgot
*na-**sey**-naa*	we forgot
***yan**-sa*	he forgets

*na-**sey**-tu **ai**-na ta-**rak**-tu mif-**taaH**-Hee.*
I forgot where I left my key.

*na-**sey**-naa an **nak**-tub al-'**un**-waan.*
We forgot to write down (record) the address.

***laa tan**-sa an **tagh**-liq al-**baab 'and**-maa **tat**-ruk al-**ghur**-fa.*
Don't forget to close the door when you leave the room.

Tips

When you learn a new verb in Arabic, it is always a good idea to go through its various conjugations—using the verb in sentences so you can remember the different ways it may be used. Start by working from the past to the present to the future, using a different sentence for each form.

***fa**-qa-da*	he lost
*fa-**qad**-tu*	I lost
***naf**-qid*	we lose

***fa**-qa-da na-THaa-**raat**-hu.*
He lost his glasses.

*fa-**qad**-tu **Haa**-fi-THa-tee.*
I lost my wallet.

*ta-**rak**-na ta-**dhaa**-kir-naa hu-**naa,** li-'**han**-na lam nu-**reed** an naf-**qid**-haa.*
We left our tickets here because we didn't want to lose them.

*wa-**jad**-naa* — we found
***wa**-ja-dat* — she found
***a**-jid* — I find

*wa-**jad**-naa sa-**yaa**-ra-tu-hu fee-al-**mow**-qif.*
We found his car in the parking lot.

*fa-**qad**-tu al-mif-**taaH,** wa-**laa**-kin-haaa **wa**-ja-**dat**-hu.*
I lost the key, but she found it.

You also may find that you need an all-purpose sentence or two. The following might help you:

*na-**sey**-naa ________________-naa. **ai**-na na-**jid**-hu/haa?*
We forgot our ________________. Where can we find that?

***ai**-na **yum**-kin an-naa **nash**-ta-**rey** ________________?*
Where is it possible for us to buy ________________?

kaa**-na min al-maf-**rooD** an na-_____________, wa-**laa**-kin ___________**-naa.
We were supposed to ________________, but we ________________.

When you start to talk about the things you may have forgotten, you might realize that you can say, "I forgot" or, "We need to find"—but you don't know the *name* of the thing you are in need of. If that happens, which of the following actions should you take?

a) Throw your hands in the air and run in circles yelling, "All is lost!"

b) Lie on the ground until someone comes to save you.

c) Try your best to explain what you mean by using the words you *do* know.

If you answered either a or b, then I believe you will have some amount of difficulty getting your problems solved. If you answered c, then you might want to keep reading to see how you might go about getting your point across. (Note: you can keep reading even if you *did* answer a or b. I won't tell anyone you got the answer wrong.)

What Do You Call That?

Have you ever had a word stuck on the tip of your tongue? This phenomenon is common when learning a foreign language.

I am trying to prevent situations like these when I keep telling you that you should try and learn your Arabic vocabulary in phrases or sentences. That way, the words have a meaning associated with them that your mind can better understand.

Still, these situations happen. What do you do? You talk your way around the word you don't know. If you are really good, you can even learn to ask questions in such a way that the people around you don't notice you are trying to learn new words. For example, you could say:

> *raa-**'hey**-tu **shey**-'han gha-**reeb** al-**yoom**. **maa**-dha tu-**sam**-mih-hu **'and**-maa …?*
> I saw something strange today. What do you call it when …?
>
> ***ya**-f'al **ha**-dhaa …*
> It does this …
>
> ***yash**-bih **ha**-dhaa …*
> It looks like this …
>
> ***maa**-dha tu-**sam**-mee **ha**-dhaa ash-**shey?***
> What do you call this thing?
>
> ***Haj**-mu-hu taq-**reeb**-an …*
> It is about this big … (Its size is about …)

> **1001 Arabian Notes**
>
> Point things out. In some cultures, it is considered rude to move too much while talking—but in Arabic, moving the hands and arms is a common method of emphasizing your speech. Use this to your advantage when trying to explain things in Arabic. Wave, sketch, and point (but not directly at strangers). Do whatever you can to get others to understand your point.

Even if you can't find the perfect word, there are certainly words you *can* find that will work. For example, let's say you were looking for your wallet but couldn't remember the word for wallet. How might you describe your wallet? Here are some suggestions.

> ***hee**-a bu-**nee**-ya wa Sa-**gheer**-a.*
> It is brown and small.
>
> *ta-**koon** nu-**qood fee**-haa.*
> There is money in it.

I think you get the idea. See what other possibilities you can come up with. And remember, it won't matter if you "cheat" a little bit in your conversation by throwing in the English word. What's most important is that you keep talking so the conversation doesn't stop. The words will come with time and practice.

Never Leave Home Without ...

So now you know how to sneak a little bit of information out of your mind—even when it doesn't cooperate as much as you might like. But you might ask, "Okay ... what can I do to prevent forgetting the words in the first place?" Well, I suppose you could memorize an Arabic dictionary. Of course, that might take a little more time.

Another option would be for you to learn the words you are most likely to need. That list of words would definitely be shorter and easier to manage. So if you were on vacation and you forgot or lost something, what words might you need? I think the following list might help you some.

*mif-**taaH**/ma-**faa**-tiH*	key/keys
***Haa**-fi-THa*	wallet
*na-THaa-**raat***	eyeglasses
*kha-**ree**-Ta*	map
***quT**-n*	cotton
***Sab**-ir*	aloe
*gha-**sool***	lotion
*Ha-**faa**-Da al-aT-**faal***	diapers
*da-**waa'h***	medicine
***aa**-la **taS**-weer*	camera
***qa**-lam*	pen
qa**-lam ra-**SaaS	pencil
wa**-ra-qa/ow-**raaq	paper/papers
*ha-**wee**-ya*	identification card
*ta-'**hak**-ka-da/ya-ta-'**hak**-kad*	ensured/he ensures
***baT**-Tar-**ree**-ya*	batteries
aT**-'aa-ma al-Hai-waan-**aat	feed the pets
saq**-a al-na-baa-**taat	water plants

***tagh**-laq al-na-**waa**-fa-dha*	close the windows
*za-**jaaj**-a*	bottle
***khuT**-Ta*	plan
khaTT**/kha-**TooT	line/lines
*maak-**yaaj***	makeup (cosmetics)
*mu-**nuTH**-THif*	detergent
*mu-**zeel** lil-ra-**waa'h***	deodorant
shaf**/sha-**foof	gauze/gauzes
*gha-**raaD***	gear
*im-daa-**daat** Tib-**bee**-ya*	medical supplies
***shaf quT**-nee*	cotton gauze
*fur-**shaa** al-is-**naan***	toothbrush
aH**-mar ash-shi-**faa'h	lipstick

Not Quite Right

Okay, so maybe you are nothing like me. Maybe you never forget to finish what you … Maybe you know exactly how to get what you want and know how to talk your way around the words that you don't know.

Well, then there probably isn't much more I can teach you. Or is there? What if the item you get is almost exactly what you want but not quite perfect? For example, let's say you really need toothpaste, so you send the concièrge to get it for you. But when you get your toothpaste, you realize that it is not your favorite brand.

Sure, you could be happy that you got something to help clean your teeth after all that great Arabic cuisine. But what if you really *need* that other type of toothpaste? What if you need a slightly different sort of the same item? What do you do? Easy. Just ask.

***aH**-taaj **shey**-'han **ak**-thar qa-**leel min** …*
I need something a little more …

***yum**-kin al-Ha-**Sool 'al**-a **ha**-dhaa **fee** ____________ **aa**-khar*
Can I get this in a different …

*mu-**naa**-sib-a*	appropriate
***shak**-l*	shape
gheyr** Sa-**HeeH	wrong (not right)
***now**-'a*	type
*kha-**Taa'h***	mistake
*akh-**Taa'h**-naa*	we went wrong
***ak**-bar*	bigger
***as**-r'a*	faster
***ab**-Taa'h*	slower
***aq**-waa*	stronger

***ha**-dhaa **laa yak**-fee. naH-**taaj ak**-thar …*
This is not enough. We need more …

ha**-dhaa **hoo**-a al-ka-**maal.
This is perfect.

***naH**-taaj **ak**-thar min **nafs** al-**now**-'a.*
We need more of the same type.

Warnings

Remember that when you travel to the Arab world, the brand names on many products in stores are likely to differ from those you are used to. Always be sure to check the ingredients listed on packaging and make your purchases through trusted sources.

Because not everything will be perfect, you will probably need some vocabulary to help explain exactly what happened and how you might get things changed.

*in-hi-**yaar***	collapse
***now**-'a*	type
***ba**-da-lan min*	instead of
***aa**-khar*	different
***thaa**-nee*	second
*mukh-**ta**-lif*	various
*ukh-**tu**-laT*	mixed
***naq**-qee*	pure

*mow-**Doo**-'a*	subject
qa-leel min	a little
*taq-**reeb**-an*	close (almost)
***kaa**-da*	almost (plus a verb)
*Sa-**gheer jid**-dan*	very small
*ka-**beer jid**-dan*	very big
***ley**-sat mu-**naa**-sib-a*	does not fit
*si-yan-**kas**-ir*	it will break
*bi-su-**hoo**-la*	easily
*in-na-**hu** mu-**San**-n'a **jey**-dan?*	Is it well made?
***Da**-yiq*	tight (fitting)
*faD-**faaD***	loose
***aq**-waa*	stronger
*mu-ta-**mey**-yiz*	specific
*khi-**laaf***	disagreement
*'a-**teeq***	old-fashioned

So now you have the foundation for getting more specific about the things you have seen and done. In the next section, we are really going to put you to the test.

Tell Me Step by Step

Trying to learn a language without being able to read or write in that language is not an easy task—but it can be done. Honestly (some might say "sadly"), over the course of my life I have met many people who can neither read nor write a particular language but who can speak and understand it just fine.

Actually, this isn't too surprising. If you think about how languages are used, most often they are used for communication between two people talking to one another. That means *speaking*, not reading or writing. And one of the most important parts of speaking is being able to recall events that have happened so that you can explain them to others.

With that in mind, in this section we will *recall* an imagined day on vacation. Hopefully, you will be able to follow the conversation without much problem. Afterward, you should see how much you can communicate about a hypothetical day in your life.

> *al-**yoom**, **kun**-tu **m'a us**-ra-tee **fee** al-ma-**dee**-na wa ra-**'hey**-naa ka-**theer** min al-ash-**yaa'h** ja-**meel**-a. **kaa**-nat al-zi-**yaa**-ra **jeyd** wa-**laa**-kin ta-**rak**-naa **b'aD** Ha-**qaa**-'hib-naa fee ma-**kaan maa.** sa-**'ha**-lat **zowj**-a-tee 'an-**nee** "**ai**-na al-Ha-**qaa**-'hib?" wa-**laa**-kin lam **a'aa**-raf. ish-ta-**rey**-naa **ai**-Daan ka-**theer** min al-ash-**yaa'h fee** as-**sooq wa ha**-dha-hi al-ash-**yaa'h kaa**-nat fee al-Ha-**qaa**-'hib.*
>
> "Today, I was in the city with my family and we saw many nice things. The visit was nice, but we left some of our bags somewhere. My wife asked me, 'Where are the bags?', but I did not know. We also bought many things in the market, and these things were in the bags."

When you are recalling events, ***qad*** is a useful word you can add to your conversation. ***qad*** is used in combination with a verb to let you know whether something has definitely happened or whether it *may* happen. When used with the past tense, ***qad*** shows that an event *did* happen. When ***qad*** is used with the present or future tense, that event *might* happen.

> ***qad** ta-kal-**lam**-naa **m'a** ash-**shur**-Ta*
> We did speak with the police
>
> *wa-**laa**-kin **laa na'a**-rif **maa**-dha si-**na**-f'al al-**aan.***
> but we do not know what we will do now
>
> *qad **na**-ta-**kal**-lam m'a al-boo-**waab.***
> We might talk with the concièrge.

It probably won't take more than a few minutes of practice for you to memorize the previous paragraph. I could write several more for you, but you will really get more from the practice if you create paragraphs of your own. When you do that, imagine you are telling a story to a friend or to someone who can help you.

And just as you tell a story in English (or in your native language), you can benefit from the use of a few "filler" words—words that fill the short pauses in conversations, or words that provide quick answers to questions.

Track 51

*a-**shuk** fee **dha**-lik*	I doubt (in) that
*mash-**kook***	doubtful
***Tab**-'aan*	of course
ley**-sa **b'ad	not yet

*fee al-ba-**daa**-ya*	at the beginning
***thu**-ma*	then
***b'ad dha**-lik*	after that
*a-**kheer**-an*	finally
***qad an**-ta-ha*	it is finished
***maa zaa**-la*	still (ongoing)
***wa**-saT*	middle
***fee** an-ni-**haa**-ya*	at the end
*kha-**TaT**-naa li*	we planned to
***thu**-ma ra-'**hey**-naa*	then we saw
***kun**-naa na-ta-**waq**-q'aa an*	we were expecting to
*bi-is-tim-**raar***	continuously

Now, you should go back through your story and see how much "flavor" you can add to it by using the phrases I have just given you. You should be surprised with the results.

Tips

When speaking in longer sentences that use ***an*** between verbs (here's an example: *u-**reed an** u-**zoor**;* "I want to visit"), when the first verb is in the past tense, the second verb will be in the present tense. (Here's another example: *a-**rad**-naa **an** na-ta-**kal**-lam;* "We wanted to talk.") This form is used for most cases and is the same as English. We wouldn't say, "We wanted to talk***ed***."

Finally, you can always benefit from the use of "all" or "some." These last two sentences should help you understand those two simple words.

*al-ta-**qey**-naa **b'aD** aS-di-**qaa'h**-naa.* (***b'aD***)
We met some of our friends. (some)

*a-**kal**-naa **kul** aT-**Ta'aaam**.* (***kul***)
We ate all of the food. (all)

Send Someone to Get It

Sometimes if you forget an item, you will have to go looking for it. And what may surprise you is that you are going to have to look for it someplace where you might not normally feel comfortable. You shouldn't be afraid to go looking for the things you need, though. You should just be prepared with the right words for the right occasion.

We have covered many terms used for many situations, and we have discussed various health issues in this book already. Certainly, there is much more that could be covered—but we only have a certain amount of time and space. That's why I thought about the things you might really *need* to say and the places you might really *need* to visit while you are on vacation.

Do you know what first came to mind? A visit to the pharmacy (drugstore). You never know when you are going to have to treat minor ailments, and I hardly expect you to have packed your luggage with the right gear (*gha-**raaD***) for every possibility.

So here you go:

***ley**-sa la-**dey**-ka …*	You don't have …
*wa-**laa**-kin aH-**taaj** …*	But I need …
***maa**-dha **aa**-f'al?*	What do I do?

***ab**-Hath **'an**-haa fee ma-**kaan thaa**-nee?*
Look for it somewhere else (in a second place)?

*wa-**laa**-kin **ai**-na?*	But where?
***fee** aS-**Sai**-dal-**lee**-ya*	in the pharmacy
***ley**-sa la-**dey**-naa.*	We don't have it.
***ley**-sa la-**dey**-hu.*	He doesn't have it.
***ley**-sa la-**dey**-haa.*	She doesn't have it.
***ley**-sa la-**dey**-hum.*	They don't have it.
*wa-**laa**-kin 'al-**ley**-naa an na-**jid**-hu.*	But we have to find it.
***Sai**-dal-**lee**-ya*	pharmacy
Tib	medicine (science)
Hab**-ba/Hab-**boob	pill/pills
***saa**-'hil*	liquid
*qin-**nee**-na/qa-**naan***	bottle/bottles (vial)

*'i-**yaa**-da Tib-**bee**-a*	medical clinic
*mas-**Hooq***	powder
*mu-**Daad** Ha-**wee**-ya*	antibiotic
***quT**-n*	cotton
*mun-ta-**jaat** an-ni-**THaa**-fa*	hygiene products
*un-tha-**wee**-ya*	feminine
***dha**-kar*	masculine
***maa**-da mu-**naTH**-THi-fa*	(a) cleaner
*is-**fan**-ja*	sponge
*ra-**dhaadh** lil-**sh'ar***	hair spray
Saq**-l lil-aTH-**faar	fingernail polish

Now you just have to remember how to politely ask the shopkeeper a few questions. If you are in a pharmacy, the person you are looking for is probably the pharmacist.

*hal **an**-ta al-**Sai**-da-**lee**?* Are you the pharmacist?

***mum**-kin tu-**saa**-'id-**nee**?* Can you help me?

Then, you can go right back into describing what you are looking for.

1001 Arabian Notes

Remember: when you are speaking with someone who is a professional, you should always address him or her politely and as his or her profession suggests. For example, if a man introduced himself as *Ta-**beeb** mar-**waan***, you would address him as *Ta-**beeb***. When meeting an Arab woman, let her decide the method of greeting (shaking hands or not)—especially if you are a man.

If you don't know your way around the town you are visiting—or you don't trust yourself to get things right—you always have one definite solution: send someone to get the item(s). Remember that society in the Arab world revolves around close relationships. If you want to gain the trust of the people you are visiting, let them do something for you.

Here's what I mean. Let's say you forgot to bring your toothpaste with you. You are staying in a small hotel, and they do not have toothpaste available at the front desk. When you were in town, you looked into several shops but didn't see toothpaste on any of the shelves. Now, it is getting late in the afternoon and you don't know what you should do. Here's what I would do: send someone to get it.

By asking someone to help you find what you need (in this case, toothpaste), you are showing that person that you trust him or her. You should be sure to ask someone you trust and someone you expect to see again. Maybe the hotel staff has someone in mind to help you already (such as the concièrge). When you ask this person (very often, it is a young boy who is looking to meet new people, have a small adventure, and impress the foreigners) and show that you trust him, he will be anxious to prove that your trust was not misplaced. If you take advantage of this method of "shopping through an intermediary," you can open the doorway to a new friendship while saving yourself the hassle of searching for something when you could be touring.

Practice Makes Perfect

Are you ready to "forget" some things? Well, maybe you shouldn't try to forget them. Instead, practice talking about the things you've forgotten.

1. Explain what *ta-waq-**q'aa**-naa* means and why.
2. Translate: *maa **zal**-naa nu-**fat**-tish **'an** mu-**zeel** lil-ra-**waa'h**.*
3. How might you tell someone, "Go. Look for it."?
4. Translate: *hal **an**-ti tas-ta-**Tey**-'u **an** tu-**sheer**-een 'al-**ey** **Sai**-dal-**lee**-ya?*
5. Translate: ***wa**-Sal-naa fee aS-Sa-**baaH** wa kha-**TaT**-naa li-**saf**-r **il**-a al-ma-**dee**-na.*
6. Translate: *qad a-ta-**kal**-lam m'a aT-Ta-**beeb**.*

The Least You Need to Know

- Don't forget that *na-**sey**-tu* means "I forgot."
- When you can't remember a particular word, try using other words to describe it.
- If all else fails, you always can describe things by using your hands.
- ***ley**-sa la-**dey**-naa* means "we don't have it."
- Recalling events is great language practice.

Part 6

Getting Things Done

Is this the final section already? Have you already come so far? I can't believe it. You must be a much better student than I was when I was just starting. Before I lose you to the study of your next language, let me remind you that you can always start this book over again.

But if you are not quite ready to give up yet, I have one last task for you: studying Part 6. In Part 6, you will take control of your Arabic skills, putting them to use to get things done.

You can start with asking for basic household services in Chapter 23. Then, in Chapter 24, you will learn how to get the word out to family and friends about your Arabic experiences. Finally, you will move beyond a casual stay and learn how to express yourself in business matters or set yourself up for a longer stay by furnishing your home. Chapter 26 contains useful phrases should you find yourself in an emergency (hopefully not). You may want to bookmark appropriate pages.

Chapter 23

Flying Carpet Services

In This Chapter

- The service advantage
- Laundry with all the "fixings"
- Personalized care
- New and various ways to say "No!"
- Finding your own help

Although they are wonderful hosts, people in the Arab world are not mind readers. So to feel truly "comfortable" during your visits with them, you may have to learn how to get some "comfort services" on your own. That's what I hope to teach you how to do in this chapter.

Whether at the laundry or the camera store, the barber shop or the beauty salon, the more you can learn about getting services, the more comfortable you are going to feel. And the more comfortable you feel, the more likely you are to try out your Arabic skills. And … the more you try out your Arabic, well … you get the idea.

In this chapter, you find out all you need to know about getting the services you need—when and where you need them. You also learn how to handle some simple problems that might arise. Before the chapter ends, I even take you a step further with your ability to say "no" and make sure you know where to find your governmental citizen services while on tour.

To Make a Claim Stick

No one really *likes* to have to take things to the cleaners or to get things fixed, but sometimes it's just unavoidable. In those instances, you have the choice of either living with a broken (*mu-**kas**-sa-ra*) or dirty (***wa**-sikh*) item (in which case you really don't need to read this chapter), or you can take it to get fixed. If you do want to learn a bit more about services, however, then I suggest you pay attention throughout this chapter. No doubt the first word you are going to want to use is "service" itself:

***kha**-da-ma/**yakh**-dim*	served/he serves
khid**-ma/khid-**maat	service/services

You might remember a word we had earlier in the book for "use" or "using." That word is *is-tikh-**daam**.* The grammar is a bit too complex to explain here, but if you investigate sometime you will see that the root *kh-d-m* is in several words, including "used," "he served," and "service." At the risk of sounding "punny" (but unfortunately not "funny"), I would have to say that *kh-d-m* is quite useful in Arabic. By the way, the Arabic word for "useful" is *mu-**feed**,* which comes from the root of the word for "beneficial."

Getting the Laundry Done

You have a shirt and shoes, but you need some service. That's not a problem. You have the vocabulary you need and the will to learn. Those two alone can take you quite far in your studies.

> **1001 Arabian Notes**
>
> Even if you can't find a traditional laundry service, you probably can find a way to get your laundry done. Sometimes people will wash and press your laundry for you in their homes as a way to supplement their income. If someone offers to do this and you are considering accepting their top-notch offer, be sure of their reputation and pay them appropriately.

Usually, if I think of a Laundromat, I picture an open-all-night, glass-fronted building filled with coin-operated machines that patrons guard like hawks. Admittedly, my mind's picture is skewed from too much television, but that is how I picture

Laundromats, self-service laundries, and launderettes—all of which are just different names for the same thing.

If you picture Laundromats the way I do and you go looking for such a shop in the Arab world, you might be surprised at what you end up finding. The following list should help you explain yourself a little better:

hal ***t'a****-rif-een* ***ai****-na yum-****kin****-a-****nee*** *an* ***aj****-jid …*
Do you (f) know where I can find a/an …

hal *t'a-****rif man*** *…*
Do you know who …

*mik-****waaa***	(an) iron
buq*-'aa*	stain
magh*-sal*	laundry (cleaner's)
gha*-sa-la/****yagh****-sal*	cleaned/he cleans
naTH*-THa-fa* ***'al****-a an-****naa****-shif*	dry clean
*ma-****Hal 'aaam*** *li-****gha****-sal ath-thi-****yaab***	laundry service (launderette)
*iy-****Saal***	receipt
*bai-****yaD***	bleach
yagh*-sil thi-****yaab***	launder clothing
ley*-sa na-****THeef***	not clean
agh*-sal yad-****wee****-an* ***fuqt***	hand wash only
*tow-****Seel***	delivery
*na-****shaa'h***	starch
*ghas-****saa****-la wa mu-****jaf****-fi*	washer and dryer (f)

After you find your way to the cleaner's, you will certainly gain confidence in your ability to move around. Why not take the next step and see whether you can take care of some of the other issues you might have?

Digital Nightmares

Technology is not advancing rapidly; it is advancing at the speed of light—literally. What I find interesting in this progression is the way that technology always seems to make my life *more* complicated, rather than less complicated. The more electronic "toys" and "gizmos" I buy, the more problems I seem to have and the more often I find myself digging into the owner's manual to figure out why I just can't take the pictures I want and show my friends when I get home.

If you have had similar experiences with technology, I'm sure you understand what I mean. Thankfully, you should have little problem finding the camera and electrical supplies you need in most Arab world locations.

The following list of words should help you with technological problems:

Track 52

*u-**reed an ash**-ta-rey …*
I want to buy …

aa**-la taS-**weer	camera
film	film
*mus-**wa**-da*	negative
***Soo**-ra*	photograph (picture)
***saa'aa** raq-**mee**-a*	digital watch
***saa'aa** mu-**nab**-bi-ha*	alarm clock
***aa**-la **see**-dee*	CD player
*ji-**haaz** as-**tir**-yoo*	stereo
***Ta**-ba-'aa/**yaT**-ba'a*	printed/he prints
***dhaa**-kir-a*	memory
*taH-**meeD***	developing (film)
***Soo**-ra*	picture
*tak-**beer** aS-**Soo**-ra*	enlarge the picture
*mu-**kab**-bir aS-**Sowt***	loud speaker
***sha**-ba-ka*	network
*Ha-**shaa/yaH**-shoo*	charged/he charges
***laa yaH**-shoo*	it won't charge
*ta-**waq**-qa-fa*	it quit (stopped)
*an-**qaT**-a'a al-**kah**-rU-**baa'h***	the electricity cut out
*al-wa-**thee**-qa maf-**qood**-a*	the document is missing

***raad**-yoo*	radio
*ha-**waa**-'hee*	antenna
***yash**-ghul*	turn on
***yow**-kif*	turn off

Get Personal with Your Care

Vacations are for relaxation. And one of the best ways to relax is to let yourself be pampered a little bit. "Pampering" means different things to different people, though. For some, it is enough to have a professional shampoo and/or their hair cut. Others prefer to have a complete makeover, from highlights to a pedicure and polished toenails.

Tips

Be sure to protect your electronic equipment from sand and temperature extremes when visiting the Arab world. That way, you can ensure that you bring home all the digital memories you record while on your vacation. Lens cleaning kits and cushioned bags help keep sensitive electronics safe from sand and heat.

Whatever you prefer, you will be able to find the personal care services that allow you to completely relax. You already know how to ask directions (***ai**-na al- …*), so you just need to know what it is you are looking for.

*tad-**leel***	pampering
*ja-**maal***	beauty
*Hi-**laa**-qa ash-**sh'ar***	haircut
***Ha**-la-qa/**yaH**-liq*	he shaved/he shaves
lown	color
*mi-**qaSS***	scissors
*taj-**meel** a-**THaa**-fir al-**yad***	manicure
***aa**-la Hi-**laa**-qa*	electric razor (clippers)
*Hal-**laaq***	barber
*Saa-**loon** Hi-**laa**-qa*	barber shop
*taj-**mee**-lee*	cosmetic

***aS**-la-'u*	bald
***ash**-'aar*	hairy
*tas-**ree**-Ha*	hairstyle
*fur-**shaaa** Hi-**laa**-qa*	shaving brush
*tad-**leek***	massage*
*mu-**dal**-lik*	masseur
mu-dal-lik-a	masseuse
***liH**-Hee-a*	beard
***shaa**-rib/sha-**waa**-rib*	mustache/mustaches
***shaa**-ma*	beauty mark (birthmark)
*taj-**'ieed daa**-'him lil ash-**sh'ar***	permanent wave (for hair)
*qa-**Seer***	short
*Ta-**weel***	long
*mu-**ja'a**-'aad*	curly
***qa**-Ta-'aa/**yaq**-ta'a*	he cut/he cuts
*qi-**naa'a***	mask
***Haa**-jib*	brow
*fur-**shaaa***	brush
***Tool** al-**kat**-if*	shoulder-length
***mib**-rad*	nail file

*Note: if asking for a massage, remember cultural considerations. It may be inappropriate for a woman to give a man a massage or vice versa. In that case, a man would ask for a masseur, and a woman would ask for a masseuse.

Okay, so you have the vocabulary … but can you put it to use? Let's see whether you can.

Tell me, "Please cut it at shoulder length." Can you think of the answer? You might want to write it out on another sheet of paper to keep yourself from looking for the answer before you know it. I suppose I will have to give you the answer anyway, so here you are:

> *ra-**jaa**-'han **taq**-ta'a-**hu** **'al**-a **Tool** al-**kat**-if.*

I don't expect you to remember all the rules of conjugation from one pass through the text, but I do hope you will use the various examples I give you in this text to create practice drills and quizzes for yourself. Now, let's take another look at the sentence I asked you to create.

The first word you should say is "Please." There are several ways to say please, and you will learn them all with practice and through discussions with friends. For this example, I chose *ra-**jaa**-'han*. That's easy enough. The second part of the sentence becomes a bit more difficult.

First, you need to know the verb "cut." In the vocabulary list you just read and the book's glossary, you can find "cut/he cuts." When you find this, you know you have located the correct verb—but you have to make it fit into your sentence. Because I asked you to tell me (K., the author, male, second person) to cut your hair, you have to change the verb from "he cuts" (***yaq**-ta'a*) to "you cut" (***taq**-ta'a*). Then you have to add an *object* to the verb to show what is being cut. In this case, the object is "hair" (***sh'ar***), a masculine noun that needs a masculine pronoun to describe it (*-hu*). That leaves you with the complete verb ***taq**-ta'a-**hu*** ("you cut it").

The only other thing you need to say is at what length your hair should be cut. In this example, the hair should be cut "at shoulder length" (***'al**-a **Tool** al-**kat**-if*). So putting all of the pieces together, you end up with the following:

> *ra-**jaa**-'han **taq**-ta'a-**hu** **'al**-a **Tool** al-**kat**-if.*
> Please cut it at shoulder length.

Congratulations! I can hear you getting better from all the way over here.

Tips

Although learning how to use and conjugate verbs is one of the hardest parts of Arabic, it is also one of the most important. You will improve your speech and learning dramatically by writing and speaking several sentences for each verb you are trying to learn. Don't repeat your example sentences, and try to think how you might use different forms of the verb in everyday conversation.

Negating: Get Out of a Word Jam

Just when you thought you were done with grammar lessons—wait a minute. You didn't *really* think you would ever be done with grammar lessons, did you? Grammar is what allows you to tell which part of a sentence belongs where. Grammar helps you speak clearly and understand exactly what others are talking about.

Unfortunately, "grammar" is often also a word that causes headaches among many language students. And there is an Arabic word that gives even intermediate and advanced Arabic students some problems: ***ley**-sa*. Fortunately for you, you are only *beginners* in Arabic and need only a basic knowledge of ***ley**-sa*. ***ley**-sa* is another way of saying "not," and we use it in cases where our other three "no" words—***laa***, ***lam***, and ***lan***—don't work.

The biggest difference between ***laa*** and ***ley**-sa* for our purposes is that on the one hand, ***laa*** and its past and future forms (***lam*** and ***lan***) are used in combination with verbs. For example:

> ***laa yadh**-hab.*
> He is not going (does not go).

***ley**-sa*, on the other hand, does not need a verb to follow it. Compare:

> ***hoo**-a **fee** al-**beyt.***
> He is in the house.
>
> ***hoo**-a **ley**-sa **fee** al-**beyt.***
> He is not in the house.

So we could say ***ley**-sa* is strong enough to stand on its own as a verb in a sentence, while ***laa*** needs to be combined with a verb. You wouldn't say ***hoo**-a **laa fee** al-**beyt.*** That would be like saying, "He is no in the house." You don't want to sound like that, so you switch to ***ley**-sa*.

"Not" in This House

So what can you do with ***ley**-sa?* Well, for starters, you want to conjugate it just like you would any other verb in Arabic. The following table shows how to conjugate ***ley**-sa* for the various ways you might need to use it.

Table 23.1

Conjugating *ley-sa*

I	***las**-tu*
You (m/s)	***las**-ta*
You (f/s)	***las**-ti*
He	***ley**-sa*
She	***ley**-sat*
We	***las**-naa*
You (m/pl)	***las**-tum*
You (f/pl)	***las**-tun-na*
They (m)	***ley**-soo*
They (f)	***las**-nna*

So if I let you look at the previous chart and then told you to tell me, "She is not in the house," do you think you could do it? Good. Tell me: "She is not in the house." The answer is not too difficult. I won't even bother breaking the sentence down for you the way I did before.

> ***hee**-a **ley**-sat **fee** al-**beyt.***
> She is not in the house.

You see … not too difficult, right? Because I want to keep things as simple as possible for you in this book, I suggest that you keep your use of ***ley**-sa* in the present tense.

However, if you think you are up to the challenge and you want to try some negation with ***ley**-sa*, here are some tips. For the past, use ***kaa**-na* first, then ***ley**-sa*, then the rest of the sentence:

> ***kun**-ta **las**-ta **fee** al-**beyt.***
> You (m/s) were not (m/s) in the house.

If you want to negate the future, you have to use ***lan*** with ***kaa**-na:*

> ***lan** ta-**koon** **fee** al-**beyt.***
> You (m/s) will not be (m/s) in the house.

Do you see what I mean about sticking to the present tense? How far you take your studies with ***ley**-sa* is entirely up to you.

"Not" That Again

You have now seen how ***ley**-sa* can be used to help you negate sentences, but what about the sentences themselves? Is there anything we can do to make the sentences a little more exciting? After all, your friends are likely to grow tired of conversation with you pretty quickly if you keep telling them things like "The cat is in the car" and "The dog is not in the car."

> **Tips**
>
> In Arabic, you can change adjectives to nouns when describing people. All you have to do is put *al* in front of the adjective. For example, *al-mow-**jood*** does not mean "present" but rather, "one who is present." Likewise, *al-m'a-**roof*** means "one who is well-known." To make plurals out of these nouns from adjectives, you add the plural ending *–oon* or *–een*.

I think I have a solution for you. Why not use ***ley**-sa* to get a little descriptive? Try the following drill for each of the following descriptive words. Use the different forms of ***ley**-sa* with each of the following adjectives to form sentences.

I'll give you one example to get started:

> ***jaa**-nat **ley**-sat mow-**jood**-a al-**yoom**.*
> Janet is not present today.

*mow-**jood***	present
*muq-**tad**-ir*	capable
*m'a-**roof***	known
***qaa**-dir/mu-ta-**mak**-kin min …*	to be able to …
*maj-**hool***	unknown
*maf-**qood***	missing
***ghaa**-'hib*	absent
***gheyr qaa**-dir*	incapable
*gha-**reeb***	strange
***'aaa**-dee*	common
***qa**-wee*	strong
***Da**-'ieef*	weak
*mus-**ta**-'id*	ready
***ley**-sa mus-**ta**-'id*	not ready

***kha**-Tir*	dangerous
***gheyr mu'h**-dhee*	harmless
*maj-**noon***	crazy
*ma'a-**qool***	sane
***il**-a al-**a**-bad*	forever
***a**-ba-dan*	never

If you can keep adding these new language tips to the Arabic dictionary in your mind, you will soon see that even if your pronunciation is a bit off now and then, your capability will outweigh any problems you might have being understood. Keep up the good work!

I Need to Send a Letter

The Internet and technological advances allow us to send messages at the speed of light, virtually anywhere in the world. But do you know what? Old-fashioned "snail mail" still has an important place in our collective hearts. Why else would kiosks in tourist locations around the world continue to sell postcards?

Depending on who you talk to, I am sure you would get different answers about what types of mail are best today—now that we can send mail from so far away so quickly. For me, electronic mail is convenient, but when I want to say something from the heart, I am much more likely to write it down and send it in a letter.

Whatever your personal motivations may be for wanting to send a letter, you aren't going to be able to do it (okay, maybe you could) if you can't explain what you need. The following list should help you take care of any postal issues you might have.

*aH-**taaj an** ur-**sil** ri-**saa**-la …*

I need to send a letter …

***keyf**-a **yum**-kin al-Ha-**Sool** 'a-**ley** …*

How is it possible to get a …

*ya-**koon daar** al-ba-**reed** qa-**reeb***

*min hu-**naa** a-**ley**-sa ka-**dha**-lik?*

There is a post office near here, isn't that so?

*ri-**saa**-la*	letter
*ba-**reed***	post (mail)
*uj-ra al-ba-**reed***	postage
*mu-**kaa**-faaa*	fee
*'un-**waan** al-i-**yaab***	return address
***da**-ra-ja **oo**-la*	first class
*ba-**reed jow**-wee*	airmail
***'ul**-ba*	package (a packet)
waq**-t al-wu-**Sool	delivery time
*bi-**Taa**-qa ba-ree-**dee**-ya*	postcard
***Taa**-bi-'aa*	(a) stamp
***shaH**-Hann*	shipping (shipment)
faaks	facsimile (fax)
*mu-**ghal**-laf*	envelope
***Sun**-dooq*	carton (box)
***ar**-sa-la/**yur**-sil*	sent/he sends
Taa**-bi-'aa ba-**reed	postage stamp
Sun**-dooq ba-**reed	postage box (mailbox)
daar** al-ba-**reed	post office

def•i•ni•tion

*a-**ley**-sa ka-**dha**-lik* literally means "Is it not like this?" In speech, we use it to verify information we have stated, such as the word "right" in English. For example, ***jaan fee** al-**beyt**, a-**ley**-sa ka-**dha**-lik?* means "John is in the house, right?" You can use *a-**ley**-sa ka-**dha**-lik* when you want to impress your friends or whenever you want to verify things you are not certain of.

If you do need to send a letter or a package, you need to remember that not only do currencies differ from country to country, but so do the taxes that will be applied to the package. Also, it is up to you to determine whether the item you are trying to send can legally be sent to your desired location.

For example, in certain countries it may be possible to purchase plant or animal products that another country does not allow. Trying to mail products like these could result in you having to give the product up—or worse, someone having to pay heavy fees or fines to pick up the package once it arrives at its destination.

Despite warnings for forbidden items, you should have little problem finding the right place and way to send your mail, letters, packages, boxes, or whatever you wish.

Take Care of It Yourself

My grandpa used to tell me over and over, "Can't never did a thing." As I grew older, I realized he was right. I also realized that he probably had to make that statement to me far more often than he should have. Oh well.

Since you bought this book, I am betting that you are the type of person who likes to solve problems for yourself. Why else would you try to teach yourself one of the most difficult languages English speakers can attempt to learn? I'm sure you understand by now that there is a lot in this book (and in learning in general) that is left completely up to you. I can only teach you so much.

But you should be proud; you're still going. I guess you already knew that "can't never did a thing." So, in the spirit of my grandpa's words, why not try to take care of a couple more of those "things" by yourself?

I Have a Problem

There is no problem so small that it goes unnoticed. If it did, I doubt we'd bother calling it a "problem." But even if a problem does exist and it bothers us to some extent, that doesn't mean the problem needs to ruin our day. We just have to talk about it. And maybe we need to explain the problem to the right person.

m'a ***man*** *yum-****kin*** *a-ta-****kal****-lam 'an* ***ha****-dha-hi al-****mush****-kil-a?*

With whom might I speak about this problem?

'and*-ee* ***mush****-kil-a ja-****deed****-a.*

I have a new problem.

***ley**-sat **mush**-kil-a*	no problem
*ba-**Seet***	simple
*ya-ta-**sar**-rab **min**-hu **ghaaz***	it is leaking gas
***hee**-a **maz**-za-qa*	it is torn
*hu-**naa**-ka **fat**-Ha **fee**-haa*	there is a hole in it
*mu-**kas**-sa-ra*	broken (cracked)
*mu-**aq**-qad*	complicated
***'and**-hu **raa**-'hi-Ha **see**-'ha*	it has a bad odor
***gheyr naq**-ee*	not fresh
*mu-ta-**'af**-fin*	rotten
*al-mi-**yaah baa**-ri-da*	the water is cold
***ley**-sa la-**dey**-haa **Hib**-r*	it has no ink
*al-ow-**raaq** muz-**da**-hi-ma*	the paper is jammed
*hoo-a Da-**'ieef***	it is weak

When you are describing your problem, remember that ***mush**-kil-a* is a feminine noun. That means any adjectives describing the problem also will have to be feminine. For example, if the problem is "complicated," it is a *mush-**kil**-a mu-**aq**-qad-a*. A further note on "problem" is that sometimes people will pronounce the word ***mush**-kil-a* and at other times they will say *mush-**kil**-a*. Both are correct.

Services for Citizens

Sometimes you may have to take care of issues that require specialized help—the type of help you can only get from a government agency. What do you think you might do in such instances? The first thing you need to realize is you should never be nervous about going to an embassy or consulate if you are in a foreign country. The entire purpose of those organizations is to provide services to citizens who are living in or visiting the country where the embassy or consulate is located.

Tips

Whenever you visit a foreign country, you are responsible for following the laws of that country. Your embassy or consulate makes an excellent resource for those laws. Therefore, you might want to schedule a trip to the embassy or consulate at the beginning of your vacation. Be sure to schedule the visit well in advance, however, as the civil servants are likely to be very busy.

There are many issues that might start you looking for an embassy or consulate:

Track 53

*si-**faa**-ra*	embassy
*qun-Su-**lee**-ya*	consulate
*sa-**feer***	ambassador
***qun**-Sul*	consul
*taa'h-**sheer**-a*	visa
***saa**-kin*	resident
***suk**-na*	residence
***rukh**-Sa*	permit
*mu-**tar**-jim*	translator
*wa-**keel***	agent
***mow**-'id*	appointment
*ij-ti-**maa'a***	meeting
***shaa**-hid*	witness
*mu-**waa**-Tin*	citizen
*taj-**deed***	renewal
*i-**Taa**-la*	extension
***ma**-da-nee*	civil
*mugh-**ta**-rib*	expatriate

Practice Makes Perfect

One more chapter down. Congratulations! A few quick questions (and as much review as you wish to make) and you will be on to the next chapter and even closer to the end of the book!

1. Translate: ***ha-dha**-a **ley**-sa al-qa-**meeS** u-**reed**-hu.*
2. How might you say, "My brother works in a Laundromat"?
3. Translate: ***kaa**-na **jeyd** wa-**laa**-kin **ley**-sa al-**aH**-san.*
4. Translate: *hal **an**-ta tu-**qaa**-dir **an** tu-**sheer** 'al-**ey** ma-**kaan** lil-taS-**leeH** **'al**-a **aa**-la taS-**weer?***
5. Translate: ***naH**-nu **mash**-ghool-**oon** al-**aan,** wa-**laa**-kin **lan** na-koon-**oon** mow-jood-**oon** fee al-mus-**taq**-bil.*
6. How might you say, "I might send this box as air mail"?

The Least You Need to Know

- There is a service for every issue. All you need to do is ask.
- If looking for a massage, be aware of cultural considerations.
- ***ley**-sa* always means "not."
- Make sure you find out where the consulate or embassy is in the area you are traveling.

Chapter 24

Getting the Word Out

In This Chapter

- Spreading the word
- More than one way to phone home
- Tell me what you really think
- Keeping things calm

You have spent almost an entire book learning how to express yourself. In this chapter, you finally get the chance to talk … and talk … and talk. This chapter is *all* about talking. Whether you are trying to use the phone or just converse with someone on the street, you are going to see how much you really can say in Arabic.

We start with a little bit of background on the phone services you can expect, then go on to learn some new vocabulary. After that, I give you the chance to express some opinions. I also show you how to work a little on your accent. Finally, you take charge of the situation and learn some words that can help you if you ever need to calm someone down. So … why wait?

Ground Control to Major Networks

This may come as no surprise to you, but depending on where you visit in the Arab world, your ability to use a telephone may be extremely limited. While using a public phone or a cellular phone in a city may present no problems at all, trying to get in touch with someone while you are on safari may prove extremely difficult. Certainly, some of you are thinking, "Of course you can't get service out in the desert. That's one of the greatest things about a safari. No one can get in touch with you!"

I wouldn't even bother mentioning the fact except that it is easy for me to imagine an unwitting tourist, angrily shaking a cell phone, saying, "Why can't I get *service* out here!" I don't want you to be that kind of tourist, so I thought it best to warn you.

Calling All Phones

Anymore, I'm sure you have come to expect that your hotel room will have a phone and Internet access. If you need a fax machine, there is one located at the front desk or in the hotel's business center. You also know, though, if you are dependent on these (or any specific amenities), it is good to ask before you book a room so that there aren't any surprises when you arrive at your destination.

Once you do arrive at your hotel and get settled in your room, you might need to use that phone to call home and check in. Here are some words and phrases to help you make that phone call home a little smoother.

Tips

If you call from a hotel to an international number, be sure you understand *all* the charges you are paying. You might pay a connection fee from the hotel and also from the local and national phone services from where you are calling. Then, you may pay an extra connection fee to the number you are calling. Such calls quickly become very expensive and it may be a good idea to use a calling card instead.

***maa**-dha tas-ta-**Tey**-'u **an** ta-**qool lee 'an** …*

What are you able to tell me about …

*hal **hoo**-a **ghaa**-lee al-Ha-**Sool 'al**-a …*

Is it expensive to get …

maa-*dha* ***a***-*f'al* ***idh***-*a* …

What do I do if …

haa-*tif*	phone
ta'a-***reef***-*a*	tariff
ma-***jaa***-*nee*	toll-free
i-ti-***Saal doo***-*lee*	international call
it-ti-***Saal*** *ma-Ha*-***lee***-*a*	local call
haa-*tif 'u*-***moo***-*mee*	public phone
khaTT khaaS	private line
sow-*fa it*-***taS***-*al* ***bi***-*ka*	I will call you
raq-*mee* ***hoo***-*a*	my number is
khaa-*raj min*-***Taq***-*a al*-***khid***-*ma*	out of the service area
bi-***Taa***-*qa* ***haa***-*tif*-***ee***-*ya*	telephone card
al-***raq***-*m* ***hoo***-*a mash*-***ghool***	the number is busy
al-it-ti-***Saal sey***-*'han*	bad connection
ley-*sa ta*-***koon khid***-*ma*	there is no service
Ta-***neen*** *al-ti*-***qaaT***	dial tone
baad-*'hi-a*	prefix

Stay on the Line

The world has definitely become smaller thanks to technology, and my personal observation is that with this shrinking world, we have less and less tolerance for the little inconveniences we may encounter. Suddenly, the Internet is too slow because we can't access our e-mail in two seconds—or a cellular phone that cuts out causes us to become just a little bit angry.

I only bring these points up because you may end up having to deal with them when traveling in or communicating with someone in the Arab world. The chances of a bad connection are slim if you are calling someone in a city or a large hotel because the phone systems and networks in those places are well established. If you are trying to connect to or from a rural area, however, the networks could be brand new—and in some cases, not more than a couple years old. Just be patient.

And to help you keep your cool (although you might be standing in the desert sun trying to make an important phone call), here are some more vocabulary words and phrases to help you explain yourself to the person on the other end of the line.

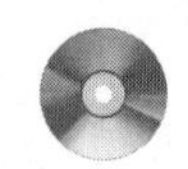

Track 54

*tash-**weesh***	static
*tash-**weesh bath** i-**dhaa**-'iee*	static interference
***'aaa**-mal al-**haa**-tif*	telephone operator
*tab-**deel***	(a) transfer
*ba-**daa**-la*	phone exchange
***haa**-tif **qam**-ree*	satellite phone
*a-**'ad** al-it-ti-**Saal bee**-ya*	return my call
***tha**-man li-da-**qeeq**-a **waa**-Hi-da*	cost per minute
*da-**qaa**-'hiq ma-**jaa-nee**-ya*	free minutes
*in-**qa**-Ta'aa al-**khaTT***	the line cut out
***ley**-sat ta-**koon khid**-ma*	there is no service
*i-**dhaa**-'aa **qa**-wee-a*	strong signal
*khaT-**Teyn***	two lines (call waiting)
*al-**baT**-Tar-**ree**-ya Da-**'ieef**-a*	battery is weak

***mum**-kin ta-**ta-Sil bee 'al**-a al-**khaTT** al-**aa**-khar?*
Can you call me on the other line?

1001 Arabian Notes

Just like during a face-to-face greeting, you should keep your phone conversations polite when dealing with Arabic speakers. While you may have to ask them to speak slowly (*raj-**jaa**-'han at-ta-**kal**-lam bi-**buT**-Ta'h*), you should always speak clearly and with your best pronunciation so they can understand you.

If you have an important phone call to make and seem to be out of luck because you can't get service on your own phone, you should remember that ever-important rule: "Ask someone to help you." If there is a way for a local citizen to help you make a phone call, he or she will do it for you. After all, think of the story that person will be able to tell his or her friends about the tourist whose phone didn't work!

Asking someone for help also will give you one more chance to practice your speaking ability—and the more chances you find, the better.

If you absolutely must be accessible by phone no matter where you are, you might want to invest in a satellite phone. With it, you can call and receive calls from virtually anywhere in the world. While that may be good for those who are on business trips, some of us are not so excited about our boss being able to call us—no matter how far away we try to go on vacation.

The Human Telegraph

One of the biggest shocks I got when I first visited the Arab world was the amount of information that is passed through conversation. Until I started talking to native speakers, I never truly understood how few *conversations* I actually had during the course of a day. I also came to realize that I was far less informed on world events than many of the people around me. That put me at a bit of a disadvantage.

Now with more experience, I have realized that the constant discussion of world and personal events—every day through continuous conversation—is just one part of an entire culture I am only now beginning to understand. There is a lot of information to be gained about a person by the way he or she talks. We can hear where he or she comes from by his or her accent. We can tell what that person likes and dislikes. We also can see what we might have in common with that person that would help strengthen our friendship. Even the most talkative English speakers I know would have a hard time keeping up with all the discussions a native Arabic speaker might have before breakfast in the morning.

You might as well be ready for plenty of talking. And do you know what? As much as I'd like to say this book has everything you need, the truth is that talking with and mimicking native speakers is the best way for you to improve your pronunciation.

If you are going to visit the Arab world, you should be prepared to answer some questions. Most likely, people will know that you are a tourist based on the way you look, the way you dress, or the way you talk to other members of your group. If you keep your cover through those evaluations, certainly the way you speak Arabic will give you away. Don't let this make you nervous. Just admit it: you are a tourist. No matter where you visit in the world, locals can spot tourists. That's the way things work.

If you are looking to get attention focused away from the fact that you are a tourist and that maybe you don't "fit in" like those around you, I discovered a great trick. After you have introduced yourself, start asking questions. I already told you that Arabic speakers love to talk, and there is nothing they would love more than to tell you their stories. This gives you a fascinating look at a world you might not otherwise see.

When you're speaking Arabic, people will naturally want to know where you learned it and where you are from. If you notice that locals are having problems understanding what you are saying (and you are nervous about your accent), you can ask them for help:

> ***keyf**-a a-**qool ha**-dhaa mith-l-**kum?***
>
> How do I say that like you (all)?

Then, you can say:

> *u-**reed an** a-**Has**-san **lah**-ja-**tee.***
>
> I want to improve my accent.

Warnings

As you begin to speak more Arabic and begin to improve your pronunciation, you may notice that your throat hurts. This symptom doesn't necessarily mean that you are becoming ill. It could be that the muscles in your throat are actually tired from learning to move and stretch in ways they have never had to before. With time, this feeling goes away.

So how are you going to keep up with conversation and all of the latest news passing through the "human telegraph"? The following list should help you.

***an**-ta a-**keed min** …*	You are certainly from …
***na**-sha-ra al-ka-li-ma*	spread the word
***shaa**-'hi-'aa*	rumor
Haq	truth
*mu-**Haa**-da-tha*	conversation
*u-**shee**-'a **an**-na …*	It is rumored that …
***sa**-m'aa/**yas**-ma'a*	he heard/he hears
*khi-**Taab***	speech (lecture)
***kadh**-ib*	(a) lie
*hal **an**-ta **mu**-ta-**'hak**-kad?*	Are you certain?
*ta-**dal**-lal **'al**-a **ha**-dhaa*	prove it

*ka-**laam***	talking
*Ha-**deeth***	speech
***maa**-dha **ya'a**-nee **dha**-lik*	What does that mean
*hal sa-**ma'aa**-ta*	Did you hear
***lam** a-**qool dha**-lik*	I didn't say that
***fee** ja-**reed**-a*	in a magazine
***ha**-dhaa **ley**-sa **maa** qa-**Sad**-tu*	That's not what I meant
*hal **yum**-kin-ka ath-**baat** **dha**-lik*	Can you prove that
***an**-a **is**-ma'a*	I am listening
ha**-dhaa Sa-**HeeH	That is true
*m'a-ka al-**Haq***	You are right
*raa-**'bey**-tu-hu **m'a** 'a-**yoon**-ee*	I saw it with my eyes
***kun**-tu **las**-tu mu-ta-**'ha**-kid*	I was not sure
***fee** aS-Sa-**Hee**-fa*	In the newspaper
*Sad-**diq**-nee*	Believe me
***man qaal**-ta **dha**-lik?*	Who told you that?
keyf**-a a-**qool ha**-dhaa mith-l-**kum?	How do I say that like you do?
***ai** qa-**naaa** akh-**baa**-ree-ya tu-**shaa**-hid?*	What news channel do you watch?

Slowly, you are developing the skills of a great storyteller. Sure, you will have to practice for more than a couple of days to get all of your details down and to start sounding like you have spent years traveling with caravans across Arabian sands—but you already knew that learning Arabic would be difficult. If you wanted "easy," you could have studied something else.

Don't Stay There

A lot of small talk is fine for a while, but you probably will get tired of it before too long. As you may already know, Arabs are fascinating to talk with and what better way to learn a language than by learning how to exchange *opinions?*

Expressing Opinions

One thing is for certain about opinions: everyone has them. By one definition, an opinion is more than an impression because you have taken the time to think about a subject. But an opinion is also not necessarily based on fact. So opinions are somewhere between impressions and facts. That makes them perfect for conversation.

> **1001 Arabian Notes**
>
> It is okay to have a difference of opinion when conversing in Arabic. In fact, many Arabic conversations are more exciting when the speakers begin to get excited as they try to prove why their opinion is correct. But you should always make sure to respect the other person—even if it means conceding part of your argument to them.

Opinions are good things—especially in the Arab world. Keep your opinions in mind when you enter into discussions, because people (lots of people!) are going to want to know them. And people are also going to want to know what you think of *their* opinions. In such situations, you might want to be a little more careful about what you say. It would be impolite to belittle someone's personal opinion.

The following list shows some opinions you might have. The list is in no way complete, but it should give you a good start.

*a'a-**ta**-qid **an**-na-**hu*** …

I believe it is …

raa**-'hey-tu **dha**-lik wa a'a-**ta**-qid **kaa-na (***kaa**-nat*, and so on) …

I saw that and I think it was …

jeyd	good
***sey**-'hi*	bad
***gheyr** muk-**ta**-rith*	indifferent
***raa**-'hee*	opinion
qool lee	tell me
***maa raa'h**-yu-ka?*	What is your opinion?
***mur**-'ib*	horrible
***maa** u-**fak**-kir …*	what I think …
*mus-**ta**-qil*	independent
*mu-**naa**-qa-sha*	discussion

***qar**-ra-ra/yu-**qar**-rir*	decided/he decides
***laa baa**-'has*	not bad
***mu**-mil*	boring
*mu-**shaw**-wiq*	interesting
*maq-**bool***	acceptable
'al**-a **maa** yu-**raam	okay (as it should be)
*mun-**fa**-rid*	lonely
*qa-**beeH***	ugly
*mah-**joor***	deserted
*ja-**meel***	pretty

Just as I explained when I told you how to improve your accent by asking someone to help you with your pronunciation, asking someone's opinion is a great way to get them to talk (and get you involved in even more conversations). All you have to do is say, "***maa raa'h**-yu-ka **'an** ...*" ("What is your opinion about ...?")—then let the other person take over.

I actually really enjoy asking questions this way. One of my favorite tricks (and you can do this in any language) is to ask someone's opinion and after they give it, ask them why they think that way (*li-**maa**-dha?*).

Don't be surprised if you ask those two questions and end up involved in a 15-minute discussion. That is the power of opinions. And finally, if you really are interested in hearing opinions (and please be careful not to offend anyone if you choose to do this), you can ask someone about something you know they do not like. Their opinion on such matters is likely to be very strong, and they will be more than ready to talk about it.

Everyone has their own opinions, and those opinions help make our individual personalities. So enjoy the opinions you have already—and as long as you are talking in Arabic, why not see whether you can pick up a new opinion or two. At the very least, try to understand how others might see things a bit differently than you do.

Giving Advice for Journeys

Luckily, there is more to be gained from opinions than just "pushing someone's buttons" to get them to talk. Opinions are also a great way to find out about locations you might want to visit on your vacation or for your new friends to get advice from you about where they should go in *your* home country.

If you have been somewhere before, you can tell others your opinion—and that might help make their decision a little easier.

Of course, in order to give someone advice, you are going to have to know what to say.

***qad kun**-tu hu-**naa**-ka min **qab**-l.*	I have been there before.
***laa tab**-qa hu-**naa**-ka!*	Don't stay there!
*aT-**T'aaam** la-**dheedh.***	The food is delicious.
***ya**-jib an tu-**shaa**-hid …*	You must see (witness) …
*yum-kin-**nee an** ow-Sa **bi** …*	I can recommend …
*ja-**deer** bil-**tha**-man*	worth the cost
*da-**khool** ma-**jaa**-nan*	entry is free
***hee**-a **magh**-laq-a aH-**Hyaa**-nan.*	It is closed sometimes.
*ta-**'ha**-khadh ma-**laa**-bis **maa**-ni-'aa lil-bu-**roo**-da.*	Take warm clothing.
*ta-**'ha**-khadh mu-**zeyd** min al-**maal m'a**-kum.*	Take extra money with you.
*ta-**jeeb maa'h.***	Bring water.
tadh**-hab **fee** al-ma-**saa'h.	Go in the evening.
***ya**-jib 'al-**ey**-kum al-is-ti-**maa'a il**-a al-**moo-see**-qa.*	You must hear the music.
*mi-**thaa**-lee-a li-'a-**waa**-'hil*	exemplary for families
***ley**-sa **fee** ai ma-**kaan aa**-khar*	not anywhere else
*hu-**naa**-ka **an**-THi-ma mal-bi-**see**-ya.*	There is a dress code.
*al-aT-**faal** gheyr mas-**mooH.***	Children are not allowed.
waa**-Hid min **now**-'a-**haa	one of a kind (unique)
*ya-jib an ta-**koon mus**-lim*	must be a Muslim

*hu-**naa**-ka* **Had aq**-*Sa li-**san**.*	There is an age limit.
*al-da-**khool** mam-**noo**-'a.*	Entry is forbidden.
*si-nu-'aa-id **il**-a hu-**naa**-ka.*	We will go back there.

Giving advice can be tricky business. I have had instances where I told someone that I had a good time at a particular place, so they went—only to have no fun at all. Then, when they came back, their experience was somehow *my fault* because I told them to go there. When your Arabic-speaking friends ask you for travel advice, be sure to consider their point of view when they will be traveling, and so on. When you ask them for advice about which sights you should see, ask what time of year is best and why. You don't want to end up on the ski slope in the summer, do you?

1001 Arabian Notes

If you want to be extremely polite when speaking in Arabic, you can refer to a singular person in the plural form. For example, when asking an opinion, you might say "***maa raa'h**-yu-kum*" instead of "***maa raa'h**-yu-ka.*" This shows that you value someone's opinion and have a high respect for them. You can see similar speech if you read Shakespearean English.

Trying to Calm Someone Down

There are many things to get excited over in life, but often we get a little more excited than necessary. Maybe we have problems dealing with stress, or maybe we just fear unknown circumstances. Whatever the cause, it is important that we try to keep from becoming too agitated.

If you are traveling to a foreign land for the first time, the experience can be overwhelming at times. When you travel to the Arab world, you are probably going to experience many things that you have not seen before. For some people, such an "unusual" experience quickly can become confusing and lead to fear. If you see this happening (perhaps with one of your children or someone in a tour group with you), you should try to help.

Here are some basic phrases that you might be able to use to try and calm someone down. (Note: naturally, you will need to combine them with the language you already know. You wouldn't just walk up to a crying child and say, "Distraction!")

is**-ta-**riH!	Relax!
***laa af**-ham.*	I don't understand.
*tu-**sak**-kin **nafs**-ka.*	Calm yourself.

laa *ta-***kha***-fa.*	Don't fear.
qa*-laq*	anxiety
*sa-***laam**	peace
maa hee*-a al-mush-***kil***-a?*	What's the problem?
tas*-lee-a*	distraction
Sar*-kha*	(a) scream
*ghaD-***baan**	angry
*qi-***taal**	(a) fight
*ta-***Had***-da-tha/ya-ta-***Had***-dath*	spoke/he speaks
*uD-***Hoo***-ka*	joke
shey*-'han lil-sha-***raab**	something to drink
*ta'a-***baan**	tired
madh*-a* ***Ha****-da-tha?*	What happened?
*mu-***Ham***-mis*	exciting
Haa*-dith*	accident
*aD-***raar**	injuries
tab*-qey hu-***naa.**	Stay here.
*ta-***na***-fas 'a-***mee***-qan.*	Breathe deeply.
*yum-***kin***-nee u-***saa***-'id-ka?*	Can I help?

1001 Arabian Notes

Remember what I wrote earlier about Arabic being an animated language? If you see two men standing on the street corner yelling at one another and you think you need to jump in and try to calm them down, you may end up looking a bit foolish. They may just be old friends talking about the weather. Be sure you understand situations before you involve yourself.

Track 56

***ai**-na **an**-ta tu-**Haa**-wil an **tadh**-hab?*
Where are you trying to go?

***man tab**-Hath **'an**?*
Who are you looking for?

*hal raa-**'hey**-ta …*
Have you seen …

*hal fa-**qad**-ta **shey**-'han?*
Have you lost something?

***ai**-na **kun**-ta **'and**-a-maa ra-**'hey-ta-haa** al-**mar**-ra al-a-**kheer**-a?*
Where were you when you last saw it?

***yum**-kin is-tib-**daal**-hu?*
Is it replaceable?

***maa man ya**-jib an ta-ta-**kal**-lam?*
Who must you speak with?

***man y'a**-rif **ai**-na **an**-ta?*
Who knows where you are?

*hal qa-**dam**-ta taq-**reer?***
Have you filed a report?

*li-**nan**-zil!*
Let's go!

***n'am hoo**-a **mu**-him.*
Yes, it is important.

***hee**-a maa **zaa**-la **am**-na.*
It is still safe.

***laa** ya-**zaal kaa**-mi-lan*
still complete

Practice Makes Perfect

So how much did you learn in this chapter? Take the quick quiz and find out. Translate the following sentences from Arabic to English and English to Arabic as appropriate. Note: your English to Arabic translations might be a bit different than mine. Don't worry about that. Just do your best.

1. ***ha**-dhaa **raq**-mee ja-**deed** ta-**Ta**-Sil **bee**-ya **ghad**-dan*
2. ***sa**-m'aa-tu **dha**-lik wa a'a-**ta**-qid **an** al-mush-**kil**-a **kaa**-nat al-**baT**-Tar-**ree**-ya*
3. "I am able to recommend more than just that restaurant."
4. "How do I know who you need to speak with?"
5. ***low tadh**-hab hu-**naa**-ka **ya**-jib an **t'a**-rif ta-**koon an**-THi-ma mal-bi-**see**-ya*
6. *yum-**kin**-nee u-**saa**-'id-ka? ta-**na**-fas 'a-**mee**-qan wa **tab**-qey hu-**naa. ab**-Hath 'an **'aaa**-'hi-**la**-tu-ka*

The Least You Need to Know

- When traveling to a different country, you may have to get used to dealing with a different level of phone service.
- In the Arab world, word of mouth is often your best source for news.
- You will not be able to hide the fact that you are a tourist for long.
- You can get a good conversation underway just by asking someone's opinion.
- You may not be allowed into all destinations.

Chapter 25

Business and Beyond

In This Chapter

- Jumping around jargon
- Processing high-speed Arabic
- Finding your way around the house
- Finding even more

It's hard to believe you have come this far already, but here you are … almost to the end of this book. Hopefully you have learned a thing or two along the way.

In this next-to-last chapter, you learn some of the language you might need as you move from just repeating sentences to actually functioning and working in Arabic (at least, at the basic level). We start out with computer and business terminology. After you learn what you need to say at meetings, we move to useful household terms and words to help you settle into the Arabic lifestyle. Finally, I give you several suggestions for finding more information about learning Arabic. The chapter ends with your very last quiz. Enjoy!

Specify Your Speech

In order to get specific about your speech, you are going to have to put some new words to use. The following list of words (prepositions, actually, but that's not the important part) will be very useful to you as you advance your Arabic studies. These are the words that you will find yourself using to fill in the quiet gaps in your conversation. You will use these and similar phrases to express your thoughts more clearly. After all, no sentence needs a prepositional phrase (refer to Chapter 7 for more prepositions), but they do improve the sentence quality when you use them.

So, here's what I would like you to do: take a look at the following list and read the terms out loud. When you have finished that, try to use each of the words in a sentence. You don't have to make the sentences complicated, but you should try to speak at an even speed—the way you have heard Arabic speakers talk. It wouldn't be much use for you to practice speaking very slowly if you were expected to speak quickly in conversation. Practice as long as you need. The rest of the chapter should still be printed on the page when you are finished.

Track 64

*bil-**rugh**-m*	despite (with the exception)
*bi-**maa'h***	including (with what)
*bil-'hi-**Daa**-fa **'il**-a*	in addition to
*bi-**sab**-ab*	because of
'al**-a **Tool	along
*bi-**jaa**-nib*	beside
*bi-**'his**-tith-**naa'h***	with exception
***waf**-qan **'il**-a*	according to
*bi-**daa**-khil*	inside
***fee** al-**khaa**-rij*	outside
*min ja-**deed***	from anew
*min **beyn***	among
*bi-khu-**SooS***	regarding
***Ha**-wa-la*	around
*min **taHt***	beneath

***naH**-wa*	facing
*ba'a-**ee**-dan **'an***	far removed
ba**-da-lan **min	instead of
*mu-**Daa**-fan **'il**-a*	plus
***naa**-qis*	minus
*bi-**waa**-Si-ta*	through (by way of)
*ya-ta-**Dam**-man*	including
Hai**-thu-**maa	wherever
kul**-la-**maa'h	whenever
***Hat**-ta*	until
***idh**-a*	if (used alone)
il**-a **an	except that

How did your sentences turn out? I hope you didn't have too many problems with them. Even more importantly, I hope that you will still remember them when you return to the lessons in this book after taking a break. And speaking of breaks, I will give you one in just a moment—right after I give you one more phrase that will help you start out your sentences.

The term ***yab**-du **an*** means "It appears that …". So:

> ***yab**-du **an**-kum mus-**ta**-'id-**oon** lil-di-**raa**-sa fee al-**qis**-m ath-**thaa**-nee!*
>
> It appears that you all are ready to study in the second section!

Well, who am I to slow you down?

At the Speed of Electrons

Today, business moves at the speed of light (literally). With a cellular phone and Internet connection, I can control business and banking transactions from almost anywhere in the world—and the transactions happen as quickly as service personnel and automation allow.

What does that mean for your Arabic ability? Well, for one thing, it means you are going to have to learn an entirely new business vocabulary than the generation before you. Instead of talking about typewriters and overhead projectors, you will be talking about processors and networks. There are plenty of other terms, as well, but why spoil the discovery when all the new words are waiting for you in just a few paragraphs?

Computer Terminology

When I was in high school, the phrase "computer terminology" as I understood it meant "language that a computer uses" or "language that a computer understands." Maybe I was way off the mark in my understanding, but these days computer terminology has made its way into our everyday world. To witness this phenomenon, I have to look no further than to my grandmother, who now speaks of computers freezing in much the same way she may have spoken of ponds freezing during her youth. Times have changed.

For you to be an effective Arabic speaker—particularly if you need Arabic for business purposes—you will need to be able to use technology and computer terms in everyday speech. That's why I am giving you some terms here.

sha-*ba-ka*	network
*a-da-****waat***	hardware
*ba-****raa****-maj*	software (programs)
faa'h-*r*	mouse
laa sil-*kee*	wireless
yad-*wee*	handheld
*koom-****byoo****-tir*	computer
*koom-****byoo****-tir maH-****mool***	laptop computer
maa-*siH Dow-****'hee***	scanner
*tab-****baa'a***	printer
sur-*'aa*	speed
Hab-*l*	cable
kaart fee-*dee-yoo*	video card
lu'u-*ba* ***fee***-*dee-yoo*	video game
*ta-****waq****-qa-fa al-koom-****byoo****-tir*	the computer froze (stopped)

***mush**-kil-a ib-ti-**daa**-'hee-a*	startup problem
*mu-**Daad** lil-**fee**-roo-**saat***	anti-virus
*mu-**'aaa**-la-ja*	processor
silk	wire
***shaa**-sha*	keyboard
***low**-Ha ma-**faa**-taH*	screen
*tan-**zeel***	download
faH**-HuS a-**maan	security check

Now, because I am certain you have already memorized this list and taken the time to commit each word to its own sentence so you can remember it better, I have a couple questions for you. What are some situations where you might find yourself needing to use the words from this list? How about the following:

*aH-**taaj b'aD** gha-**raaD li**-koom-**byoo**-tir-**nee**.*

I need some gear (equipment) for my computer.

***hal 'and**-kum **kaart** li-**sha**-ba-ka **laa sil**-kee-ya?*

Do you have a card for a wireless network?

I've shown you just two examples. How many can you create? Try to turn your answers into a story in order to practice developing your speech patterns so that they take on a more natural flow. Note: I understand this may be difficult at first, but with practice you will get there in no time.

Be a Team Player

I'll never forget the time when, during halftime of a high-school basketball game, our coach reminded us of the common saying: "There is no 'I' in 'team'." I will never forget it, because the boy standing next to me whispered just loud enough for me (but not our coach) to hear, "There's no 'I' in 'sauerkraut', either." Well, they were both right.

These days, a lot of work is done on a per-project, per-assignment basis. "Teams" are made up of specialists in various fields who come together, put a package (product) together, and go their separate ways when the project is finished.

Experience has shown me that the best team members are those who are willing to learn from one another. After all, as the saying goes, you cannot teach someone who already knows everything. You are still reading this book, so I'm betting you don't feel like you know everything. Well, even if I can't teach you everything, I can teach you a few more words so that you can go out and be the best team player possible.

*bar-**naa**-maj*	program
***khuT**-Ta*	project
***fir**-qa*	team
*ma-**ham**-ma*	assignment
***fat**-ra*	term
***Had za**-ma-nee*	deadline
*taq-**reer***	report
*takh-**TeeT***	draft
***nus**-kha*	copy
*mu-**deer***	manager (director)
*qi-**yaa**-da*	leadership
***'u**-Doo*	member
***za'a**-eem*	leader
*ra-**'hees***	president (boss)
naa**-'hib ra-**'hees	vice president
*sak-ra-**teer***	secretary
***Saa**-Hib*	owner (also "friend")
*ij-ti-**maa'a***	meeting
*mu-**qaa**-ba-la*	interview
*tas-**weeq***	marketing
bu**-yu'u-**aat	sales
*Si-**naa'a***	production
*taH-**leel***	analysis

*takh-**TeeT***	planning
*ti-**jaa**-ra*	business (trade)
*tak-**nee**-kee*	technical
***qis**-m*	section/division
***shugh**-l*	business (work)
*man-**tooj***	product
***m'a**-aan*	together

No team is complete without a "chief." As you can see from the previous list, there is more than one word you can use for *leader* in Arabic. While *ra-**'hees*** is listed as meaning "president," the term—like many others in Arabic—can have several meanings. For example, *ra-**'hees*** can be used when someone is the president of a committee (*ra-**'hees** al-**laj**-na*) or it can be used for the "chief" problem (*al-mush-**kil**-a ar-**ra**-'hee-**see**-ya*).

Tips

Although it is important to continually review the new words you have learned, the vocabulary in this section will help you if you decide to return to Chapter 12, where you learned to talk about yourself. For a good practice drill, return to Chapter 12 and see whether you know more about yourself now that you have more business vocabulary.

Caught in a Web

Have you ever watched an episode of a criminal or medical television show and felt a little silly because all of the characters were using terms you had never heard? Did you pretend you understood what they were saying, only to run for the dictionary when no one was looking so that you could look things up? If so, then it is likely that the characters in the show were using *jargon* in their dialog.

Jargon has its appropriate use, but if you are speaking to a group unfamiliar with the terms, jargon quickly becomes confusing. So what does jargon have to do with you learning Arabic? Don't worry, I'm not going to try

def•i•ni•tion

Jargon is language that is difficult for people to understand in everyday conversation because it is confusing or because the terms are used and understood by a specific group. While learning Arabic, you will be better off learning common words first and jargon *after* you have a command of the language basics.

to teach you several pages worth of jargon so that you can impress your colleagues. Instead, you'll be relieved to know you won't have to worry about learning jargon—because jargon in Arabic often is borrowed from English.

So instead of seeing ***shaa**-sha mu-**saT**-Ta-Ha* for "flat-screen," you might hear the Arabic/English-sounding "***al** see **dee**,*" which would be "LCD" (a type of flat-screen monitor or television). Do you understand? Good. I thought so. Remember, avoid jargon when you are speaking—and the jargon you do hear may just be an Arabic version of a word you already know.

So, without further delay, I present your next list:

in**-tir-**nat	Internet
***sha**-ba-ka*	web
***aa**-la **Haa**-si-ba*	computer
*ba-**reed** i-**lak**-**troo**-nee*	e-mail
mow**-q'i al-**in**-tir-**nat	website
***'un**-waan*	address
***'al**-a ash-**sha**-ba-ka*	online
***dar**-da-sha*	chat (casual discussion)
***mu'h**-ta-mar **fee**-dee-yoo*	video conference
***am**-n*	security
***raq**-m **shakh**-See*	Personal Identification Number (PIN)
*Hi-**saab***	account
***Sun**-dooq al-**waa**-rid*	inbox
*zu-**baa**-la*	trash (garbage)
khid**-ma ban-**kee**-ya **'al**-a al-**in**-tir-**nat	online banking
*tas-**weeq** **'al**-a al-**in**-tir-**nat***	online marketing
*Ha-jooz-**aat** **'al**-a al-**in**-tir-**nat***	online reservations
*mu-**taa**-jir **'al**-a al-**in**-tir-**nat***	online trading
taa**-jir **'al**-a al-**in**-tir-**nat	online merchant
sur**-a'aa **'aaa**-lee-ya li-'hit-ti-**Saal	high-speed connection

By now, some of you are probably thinking, "Lists, lists, *lists!* All I do is learn vocabulary words. When are we going to get to the *talking?*" Well, I hope I am not disappointing you when I tell you that you have already learned much of what you need to know to speak a large amount of Arabic at a basic level. At this point, I believe you are better at putting sentences together than I am at putting them together for you. I also believe the space that I would use putting together sentences for you is better used teaching you new vocabulary. That being said, here is a quick test. See whether you can tell me what is strange with the following words. (If you want the test to work, don't cheat and try to look back for the answer.)

*al-**in**-tir-**nat** **'al**-a at-**taa**-jir*

Can you tell what is wrong? Check the word order. If you know that "***'al**-a*" means "on," then can you tell me what item is on what? Actually, "*al-**in**-tir-**nat** **'al**-a at-**taa**-jir*" means "The Internet is on the merchant."

I'm not sure how you might use that sentence and not have it sound strange. The term I mixed for you, ***taa**-jir **'al**-a al-**in**-tir-**nat**,* means "merchant on the Internet" or "online merchant." I highlight this usage because it is interesting to see how changing the word order in Arabic can have a drastic effect on sentence meaning. There. Now you have learned even a little bit more. But I still think we should move on to the next section.

Around the House

You may be asking yourself how I could leave items for around the house until almost the end of the book, when they are things you will deal with every day when you are on vacation or speaking with Arabic friends. There are actually a few reasons why.

Household items are generally personal because they belong to your private life. Although you may use them every day, I'm fairly certain you would not meet a new Arab friend and say "***ah**-lan, is-mee **jaan**. u-**fat**-tish 'an mil-'**aa**-qa.*" While your friend may appreciate you introducing yourself, I doubt that he or she will be interested to know that you are looking for a spoon.

Here are some common words to get you started talking about your home.

baab	door
***mad**-khal*	entrance
***Taa**-wi-la*	table

***kur**-see*	chair
***naa**-fi-dha*	window
*a-**ree**-ka*	sofa
mis**-nad lil-qa-da-**meyn	footstool
farn	oven
*foo-**ta**-ya*	armchair
*khi-**zaa**-na*	cupboard
*ru-**foof***	shelves
*tha-**laa**-ja*	refrigerator
*mu-**jam**-mad*	freezer
HowD	sink
*fin-**jaan***	cup
***SaH**-n*	plate
***Taa**-sa*	bowl
*sik-**keen***	knife
***kaa**-'has*	glass (tumbler)
***show**-ka*	fork
*mil-**'aa**-qa*	spoon
*bar-Ta-**maan***	jar (for canning)
*ib-**reeq***	pot
*i-**naa'h***	pan
durj	drawer
*fi-**raash***	bed
*koo-moo-**dee**-noo*	night table (commode)
*khi-**zaa**-na*	closet
***shur**-fa*	terrace (balcony)
*ar-**Dee**-a*	floor (ground level)

suq-*f*	ceiling
ji-***daar***	wall
si-***taar***	curtain
mir-*wa-Ha as*-***suq***-*f*	ceiling fan
na-baa-***taat***	plants
zu-***hoor***	flowers
man-***fadh***	outlet
saj-***jaa***-*da*	carpet
baT-***Taa***-*nee-ya*	rug (also blanket)
saT-*H*	roof

1001 Arabian Notes

You may have seen that many homes in Arab lands are built of brick and have flat roofs. The bricks serve as great insulation from the sun, and the flat roofs make great locations for a quiet (or not so quiet) evening outside. With little rain to worry about, the roofs provide extra utility space, too.

Settling In

You have finished your vacation and decided you just can't go home—at least, not yet. You want to settle in for a longer stay, and I can't say I blame you. Naturally, you will want to make sure you have everything you need.

"Everything you need," of course, means you will have to find out about residency permits from your host territory, state, or country. You should also use your own government services to confirm your plans. But aside from those "minor details," I want to make sure you have—or can get—all of the things you might really need to relax and enjoy yourself for as long as you decide to stay.

If you plan to stay a lifetime or you just want to have a second home in an Arabic-speaking land, you should try to be as familiar with the culture and customs as you are with your own. By showing that you care to learn, you will show your Arabic-speaking friends that you truly care about becoming part of their community. Maybe that means getting involved in social clubs; perhaps it means hosting dinners in your own home (which shouldn't be a problem anymore, right?).

And most importantly, you should *learn to speak Arabic*. There is no better method of learning the language than surrounding yourself with books, videos, movies, and friends who all use Arabic. If it is feasible, you will also want to enroll in some sort of Arabic language course. But this is all in the future. For now, you just want to learn a few more words before you put this book down one more time. I understand. I often felt the same way while learning Arabic. So here is one last heavy dose of vocabulary. May it serve you well in your studies.

mu**-da al-Ha-**yaaa	lifetime
***Haa**-na*	bar (pub)
*a-**thaath***	furniture
***uj**-ra*	rent
*shi-**raa'h***	(a) purchase
*Ha-**dee**-qa*	garden
*mus-**tan**-bat zu-**jaa**-ja*	greenhouse
*aS-di-**qaa'h***	friends
*ta-**zey**-yan*	decorations
*na-**seej***	tapestry
'aeyn	fountain
*Ha-**maam***	doves
jaar	neighbor
*ji-**waar***	neighborhood
*muj-**ta**-ma'a*	community
***an**-sha-Ta*	activities
*tan-**THeem***	organization
*maj-**moo**-'aa*	group
*Ha-**yaaa** ja-**deed***	new life
***maD**-Dee **waq**-t*	spend time
*is-**tak**-sha-fa/yas-**tak**-shif*	he explored/he explores
*iq-**ta**-sa-ma/yaq-**ta**-sim*	he shared/he shares

***'ish**-ra*	companionship (company)
***maa**-ri-fa*	acquaintance
***da'a**-wa*	invitation
*yoo-**mee**-yan*	daily
*us-boo-'a-**ee**-yan*	weekly
*shah-**ree**-yan*	monthly
*san-a-**wee**-yan*	yearly
*'a-**waa**-'hid*	habits
*tas-**lee**-a*	pastime
***ath**-tha-tha/yu-**'hath**-thath*	furnished/he furnishes
***naq**-l*	movement
***na**-qa-la/**yan**-qul*	moved/he moves
***'aaa**-sha/**y'a**-ash*	lived/he lives
***man**-zil*	home
***wa**-Tan*	homeland
***thaa**-bit*	settled
*mus-**tow**-Ta-na*	settlement
*Sa-**daa**-qa*	friendship

Tips

Speaking of studies, you should try to study Arabic in a setting with as few distractions as possible. Remember, you are trying to teach your mind something it has never tried to learn before. Distractions around you will keep you from reaching the deep level of concentration your brain needs to hold on to everything you are teaching it. Believe me, it is worth the effort. The distractions will still be there when you are done.

I can think of little else to say before we finish. Although it may seem like there were too few lessons (or maybe not; I'm not sure how you feel about it), you should keep in mind that by now, you actually know *hundreds* of words in Arabic. If you think about how you can conjugate single verbs to create entire sentences, your Arabic-mind dictionary holds *thousands* of words. That is no small feat for a few hundred pages of reading.

It is almost time for you to congratulate yourself … but not quite yet.

Next Step: Further Reading

I want to tell you a little bit about some resources you can use to learn more Arabic. Chapter 26 is reserved for emergency situations, and I don't want to put things there that might distract you.

So where can you go when you have an insatiable appetite for Arabic? There are lots of places.

- **The Internet.** The Internet is a great resource for learning Arabic, with hundreds of excellent websites dedicated to teaching you how to learn this difficult language. Simply searching for "learn Arabic" will likely result in references to product pages expecting you to make a purchase, so I would recommend you enter one of the easy words you learned from this book. For example, search for "*ahlan wa sahlan*." Hopefully that will help narrow your search.
- **Your local library.** If you do not have the Internet, or if you prefer to visit your library, the staff there can help you find resource materials to help you. Be prepared, though—it may take a while to get exactly what you are looking for.
- **Your friends.** If you live in a large city, there is a good chance your city might have an Arabic population. For many of you, this is exactly why you chose to learn Arabic. Use these native speakers, as they will be your best "learning how to speak Arabic" resource of all.
- **The radio.** If you live in a large city or have access to satellite radio, you may be able to receive Arabic radio broadcasts.
- **Internet radio.** If you spend hours a day on a computer, why not tune in to a station covering news or television in Arabic? There are sources available from around the world where you can learn about news, sports, entertainment, culture, history—whatever you choose.
- **Television.** As with radio, Arabic television programs can help you strengthen your skills. Be aware, though, that depending on the channel, you may hear different dialects of Arabic.

- **Movies.** The world is smaller. Products from Arab lands are now available virtually everywhere. Some of those products are Arab movies. Learn to like famous stars from another land while learning more Arabic. You should know, though, that much Arabic film and television is produced in Egypt, so you may hear Egyptian dialect spoken more than others.
- **Your favorite *Complete Idiot's Guide.*** You've read this book once. Why not go back and read it again? I'm sure you will find things you have missed.

Practice Makes Perfect

You have now arrived at your last introduction to your last practice quiz. When you picked up this book the first time, did you think you would make it this far? I knew you could. If I can learn Arabic, anyone can. Enjoy your final quiz.

1. How might you translate, "Hello, and welcome to our meeting. Today, we will study a little about the computer."?
2. Translate: "I have a technical problem. I am not certain if it is the keyboard or the screen."
3. Translate: "The manager is responsible for this problem. The owner is only responsible for travel."
4. Translate: *al-**yoom** **kaa**-na 'al-**ley**-ya (upon me) **an adh**-hab **il**-a as-**sooq** li-shi-**raa'h** **b'aD** ash-**yaa'h** min hu-**naa**-ka.*

The Least You Need to Know

- Prepositions improve your speech.
- Most jargon already will be in English.
- Business terms will help you become the *ra-**'hees.***
- You are surrounded by Arabic language resources.
- You have scarcely begun your Arabic learning.

Chapter 26

Emergencies

In This Chapter

- Know your government representatives
- Medical and other emergency-related vocabulary
- Basic statements
- Fill in the blank

The last thing anyone wants to do while on vacation is to witness or become involved in an emergency. Unfortunately, we don't always get to choose the events that affect us. Knowing that you may find yourself suddenly in the middle of a perhaps confusing and frightening situation, I have written some tips that may help you say what you need to say in order to take charge of the situation.

This chapter is broken down into three short sections. The first section covers less-serious issues, including making initial contact to a consulate or a specific public service. The second section covers vocabulary you might need in an emergency. The third and final section you will likely use most often. This section contains fill-in-the-blank sentences you can use to quickly get your message across.

Contacting Citizen and Public Services

You should be familiar with the government and public services that are available to you *before* you travel so that if an unplanned event does happen, you know where you can go to get whatever help you may need.

Here are some of the questions you should be able to answer before you travel:

- Where is the nearest consulate or embassy?
- What are their operating hours?
- What is their phone number?
- Who is a point of contact there?
- What services can they provide?
- What is the fastest way to get there?
- How long am I allowed to stay (for visa issues)?
- What does my government say about travel to this location?
- Who knows where I am going and how long I plan to stay?
- What is the emergency phone number in my location (911 in the United States and Canada, or 112 in Europe, for example)?
- Where is the police station, and how do I contact the authorities?
- What medical facilities are available, and where are they?

Tips

It is a good idea to get a copy of all the information in this section and leave it with a friend or relative who knows your travel plans. You may also want to carry this information with you in your purse or wallet.

Here are some questions you will want to have answered before you travel. Be sure to learn how to say them smoothly.

Track 57

***ai**-na …*	Where is …
*Mu-**HuT**-Ta ash-**shur**-Ta*	the police station
*al-mus-**tash**-fa*	the hospital

as-*si-**faa**-ra*	the embassy
*al-qun-Su-**lee**-ya*	the consulate

***maa hoo**-a **raq**-m **haa**-tif aT-Ta-**waa**-ri'h?*
What is the emergency telephone number?

If you have to contact the police, fire department, or an ambulance, you will want to explain clearly what happened. By keeping your statement short, you can avoid confusion.

***kaa**-na hu-**naa**-ka **Haa**-dith.*
There was an accident.

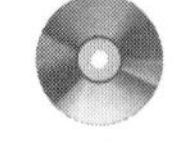

Track 57

*shaa-**hid**-tu-haa.*
I witnessed it.

kaa**-nat hu-**naa**-ka i-Saa-**baat.
There were injuries.

naH**-taj mu-**saa**-'i-dat-**kum.
We need your help.

Medical Emergencies

Don't let medical emergencies take you by surprise. The list below is organized by the beginning of a statement, then by illness, then by symptom.

*u-**fak**-kir 'and-hu …*	I think he has …
***kaa**-na **'and**-hu/haa …*	he/she had; or: has *had* …
***fee** al-**maa**-Dee …*	In the past …
***hoo**-a …*	He is …
***hee**-a …*	She is …

Illnesses and Conditions:

*Has-**saas**-ee*	allergic
*mu-**jaf**-faf*	dehydrated
Dur**-bat ash-**shams	sunstroke
*tas-**meem** al-gha-**dhaa**-'hee*	food poisoning
***rab**-boo*	asthma
inf-loo-in-zaa	influenza
*Has-**saa**-see **min** ban-**sleen***	allergic to penicillin

***ma**-raD as-**sak**-kar*	diabetes
*sha-**laal Tif**-li*	polio
*ju-**da**-ree*	smallpox
***ma**-raD **naqS** al-ma-**naa**-'a al-muk-**ta**-sab*	A.I.D.S.
wa-ram	tumor
ma-laa-ri-yaa	malaria
naqS al-maa'h	lack of water
a'a-ma	blind
aT-ra-su	deaf
*Has-**saa**-see min al-**naH**-l*	allergic to bees
*Has-**saa**-see min **fool** soo-**daa**-nee*	allergic to peanuts
*sa-ra-**Taan***	cancer
***jal**-Ta*	a stroke
***now**-ba qal-**bee**-a*	a heart attack
***dagh**-a **dam** mur-**taf**-'i*	high blood pressure
***daa'h** sha-**qeeq**-a*	migraine
*ma-**reeD***	sick (ill)
*ta-**Saa**-dum*	shock

Symptoms:

ley**-sa mus-ta-**jeeb	not responsive
***waa**-'in*	aware
***dow**-ja*	dizziness
*ta-**sam**-man*	poisoning
*Su-**daa'a***	headache
*gha-sha-**yaan***	nausea
***Hak**-ka jil-**dee**-a*	itching
***'aT**-sa*	sneezing
*is-**haal***	diarrhea
*im-**saak***	constipation
***ar**-aq*	insomnia
***Hum**-ma*	fever
*i-**Saa**-ba qa-**deem**-a*	old injury
*i-**Saa**-ba ja-**deed**-a*	new injury
*maj-**rooH***	wounded/injured

jurH/*aj*-***raH***	wound/wounds
ath-*r aj*-***jurH***	scar
nafs *al-mush*-***kil***-*a*	the same problem
dam	blood

an-*ta ti*-***taS***-*il bish*-***shur***-*Ta! al*-***aan!***
You! Call the police, now!

Fill in the Blank

If you find yourself in an emergency, you need to communicate quickly and effectively. If you are the first person at an emergency scene, you may be the only one who can help those who may be in danger. If you are afraid to provide help because of legal action that may be taken against you by an injured person who you tried to help, remember that there are so-called "good Samaritan laws" that are designed to prevent you from such action. Basically, if you find yourself witnessing an emergency and you can help, you should. After all, if you needed the help, wouldn't you want someone to help you?

Stay calm and do what you can. Do not put yourself in danger, find what help you can, and do not leave until proper authorities have taken over.

In order to "get your point across," especially if you are surrounded by people who don't speak the same language as you, you may have to rely on hand signals. If so, make sure your hand signals are direct and easy to understand.

naH-*taaj …*	We need …
tadh-*hab wa* ***ta***-*jid …*	Go and find …
naH-*nu* ***fee …***	We are at …
naH-*nu qa*-***reeb min*** *…*	We are near …

sa-***yaa***-*ra is*-***'aaaf***	an ambulance
ash-***shur***-*Ta*	the police
naq-***qaa***-*la*	a stretcher
mu-***saa***-*'i-da*	help (assistance)
Ta-***beeb***	a doctor
ba-Ta-***Teen***	blankets
is-***'aaaf*** *ow-wa-lee*	first aid
li-faa-***faat***	bandages (wraps)
Ta-***faa***-*ya*	a fire extinguisher

***haa**-tif*	a telephone
thalj	ice
*ri-**jaal** ma-**Taa**-fi'h*	(a) fire department
*sa-**yaa**-ra iT-**faa'h***	a fire truck
ak**-thir min al-**maa'h	more water
*hu-**naa**-ka …*	There is …
***kaa**-na hu-**naa**-ka …*	There was …
*ta-**koon** …*	It is …
***kaa**-nat …*	It was …
***sa**-ri-qa*	a robbery
***Haa**-dith sa-**yaa**-ra*	a car accident
*Ha-**reeq***	a fire
*ki-**taal***	a fight
*iq-ti-**Haam***	a break-in
***shaa**-hid*	a witness
dam	blood
*mu-**Saa**-baat*	injured people
***shakhS faa**-qid al-**wa**-'iee*	an unconscious person
jurh** na-**zeef	a bleeding wound
al**-am sha-**deed	severe pain
*maa-**zaa**-la hu-**naa**-ka **kha**-Tar*	there is still danger
naas** ka-**theer	many people
*aT-**faal** mu-Saa-**boon***	injured children
Hashd** ka-**beer	a large crowd

Track 58

***hee**-a ta-**Da'u Tif**-l.*
She is having a baby.

*as-sa-**yaa**-ra is-**Ta**-da-mat bi-hu.*
The car hit him.

*fa-**qad** ta-**saaa**-qa-**Ta.***
He (simply) collapsed.

***hee**-a laa **taq**-dar **an** ta-ta-**Har**-rak.*
She is not able to move.

*a'a-**ta**-qid **an**-na-**haa** in-**qa**-sa-rat.*
I believe it is broken.

***Ta**-la-bat **'an** mu-**saa**-'i-da.*
She asked for help.

qad taH**-taaj **dam.
She might need blood.

qad yaH**-taaj in-soo-**leen.
He might need insulin.

maa**-dha a-**f'al?
What should I do?

***hee**-a fiq-**daan**-a adh-**dhaak**-ra.*
She lost her memory. (She doesn't remember.)

***laa yaq**-dar **an** ya-ta-**kal**-lam.*
He is not able to talk.

laa naq**-dar **an** naq-**ta**-rib-**haa.
We cannot approach her (it).

***ai**-na a-**jeeb**-haa?*
Where do I bring her?

***taH**-taaj **Haq**-nan.*
She needs an injection.

The Least You Need to Know

- In an emergency, make sure you make your point quickly and be prepared to back it up with hand signals.
- Make sure you know how to contact your government and consulate before you leave.
- Remember to stay calm.
- Take the time to learn some common, basic emergency phrases.

Appendix A

Making the Sounds

All of the following sounds are the same in Arabic and English. (An example of the sound appears in parentheses after the sound.)

b (as in: boy)	***t*** (take)	***th*** (thing)
j (jeans)	***d*** (dog)	***dh*** (this)
r (radio)	***z*** (zoo)	***s*** (sink)
sh (shoe)	***f*** (film)	***k*** (keep)
ow (cow)	***l*** (left)	***m*** (mine)
n (new)	***h*** (help)	***w*** (wake)
y (yes)	***a*** (had)	***aa*** (father)
oo (soon)	***ee*** (keep)	***ey*** (hey)
ai (Thai)	***i*** (fit)	***u*** (push)

These sounds are new (see Chapter 2):

T: Hard "t"; sound made with the entire tongue and roof of the mouth, not the front of the tongue and the teeth

TH: Heavier '*dh*' sound; constrict the throat and soft palate; the sound comes from the entire mouth

D: Hard "d"; the sound is made between the tongue and soft palate, not the tongue and teeth (as with "d")

S: Hard "s"; air escapes between the tongue and soft palate; farther back in the mouth than "s"

H: Constrict the windpipe and say, "Ha" or "Ho"

kh: Like "***H***"; constrict the windpipe and bounce the uvula off the back of the tongue

'a/'u/'i: Constrict the throat and allow only a little air through as if saying, "Ahh"; change the vowel as appropriate

gh: Constrict the throat and say, "***ghei***"; like gargling or purring

'h: Close and open the airway, as in a light cough; sounds like the middle of "huh'uh"

q: Harder than the English "***q***"; make the "***k***" sound with the back of the tongue and the soft palate

Verb Conjugations

Past-Tense Conjugations (*ka-ta-ba* = he wrote)

I	***ka-tab*** ... *tu*
We	***ka-tab*** ... *naa*
You (s/m)	***ka-tab*** ... *ta*
You (s/f)	***ka-tab*** ... *ti*
You (p/m)	***ka-tab*** ... *tum*
You (p/f)	***ka-tab*** ... *tun-na*
He	no ending (***ka****-ta-ba*)
She	***ka-ta*** ... bat
They (m)	***ka-tab*** ... oo
They (f)	***ka-ta*** ... *ban-na*

Present-Tense Conjugations (*da-ra-sa* = he studied)

I	***ad*** ... *ras*
We	***nad*** ... *ras*
You (s/m)	***tad*** ... *ras*
You (s/f)	***tad*** ... *ras* ... ***een***
You (p/m)	***tad*** ... *ras* ... ***oon***
You (p/f)	***tad*** ... *ras* ... ***n-na***
He	***yad*** ... *ras*
She	***tad*** ... *ras*
They (m)	***yad*** ... *ras* ... ***oon***
They (f)	***yad*** ... *ras* ... ***n-na***

Useful Phrases and Numbers

"Hello, and welcome!"	***ah**-lan wa **sah**-lan*
"My name is …"	***is**-mee …*
"What is your name?"	***m'a** is-mu-**ka/ki***
"Who …"	***man** …*
"What …"	***maa**-dha/**maa** …*
"Who …"	***man** …*
"What …"	***maa**-dha/**maa** …*
"Where …"	***ai**-na …*
"Why …"	*li-**maa**-dha …*
"How much/many …"	***kam** …*
"When …"	***mat**-a …*
"How …"	***keyf**-a …*
"Yes …"	***n'am** …*
"Perhaps"	***ru**-bim-aa*
"Sometimes"	*aH-**Hyaa**-nan*
"Never"	***ab**-i-dan*
"Of course"	***Ta**-b'a-'an*
"No problem"	***laa** mush-**kil**-a*
"No"	***laa***
"There is …"	*hu-**naa**-ka …*
"Excuse me/Please"	***'af**-wan*
"Thank you"	***shu**-kraan*
"Goodbye (go with peace)"	***m'a** sa-**laam**-a*
"I am …"	***an**-a …*
"Good morning (greeting)"	*Sa-**baaH** al-**kheyr***
"Good morning (response)"	*Sa-**baaH** an-**noor***
"Good evening (greeting)"	*ma-**saa'h** al **kheyr***
"Good evening (response)"	*ma-**saa'h** an-**noor***
"One moment …"	***la**-Ha-THa …*
"Not bad …"	***laa ba**-'his*
"Good …"	***jeyd** …*
"Very good …"	***jeyd jid**-din …*
"Great!"	*'a-**THeem***

"Long"	*Ta-**weel***
"Big"	***ka**-beer*
"Small"	*Sa-**ghair***
"Stop!"	***qif!***
"Eat!"	***kul!***
"Quiet!"	***is**-kut!*
"Stand!"	***qoom**!*
"Walk!"	***im**-shee!*
"Drink!"	***ish**-rab!*
"Go!"	***idh**-hab!*
"Sit!"	***ij**-las!*
"Listen!"	***is**-m'a!*
"Look!"	***in**-thur!*
"I lost …"	*fa-**qad**-tu …*
"I am searching for …"	***ab**-Hath **'an** …*
"I want to buy …"	*u-**reed an ash**-ta-rey …*
"I must see (witness) …"	***ya**-jib an u-**shaa**-hid …*
"Have you seen …"	*hal raa-**'bey**-ta/ti …*
"I need …"	***aH**-taaj …*
"money …"	*nu-**qood** …*
"Zero …"	***Sif**-r …*
"One …"	***waa**-Hid …*
"Two …"	*ith-**neyn** …*
"Three …"	***tha-laa-tha** …*
"Four …"	***ar**-b'a-a …*
"Five …"	***kham**-sa …*
"Six …"	***sit**-ta …*
"Seven …"	***sab**-'a-a …*
"Eight …"	*tha-**maan**-ya …*
"Nine …"	***tis**-'a-a …*
"Ten …"	***'ash**-a-ra …*
"Twenty …"	*'ish-**roon** …*

"Thirty ..."	*tha-laa-**thoon*** ...
"Forty ..."	*ar-b'a-**oon*** ...
"Fifty ..."	*kham-**soon*** ...
"Sixty ..."	*sit-**toon*** ...
"Seventy ..."	*sa-b'a-**oon*** ...
"Eighty ..."	*tha-maa-**noon*** ...
"Ninety ..."	*tis-'a-**oon*** ...
"One hundred ..."	***mi**-'ha* ...
"Two hundred ..."	*mi-'ha-**teyn*** ...
"One thousand ..."	***alf*** ...
"Two thousand ..."	*alf-**eyn*** ...

Appendix B

Introduction to Written Arabic

In this appendix, I finally give you the chance to look at some written Arabic. You will learn about the Arabic alphabet and how to recognize the different ways Arabic letters can be written. Even if Arabic is the first foreign language you've studied (I only had one day of high school French but still learned Arabic when I was in my mid-twenties, so don't give up hope!), before you are done working through these next pages you will be able to read some simple Arabic words, recognize and read Arabic numbers, and order your favorite Arabic foods.

The information in this appendix is presented without much space given for practice writing drills. I did this in order to fit as much material into the appendix as possible. Also, you will soon see that you can create your own writing exercises by taking any of the vocabulary words in this book and changing the English letters into the corresponding Arabic letters. That way, you can teach yourself a bit of writing. The only difference you'll find in spelling things out in Arabic script is that the "*a*" sound at the end of words may be created with different Arabic letters. Still, with this appendix and the rest of the book, you can create enough practice writing drills to get off to a good start with writing Arabic.

The final piece of information you need before you continue with your writing lesson is that you now have to think in Arabic style. That means you will read from right to left, top to bottom. No, not "backward." Maybe English is the language that's backwards, after all. Start at the top right and work your way to the left. When you reach the end of the line, go to the next lower line and read from right to left. I've even given you some helpful practice. From now on, all of the *pronunciations* you read will be written from right to left as well, just below the Arabic script. You will see what I mean soon enough. So … have *fun*!

The Arabic Alphabet

The Arabic alphabet is not actually an alphabet. Arabic uses an *abjad*, which means that sounds are made in consonant/vowel pairs. Each written consonant has a vowel sound that comes with it, and we will get to the vowel sounds in a moment. For now, you should know that Arabic uses 28 consonants. Three of these consonants (a, y, and w) sometimes double as vowels depending on how they are pronounced.

The following list shows the 28 Arabic consonants as they look when they are standing alone (which they don't do very often). Don't forget: read from the top right to the bottom left of the list!

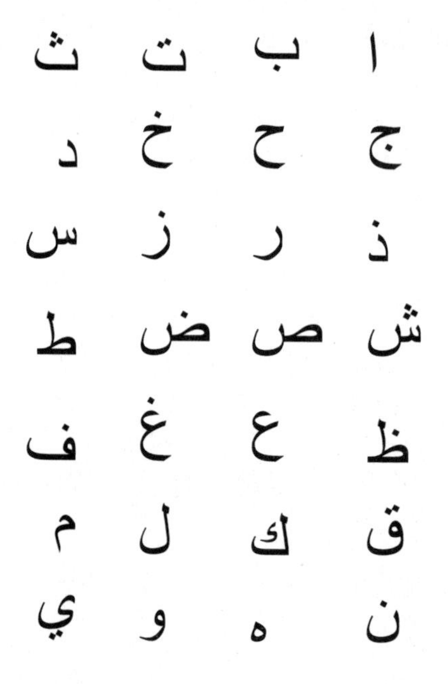

That's it! The 28 letters you just looked at are really all it takes to make up the entire Arabic language that you want to learn. Now that you've seen the letters, take out a blank sheet of paper and practice copying each one at least three times.

Right now, you're probably thinking the same thing I did when I started learning Arabic: "Right to left? How will I ever be able to learn to read *backward?*" First of all, in defense of the beautiful Arabic language, I must say that Arabic is not written "backward" but rather from right to left. A native Arabic speaker could just as easily say that we native English speakers write backward. But semantic arguments aside, you still want to know what secret formula will lead you to success in learning Arabic. Well, there is no magic formula I know of, but when you start with small steps and practice, you'll find it's not as hard as you thought.

Tips

Arabic punctuation is much like English, only you will find less of it—because Arabic grammar allows for much longer sentences than we're used to in English. Apart from the punctuation you are used to, look for the symbol ۏ separating sentences in Arabic.

I mentioned earlier that you will rarely use Arabic letters in a standalone form. That is because Arabic is *always* written in what I would call "cursive" or "script." That is, almost every letter in a word connects to the letters before and after it. Words are separated by a space. (Note: there are six exceptions to the connected letters, and I will get to them shortly.)

To read Arabic, you have to tell the difference between letters when you look at them on a page. And in order to do that, you must know there are four ways each letter can be written. Does that scare you? It shouldn't. We have four ways letters can be written in English as well: capitalized in print, lowercase in print, capitalized in cursive, and lowercase in cursive. When I think about all the different ways I've seen the letters "a" and "s" written in English, I wonder whether Arabic is actually the simpler language to read.

Now we come to the most important table you can use when trying to learn how to read Arabic. This table identifies all of the ways Arabic letters will be written, depending on where they appear in a word. If it seems daunting at first, remind yourself that this language is new to you. If you feel you are going too slowly, remember that studying well does not always mean studying fast.

When looking at the following table, remember that there is a difference between lowercase and capital letters. For example, "t" and "T" have different pronunciations (you should remember this from learning the sounds back in Chapter 2). In the following table, from right to left, you see:

- Eng.: The letter's name in English
- Ar.: The letter's name in Arabic

- Pron.: The pronunciation (from Chapter 2)
- Alone: How the letter looks when standing alone
- Begin: How the letter looks at the beginning of a word
- Middle: How the letter looks in the middle of a word
- End: How the letter looks at the end of a word

Table A.1

The Arabic Alphabet

End	Middle	Begin	Alone	Pron.	Ar.	Eng.
ـا	ـاـ	اـ	ا	*a/aa*	الف	***al-if***
ـب	ـبـ	بـ	ب	*b*	باء	***baa'h***
ـت	ـتـ	تـ	ت	*t*	تاء	***taa'h***
ـث	ـثـ	ثـ	ث	*th*	ثاء	***thaa'h***
ـج	ـجـ	جـ	ج	*j*	جيم	***jeem***
ـح	ـحـ	حـ	ح	*H*	حاء	***Haa'h***
ـخ	ـخـ	خـ	خ	*kh*	خاء	***khaa'h***
ـد	ـدـ	دـ	د	*d*	دال	***daal***
ـذ	ـذـ	ذـ	ذ	*dh*	ذال	***dhaal***
ـر	ـرـ	رـ	ر	*r*	راء	***raa'h***
ـز	ـزـ	زـ	ز	*z*	زاي	***zey***
ـس	ـسـ	سـ	س	*s*	سين	***seen***
ـش	ـشـ	شـ	ش	*sh*	شين	***sheen***
ـص	ـصـ	صـ	ص	*S*	صاد	***Saad***
ـض	ـضـ	ضـ	ض	*D*	ضاد	***Daad***
ـط	ـطـ	طـ	ط	*T*	طاء	***Taa'h***

ـظ	ـظـ	ظـ	ظ	*TH*	ظاء	***Thaa'h***
ـع	ـعـ	عـ	ع	*'a/'i/'u*	عين	***'aain***
ـغ	ـغـ	غـ	غ	*gh*	غين	***ghain***
ـف	ـفـ	فـ	ف	*f*	فاء	***faa'h***
ـق	ـقـ	قـ	ق	*q*	قاف	***qaaf***
ـك	ـكـ	آـ	ك	*k*	آاف	***kaaf***
ـل	ـلـ	لـ	ل	*l*	لام	***laam***
ـم	ـمـ	مـ	م	*m*	ميم	***meem***
ـن	ـنـ	نـ	ن	*n*	نون	***noon***
ـه	ـهـ	هـ	ه	*h*	هاء	***haa'h***
ـو	ـوـ	وـ	و	*w/oo*	واو	***wow***
ـي	ـيـ	يـ	ي	*y/ee*	ياء	***yaa'h***

What do you think? Can you do it? Of course you can. Does it look a little scary? Perhaps. But believe me, a little practice and you will get it. Oh, and so you don't get discouraged … it took me more than three weeks, eight hours a day, to become familiar with the abjad (admittedly, I'm not always the fastest learner).

So … what can you do as a beginner? How are you going to distinguish one letter from the others? Well, I have some tips for you. First, pay attention to the *dots*. If you look at the number of dots a letter has and where those dots are, then combine those two facts with the shape of the letter itself—you will be able to tell all the letters from one another regardless of where in a word the letter comes. For example, the letters ***baa'h*** ـب, ***taa'h*** ـت, ***thaa'h*** ـث, ***noon*** ن, ***and yaa'h*** ي all look the same in the middle of the word, but if you look at the dots, you can tell which letter is which.

Second tip: don't worry about how much space comes between one letter and the next, because the horizontal lines aren't as important as the vertical "notches" that indicate a letter. Don't let it bother you the way it used to bother me. For example,

> **Tips**
>
> These six Arabic letters *never* connect to the letters that follow them: ا, د, ذ, ر, ز, و. Don't be tricked by those tricky letters.

naH-nu نحن, which is Arabic for "we," is written with the same three letters whether they appear "نحن" or if they appear "نـــــحـــــن".

A Longer Look at Vowels

There are only three long vowels in Arabic. And just what is a long vowel? Well, for writing purposes, a long vowel is a vowel that is actually written. The three long vowels in Arabic are as follows:

- ا : The ***al-if***. ***al-if*** is easily recognizable because it goes straight up into the air and doesn't connect to the letter that comes after it. ***al-if*** as a long vowel has the ***a*** or ***aa*** sound.
- ي : The ***yaa'h***. ***yaa'h*** is recognized by two dots underneath it. ***yaa'h*** sounds like ***ee***.
- و : The ***wow***. ***wow*** is easy to recognize because it looks like the small English printed letter "g." ***wow*** is often seen by itself (meaning the word "and") or joining two sentences. ***wow*** never connects to the letter that follows it.

The Hamza: Almost a Vowel

The ***ham-za*** (ء) is not quite a vowel, not quite a consonant. It looks like a tiny "S" or perhaps a "5," but it is neither of those. The hamza (Arabic "***az-mah***/همزة") indicates a glottal stop, which is a sound that is easy to make but more difficult to spell. Imagine a glottal stop as the sound in the middle when someone tells you they're doing "nuh'in." The ***ham-za*** is sometimes considered a vowel, sometimes not. The hamza is not considered one of the 28 main letters of the Arabic alphabet. The use of the hamza developed with the modern Arabic language as a way to indicate how the long vowels are to be used. But you need not worry about that.

You just want to know what the ***ham-za*** is going to make things sound like. For this book, I indicated almost every ***ham-za*** with the symbol "***'h***". The only exceptions were at the beginning of some words that started with a ***ham-za***. The following list shows the different ways you will see the ***ham-za*** used.

- ء : Standing alone, the ***ham-za*** indicates a full glottal stop. The sound is unvoiced and resembles a very light cough or the beginning of our sneeze-word "*achoo*."

The *ham-za* can also be used to support one of the long vowels. In such cases, the glottal stop is connected to the sound of the vowel and the *ham-za* becomes a diacritical mark for the vowel. (A diacritical mark is just a mark above or below a written Arabic letter that shows which short vowel sound to say with the consonant sound.) We cover other diacritical marks later in this chapter. Here are the ways you will see the *ham-za* paired with long vowels:

- أ/إ : Above and below the *al-if*. Above the *al-if the ham-za creates the* ***'ha*** sound. Below the *al-if*, it creates the ***'hi*** sound.
- ؤ : Above a *wow*. Here, the *al-if* creates the ***'hu*** sound.
- ئ : Above the letter ***yaa'h***. Here, you can see that the two dots disappear from the ***yaa'h***. The resulting sound is ***'hey***.

Condition Diacritical

In English, to recognize the difference between long and short vowels, you need to have a strong grasp of the language and understand as many exceptions as rules. That's because long vowels and short vowels are spelled the same, but pronounced differently. In Arabic, it's a bit easier. Long vowels and short vowels are pronounced differently *and* they're written differently. To be specific, short vowels aren't usually written. When they are written, they are written as one of nine different diacritical marks, above or below the consonant with which they are paired.

I have now mentioned Arabic has nine diacritical marks. What does that mean? Do you remember how the Arabic alphabet is based on 28 consonants? In Arabic words, only the consonants are written; diacritical marks are used to show you how to pronounce the short vowels that occur between the consonants within a word. The marks developed as a way for non-native Arabic speakers to be able to read the text of the Qur'an (*qur-****aan***). You'll be thankful for the marks when you start seeing how much of a difference they can make in a word's meaning.

So how are you going to recognize short vowels? Easily. They're not as tall as their kinfolk. Okay, that was a poor joke, I admit, but as you speak more and more Arabic, you will see that my bad joke actually makes sense. As you familiarize yourself with the language, you'll begin to hear how short vowels really are "shorter" than the long vowels. As soon as you begin to hear the difference, you will be able to start spelling Arabic words with more accuracy. Short vowels are always used in pairs with consonants. When they are written (usually they are only found in religious text), the short vowels are indicated as diacritical marks above or below their consonants. The short vowels are:

- *fat-ha* (َ) : the *fat-ha* is placed above the consonant and gives the consonant the ***a*** sound. Example: تَ is pronounced "***ta***."
- ***kas-ra*** (ِ) : the ***kas-ra*** is placed below the consonant and gives the consonant the ***i*** sound. Example: تِ is pronounced "***ti***."
- ***dum-ma*** (ُ) : the ***dum-ma*** is placed above the consonant and gives the consonant the ***u*** sound. Example: تُ is pronounced "***tu***."
- *su-**koon*** (ْ) : The ***fat-ha*** gives us the ***a*** sound. The ***kas-ra*** gives us the ***i*** sound. The ***dum-ma*** gives us ***u***. The *su-**koon*** is different. It tells us that there is no sound at all. You can see a quick example of how the consonants are written and how diacritical marks are used for the short vowels by looking at the word *naf-su-**ki***, which means "yourself" in the feminine sense.

نَفْسُكِ Notice how in the example *naf-su-**ki***, there are only four letters written in Arabic: ***n-f-s-k***. But when combined with the diacritical marks for the short vowels, you end up with eight letters (seven if you don't count the silent *su-**koon***). This gives you the end *naf-su-**ki***.

In addition to the short vowels, Arabic script contains the ***tan-ween***, which are doubled-up short vowels, and a couple other marks, the ***shad-da*** and ***mad-da***. I present them here, so you know what they look like and recognize them when you see them.

- ً : The doubled ***fat-ha*** is located above the consonant and gives the accented letter the pronunciation ***an***. Example: تً is pronounced "***tan***."
- ٍ : The doubled ***kas-ra*** is located under the consonant and gives the accented letter the pronunciation ***in***. Example: تٍ is pronounced "***tin***."
- ٌ : The doubled ***dum-ma*** is located above the consonant and gives the accented letter the pronunciation ***un***. Example: تٌ is pronounced "***tun***."
- ّ : The ***shad-da*** is the 'w'-looking symbol. It is located above the consonant and signifies the consonant sound is made twice. Example: حبّ is pronounced ***Ha-ba-ba***.
- آ : The ***mad-da*** can only be written above the ***al-if***, and it indicates a long ***aa*** sound.

That does it for the short vowels and diacritical marks. There are only a couple other marks that I want to show you. Do you remember how I told you earlier that for other than a few exceptions you could write the Arabic based on the pronunciation I gave you? The exceptions are largely caused by the ***taa'h** mar-**boo**-Ta* ("tied ***taa'h***") and the ***al**-if maq-**Soor**-a* ("shortened ***al**-if*"):

> **1001 Arabian Notes**
>
> If you think it's difficult to spot the differences in Arabic letters today, imagine the letters with no dots or vowel markings. That's how the letters were written originally!

- ة : ***taa'h** mar-**boo**-Ta* is used most often to show that a noun is feminine. I don't want to confuse you right now with too much explanation. Just understand that the ***taa'h** mar-**boo**-Ta* looks like this: (ـة), is built from the ***taa'h***, and you will find it at the end of words. The name ***taa'h** mar-**boo**-Ta* means "tied ***taa'h***." You can remember the symbol by thinking of the letter ت and imagining the two ends tied, leaving you with a circle that has two dots over it (ة).
- ى : ***al**-if maq-**Soor**-a* is trickier to define than the ***taa'h** mar-**boo**-Ta*, so it's a good thing you don't need to worry about defining it. What you need to know is that the ***al**-if maq-**Soor**-a* is built from the ***al**-if*, comes at the end of a word, and looks like the symbol ي with the dots removed.

There's just one thing left to say … *whew!!!!* And you can say it again. I realize some of this may be a bit advanced for an introduction, but the further I can bring you in this volume, the better off you will be in your studies.

No One Prints Anymore

Arabic, like any other language, has characteristics that are easy to learn and characteristics that are more difficult. For example, Arabic is always in "script" and there are *zero* upper and lowercase letters. Those are the easy parts of writing Arabic. What's more difficult is that only rarely (most often in older or religious texts) are the short vowels written, which means you have to know how to say the word before you can correctly read it.

Unlike English, Arabic text is written from right to left, top to bottom. That means that when you've finished with this book and you decide to read a book written completely in Arabic, you will find the cover opens opposite of what you are used to, and that the spine of the book is on your right. When you find a book this way, do not be alarmed. The book is supposed to be like that. Just open up the cover and begin reading as you've learned, from the beginning at the top right, to the end at the bottom left.

Here is your first example text; see if you can find the beginning and the end of the following:

مرحبا، إسمي "كي." اشكرآم للشراء هذا الكتاب و أنا
متحمس تريدون تعلم اللغة العربية!

Did you figure out where the text ends and where it begins? That wasn't so hard now, was it? And just so you know, the text says:

> "Hello, my name is 'K.' Thank you for buying this book and I am excited that you want to learn the Arabic language!"

Now, use the sample text to see whether you can identify the different letters. Remember to focus on the dots, and remember how the letters fit together differently, depending on where they are in the word.

There is no easy way around some of the struggles in Arabic, and it's not fair of me to start you out with an entire sentence. So what we can do instead is focus on how you might see some common words, the easy ones. By looking at the English pronunciation, you should be able to see how many letters are in the word. By practicing a bit of writing, you can see how the letters fit together (and how your hand is going to think you are strange for making it go the other direction). Remember, the pronunciation is written from right to left …

هل
lah
Question word

ال
la
The

لا
aal
No

مِن
nim
From

مَن
nam
Who

أين
an-ia
Where

آيف
fyek
How

إسمي
eem-si
My name is

انا
a-na
I am

Practice writing these easy words and if you feel you need a break, take one. I'll be waiting for you with something easier in the next section.

Shiver Me Numbers

I discovered an interesting point in my research about the numbers used in the Arabic language. It turns out Arabic language uses numbers that came from East of the Arabic world and are often called "Hindu-Arabic" numerals. The numbers we are used to using (I'm talking about 1, 2, 3, etc.), are actually called "Arabic Numerals." Don't get confused.

You just want to know what symbols to expect on the signs when you are visiting an Arab land, right? Good. Then for our purposes, I will call the numbers you already know (1, 2, 3 ...) "European Numbers" and the new symbols you are to learn, "Arabic Numbers." The following list shows European and Arabic numbers right above one another, so you can closely examine the differences.

European	0	1	2	3	4
Arabic	٠	١	٢	٣	٤
European	5	6	7	8	9
Arabic	٥	٦	٧	٨	٩

Whether or not you noticed when you were looking at the list above, there are many similarities between the numbers you already know and the numbers you are trying to learn. To help you remember them better, though, I thought it would be a good idea for me to tell you how I remember all the numbers.

First of all, neither set of numbers (neither "language" if you prefer) uses "cursive numbers." I mean that a number will never connect to the number or letter that comes before or after it. So far, so good.

The Arabic zero is a centered dot (٠). There is nothing in the dot, so you remember, "Zero has nothing inside."

The Arabic 1 ١ is the same as our 1. Therefore, at least "that one is the same."

Two and three (٢, ٣) can be counted by the number of points they have on top.

Four (٤) looks like a backwards three.

Five (٥) looks like an inflated zero.

Six (٦) looks like seven, so be sure to "subtract one."

Seven (٧) looks like the Roman Numeral "five" (V), so don't confuse that one.

Eight (٨) is an upside-down seven. Remember that the eight is more, so it points upwards.

And nine (٩). Nine is easy—it looks like a nine.

And there you have them, the "Arabic" numbers. Try them out on your own or with a friend. One final tip before you go: if you are looking at a date, you will usually find it written with the year first, then the month, then the day, written, of course, from left to right.

Get Back on the Menu

We are almost out of room, but if you are looking for a good start into Arabic writing, there are two great sources of basic writing you will want to consider. The first are the print materials such as postcards and souvenir pamphlets you will find at any tourist location. The second great source of some basic Arabic reading is the menu at your favorite restaurant.

With that in mind, use what you know about how Arabic letters connect with one another and take another look at these restaurant vocabulary words from earlier in the book (Remember, the pronunciation directly under the word is written from right to left. For example, "like this" would be written, "siht ekil". The English is found on the third line.):

فلافل *laf-**aal**-af* falafel	سندويش ***hseewd**-nas* sandwich	مياه معدنية *ay-**een**-ad-a'am **haay**-im* mineral water
كباب ***baab**-ak* kebab	سجق ***quj**-us* sausage	بيرة *a-**reeb*** beer
غداء ***h'aad**-ahg* lunch	سلطة *aT-**al**-as* salad	نبيذ ***hdeeb**-an* wine
رز ***zzur*** rice	بطاطة *aT-aaT-**ab*** potatoes	شرب الليمون ***noom**-eel-al **baar**-hsa* lemonade

معكرونة *an-**oor**-ak-**a'm*** noodles	شوارمة *am-**raaw**-ahs* shawarma	حليب ***beel**-aH* milk
آوسكوس *sook-**sook*** couscous	خروف ***foor**-ahk* lamb	شوكولاتة ساخنة *an-ihk-**aas** at-**aal**-ook-**oohs*** hot chocolate
مشوي *eew-**hsam*** grilled	لحوم/لحم ***mooH**-ul/m-**Hal*** meats/meat	عصير برتقال ***laaq**-ut-rub **reeS**-a'* orange juice
عشاء ***h'aahs**-a'* dinner	كولا *aal-**ook*** cola	دجاج مخبوز ***zoob**-hkam **jaaj**-ad* baked chicken

And there you have it, your basic introduction to the Arabic language. You've gotten a little bit of writing, (hopefully) a lot of speaking, and a lot of work ahead of you. Don't be discouraged, though. You've got an amazing amount of work behind you as well.

And since you have been such a good student/reader, I will give you a couple more tips before I close. When learning how to write Arabic, the best drills you can complete will be to practice with the table at the beginning of this appendix. By learning all the ways a letter can be written, there is nothing stopping you from picking up an Arabic text and "sounding out" the words that are written there. Sure, you probably will miss at least as many pronunciations as you get correct, but you will *succeed* in learning to continue with your studies. And like I've said before, the more you practice, the better you will become.

Another good writing drill would be to try and write some of the vocabulary in this book by putting it into the format shown at the beginning of this appendix. If you have access to the Internet, you may even be able to plug the English word into your favorite translator (there are several cost-free translation sites available), and see how close your translation (or picture, if you prefer) matches to the translation the computer gives you.

There is much, much more advice I could give you, but alas, it will have to wait for (perhaps) another volume. Until that time, I can only tell you that you, the reader, have made this writing worthwhile for me and I hope you have learned as much from the experience as I have. مع السلامة (***m'a** as-sa-**laa**-ma*), or in English, "With peace, I bid you farewell."

Appendix C

English to Arabic Dictionary

1	*__waa__-Hid*
2	*ith-__neyn__*
3	*tha-__laa__-tha*
4	*__ar__-b'a-a*
5	*__kham__-sa*
6	*__sit__-ta*
7	*__sab__-'a-a*
8	*tha-__maan__-ya*
9	*__tis__-'a-a*
10	*__'ash__-a-ra*
11	*a-__Had__-a __'ash__-ar*
12	*ith-__naa 'ash__-ar*
13	*tha-__laa__-tha-ta __'ash__-ar*
14	*ar-__b'a__-a-ta __'ash__-ar*
15	*__kham__-sa-ta __'ash__-ar*
16	*__sit__-ta-ta __'ash__-ar*
17	*sab-__'a__-a-ta __'ash__-ar*
18	*tha-__maan__-ya-ta __'ash__-ar*
19	*tis-__'a__-a-ta __'ash__-ar*
20	*'ish-__roon__*
30	*tha-laa-__thoon__*
40	*ar-b'a-__oon__*
50	*kham-__soon__*
60	*sit-__toon__*
70	*sa-b'a-oon*
80	*tha-maa-__noon__*
90	*tis-'a-__oon__*
100	*__mi__-'ha*
300	*tha-__laath mi__-'ha*
400	*__ar__-b'a __mi__-'ha*
500	*__kham__-is __mi__-'ha*
600	*__sit mi__-'ha*
700	*__sab__-'a __mi__-'ha*
800	*tha-maan mi-'ha*
900	*__tis__-'a __mi__-'ha*
1,000 apologies	*__alf as__-if*
1,000 thanks	*__alf shu__-kir*
3,000	*tha-__laa__-tha aal-__aaf__*
10,000	*__'ash__-a-ra aal-__aaf__*
90,000	*tis-'a-__een alf__*
a cold	*zu-__kaam__*
a little	*qa-__leel min__*
a little less …	*__taq__-l qa-__lee__-lan __min__ …*
a second time	*__mar__-ra __thaa__-nee-a*

aboard *'**al**-a **mat**-n*
above ***fowq***
above zero ***fowq** aS-**Sif**-r*
absent ***ghaa**-'hib*
acceptable *maq-**bool***
accident ***Haa**-dith*
according to ***waf**-qan **'il**-a*
account *Hi-**saab***
account balance *ra-**Seed** al-Hi-**Saab***
account number ***raq**-m al-Hi-**Saab***
aching ***al**-am*
acquaintance ***maa**-ri-fa*
across ***'a**-ba-ra*
across from the ... ***'ab**-ra min al ...*
activities ***an**-sha-Ta*
added/he adds *a-**Daaf**/yu-**Deef***
addition *i-**Daa**-fa*
additional fees *ru-**soom** i-**Daa**-fee-a*
address ***'un**-waan*
adjustment *ta'a-**deel***
administration *i-**daa**-ra*
adult pool ***bir**-ka al-ku-**baar***
adventure *mu-**ghaa**-mir-a*
after ***b'ad***
after that ***b'ad dha**-lik*
after the ... ***b'ad** al ...*
after work ***b'ad** al-**'am**-l*
after/when ***lam**-ma*
afternoon ***b'ad** aTH-**THuh**-r*
again/two times *mar-ra-**teyn***
against ***Didd***
age ***'um**-r*
agent *wa-**keel***
agreed ***waa**-fa-qa/yu-**waa**-fiq*
air conditioner *mu-**keyf** al ha-**waa'h***
air filter *mu-**rash**-shiH al-ha-**waa'h***
air mail *ba-**reed jow**-wee*
airline company ***sha**-ri-kat Tai-**raan***
airlines *khu-**TooT** joo-**wee**-a*
airplane ***Taa**-'hi-ra*
airport *ma-**Taar***
airport lounge ***Saal**-at al-ma-**Taar***
aisle ***ma**-mar*
alarm clock ***saa'aa** mu-**nab**-bi-ha*
alchemy/chemistry *al-kee-**mee**-a'h*
alcohol *al-ku-**Hool***
Alexandria *as-**skan**-dir-ee-a*
alfalfa *al-**fuS**-fuS-a*
algebra *al-**jab**-ir*
Algeria *al-ja-**za**-'hir*
all over (everywhere) ***fee kul** ma-**kaan***
all-inclusive ***yash**-mal aj-jam-**ee**-'a*
allergic *Has-**saas**-ee*
allergic to bees *Has-**saa**-see **min** al-**naH**-l*
allergic to penicillin *Has-**saa**-see min ban-**sleen***
alley/side street *zu-**qaaq***
almost (plus a verb) ***kaa**-da*
aloe ***Sab**-ir*
alone *wa-**Heed**-an*
along ***'al**-a **Tool***
also ***ai**-Daan*
altered/he alters *ta-**ghey**-ya-ra/ya-ta-**ghey**-yar*
although ***wa**-'hin*
always ***daa**-'hi-man*
always hurts *yu-**al**-lim **daa**-'hi-man*
ambassador *sa-**feer***
amber *kah-ra-**maan***

ambulance	*sa-**yaa**-ra is-**'aaf***
American	*am-ree-**kee***
amid/between	***beyn***
amid/in the middle	***wa**-sa-Ta*
Amir, Emir	***a**-meer*
among	*min **beyn***
among the	***min** al*
amount	***mab**-lagh*
analysis	*taH-**leel***
and	***wa***
angry	*ghaD-**baan***
animal/animals	*Hai-**waan**/Hai-**waan**-aat*
another time	***mar**-ra **ukh**-ra*
antenna	*ha-**waa**-'hee*
anti-virus	*mu-**Daad** lil-**fee**-roo-**saat***
antibiotic	*mu-**Daad** Ha-**wee**-ya*
antiques	***tuH**-fa*
anxiety	***qa**-laq*
apartment	***shaq**-qa*
appeared/he appears	***THa**-ha-ra/**yaTH**-har*
appendix	***zaa**-'hi-da doo-**dee**-a*
apple/apples	*tu-**faaH***
apple juice	*'a-**Seer** tu-**faaH***
appointment	***mow**-'id*
appropriate	*mu-**naa**-sib-a*
apricot	***mish**-mish*
April	*ab-**reel**/nee-**saan***
Arabic (language)	*al-**'ar**-ra-**bee**-a*
are you able to …	*tas-ta-**Tey**-'u **an***
area (region)	*min-**Ta**-qa*
arm	*dhi-**raa'a***
armchair	*foo-**ta**-ya*
around	***Ha**-wa-la*
arrival	*wu-**Sool***
arrival terminal	***Saal**-at wu-**Sool***
arrived/he arrives	***wa**-Sa-la/**ya**-Sil*
art	*al-**fann***
as (before a verb)	*ka-**maa***
as it were	*ka-**'han**-na*
asked/he asks	***sa**-'ha-la/**yas**-'hal*
aspirin	*as-pir-**een***
assignment	*ma-**ham**-ma*
asthma	***ma**-raD ar-**rab**-boo*
Aswan Dam	*sad as-**waan***
at all times	***fee kul** al-ow-**kaat***
at the beginning	*fee al-ba-**daa**-ya*
at the end	***fee** an-ni-**haa**-ya*
ate/he eats	***a**-ka-la/ya-**'ha**-kal*
Atlantic Ocean	*al-mu-**HeyT** al-**aT**-las-ee*
attendant/steward	*mu-**Deyf**(-a)*
attire	*li-**baas***
August	*a-**ghus**-Toos/**ab***
Automatic Teller Machine (ATM)	*ji-**haaz** li-**Sarf** al-**aa**-lee*
autumn	*kha-**reef***
available	*mu-ta-**waf**-fir(-a)*
available services	*khid-**maat** mu-ta-**waf**-fir-a*
average/normal (the)	*al-**'aaa**-dee*
aware	***waa**-'in*
away from/after/for	***'an***
baby boy, child	***Tif**-l*
Babylon	***baa**-bil*
back	***THah**-ra*
backward	***il**-a al-wa-**raa'h***
bad	***sey**-'hi*
bad connection	*al-it-ti-**Saal sey**-'han*
bag of ice	***keys** ath-**thalj***
baggage	*am-**ti'aa***

Bahrain	*al-ba-**Hreyn***
baked	*makh-**booz***
baked chicken	*da-**jaaj** makh-**booz***
baklava (baklawa)	*bak-**laa**-wa*
bald	***aS**-la-'u*
ballet (also baa-**lee**-a)	*raqS tam-**thee**-lee*
banana	***mowz***
bandage	*Da-**maa**-da*
bandages (wraps)	*li-faa-**faat***
bank	***maS**-rif*
banquet	***maa'h**-du-ba*
bar (pub)	***Haa**-na*
barbecue (grill party)	***Haf**-la ash-shi-**waa'h***
barber	*Hal-**laaq***
barber shop	*Saa-**loon** Hi-**laa**-qa*
barley	*sha-**'ieer***
barracks	***thuk**-na*
baseball	***lu'u**-ba **bees**-bool*
basically	*a-saas-**see**-an*
basket/baskets	***sal**-la/si-**laal***
bathing	*is-ti-**Haam***
bathing suit	***thowb** as-si-**baa**-Ha*
bathroom/WC/bath	*Ham-**maam***
bathtub	***baan**-yoo*
batteries	***baT**-Tar-**ree**-ya*
battery is weak	*al-**baT**-Tar-**ree**-ya Da-**'ieef***
beach/shore	***shaa**-Ti'h*
bead/beads	***ja**-ra-za/**ja**-raz*
beard	***liH**-Hee-a*
beauty	*ja-**maal***
beauty mark (birthmark)	***shaa**-ma*
because	*li-**'han**-na*
because of	*bi-**sab**-ab*
bed	*fi-**raash**/**sa**-reer*
bed linens	***shar**-shaf*
beef	***laH**-m **baq**-ar*
beer	***beer**-a*
before (in front of)	*am-**aam***
before (in place)	*qu-**daam***
before (in time)	***qab**-l*
before noon	***qab**-l aTH-THuh-r*
before the …	***qab**-la al …*
behind the …	*wa-**raa'h** al …*
behind/beyond	*wa-**raa'h***
Belgian	*bal-**jee**-kee*
believe me	*Sad-**diq**-nee*
believed/he believes	*i'a-**ta**-qa-**da**/ya'a-**ta**-qid*
belly	***baT**-n*
below zero	***taHt** aS-**Sif**-r*
belt/belts	*Hi-**zaam**/**aH**-zi-ma*
beneath	*min **taHt***
beside	*bi-**jaa**-nib*
beside the …	*bi-**jaa**-nib al …*
better than	***aH**-san **min***
bicycling	*ad-dar-**raj**-a*
big (m/f)	*ka-**beer**/ka-**beer**-a*
bigger	***ak**-bar*
bigger than	***ak**-bar **min***
billion/billions	*mil-**yaar**/mil-yaar-**aat***
biology	***'al**-m al-a-**Hyaa'h***
birthing clinic	***daar** at-tow-**leed***
black	***as**-wad/sow-**daa'h***
blanket/blankets	*baT-Taa-**nee**-ya/ba-Ta-**Teen***
bleach	*bai-**yaD***
bleeding wound	***jurh** na-**zeef***
blind	***a'a**-ma*
blood	***dam***

blouse	***blooz**-a*
blue	***az**-raq/zar-**qaa'h***
boat	***zow**-raq*
boiled	***mas**-looq*
bone/bones	***'aTH**-m/'i-**THaam***
book/books	*ki-**taab**/**ku**-tub*
boring	***mu**-mil*
bottle/bottles (vial)	*qin-**nee**-na/qa-**naan***
bottle (soda bottle)	*za-**jaaj**-a*
bought/he buys	*ish-**ta**-ra/yash-**ta**-rey*
bowl	***Taa**-sa*
bowling	***boo**-leengh*
box (carton)	*Sun-**dooq***
boxing	*mu-**laa**-ka-ma*
boy/boys	***wa**-lad/ow-**laad***
bracelet/bracelets	*si-**waar**/a-**saa**-wir*
brain	*di-**maagh***
branch	***far**-'a*
brass	*nu-**Haas aS**-far*
bread	***khubz***
break (it will break)	*si-yan-**kas**-ir*
break-in	*iq-ti-**Haam***
breakfast	*fu-**Toor***
breathe deeply	*ta-**na**-fas 'a-**mee**-qan*
bride	*'a-**roos***
bring water	*ta-**jeeb maa'h***
British pound	***jun**-ya bree-Taa-**nee**-ya*
Briton	*bree-**Taa**-nee*
broiled	*mun-**sha**-wee*
broken	*mu-**'aT**-Tal(-a)*
broken (cracked)	*mu-**kas**-sa-ra*
broken arm	***kas**-r adh-dhi-**raa'a***
bronchitis	*il-ti-**haab** al-qa-Sa-**baat***
brother/s	***akh**/ikh-**waan***
brow	***Haa**-jib*
brown	***bu**-nee/bu-**nee**-ya*
brush	*fur-**shaaa***
building/buildings	*bi-**naa**-ya/bi-naa-**yaat***
bus	***Haa**-fil-a/**baaS***
business (trade)	*ti-**jaa**-ra*
business (work)	***shugh**-l*
busy	*mash-**ghool***
But I need …	*wa-**laa**-kin aH-**taaj** …*
But where?	*wa-**laa**-kin **ai**-na?*
but/yet	*wa-**laa**-kin*
butter	***zub**-d*
by yourself	*bi-**nafs**-u-ka/ki*
cable	***Hab**-l*
café	***maq**-ha*
Cairo	*al-**qaa**-hir-a*
camel	***jam**-al*
camera	***aa**-la **taS**-weer*
camping	***khey**-yam*
Can I help you?	*yum-**kin**-nee u-**saa**-'id-ka?*
Canadian	*ka-**na**-dee*
cancellation	*il-**ghaa'h***
cancer	*sa-ra-**Taan***
candy/sweets	*Hal-wa-**yaat***
capable	*muq-**tad**-ir*
car/cars (auto)	*sa-**yaa**-ra/sa-yaa-**raat***
car accident	***Haa**-dith sa-**yaa**-ra*
car park/parking lot	***mow**-qif as-sa-yaa-**raat***
caramel	*ka-ra-**mil**-laa*
carat	*qee-**raat***
cardamom	***heyl***
carpet	*saj-**jaa**-da*
carried/he carries	***Ha**-ma-la/**yaH**-mil*
cart (wagon)	***'a**-ra-ba*

Casablanca	*__daar__ al-bai-__Daa'h__*
cashier	*Sar-__raaf__*
casino	*kaa-__zee__-noo*
castle (palace)/castles	*__qaS__-r/qu-__Soor__*
casual	*__'a__-ra-Dee*
cat (m/f)	*__qiTT/qiT__-Ta*
CD player	*__aa__-la __see__-dee*
ceiling	*__suq__-f*
ceiling fan	*__mir__-wa-Ha as-__suq__-f*
cellular phone	*__haa__-tif __kha__-la-wee*
cemetery/cemeteries	*__maq__-ba-ra/ma-__qaa__-bir*
Centigrade	*mi-'ha-__wee__-a*
certain (m/f)	*mu-ta-__'ha__-kid/ mu-ta-__'ha__-kid-a*
chair	*__kur__-see*
change (switch)	*ta-__gheyr__*
change (the remainder)	*al-__baa__-qee*
changed/he changes	*__bad__-da-la/yu-__bad__-dil*
charged/he charges	*Ha-__shaa/yaH__-shoo*
charges (costs)	*ta-ka-__leef__*
chat (casual discussion)	*__dar__-da-sha*
check	*__sheek__*
checked/he checks	*ta-__Haq__-qa-qa/ya-ta-__Haq__-qaq*
checking account	*Hi-__Saab jaa__-ree*
checkout	*mu-__ghaa__-dar-a*
cheese	*__jub__-na*
chest	*__Sud__-r*
child/children	*Tif-l/aT-__faal__*
child's bed (crib)	*sa-__reer Tif__-l*
children's pool	*__bir__-ka al-aS-Si-__Ghaar__*
Chinese	*__See__-nee*
chocolate	*__shoo__-koo-__laa__-ta*
church/churches	*ka-__nees__-a/ka-__naa__-'his*
cinema	*__see__-na-maa*
cinnamon	*__qir__-fa*
circulation	*dow-a-__raan__*
citizen	*mu-__waa__-Tin*
citrus	*Ham-dee-__yaat__*
city/cities	*ma-__dee__-na/__mu__-dun*
civil	*__ma__-da-nee/'u-__moom__-ee*
cleaned/he cleans	*__gha__-sa-la/__yagh__-sal*
cleaner	*__maa__-da mu-__naTH__-THi-fa*
climate	*__jow__*
clinic	*'i-__yaa__-da*
close (almost)	*taq-__reeb__-an*
closed (not open)	*__magh__-laq*
closet/cupboard	*khi-__zaa__-na*
cloth	*qu-__maash__*
clothing	*ma-__laa__-bis*
clouds	*__ghaa__-'him/__su__-Hub*
coat (clothing)	*__mi'i__-Taf*
coffee	*__qah__-wa*
coins (small change)	*__'um__-la __m'a__-din-__nee__-a*
cold and icy	*__ba__-rid wa mu-__thal__-laj*
cold water	*__maa'h ba__-rid*
collapse	*in-hi-__yaar__*
college	*kil-__lee__-a*
color	*__lown__*
comb (for hair)	*__mushT__*
come with me	*__ta'h__-tee __m'a__-ee*
common	*__'aaa__-dee*
community	*muj-__ta__-ma'a*
companionship (company)	*__'ish__-ra*
company funds	*um-__waal__ shi-ree-__kee__-a*
complicated	*mu-__aq__-qad*
computer	*__aa__-la __Haa__-si-ba*

concert *__Haf__-la moo-see-__qee__-ya*

conductor (for tickets) *__qaa__-T'i at-ta-__dhaa__-kir*

conference room *__ghur__-fa li-__mu'h__-tam-ar-__aat__*

confirmation number *__raq__-m at-ta'h-__keed__*

connection *'hit-ti-__Saal__*

consequently *__fa__*

constipation *im-__saak__*

consul *__qun__-Sul*

consulate *qun-Su-__lee__-ya*

consulted/ he consults *__raa__-ja'aa/yu-__raa__-ji'u*

contains *__yaH__-wee*

continuously *bi-is-tim-__raar__*

contract *__'aq__-d*

conversation *mu-__Haa__-da-tha*

cooking utensils *ad-a-__waat__ aT-__Tabkh__*

copy *__nus__-kha*

corner/corners *__ruk__-n/ar-__kaan__*

correspondent *__mu__-kaa-tib*

cosmetic *taj-__mee__-lee*

cost per minute *__tha__-man li-da-__qeeq__-a __waa__-Hi-da*

cotton *__quT__-n*

cotton gauze *__shaf quT__-nee*

cough *su-__'aaal__*

country (nation) *__bal__-ad*

country (rurality) *ar-__reef__*

country area/ rural area *min-__Ta__-qa ree-__fee__-a*

couscous *__koos__-koos*

covered/he covers *__ghaT__-Ta/__yigh__-Tee*

crazy *maj-__noon__*

creative (m/f) *mub-__di'a__/mub-__di'a__-a*

credit card *bi-__Taa__-qa 'i-ti-__maad__*

crew *__Taa__-qim*

crowd/crowds *jum-__hoor__/ja-__maa__-heer*

crowded *maz-__da__-Him-a*

cruise *__jow__-la ba-Har-__ree__-a*

cuff links *__zur kum__ al-qa-__mees__*

cultural events *aH-__daath__ tha-qaa-__fee__-ya*

cup *fin-__jaan__*

curly *mu-__ja'a__-'aad*

currency *__'um__-la*

currently *Haa-__lee__-yan*

curtain *si-__taar__*

customs *ja-__maa__-rik*

customs office *__mak__-tab aj-ja-__maa__-rik*

customs officer *mun-__doob__ aj-ja-__maa__-rik*

cut/he cuts *__qa__-Ta-'aa/__yaq__-Ta'a*

daily *yoo-__mee__-yan*

Damascus *da-__mashq__*

danced/he dances *__ra__-qa-Sa/__yar__-qaS*

danger *__kha__-Tar*

dangerous *__kha__-Tir*

dark *__muTH__-lim*

dark room *__ghur__-fa __muTH__-lim-a*

date (fruit) *__tam__-ra*

date of arrival *taa-__reekh__ al-wu-__Sool__*

date palm trees *__nakh__-la*

dates (fruit) *__nakh__-la*

daughter/s *__ib__-na/ib-__naat__*

daydream *__Halm__ al-ya-__qa__-THa*

Dead Sea (The) *al-__ba__-Hr al-__meyt__*

deadline *__Had za__-ma-nee*

deaf *__aT__-ra-su*

debit/credit card *bi-__Taa__-qa i'i-ti-__maad__*

December *di-__seem__-bir/ kaa-__noon__ al-__ow__-wal*

decided/he decides *__qar__-ra-ra/yu-__qar__-rir*

deck of the ship **THa**-hr as-sa-**fee**-na
decorations ta-**zey**-yan
deep sea **ba**-Hr al-'a-**meeq**
dehydration taj-**feef**
delay (noun) ta'h-**kheer**
delivery tow-**Seel**
delivery/arrival time **waq**-t al-wu-**Sool**
dentist Ta-**beeb** al-is-**naan**
deodorant mu-**zeel** lil-ra-**waa'h**
departed/he departs **ghaa**-da-ra/yu-**ghaa**-dir
departure iq-**laa'a**
dependable (m/f) moo-**thooq**/moo-**thooq**-a
deposited/he deposits **ow**-da-'a/ya-**wad**-'a
dermatologist Ta-**beeb** am-**raaD** jil-**dee**-a
desert Sa-Hraa'h
deserted mah-**joor**
despite bil-**rugh**-m
dessert taH-**lee**-a
destination **maq**-Sid
detergent mu-**nuTH**-THif
developing (film) taH-**meeD**
diabetes **ma**-raD as-**sak**-kar
diagnosis tash-**kheeS**
dial tone Ta-**neen** al-ti-**qaaT**
diamond **maa**-sa
diapers Ha-**faa**-Da al-aT-**faal**
diarrhea is-**haal**
did/he does **fa'a**-la/**ya**-f'al
did you hear hal sa-**ma'aa**-ta
different **aa**-khar
difficult **S'ab**
digital watch **saa'aa** raq-**mee**-a
dinar dee-**naar**
dinner (supper) 'a-**shaa'h**
directions/instructions ta'a-lee-**maat**
director mu-**deer**
dirham/dirhams (money) dir-**haam**/di-**raa**-him
dirty (m/f) mu-**tas**-sikh/mu-**tas**-sikh-a
disagreement khi-**laaf**
disappears suddenly yakh-**taf**-ee **faj**-'ha-tan
discount takh-**feeD**
discovered/he discovers ik-**ta**-sha-fa/yak-**ta**-shif
discussion mu-**naa**-qa-sha
diving (sport diving) **ghowS**
dizziness **dow**-kha
doctor Ta-**beeb**
dog **kalb**
dog racing si-**baak** al-ki-**laab**
dollar doo-**laar**
donkey Hi-**maar**
door **baab**
door locks aq-**faal** al-ba-**waab**
doorman/concièrge boo-**waab**
dormitory ma-**naa**-ma
doubtful mash-**kook**
doves/pigeons Ha-**maam**
draft takh-**TeeT**
drank/he drinks **sha**-ra-ba/**yash**-rab
drawer **durj**
drawing (a sketch) **ras**-m
dress fus-**taan**
drew/he draws (sketch) **ra**-sa-ma/**yar**-sum
Drink! **ish**-rab!
drink/drinks sha-**raab**/mash-roo-**baat**
drinking water **maa'h lil** sha-**raab**
driver **saa**-'hiq
driver's license **rukh**-Sa si-**yaa**-qa
drove/he drives **saa**-qa/ya-**sooq**

dry clean	***naTH**-THa-fa **'al**-a an-**naa**-shif*
dry cleaning	*tan-**Theef jaaf***
dry/arid	***jaaf***
duration of the stay	***mud**-a al-i-**qaa**-ma*
Dutch (of Holland)	*hoo-**lan**-dee*
dwelling	***daar***
ear infection	***'ad**-wa al-**udh**-n*
ear/ears	***udh**-n/aa-**dhaan***
early	***baa**-kir-an*
earned/he earns	***ka**-sa-ba/**yak**-sib*
earnings	*ma-**kaa**-sib*
earring/earrings	***Ha**-laq/Ha-laq-**aan***
easily	*bi-su-**hoo**-la*
east	***sharq***
easy (m/f)	***sah**-l/**sah**-la*
Eat!	***kul!***
economy class	***da**-ra-ja iq-ti-**Saa**-dee-a*
egg/eggs	***bai**-Da/**baiD***
Egypt	***maS**-r*
eighth (m/f)	***thaa**-min/**thaa**-min-a*
elbow	***mir**-faq*
electric razor (clippers)	***aa**-la Hi-**laa**-qa*
electronic transfer	*taH-**weel** al-am-**waal***
electronics	*al-i-lak-troo-nee-**yaat***
elementary	*ib-ti-da-**'bee**-a*
elementary school	***mad**-ra-sa ib-ti-da-**'bee**-a*
elevator	***miS**-'ad*
eleventh (m/f)	***Haa**-dee **'aaa**-shir/ Haa-**dee**-a-ta 'aaa-shir*
e-mail	*ba-**reed** i-**lak**-**troo**-nee*
embassy	*si-**faa**-ra*
emerald	*zu-**mur**-rud*
emergency	*Ta-**waa**-ri'h*
emergency situation	***Haal**-a Ta-**waa**-ri'h*
employee	*mu-**waTH**-THif*
empty	***faa**-ragh*
engine fan	***mir**-wa-Ha al-mu-**har**-rik*
engineer	*mu-**han**-dis*
English	*al-**an**-klee-**zee**-a*
engraved/he engraves	***na**-Ha-ta/**yan**-Hat*
enlarge the picture	*tak-**beer** aS-**Soo**-ra*
enlarged/he enlarges	***kab**-ba-ra/ya-**kab**-ba-ra*
ensured/he ensures	*ta-'**hak**-ka-da/ya-ta-**'hak**-kad*
entered/he enters	*da-kha-la/**yad**-khul*
entrance	***mad**-khal*
entry is forbidden	*al-da-**khool** mam-**noo**-'a*
envelope	*mu-**ghal**-laf*
equipment	*taj-**heez**-a*
Euphrates River	***na**-hr al-far-**aat***
event	***Haa**-dith-a*
everything is okay	***kul shey 'al**-a **maa** yu-**raam***
exact	*maD-**booT***
exactly	*bil-**Dab**-T*
examined/ he examines	**'aaa**-ya-na/yu-**'aaa**-yi-nu
excellent	*mum-**taaz***
except that	***il**-a **an***
exception	*is-tith-**naa'h***
exceptionally	***Ha** -san-nan*
exchange	*taH-**weel***
exchange (act of exchanging)	*mu-**baa**-da-la*
exchange rate	***si'r** aS-**Sarf***
exchanged/ he exchanges	*ta-**bad**-da-la/ya-ta-**bad**-dal*
exciting (agitating)	*ma-**theer***
exciting (thrilling)	*mu-**Ham**-mis*
excuse me/please	*'af-**waan***

exercise	*tam-**reen***
exercise room	***ghur**-fa ri-yaa-**Dee**-a*
exit	***makh**-raaj*
expatriate	*mugh-**ta**-rib*
expected/he expects	*ta-**waq**-q'aa/ya-ta-**waq**-q'aa*
expenditures	*mun-**Sar**-af*
expensive	***ghaa**-lee(-a)*
expert	*kha-**beer***
explored/he explores	*is-**tak**-sha-fa/yas-**tak**-shif*
extension	*i-**Taa**-la*
extra bed	*sa-**reer** i-**Daa**-fee*
extra cost	***tak**-lif-a i-Daa-**fee**-a*
extra gasoline (petrol)	***ban**-zeen i-**Daa**-fee*
extra water	***maa'h zaa**'hid-a*
extreme heat	*Ha-**raar**-a sha-**deed**-a*
eye doctor	*Ta-**beeb** 'u-**yoon***
eye/eyes	***'aeen**/'u-**yoon***
eyeglasses	*na-THaa-**raat***
facing	***naH**-wa*
facsimile (FAX)	***faaks***
Fahrenheit	***fah**-ran-**haa**-yit*
fainting	*ghey-**boob**-a*
falafel	*fa-**laa**-fal*
falconry	***Said** bil-bu-**'booz***
families	*'a-**waa**-'hil/a-hil-**oon**/**us**-ar*
family	*'aaa-'hi-la/**a**-hil/**us**-ra*
family/families	***us**-ra/**us**-ar*
fan	***mar**-wa-Ha*
fan belts	***aH**-zim-a al-**mir**-wa-Ha*
far	*b'a-**eed**-an*
far removed	*ba'a-**ee**-dan **'an***
farming	*zu-**raa'aa***
faster	***as**-r'a*
father/s	***ab**/aab-**aa'h***
February	*fib-**raa**-yir/sh-**baaT***
fee	*mu-**kaa**-faaa*
feed the pets	***aT**-'aa-ma al-Hai-waan-**aat***
fell down/he falls	***sa**-qa-Ta/**yas**-qaT*
felt/he felt	***'aa**-sha-ra/**ya'a**-shur*
feminine	*un-tha-**wee**-ya*
fever	***Hum**-ma*
few people	*qa-**leel** min an-**naas***
Fez	***faas***
fifth (m/f)	***khaa**-mis/**khaa**-mis-a*
fig	***tee**-na*
fight	*qi-**taal***
film/films	***film**/af-**laam***
finally/recently	*a-**kheer**-an*
finger	***iS**-b'a*
fingernail polish	***Saq**-l lil-aTH-**faar***
fire	*Ha-**reeq***
fire department	*ri-**jaal** ma-**Taa**-fi'h*
fire extinguisher	*Ta-**faa**-ya*
fire truck	*sa-**yaa**-ra iT-**faa'h***
first (m/f)	*ow-wal/**oo**-la*
first aid	*is-**'aaaf** **ow**-wa-lee*
first class	***da**-ra-ja **oo**-la*
fish	***sam**-ak*
fishing	*aS-**Said** as-**sam**-ak*
fit (the size)	*al-ma-**qaas***
flat-screen	***shaa**-sha mu-**saT**-Ta-Ha*
flight	*Tai-**raan***
flight number	***raq**-m ar-**riH**-la*
flight plan	***khuT**-Ta aT-Tai-**raan***
floor (ground level)	*ar-**Dee**-a*
floor/story	***Taa**-biq*
flour	*Ta-**Heen***
flower/flowers	***zah**-ra/zu-**hoor***

flying	***Taa***-*'hir*
fog	*Da-**baab***
followed/he follows	*ta-**tab**-b'a/**ya**-ta-**tab**-b'a*
food	***Ta'aaam***
food poisoning	*tas-**meem** al-gha-**dhaa**-'hee*
foot/feet	***qad**-am/aq-**daam***
football (soccer)	***lu'u**-ba **kur**-a **qa**-dam*
footstool	***mis**-nad lil-qa-da-**meyn***
for example	***mith**-lan*
for/to/on account of	*li-*
forest	***ghaa**-ba*
forever	***il**-a al-**a**-bad*
forgot/he forgets	***na**-si-ya/**yan**-sa*
fork	***show**-ka*
formal	***ras**-mee*
fortress/fortresses	***HiS**-n/Hu-**Soon***
forward	*mu-**qad**-dim-a*
found/he finds	***wa**-ja-da/**ya**-jid*
fountain	***'aeyn***
fourth (m/f)	***raab**-'i/**raab**-'i-a*
free entry	*da-**khool** ma-**jaa**-nan*
free minutes	*da-**qaa**-'hiq ma-**jaa-nee**-ya*
freezer	*mu-**jam**-mad*
French	*fa-**ran**-see*
fried	*maq-**lee***
friend (m/f)/friends	*Sa-**deeq**/Sa-**dee**-qa/ aS-di-**qaa'h***
friendship	*Sa-**daa**-qa*
from anew	*min ja-**deed***
from/on account of	***min***
fruit	***faa**-ki-ha/fa-**waa**-kih*
fund/balance	*ra-**Seed***
funny (m/f)	***muD**-hiq/**muD**-hiq-a*
furnished/ he furnishes	***ath**-tha-tha/yu-**'hath**-thath*
furniture	*a-**thaath***
game	***lu'u**-ba*
garden	*Ha-**dee**-qa*
garlic	***thoom***
gate	*ba-**waa**-ba*
gauze/gauzes	***shaf**/sha-**foof***
gave/he gives	***a'a**-Taaa/yu-'a-Tee*
gear	*gha-**raaD***
general practitioner	*Ta-**beeb 'aam***
generalized pain	***al**-am **'aaa**-mee*
genuine	*Sa-**HeeH***
German	*al-**maa**-nee*
gift/gifts	*ha-**dee**-a/ha-**daa**-yaa*
gifted/he gifts	***wa**-ha-ba/ya-**hib***
girl	***bint***
girls	*bi-**naat***
glass (tumbler)	***kaa**-'has*
glory/majesty	***sub**-Ha*
Go!	***idh**-hab!*
God willing	*in-**shaa'h** al-**lah***
gold	***dha**-hab*
gold market	***sooq dha**-hab-ee*
golden	***dha**-ha-bee/dha-ha-**bee**-ya*
good	***Ha**-san*
good	***jeyd***
good evening (greeting)	*ma-**saa'h** al-**kheyr***
good evening (response)	*ma-**saa'h** an-**noor***
good morning (greeting)	*Sa-**baaH** al-**kheyr***
good morning (response)	*Sa-**baaH** an-**noor***
goodbye (go with peace)	***m'a** sa-**laam**-a*

government *Ha-**koo**-ma*
grade ***Suf***
gram/grams ***ghraam**/ghraam-**aat***
granddaughter/s ***Ha**-feed-a/Ha-fee-**daat***
grandfather/s ***jadd**/aj-**daad***
grandmother/s ***jad**-da/jad-**daat***
grandson/s ***Ha**-feed/aH-**faad***
grave/tomb ***qab**-r/Da-**reeH***
gray/grey *ra-**Saa**-See/ra-Saa-**See**-ya*
Great! *'a-**THeem!***
green ***akh**-Dar/khaD-**raa'h***
greenhouse *mus-**tan**-bat zu-**jaa**-ja*
greeted/he greets ***qaa**-ba-la/yu-**qaa**-bil*
greeting *qa-**bool***
greeting *Sa-**baaH** al-**kheyr***
grilled ***mash**-wee*
groom *'a-**rees***
ground/earth ***arD***
group *maj-**moo**-'aa*
guest ***Daif***
guinea ***jun**-ya*
gynecologist *Ta-**beeb** am-**raaD** in-nis-**saa'h***

habits *'a-**waa**-'hid*
hair ***sh'ar***
hair brush *fur-**shaa sha'a**-ra*
hair dryer *mu-**jaf**-faf ash-**sh'ar***
hair spray *ra-**dhaadh** lil-**sh'ar***
haircut *Hi-**laa**-qa ash-**sh'ar***
hairstyle *tas-**ree**-Ha*
hairy ***ash**-'aar*
half an hour ***niSf saa'a***
hallway/corridor ***ma**-mar*
hand luggage *Ha-**qaa**-'hib yad-a-**wee**-a*
hand wash only ***agh**-sal yad-**wee**-an **fuq**-T*
hand/hands ***yad/ai**-da*
handheld ***yad**-wee*
handkerchief *min-**deel***
handsome, pretty (m/f) *ja-**meel/ja**-meel-a*
happy (m/f) *sa'a-**eed**/sa'a-**eed**-a*
hard (difficult)(m/f) ***Sa**-'ab/**Sa**-'ab-a*
hardware *a-da-**waat***
harmless ***gheyr mu'h**-dhee*
hat ***qub**-ba'aa*
Have you seen … *hal raa-**'hey**-ta …*
having/with ***'and**/la-**dey***
he/he is ***hoo**-a*
he is from/ she is from ***hoo**-a min/**hee**-a min*
head ***ra**-'his*
headache *Su-**daa'a***
heals ***yash**-fee*
health *aS-**SuH**-Ha*
heard/he hears ***sa**-m'aa/**yas**-ma'a*
heart ***qalb***
heart attack ***now**-ba qal-**bee**-a*
heat *Ha-**raar**-a*
heat waves *moo-**jaat** al-Ha-**raar**-a*
heater *ji-**haaz** tad-fi-**'ha**/sa-**khaan***
hello ***ah**-lan*
hello and welcome ***ah**-lan wa **sah**-lan*
help (assistance) *mu-**saa**-'i-da*
here *hu-**naa***
herself *naf-su-**haa***
hidden fee *at-**'aaab** kha-**fee**-ya*
high blood pressure ***dagh**-a **dam** mur-**taf**-'i*
high-speed ***sur**-'aa **'aaa**-lee-ya*
highway *Ta-**reeq** as-sa-**ree**-a'a*

himself *naf-su-**hu***
historical sites *ma-**waa**-qi'i **taa**-ree-**khee**-ya*
history *at-taa-**reekh***
hobby/hobbies *hi-**waa**-ya/hi-waa-**yaat***
home ***man**-zil*
homeland ***wa**-Tan*
honest (m/f) *sha-**reef**/sha-**reef**-a*
honey *'a-**sal***
honored (m/f) ***ka**-rim/**ka**-rim-a*
horrible ***mur**-'ib*
horses ***far**-as*
hospital *mus-**tash**-fa*
host *mu-**Daif***
hot chocolate ***shoo**-koo-**laa**-ta **saa**-khi-na*
hotel/hotels ***fun**-duq/fa-naa-**diq***
hour/hours ***saa'a**/saa'a-**aat***
house ***beyt***
house number ***raq**-m al-**beyt***
how is/are ***keyf**-a*
how many times … ***kam** mar-**raat** …*
how much/how much ***kam***
huge (m/f) ***Dakhm**/**Dakhm**-a*
humidity *ru-**Too**-ba*
hundreds *mi-**'haat***
hungry *jow-**'aaan***
hunting ***Said***
hurt/it hurts ***al**-la-ma/yu-**al**-lim*
hurts sometimes *yu-**al**-lim aH-**Hyaa**-nan*
husband ***zowj***
hygiene products *mun-ta-**jaat** an-ni-**THaa**-fa*
I ***an**-a*
I am ***an**-a*
I am fine ***an**-a bi-**kheyr***
I am listening ***an**-a **is**-ma'a*
I can recommend *yum-kin-**nee an** ow-Sa **bi** …*
I don't know *laa **a'a**-rif*
I don't understand ***laa af**-ham*
I doubt (in) that *a-**shuk** fee **dha**-lik*
I find ***a**-jid*
I forgot *na-**sey**-tu*
I have ***'and**-ee*
I lost *fa-**qad**-tu*
I prefer something … *u-**faD**-Dil **shey**-'han …*
I want to … *u-**reed an** …*
I wrote *ka-**tab**-tu*
ice cream (frozen cream) ***boo**-za Ha-**leeb***
ice cream (frozen treat) *math-looj-**aat***
ice machine ***aa**-la ath-**thalj***
identification card *ha-**wee**-ya*
if (used with "***laa***") ***low***
if (used alone) ***idh**-a*
if not *low laa*
important (m/f) *mu-**him**/mu-**him**-a*
impossible *mus-ta-**Heel***
improved/it improves *ta-**Has**-sa-na/ya-ta-Has-san*
in a magazine ***fee** ja-**reed**-a*
in addition to *bil-'hi-**Daa**-fa **'il**-a*
in the coming (next) month … *fee ash-**sha**-hr al-**qaa**-dim …*
in the daytime *fee an-na-**haar***
in the early morning *fee aS-Sa-**baaH** al-**baa**-kir*
in the evening *ma-**saa**-'han/feeal- ma-**saa'h***
in the house ***fee** al-**beyt***
in the month of … *fee **sha**-hr …*
in the morning *Sa-**baa**-Han/fee aS-Sa-**baaH***
in the past … ***fee** al-**maa**-Dee …*

in the season of … *fee* ***faS****-l …*

in the summer *fee aS-****Saif***

in this way ***fee ba****-dhaa aT-Ta-****reeq***

in your opinion … ***fee raa'b****-yu-ka/ki …*

in/at/near/by/ with/through ***bi-***

in/into/among ***fee***

inbox ***Sun****-dooq al-****waa****-rid*

incapable ***gheyr qaa****-dir*

inch/inches ***booS****-a/booS-****aat***

included *mu-****Dam****-man*

including *ya-ta-****Dam****-man*

including (with what) *bi-****maa'b***

income tax *Da-****reeb****-a ad-****dakh****-l*

independent *mus-****ta****-qil*

indicated/he indicates *bey-****ya-na/tu-bey****-yin*

indifferent ***gheyr*** *muk-****ta****-rith*

industry *Si-****naa'aa***

infection ***'ad****-wa*

inflammation *il-ti-****haab***

influenza *inf-****loo****-in-****zaa***

information desk/office ***mak****-tab al-****m'a****-loo-maat*

informed/he informs ***khab****-ba-ra/yu-****khab****-bir*

injection ***Haq****-nan*

injured children *aT-****faal*** *mu-Saa-****boon***

injured people *mu-****Saa****-baat*

injury (detriment) *aD-****raar***

injury/injuries (wounds) *i-****Saa****-ba/i-Saa-****baat***

inside *bi-****daa****-khil*

insomnia ***ar****-aq*

instead of ***ba****-da-lan* ***min***

instrument/ instruments *ad-****aaa****/ad-a-****waat***

insulin *in-soo-****leen***

interest (banking) ***faa****-'hi-da*

interesting *mu-****shaw****-wiq*

international call *i-ti-****Saal doo****-lee*

Internet ***in****-tir-****nat***

Internet café ***muq****-ha al-****in****-tir-****nat***

intersection/crossroad *muf-****ta****-raq aT-Ta-****reeq***

interview *mu-****qaa****-ba-la*

introduced/ he introduces ***'ar****-ra-fa/yu-****'ar****-rif*

introduction *t'ar-****reef***

investigated/ he investigates ***fat****-ta-sha/yu-****fat****-tish*

invitation ***da'a****-wa*

Iraq *al-'ar-****aaq***

Iraqi *'i-****raa****-qee*

iron (clothing press) *mik-****waaa***

Islamic clothing *mu-****laa****-bis is-laa-****mee****-ya*

Islamic/Hijri calendar *al-****taq****-weem al* ***hij****-ree*

island/islands *ja-****zee****-ra/****juz****-ur*

it ***hoo****-a/****hee****-a*

it is … *ta-****koon*** *…*

it is finished ***qad an****-ta-ha*

it's not far ***ley****-sat* ***b'a****-ee-da*

itching ***Hak****-ka jil-****dee****-a*

ivory ***'aaaj***

jack (car lifter) *raa-****f'i****-a as-sa-yaa-****raat***

jacket *jaa-****keet***

jam/jams (noun) *mi-****rab****-ba/mi-rab-ba****at***

January *ya-****naa****-yir/kaa-****noon*** *ath-****thaa****-nee*

Japanese *yaa-****baa****-nee*

jar (for canning) *bar-Ta-****maan***

jasmine *yaas-****meen***

jeans (pants) *ban-Ta-****loon jeenz***

jewel/jewels	*jow-ha-ra/ja-**waa**-hir*
jewelry (gems)	*mu-**jow**-ha-**raat***
jewelry (trinket)	*Hu-**lee***
jogging (trotting)	***khab**-ba*
joke	*uD-**Hoo**-ka*
Jordan	*al-**'ur**-dun*
juice	*'a-**Seer***
July	***yul**-yoo/tam-**mooz***
jumped/he jumps	***qa**-fa-za/**yaq**-faz*
June	***yun**-yoo/Hu-zey-**raan***
kebab	*ka-**baab***
key/keys (for unlocking)	*mif-**taaH**/ma-**faa**-tiH*
keyboard	***shaa**-sha*
kidney	***kul**-ee-a (or) **kul**-wa*
kilogram/kilograms	*keel-o-ghraam/ keel-o-ghraam-**aat***
kilometer/kilometers	*kee-**loo**-mit-r/ kee-loo-mit-ar-**aat***
kindergarten	***row**-Da*
king-size bed	*sa-**reer** ka-beer*
knee	***ruk**-ba/**ru**-kab*
knew/he knows	***'a**-ra-fa/**y'a**-rif*
knife	*sik-**keen***
known	*m'a-**roof***
Kuwait	*al-koo-**weyt***
lack of water	***naqS** al-**maa'h***
lake	*bu-**Hey**-ra*
lamb	*kha-**roof***
lamp/lamps	*mis-**baaH**/ma-**saa**-biH*
language/languages	***lugh**-a/al-lugh-**aat***
laptop computer	*koom-**byoo**-tir maH-**mool***
large crowd	***Hashd** ka-**beer***
last one (final)	*al-a-**kheer***
launder clothing	***yagh**-sil thi-**yaab***
laundry (cleaner's)	***magh**-sal*
LCD	***al** see **dee***
leader	***za'a**-eem*
leadership	*qi-**yaa**-da*
learned/he learns	*ta-**'al**-lam/ya-**ta'al**-lam*
leather goods	*ba-**Daa**-'hi'i jil-**dee**-ya*
Lebanese	*lub-**naa**-nee*
Lebanon	*lub-**naan***
left (direction)	*ya-**saar***
left/he leaves (a thing)	***ta**-ra-ka/**yat**-ruk*
leg	***rij**-l/ir-**jaal***
lemon	*lee-**moon***
lemonade	*sha-**raab** al-lee-**moon***
Let's go!	*li-**nan**-zil!*
letter	*ri-**saa**-la*
library	***mak**-ta-ba/mak-ta-**baat***
Libya	***leeb**-yaa*
license plate	***loo**-Ha as-sa-**yaa**-ra*
lie	***kadh**-ib*
lifetime	***mu**-da al-Ha-**yaaa***
lighter (weight)	***akh**-faf*
like (comparative)	***mith**-la*
like (such as)	***mith**-l*
like that	*ka-**dha**-lik*
limited distance	*ma-**saaf**-a maH-**dood**-a*
line/lines	***khaTT**/kha-**TooT***
lipstick	***aH**-mar ash-shi-**faa'h***
liquid	***saa**-'hil*
lira	***lee**-ra*
Listen!	***is**-m'a!*
liter/liters	***li**-tir/li-tir-**aat***
lived/he lives	***'aa**-sha/**ya'a**-eesh*
liver	***ka**-bid*
loan	***qarD***

lobby (waiting hall)	***Saal**-a lil-in-ti-**THaar***
local call	*it-ti-**Saal** ma-Ha-**lee**-a*
local currency	***'um**-la maH-**lee**-ya*
lock	***quf**-l*
lonely	*mun-**fa**-rid*
long (m/f) (and) tall (m/f)	*Ta-**weel**/Ta-**weel**-a*
longer	***aT**-wal*
longer than	***aT**-wal **min***
Look!	***in**-THur!*
loose	*faD-**faaD***
lost/he loses	***fa**-qa-da/yaf-qid*
lotion	*gha-**sool***
loud	***Saa**-khib*
loud speaker	*mu-**kab**-bir aS-**Sowt***
lunch	*gha-**daa'h***
lung/(2) lungs	***ri**-ha/ri-'ha-**taan***
lying (lounging)	*is-**taq**-la*
main office	***mak**-tab ra-**'bee**-see*
makeup (cosmetics)	*maak-**yaaj***
malaria	*ma-**laa**-ri-**yaa***
man	***raj**-al*
manager (director)	*mu-**deer***
manicure	*taj-**meel** a-**THaa**-fir al-**yad***
many people	*ka-**theer** min an-**naas***
map	*kha-**ree**-Ta*
March	***maa**-ris/aa-**thaar***
market/markets	***sooq**/as-**waaq***
marketing	*tas-**weeq***
Marrakesh	*mar-**raa**-kash*
married	*mu-ta-**zow**-waj/ mu-ta-**zow**-waj-a*
masculine	***dha**-kar*
mask	*qi-**naa'a***
massage	*tad-**leek***
masseur	*mu-**dal**-lik*
masseuse	*mu-**dal**-lik-a*
maternal aunt/s	***khaal**-a/khaal-**aat***
maternal uncle/s	***khaal**/ukh-**waal***
math	*ar-ri-**yaa**-Dee-**aat***
Mauritania	*moor-ee-**taan**-yaa*
May	***maa**-yoo/a-**yaar***
measurement	*qee-**yaas***
meat/meats	***laH**-m/lu-**Hoom***
medical clinic	*'i-**yaa**-da Tib-**bee**-a*
medical supplies	*im-daa-**daat** Tib-**bee**-ya*
medicine	*da-**waa'h***
medicine (science)	***Tib***
meditated/ he meditates	*ta-**'ham**-mal/ya-ta-**'ham**-mal*
meeting	*li-**qaa'h***
meeting (official)	*ij-ti-**maa'a***
melon	*baT-**Teekh***
member	***'u**-Doo*
memory	***dhaa**-kir-a*
menu (list of foods)	***qaa**-'hi-ma al-**aT**-T'im-a*
Mesopotamia	***beyn** al-na-**hreyn***
meter/meters	***mat**-r/am-**taar***
method/means	*Ta-**reeq**-a*
Mexican	*mak-**see**-kee*
middle school	***mad**-ra-sa mu-ta-wa-siT-a*
might/did	***qad***
migraine	***daa'h** sha-**qeeq**-a*
mile	***meel**/am-**yaal***
milk	*Ha-**leeb***
million/millions	*mil-**yoon**/mil-aa-**yeen***
mineral water	*mi-**yaah** ma'a-da-**nee**-ya*
mint	*na'a-**naa'a***
minus	***naa**-qis*

minute/minutes *da-**qee**-qa/da-**qaa**-iq*
mirage *sa-**raab***
mirror/mirrors *mi-**raaa**/ma-**raa**-yaa*
missing (m/f) *maf-**qood**/maf-**qood**-a*
mistake *kha-**Taa'h***
mixed *mukh-**tu**-laT*
molasses ***dibs** as-**suk**-kar*
moment ***la**-Ha-THa*
monetary ***naq**-dee*
monetary penalty *'u-**qoo**-ba maa-**lee**-a*
money ***maal**/ nu-**qood**/fu-**loos***
money order (transfer) *Ha-**waal**-a maa-**lee**-a*
month ***sha**-hr*
monthly *shah-**ree**-yan*
moon ***qam**-ar*
more water ***ak**-thar min al-**maa'h***
Moroccan *magh-**rab**-ee*
Morocco *al-**magh**-rib*
mosque (gathering place) ***jaam**-'i*
mosque/mosques ***mas**-jid/ma-**saa**-jid*
mother/s ***umm**/um-mu-**haat***
motor vehicle tax *Da-**reeb** as-sa-yaa-**raat***
motorcycle *dar-**raa**-ja*
Mountain of Moses ***jab**-il **moo**-sa*
mouse ***faa'h**-r*
mouth ***fam***
moved/he moves (provoke) ***Har**-ra-ka/yuH-**Har**-rik*
moved/he moves (transport) ***na**-qa-la/**yan**-qul*
movement ***naq**-l*
muscle/muscles *'**a**-Da-la/'**a**-Da-**laat***
museum/museums ***mat**-Haf/ma-**taa**-Hif*
mustache/mustaches ***shaa**-rib/sha-**waa**-rib*
myself ***naf**-see*
nail file ***mib**-rad*
name/names ***is**-m/as-**maa'h***
nausea *gha-sha-**yaan***
navigation system *ji-**haaz** al-mi-**laa**-Ha*
near *qa-**reeb***
neck ***'u**-nuq*
necklace/necklaces ***'iq**-d/'u-**qood***
needed/he needs *iH-**taa**-ja/**yaH**-taaj*
negative *mus-**wa**-da*
negotiate *ta-**faa**-wa-Da*
neighbor ***jaar***
neighborhood *ji-**waar***
network ***sha**-ba-ka*
neurologist *Ta-**beeb** a'a-**Saab***
never ***a**-ba-dan*
new (m/f) *ja-**deed**/ja-**deed**-a*
new life *Ha-**yaaa** ja-**deed***
newspaper *Sa-**Hee**-fa*
night club ***naa**-dee ley-**lee**-a*
night table (commode) *koo-moo-**dee**-noo*
night/nights ***leyl**/li-yaal*
nights *li-**yaal***
Nile *an-**neel***
ninth (m/f) ***taa**-s'i/**taa**-s'i-a*
no ***laa***
no problem ***laa** mush-**kil**-a*
no way ***kal**-laa*
non-/not/ other than … ***gheyr***
nonsmoking ***gheyr** tad-**kheen***
nonstop (fast) *sa-**ree**-a*
noodles ***m'a**-ka-**roo**-na*

normal/natural	*Ta-bee-'iee*
north	*sha-**maal***
nose	***unf***
not	***ley**-sa*
not a problem	***ley**-sat mush-**kil**-a*
not bad	***laa baa**-'bas*
not clean	***ley**-sa na-**THeef***
not fresh	***gheyr naq**-ee*
not ready	***ley**-sa mus-**ta**-'id*
not responsive	***ley**-sa **mus**-ta-**jeeb***
not so (not that way)	***ley**-sa ka-**dha**-lik*
not yet	***ley**-sa **b'ad***
November	*noo-**fim**-bir/**tash**-rin ath-**thaa**-nee*
now	*al-**aan***
number (numeral)	***raq**-m*
number (quantity)	***ad**-ad*
nurse (f)	*mu-**mar**-riD-**a***
nutmeg	***jowz** aT-**Teen***
oasis	***waa**-Ha*
observed/he observes	***laa**-Ha-THa/yu-**laa**-Hith*
October	*uk-**too**-bir/**tash**-rin al-ow-wal*
of course/naturally	***Tab**-'aan*
office/offices	***mak**-tab/ma-**kaa**-tib*
officer	***Daa**-biT*
often	*ka-**theer**-an*
oil level	***mus**-ta-wa an- **nafT***
okay	***Taa**-yib*
okay (as it should be)	***'al**-a **maa** yu-**raam***
okra	***baam**-yaa*
old-fashioned	*'a-**teeq***
olives	*zey-**too**-na*
Oman	*'um-**aan***
omelet	***'uj**-ja **beyD***
on board (aboard)	***'al**-a **mat**-n*
on/onto/over	***'al**-a*
one-of-a-kind (unique)	***waa**-Hid min **now**-'a-**haa***
one-way	*dhi-**haab fuq**-T*
onion	***ba**-Sa-la*
online	***'al**-a ash-**sha**-ba-ka*
only	***fuq**-T*
open (not closed)	*maf-**tooH***
opera	*mas-ra-**Hee**-ya ghi-**naa**-'bee-ya*
operated/he operates	*ish-ta-gha-la/yash-ta-ghil*
operation	*'a-ma-**lee**-a*
opinion	***raa**-'hee*
or	***ow***
orange (color) (m/f)	*bur-tu-qaa-**lee**(-ya)*
orange juice	*'a-**Seer** bur-tu-**qaal***
orange/oranges	*bur-tu-**qaal**/bur-tu-**qaan***
organization	*tan-**THeem***
oryx	*ow-**reeks***
other identification	*ha-**wee**-a **akh**-ra*
ourselves	*naf-su-**naa***
out of the service area	***khaa**-raj min-**Ta**-qa al-**khid**-ma*
outlet	*man-**fadh***
outside	***fee** (**bi**-) al-**khaa**-rij*
outside line	***khuT khaa**-rij-**ee**-a*
oven	***farn***
owner (also "friend")	***Saa**-Hib*
package (a packet)	***'ul**-ba*
page	***Suf**-Ha*
paid/he pays	***da**-fa-'a/**yad**-f'aa*
painkillers	*ha-**boob** ma-**sak**-an-a*
painted/he paints	***low**-wa-na/ya-**low**-wan*
paler	***af**-taH*
pampering	*tad-**leel***
pan	*i-**naa'h***

paper money (bills)	*fu-**loos** **wa**-ra-qee*
paper/papers	***wa**-ra-qa/ow-**raaq***
parachuting (skydiving)	*ha-**booT** bil-ma-THa-**laat***
parent/s	***waa**-lad/waa-lad-**doon***
park	*Ha-**dee**-qa*
party/parties (event)	***Haf**-la/Haf-**laat***
passenger list	***qaa**-'hi-ma ar-ru-**kaab***
passenger/passengers	*raa-**kib**/ruk-**kaab***
passport (travel pass)	*ja-**waaz** as-**saf**-r*
pastime/entertainment/distraction	*tas-**lee**-a*
pastry	*mu-'aj-jan-**aat***
paternal aunt/s	***'am**-ma/'am-**maat***
paternal uncle/s	***'am**/i'am-**aam***
path	*Ta-**reeq***
patient (m/f)	*Sa-boor/Sa-**boor**-a*
paused/he pauses	*ta-**waq**-qa-fa/ya-ta-**waq**-qaf*
payment	***mad**-fu'u*
payments/disbursements	*Sar-fee-**yaat***
peace	*sa-**laam***
peaceful	*sal-am-**mee**-a*
pearl	***lu'h**-lu'h*
pediatrician	*Ta-**beeb** aT-**faal***
pen	***qa**-lam*
pencil	***qa**-lam ra-**SaaS***
people	***naas***
pepper	***fal**-fal*
perfume/perfumes	***'iT**-r/'u-**Toor***
perhaps	***ru**-bim-aa*
permit	***rukh**-Sa*
person	***shakhS***
personal	***shakh**-See*
Personal Identification Number (PIN)	***raq**-m **shakh**-See*
personal things	*ash-**yaa'h** shakh-**See**-ya*
pharmacy	***Sai**-dal-**lee**-ya*
phone	***haa**-tif*
phone exchange	*ba-**daa**-la*
photograph (picture)	***Soo**-ra*
physical therapy	*'a-**laaj** Ta-bee-'iee*
picture/pictures	***Soo**-ra/**Sa**-war*
piece/pieces	***qiT**-'aa/**qiT**-'a*
pill/pills	***hab**-ba/ha-**boob***
pillow	*wi-**saa**-da*
pills	***Hab**-ba/Hab-**boob***
pilot	*Tai-**yaar***
pink	***war**-dee/war-**dee**-ya*
plan/project	***khuT**-Ta*
planning	*takh-**TeeT***
plants	*na-baa-**taat***
plate	***SaH**-n*
platform/sidewalk	*ra-**Seef***
platinum	*blaa-**teen***
played/he plays	***la**-'ib-ba/**yal**-'aab*
playground	***mal**-'aab*
playing	***la**-'ib*
playing cards	***la**-'ib ow-**raaq** al-**l'ab***
playing guitar	***'iaa**-zif al-ghee-**taar***
please	*ra-**jaa**-'han*
pleasure/fun/enjoyment	*tas-**lee**-a*
pleasured (m/f)	*mus-**roor**/mus-**roor**-a*
plus	*mu-**Daa**-fan **'il**-a*
pocket	***jeeb***
pocketwatch	***saa'aa** lil-**jeyb***
poisoning	*ta-**sam**-man*
police	***shur**-Ta*
police officer	***Daa**-biT **shur**-Ta*
police station	*Mu-**HuT**-Ta ash-**shur**-Ta*

policeman/ policewoman	***shur**-tee/shur-**tee**-a*
polio	*sha-**laal** **Tif**-li*
polite (m/f)	*mu-**'had**-dab/mu-**'had**-dab-a*
pork	***laH**-m **khin**-zeer*
porridge	*'a-**See**-da*
port	*mee-**naa'h***
porter	*Ham-**maal***
Portugal	*bur-tu-**ghaal***
possibly	*min al-**mum**-kin*
post (mail)	*ba-**reed***
post office	***daar** al-ba-**reed***
postage	***uj**-ra al-ba-**reed***
postage box (mailbox)	***Sun**-dooq ba-**reed***
postage stamp	***Taa**-bi-'aa ba-**reed***
postcard	*bi-**Taa**-qa ba-ree-**dee**-ya*
pot	*ib-**reeq***
potato	*ba-**Taa**-Ta*
powder	*mas-**Hooq***
Praise be to God	*al-**Ham**-du lil-**laah***
prayed/he prays	***Sal**-la/yu-**Sal**-lee*
prayer/prayers	*Sa-**laaa**/Sa-la-**waat***
precious stone	***Ha**-jar ka-**reem***
precisely (perfect)	*ta-**maa**-man*
prescription	***waS**-fa*
present (here)	*mow-**jood***
president (boss)	*ra-**'hees***
price	***si'r***
prince	***a**-meer*
printed/he prints	***Ta**-ba-'aa/**yaT**-ba'a*
printer	*tab-**baa'a***
private cabin	***qam**-ra **khaa**-Sa*
private line	***khaTT khaaS***
problem	*mush-**kil**-a*
processor	*mu-**'aaa**-la-ja*
product	*man-**tooj***
production	*Si-**naa'a***
professor (m/f)	*us-**taadh**/us-**taadh**-a*
program	*bar-**naa**-maj*
proper	*mu-**naa**-sib*
protected/he protects	***sal**-la-ma/yu-sal-lim*
province	*mu-**qaa**-T'aa*
psychology	***'al**-m an-**nafs***
pub	***Haa**-na*
public phone	***haa**-tif 'u-**moo**-mee*
public road	*Ta-**reeq** al-**'aam***
pudding	*Hal-wee-**yaat***
purchase	*shi-**raa'h***
pure	***naq**-qee*
purple	*ur-ju-**waa**-nee/ ur-ju-waa-**nee**-ya*
purse (money tote)	***kees** an-nu-**qood***
pyramids	*ah-**raam***
Qatar	***qaT**-ar*
quarter	***rub**-'a*
question/questions	*soo-**'hal**/as-'hi-la*
quiet (m/f)	***haa**-di'h/haa-di'h-a*
Quiet!	***is**-kut!*
quit/he quits (stop/pause)	*ta-**waq**-qa-fa/ya-ta-**waq**-qaf*
race/races	*si-**baaq**/si-baaq-**aat***
radiator (engine cooler)	*tab-**reed** al-mu-**har**-rik*
radio	***raad**-yoo*
railways	***sik**-ka Ha-**deed**-a*
rains	*am-**Taar***
ran/he runs	***ra**-ka-da/**yar**-kuD*
razor	***moo**-sa al-Hi-**laaq**-a*
reading	*qi-**raa'h***
ready	*mus-**ta**-'id*
real estate tax	*Da-**reeb**-a 'a-**qaa**-ree-a*

really	*fi-’**al**-an*
rebate	***khaS**-m*
receipt	*iy-**Saal***
received/he receives	*is-**taq**-ba-la/yis-taq-bil*
reception	*is-tiq-**baal***
recreation	***nuz**-ha*
red (m/f)	***aH**-mar/Ham-**raa’h***
Red Sea (The)	*al-**ba**-Hr al-**aH**-mar*
refrigerator	*thal-**laaj**-a*
regarding (as for)	***am**-ma fa*
regarding (in particular)	*bi-khu-**SooS***
relative/relatives	*a-**qaa**-rib/aq-ri-**baa’h***
relaxation	***is**-tir-**khaa’h***
removed/he removes	***na**-za-’aa/**yan**-za’a*
renewal	*taj-**deed***
rent	***uj**-ra*
rental	*ee-**jaar**-ee*
rental car	*sa-**yaa**-ra ee-**jaar**-a*
repaired/he repairs	***aS**-la-Ha/**yuS**-liH*
report	*taq-**reer***
request	***Ta**-lab*
reservation	***Haj**-z*
reserved/he reserves	***Ha**-ja-za/**yuH-jiz***
resided/he resides	***sa**-ka-na/**yas**-kun*
residence	***suk**-na*
resident	***saa**-kin*
responsible (m/f)	*mas-’**hool**/mas-’**hool-a***
restaurant	***maT**-’am*
return address	*’un-**waan** al-i-**yaab***
returned/he returns	*’**aaa**-da/yu-’**aa**-id*
rice	***ruzz***
riding	*ar-ra-**koob***
right (direction)	*ya-**meen***
ring	***khaa**-tim*
river	***na**-hr*
robbery	***sa**-ri-qa*
rock climbing	*tas-**sal**-laq aS-Su-**khoor***
rode/he rides	***ra**-ka-ba/ya-**rak**-ab*
roof	***saT**-H*
room service	***khid**-ma al-**ghur**-fa*
room/s (in a building)	***ghur**-fa/**ghu**-raf*
rosemary	*ik-**leel***
rotten	*mu-ta-’**af**-fin*
round	*daa-’**hir**-ee*
ruby	*yaa-**qoot aH**-man*
rug (also blanket)	*baT-**Taa**-nee-ya*
ruins	*kha-**raa**-’hib*
rumor	***shaa**-’hi-’aa*
runway	*mad-**dar**-aj*
Russian	***roo**-see*
rye	***jaaow**-daar*
saffron	*za’af-**raan***
said/he says	***qaa**-la/ya-**qool***
sailboat	*sha-raa-’**iee**-a*
sailing	*ib-**Haar***
salad	*sa-**la**-Ta*
sale (reduced price)	***rukh**-Sa*
sales	***bu**-yu’u-**aat***
salt	***milH***
sand	***ram**-l*
sand dunes	*kuth-**baan** ar-ra-**maal***
sandal/sandals	***na’al**/ni-’**aaal***
sandstorms	*ri-**yaaH** ram-**lee**-a*
sandwich	*san-**dweesh***
sane	*ma’a-**qool***
sapphire	***Ha**-jar as-sa-**feer***
satellite phone	***haa**-tif **qam**-ree*
Saudi Arabia	*as-s’aoo-**dee**-a*
sausage	*su-**juq***

savings account	*Hi-**Saab** tow-**feer***
saw/he sees/I saw	***raa**-'ha/**ya**-ra/raa-'**hey**-tu*
scanner	***maa**-siH Dow-**'hee***
scar	***ath**-r aj-**jurH***
scheduled/ he schedules	***had**-da-da/yu-**had**-did*
school	***mad**-ra-sa*
science	*al-'**al**-m*
scissors	*mi-**qaSS***
scream (noun)	***Sar**-kha*
screen	***low**-Ha ma-**faa**-taH*
sea	***ba-Hr***
searched/he searches	***ba**-Ha-tha/ **yab**-Hath (with **'an**)*
seat/seats	***maq**-'ad/ma-**qaa**-'id*
seatbelts	***aH**-zim-a ma-**qaa**-'id*
second (m/f)	***thaa**-nee/**thaa**-nee-a*
second/seconds	***thaa**-nee-a/tha-**waa**-nee*
secondary school	***mad**-ra-sa thaa-na-**wee**-a*
secretary	*sak-ra-**teer***
section/division	***qis**-m*
security	***am**-n*
security box	***khaz**-na al-**Hif**-iTH*
security screening	*faH-s **am**-an-nee*
self/selves	***naf**-s/nu-**foos***
sent/he sends	***ar**-sa-la/**yur**-sil*
sentence	***jum**-la*
September	*sib-**tim**-bir/ay-**lool***
served/he serves	***kha**-da-ma/**yakh**-dim*
service/services	***khid**-ma/khid-**maat***
sesame	***sim**-sim*
settled	***thaa**-bit*
settlement	*mus-**tow**-Ta-na*
seventh (m/f)	***saa**-b'i/**saa**-b'i-a*
severe pain	***al**-am sha-**deed***
sewed/he sews	***khaa**-Ta/ya-**kheet***
shade from the sun	***THul** min ash-**shams***
shampoo	***shaam**-boo*
shape/shapes (also) form/forms	***shak**-l/ash-**kaal***
shared/he shares	*iq-**ta**-sa-ma/yaq-**ta**-sim*
shaved/he shaves	***Ha**-la-qa/**yaH**-liq*
shaving brush	*fur-**shaaa** Hi-**laa**-qa*
shawarma (sandwich)	*sha-**waar**-ma*
shawl	***shaal**/shaal-**aat***
she (is)	***hee**-a*
shelves	*ru-**foof***
ship	*sa-**fee**-na*
shipping (shipment)	***shaH**-Hann*
shirt/shirts	*qa-**meeS**/qum-**Saan***
shock	*ta-**Saa**-dum*
shoe/shoes	*Hi-**dhaa'h**/aH-**dhee**-a*
shopping center	***mar**-kaz at-ta-**saw**-wuq*
short (m/f)	*qa-**Seer**/qa-**Seer**-a*
shorter	***aq**-Sar*
shorts (short pants)	*ban-Ta-**loon** qa-**Seer***
shoulder/shoulders	***kat**-if/ak-**taaf***
shoulder-length	***Tool** al-**kat**-if*
shower	***doosh***
sick (ill)	*ma-**reeD***
sight (spectacle)	***maTH**-har/**mash**-had*
signals	*i-shaa-**raat***
silence	***Sumt***
silver	***fiD**-Da*
silver-colored	***fiD**-Dee/fiD-**Dee**-ya*
silverware	*a-**waan** fiD-**Dee**-ya*
simple	*ba-**Seet***
since	***mun**-dhu*
singing	*ghi-**naa'h***
single (m/f)	***a'a**-zib/**a'a**-zib-a*

sink	***HowD***
sir/lady	*sa*-***eed****/sa*-***eed***-*a*
sister/s	***ukht****/ukh-a*-***waat***
Sit!	***ij***-*lis!*
site (location)	***mow***-*q'i*
sitting	*ju*-***loos***
situation	***Haal***-*a*
sixth (m/f)	***saa***-*dis/****saa***-*dis-a*
size	***Haj***-*m*
skin	***jild***
skirt	*tan*-***noor***-*a*
skyscraper	***naa***-*Ti-Hat sa*-***Haab***
sleeping	***nowm***
slower	***ab***-*Taa'h*
slowly	*bi*-***buT***-*Ta'h*
small (m/f)	*Sa*-***gheer****/Sa*-***gheer***-*a*
small car	*sa*-***yaa***-*ra Sa*-***gheer***-*a*
smaller	***aS***-*ghar*
smallpox	*ju*-***da***-*ree*
smart (m/f)	***dha***-*kee/dha*-***kee***-*a*
smoking	*tad*-***kheen***
sneezing	***'aT***-*sa*
snow skiing	*ta*-***zal***-*laj* ***'al***-*a al*-***thalj***
snow/ice	***thalj***
so (thus)	***ha***-*ka-dha*
soap	***Saa***-*boon*
soccer	***kur***-*a al*-***qad***-*am*
socks	***jow***-*rab qa*-***Seer***
soda	***Soo***-*daa*
sofa	*a*-***ree***-*ka*
soft (m/f)	***naa***-*'im/****naa***-*'im -a*
software (programs)	*ba*-***raa***-*maj*
sold/he sells	***baa***-*'aa/ya*-***bee***-*'u*
some	***b'aD***
someday	***yoom***-*an* ***maa***
someplace	*ma*-***kaan*** *maa*
something to drink	***shey***-*'han lil-sha*-***raab***
sometimes	*aH*-***Hyaa***-*nan*
son/sons	***ib***-*n/ib*-***naa'h***
soon (nearby)	*qa*-***reeb***-*an*
sore throat	***al***-*am al*-***Halq***
sorry (m/f)	***as***-*if/****as***-*if-a*
soup	***shoor***-*ba*
south	*ja*-***noob***
souvenir	*tadh*-***kaar***
Spanish (language)	*al*-***as***-*baa*-***nee***-*a*
Spanish (person)	*as*-***baa***-*nee/as*-***baa***-*nee-a*
spare (reserve) tire	***'aj***-*la iH-tee-yaa*-***Tee***-*a*
special/personal	***khaaS***-*(-a)*
specific	*mu-ta*-***mey***-*yiz*
speech (conversation)	*Ha*-***deeth***
speech (lecture)	*khi*-***Taab***
speed	***sur***-*'aa*
spend time	***maD***-*Dee* ***waq***-*t*
spent/he spends (money)	***Sa***-*ra-fa/****yaS***-*rif*
Sphinx	***ab***-*oo al-ha*-***lool***
spice/spices	***taa***-*bil/ta*-***waa***-*bil*
spoke/he speaks	*ta*-***Had***-*da-tha/ ya-ta*-***Had***-*dath*
sponge	*is*-***fan***-*ja*
sponsor	*mu-ta*-***kal***-*lif*
spoon	*mil*-***'aa***-*qa*
sport/sports	*ri*-***yaaD***-*a/ri*-***yaaD***-*aat*
sports	*ar-ri*-***yaa***-*Da*
spread the word	***na***-*sha-ra al-ka-li-ma*
spring	*rab*-***bee***-*i'*
square	*mu*-***rab***-*b'a*
stain	***buq***-*'aa*
staircase	*sul*-***lam***

stairway	*da-ra-ja*
stamp	*Taa-bi-'aa*
Stand!	*qoom!*
star/stars	*naj-m/nu-joom*
starch	*na-shaa'h*
stars	*nu-joom*
startup problem	*mush-kil-a ib-ti-daa-'hee-a*
state/nation	*wa-laa-ya/dow-la*
static	*tash-weesh*
static interference	*tash-weesh bath i-dhaa-'iee*
station	*ma-HaT-Ta*
stay here	*tab-qey hu-naa*
stereo	*ji-haaz as-tir-yoo*
stew	*yakh-na*
still (ongoing)	*maa zaa-la*
stomach	*ma-'i-da*
stop (as in bus stop)	*mow-qif*
stop sign	*laa-fi-ta at-taw-waq-qif*
Stop!	*qif!*
store (shop)/stores	*duk-kaan/da-kaa-neen*
storm/storms	*'aaa-Si-fa/'a-waa-Sif*
straight ahead	*qu-du-man*
Strait of Gibraltar	*ma-Daiq jab-il Taa-riq*
strange	*gha-reeb*
strawberry	*fa-raaow-la*
stream	*jad-wal*
street lamp	*mis-baaH ash-shaa-r'i*
street/streets	*shaa-r'i/sha-waa-r'i*
stretcher	*naq-qaa-la*
stroke (illness)	*jal-Ta*
strong (m/f)	*qa-wee/qa-wee-a*
strong signal	*i-dhaa-'aa qa-wee-a*
stronger	*aq-waa*
student	*Taa-lib*
studied/he studies	*da-ra-sa/yad-rus*
studies	*di-raa-sa*
subject	*mow-Doo-'a*
suburbs	*Du-waa-Hee*
Sudan	*as-soo-daan*
sudden pains	*aa-laam mu-faa-ji-'ha*
suffices	*yak-fee*
sugar	*suk-kar*
suit	*badh-la*
suitcase	*Ha-qee-ba/Ha-qaa-'hib*
suite	*ja-naaH*
summer	*Saif*
sun	*shams*
sunburn	*Ha-rooq ash-shams*
sunglasses	*na-Thaa-raat sham-see-ya*
sunstroke	*Darb-at ash-shams*
supplies	*tam-ween*
support (backing)	*mu-naa-Sa-ra*
surgeon	*jar-raaH*
surgery	*ji-raa-Ha*
swam	*si-baa-Ha*
swam/he swims	*sa-ba-Ha/yas-baH*
sweat	*'ar-aq*
sweater	*kan-za*
swelling	*war-ram/in-ti-faakh*
swimming	*as-si-baa-Ha*
swimming pool	*mas-baH*
Syria	*soo-ree-a*
table	*maa-'hi-da*
table (cognate)	*Taa-wi-la*
talked/he talks	*ta-kal-la-ma/ya-ta-kal-lam*
talking	*ka-laam*
Tangier (Tangiers)	*Tan-ja*
tapestry	*na-seej*
tariff	*t'a-ree-fa*
Tariq's Mountain	*jab-il Ta-riq*

tax	*Da-**reeb**-a*
tax-free (free of taxes)	***m'u**-fee min aD-Da-**raa**-'bib*
tea	***shaai***
tea set (tea service)	***Taq**-m ash-**shaai***
teacher	*mu-**dar**-ris/mu-**'al**-lim*
teacup	*fin-**jaan shaai***
team	***fir**-qa*
teapot (kettle)	*ib-**reeq** ash-**shaai***
technical	*tak-**nee**-kee*
technical school	***mad**-ra-sa tak-nee-**kee**-a*
telephone	*ta-li-**foon/haa**-tif*
telephone card	*bi-**Taa**-qa **haa**-tif-**ee**-ya*
telephone operator	***'aaa**-mal al-**haa**-tif*
tell me	***qool lee***
temperature	***da**-ra-ja al-Ha-**raar**-a*
temples	*ma-**'aaa**-bid*
tennis	***kur**-a al-**miD**-rab/**tan**-is*
tenth (m/f)	***'aaa**-shir/**'aaa**-shir-a*
term	***fat**-ra*
terrace (balcony)	***shur**-fa*
thank you	*shu-**kraan***
thankful	*mush-**koor**/mush-**koor**-a*
that (f/that one)	*til-**ka***
that (m/that one)	***dha**-li-ka*
that is true	***ha**-dhaa Sa-**HeeH***
that/in order that	***an***
the	***al***
the best	*al-**aH**-san*
theater (stage)	*mas-ra-**Hee**-ya*
themselves (f)	*naf-su-**hun**-na*
themselves (m)	*naf-su-**hum***
then	***thu**-ma*
There is …	*hu-**naa**-ka …*
there is no service	***ley**-sat ta-**koon khid**-ma*
therefore	***fa***
thermometer	*mey-**zaan** al-Ha-**raar**-a*
these (m/f)	*ha-'hu-**laa'h***
they (d/f)	*hum-**aa***
they (d/m)	*hum-**aa***
they (f)	*hun-na*
they (m)	***hum***
thicker	***ath**-khan*
thing/things	***shey**/ash-**yaa'h***
thinner	***ar**-qaq*
third (m/f)	***thaa**-lath/**thaa**-lath-a*
thirsty	*'aT-**shaan***
this (f)	***ha**-dha-hi*
this (m)	***ha**-dhaa*
this month …	***ha**-dhaa ash-**sha**-hr …*
those (m/f)	*oo-**laa**-'hi-ka*
thought/he thinks	***fak**-ka-ra/yu-**fak**-kir*
thousand/thousands	***alf**/aal-**aaf***
throat	***Halq***
through (by way of)	*bi-**waa**-Si-ta*
thyme	***za'a**-tar*
ticket	*bi-**Taa**-qa as-**saf**-r*
ticket	*b-**Taa**-qat/**tadh**-kir-a*
ticket for the day	***tadh**-kir-a lil-**yoom***
ticket office/desk	***mak**-tab at-**tadh**-kir*
tight (fitting)	***Da**-yiq*
Tigris River	***na**-hr **dij**-la*
time/times	***waq-t**/ow-**qaat***
tip (gratuity)	***baq**-sheesh*
tire wrench	*mif-**taaH rab**-T lil-'aj-**laat***
tire/tires	***'aj**-la/'aj-**laat***
tired	*ta'a-**baan***
to	***il**-a*
to be (verb)	***kaa**-na*
to be able to …	***qaa**-dir/ mu-ta-**mak**-kin min …*

today	*al-**yoom***
toe	***iS**-b'a al-**qad**-am*
together	***m'a**-aan/sa-**wee**-an*
toilet	*twaa-**leet***
toll-free	*ma-**jaa**-nee*
tomato	*Ta-**maa**-Ta*
Tomb of Saladin	***qab**-r Sa-**laaH** ad-**deen***
tomorrow	***ghad**-dan*
tongue	*li-**saan***
took/he takes	***a**-kha-dha/yu-**a**-khad*
tooth/teeth	***sinn**/is-**naan***
toothbrush	*fur-**shaa** al-is-**naan***
toothpaste	*m'a-**joon** al-is-**naan***
torn	***hee**-a **maz**-za-qa*
total price	***si'r** al-**kaa**-mil*
tour	***jow**-la*
tour bus	***Haa**-fil-a see-yaa-**Hee**-a*
tourism	*si-**yaa**-Ha*
tourist/(f)	*si-**yaa**-Hee/Hee-a*
tournament	*mu-**baa**-raa*
towel	***min**-sha-fa*
tower	***burj***
town/village	*qa-**ree**-a*
toy/toys	***lu'u**-ba/lu'u-**baat***
traditional costumes	*az-**yaa'h taq**-lee-**dee**-ya*
traffic	***Ha**-ra-kat al-mu-**roor***
traffic circle/ roundabout	*da-**waar***
traffic jam	*zi-**Haam***
traffic light	*i-**shaa**-ra al-mu-**roor***
traffic police	***shur**-Ta al-mu-**roor***
train	*qi-**Taar***
train(s) station	*ma-**HaT**-Ta al-qi-Taar-**aat***
training (jogging) suit	***badh**-la tad-ree-**bee**-ya*
training (practice)	*tad-**reeb***
transaction fee	*mu-**kaa**-faa-'ha **Saf**-qa*
transfer	*tab-**deel***
transferred/ he transfers	***Haw**-wa-la/yu-**Haw**-wil*
translator	*mu-**tar**-jim*
trash (garbage)	*zu-**baa**-la*
travel (noun)	***saf**-r*
traveled/he travels	***saa**-fa-ra/yu-**saa**-fir*
traveler	*mu-**saa**-fir*
travelers' checks	***Suk** see-**yaa**-Hee*
tree	***sha**-ja-ra*
triangle	*mu-**thal**-lath*
tried/he tries	***Haa**-wa-la/yu-**Haa**-wil*
Tripoli	*Tu-**raab**-lis*
trousers	*sa-raa-**weel***
truth	***Haq***
tumor	***wa**-ram*
Tunis	***too**-nis*
Tunisia	***too**-nis*
turkey	***deek roo**-mee*
Turn!	***door**!*
turned/he turns	***daa**-ra/ya-**dowr***
turn-off	***yow**-kif*
turn-on	***yash**-ghul*
turquoise	*fey-**rooz***
twelfth (m/f)	***thaa**-nee **'aaa**-shir/ thaa-**nee**-a **'aaa**-shir*
type	***now**-'a*
typewriter	*mik-**taab***
ugly	*qa-**beeH***
umbrella	*mi-**THal**-la*
unconscious person	***shakhS faa**-qid al-**wa**-'iee*
under/below	***taHt***
underwear	*ma-**laa**-bis daakh-**lee**-ya*
university	***jaa**-m'ia*

unknown	*maj-**bool***
until/as far as	***Hat**-ta*
upgrade	*tar-**qee**-a*
used/he uses	*is-**ta'am**-al/yas-**ta'a**-mil*
used/he uses	*is-**takh**-da-ma/yas-**takh**-dim*
useful	*mu-**feed***
using/the use	*is-ti'i-**maal (or)** is-tikh-**daam***
value/fare/cost	***tha**-man*
various	*mukh-**ta**-lif*
vases	*maz-ha-**ree**-ya*
vegetables	*khud-ru-**waat***
vehicle	***'a**-ra-ba*
ventilator	*ji-**haaz** at-tah-**wee**-a*
verily	***yaa***
very	***jid**-dan*
very big	*ka-**beer jid**-dan*
very good	***jeyd jid**-dan*
very hot	***Haar jid**-dan*
very small	*Sa-**gheer jid**-dan*
vice president	***naa**-'hib ra-**'hees***
video card	***kaart fee**-dee-yoo*
video conference	***mu'h**-ta-mar **fee**-dee-yoo*
video game	***lu'u**-ba **fee**-dee-yoo*
view (noun)	***man**-THar*
viewed/he views	***na**-THa-ra/**yan**-THar*
visa	*taa'h-**sheer**-a*
visit (noun)	*zi-**yaa**-ra*
visited/he visits	***zaa**-ra/yu-**zoor***
vocational	*ma-ha-**nee**-a*
vocational school	***mad**-ra-sa ma-ha-**nee**-a*
volcano	*bur-**kaan***
volleyball	***kur**-a aT-**Taa**-'hir-a*
waist	***kha**-Sir*
waited/he waits	*in-**ta**-THa-ra/yan-**ta**-THar*
Walk!	***im**-shee!*
walked/he walks	***mash**-a/**yam**-shee*
walking	*al-**mash**-ee*
wall	*ji-**daar***
wallet	***Haa**-fi-THa*
war	***Harb***
warmer/hotter	*a-**Harr***
was/it is	***kaa**-na/ya-**koon***
washer and dryer	*ghas-**saa**-la wa mu-**jaf**-fif*
watch (timepiece)	***saa'aa***
water plants	***saq**-a al-na-baa-**taat***
water/waters	***maa'h**/mi-**yaah***
waterfall	*sha-**laal***
we	***naH**-nu*
weak (m/f)	*Da-**'ieef**/Da-**'ieef-a***
weather	***Taqs***
website	***mow**-q'i al-**in**-tir-**nat***
wedding	*zi-**faaf***
week/weeks	*us-**boo**-'a/a-**saa**-bee-'a*
weekly	*us-boo-**'aee**-yan*
weight	***waz**-n*
welcome	***mar**-Ha-ban*
went/he goes	***dha**-ha-ba/**yadh**-hab*
west	***gharb***
what	***maa**-dha/**maa***
What do I do?	***maa**-dha **af**-'al?*
What happened?	***maa**-dha **Ha**-da-tha?*
what I think …	***maa** u-**fak**-kir …*
What's the problem?	***maa hee**-a al-mush-**kil**-a?*
wheat	***qamH***
wheelchair	***kur**-see al-mu-ta-**Har**-rak*
when	***mat**-a*
when (statement)	***'and**-a-maa*
When are you (pl/m) …	***mat**-a an-**tum** …*
when/since	***in**-na*

whenever	***kul***-*la*-***maa***
where	***ai***-*na*
wherever	***Hai***-*thu*-***maa'h***
which	***ai***
whipped cream	***kree***-*ma makh*-***fooq***-*a*
white	***ab***-*yaD/bai*-***Daa'h***
White House	***beyt*** *al*-***ab***-*yaD*
who	***man***
why	*li*-***maa***-*dha*
Why?	*li*-***maa***-*dha?*
why not	*li*-***maa laa***
wife	***zow***-*ja*
wife (also "woman")	***mur***-*ra*
wildlife	*Hi*-***yaa*** *bu*-***ree***-*a*
window	***naa***-*fi*-*dha*
windows	*na*-***waa***-*fa*-*dha*
winds (that blow)	*ri*-***yaaH***
windshield wipers	*mas*-***saa***-*Ha az*-*zu*-***jaaj***
wine	*na*-***beedh***
winter	*shi*-***taa'h***
wire	***silk***
wireless	***laa sil***-*kee*
with	***m'a***
with me	***m'a***-*ee*
with/having	*la*-***dey***
withdrew/withdraws	***sa***-*Ha*-*ba*/***yas***-*Hab*
without	*bi*-***doon***
witness	***shaa***-*hid*
witnessed/ he witnesses	***shaa***-*hi*-*da*/***yash***-*hid*
woke/he wakes	*is*-***tey***-*qa*-*THa/yas*-***tey***-*qaTH*
woman	*im*-***ra***-*'ha*
won (he won)	***faa***-*za*
wool/wools	***Soof***/*aS*-***waaf***
work (noun)	***'am-l***
workday	***yoom*** *al*-***'am***-*l*
worked/he works	***'aa***-*mi*-*la*/***ya'a***-*mal*
worth the cost	*ja*-***deer*** *bil*-***tha***-*man*
wound/wounds	***jurH***/*aj*-***raH***
wounded/injured	*maj*-***rooH***
wrist	***rusgh***
writer/writers	***kaa***-*tib*/***ku***-*tub*
writing	*ki*-***taa***-*ba*
written	*mak*-***toob***
wrong (not right)	***gheyr*** *Sa*-***HeeH***
wrote/he writes	***ka***-*ta*-*ba*/***yak***-*tub*
yacht	***yakht***
yard/yards	***yaard***/*yaard*-***aat***
year	***san***-*a*
yearly	*san*-*aw*-***wee***-*yan*
yellow	***aS***-*far/Saf*-***raa'h***
Yemen	*al*-***yam***-*in*
yes	***n'am***
yogurt	***lab***-*an*
you (d/f)	*an*-*tum*-***aa***
you (d/m)	*an*-*tum*-***aa***
you (p/f)	*an*-***tun***-*na*
you (p/m)	***an***-*tum*
you (s/f)	***an***-*ti*
you (s/m)	***an***-*ta*
you are right	*m'a*-*ka al*-***Haq***
yourself (f)	*naf*-*su*-***ki***
yourself (m)	*naf*-*su*-***ka***
yourselves (f)	*naf*-*su*-***kun***-*na*
yourselves (m)	*naf*-*su*-***kum***
youth center	***mar***-*kaz ash*-*sha*-***baab***
zero	***Sif***-*r*
zoo	*Ha*-***dee***-*qa al*-***Hai***-*waan*

Appendix D

Answers to "Practice Makes Perfect"

Chapter 1

1. *al-**magh**-rib*
2. Egypt
3. Iraq, Jordan, Saudi Arabia, Bahrain, Qatar, the United Arab Emirates (UAE), Oman, and Yemen
4. The Red Sea

Chapter 2

1. *kaf-an; hoop* or *howp*
2. The Arabic *u* sounds more like the vowels in the English words "good" and "hood" than in words like "under" and "but."
3. Arabic does not have the "short e" sound, so the words should probably be written "Maghrib" and "Marrakash."

4. Arabic has three long vowels, three short vowels, and two diphthongs. The vowel sound *ee* can sometimes sound like *ai* or *ey*.

5. None of the Arabic sounds will be difficult once you practice enough, but for me, *gh* was the hardest sound to learn because it is a vocalized form of *kh*.

Chapter 3

1. ***wa, al, yaa, laa***

Track 4

2. *ar-**raj**-al laa im-**ra**-'ha*. Remember that "r" is a Sun Letter, so the "l" on ***al*** is not pronounced. Don't worry if you miss that little piece. It wouldn't affect someone's ability to understand you.

3. ***qiT**-Ta* is Arabic for "cat (f)," so using the ***–aat*** rule we get ***qiT**-Taat* as the plural, "cats."

4. Sun Letters cause the "l" in the definite article "***al***" to not be heard. With Moon Letters, you hear the "l."

5. *al-**fuS**-fuS-a* means "alfalfa," and the words are examples of cognates.

6. *di-**mashq*** is a cognate for Damascus, which is in Syria.

7. is, are, a, an

Chapter 4: Whose Numbers Are They?

1. 194 = ***mi**-'ha **ar**-b'a-a wa tis-'a-**oon***

   283 = *mi-'ha-**teyn** tha-**laa**-tha wa tha-maa-**noon***

   56 = ***sit**-ta wa **kham**-soon*

2. An ordinal number is used to determine order (for example, "fifth").

3. The numbers 3 to 10 get plural nouns; all nouns after that are singular.

4. *tha-**laa**-tha wa **nuS**-uf*

5. ***sab**-'a-a **il**-a **rub**-'a*

6. *tha-**laa**-tha da-**qaa**-iq*

7. *a-**Had**-a **'ash**-ar **thaa**-nee-a*

8. ***sab**-'a-a am-**taar***

Chapter 5

1. First person (I), second person (you), third person (they)
2. Three
3. *ra-**kab**-tu*
4. *si-ya-**rak**-ab-**oon***
5. ***zur**-tu al-**mak**-tab-a*

Track 12

Chapter 6

1. ***an**-a*
2. *ta-**rak**-a-hu* (the final syllable shows the "it")
3. *ta-rak-a-**haa*** (Tricky: the third-person feminine singular is similar to second-person male singular)
4. ***dha**-hab-at as-sa-yaa-**raat*** (Plural nonhuman is conjugated like third-person feminine singular; the verb doesn't necessarily need to be first)
5. When you are looking at nouns. The dual is uncommon in everyday speech or writing.

Chapter 7

1. *sa-**yaa**-ra **mu-tas**-sikh-a*

Track 19

2. ***hee**-a 'i-raa-**qee**-a*
3. It has *–**an*** as its ending.
4. A preposition with a noun (example: "with speed" instead of "quickly")
5. ***hee**-a **fee** al-**beyt***. Note: you can change the preposition to whatever you wish in order to practice speaking.
6. that, and, therefore, because, but
7. John's car, or "the car of John"

Chapter 8

1. ***hal***
2. ***hal tadh****-hab-****oon****?*
3. Who = ***man;*** what = ***maa/maa****-dha;* where = ***ai****-na;* when = ***mat****-a;* why = *li-****maa****-dha;* how = ***keyf****-a;* which = ***ai;*** how much/many = ***kam***
4. ***ai*** *im-****raa****-'ha* ***dha****-hab-at.*
5. We stopped at the restaurant.
6. ***an****-a a-****ta'al****-lam al-'****ar****-ra-****bee****-a. raj-****jaa****-'han at-ta-****kal****-lam bi-****buT****-Ta'h.*

Chapter 9

1. The verb comes first.
2. ***lan tad****-ras*
3. ***min*** *al-****ak****-mal*
4. Turn (feminine/singular) to the left.
5. ***qoom****-oo*
6. ***aq****-rab; al-****aq****-rab*

Chapter 10

1. *ma-****saa'h*** *an-****noor;*** good evening
2. ***keyf****-a* ***SuH****-tu-ka* ***yaa ukh****-ee*
3. Because ***qalb****-ee* (my heart) is very close to ***kalb****-ee* (my dog)
4. ***'af****-wan sa-****eed****-a* (Note: to say "my lady," you say *sa-****eed****-a-tee).*
5. ***jeyd jid****-din*
6. ***ukh****-ee* ***raj****-al* ***dha****-kee* ***jid****-din.* (My brother, man, smart, very)

Chapter 11

1. ***ha**-dha-**bi um**-mee.*
2. How are you (how is your situation) today?
3. ***an**-a as-**baa**-nee-ya wa **zowj**-ee am-**ree**-kee.*
4. This is a trick question. If it were a joke, the answer might be "very carefully." I learned that it is impolite to ask a woman her age (the Arab women I asked told me as much when I inquired). If you insist, the answer would be: ***kam 'um**-ru-ki.*
5. "Meet me in the airport."

Chapter 12

1. ***an**-a min qa-**ree**-a Sa-**ghee**-ra **jid**-dan*
2. Have you worked there for a long time?
3. ***maa**-dha **ta**-f'al **b'ad** al-**'am**-l*
4. Is there a playground near here?
5. ***m'a hoo**-a **raq**-m ta-li-**foon**-u-ki* (Note: use this with caution. You do not want to offend anyone!).

Chapter 13

1. The weather today is very hot.
2. ***da**-ra-ja al-Ha-**raar**-a al-**yoom hee**-a tha-**laa**-tha wa ar-b'a-**een da**-ra-ja mi-'ha-**wee**-a*
3. *hal ta-**faD**-Dal-ee al-Ha-**raar**-a **ak**-thar min al-ba-**roo**-da?*
4. *ri-**yaaH** ar-ra-**maal**; **'aaa**-Si-fa ar-**ram**-l*
5. Either: *u-**reed** as-si-**baa**-Ha fee al-bu-**Hey**-ra*

   I want (the swimming) in the lake.

   or:

   *u-**reed** an **as**-baH fee al-bu-**Hey**-ra.*

   I want (that I swim) in the lake.

Chapter 14

1. ***'and**-ee Su-**daa'a** sha-**deed** wa yu-al-**lim**-nee **daa**-'hi-man.*
2. *a'a-**ta**-qid la-**dey** ('**and**-ee) '**ad**-wa as-**sinn***
3. Lay on (the) back and open (the) mouth.
4. *She* consulted a specialist. (Notice the feminine ending on the verb.)
5. You are in need of a surgical operation and physical therapy.
6. Take (f) two of these and call (f) me in the morning!

Chapter 15

1. *u-**reed** an **a**-ra ah-**raam***
2. *u-**reed** an u-**zoor** al-**magh**-rib*
3. *ra-ma-**Daan***
4. *Hu-zey-**raan***
5. *u-**reed** as-**saf**-r*
6. ***ai**-na **adh**-hab*
7. who = ***man;*** what = ***maa**-dha/maa;* when = ***mat**-a;* where = ***ai**-na;* why = *li-**maa**-dha;* how = ***keyf**-a;* is/are = *hal* (Note: I just included this for review, not to trick you.)
8. ***mat**-a iq-**laa'a***

Chapter 16

1. air conditioner; tires; mirrors; impossible
2. *hal a-**khadh**-ti **ha**-dha-hi ar-**riH**-la min **qab**-l?*
3. What is the location of the first stop?
4. Are there additional fees, or is this the complete price?
5. *al-**Haa**-dith **ley**-sat kha-**Taa'h** min-**nee wa** u-**reed** sa-**yaa**-raa ja-**deed**-a.*

Chapter 17

1. *u-**reed** an **uH**-jiz **ghur**-fa **fee** fun-**duq**-kum*
2. ***ghur**-fa **gheyr** tad-**kheen m'a** sa-**reer**-teyn wa **man**-THar ja-**meel***
3. ***yoom**-an **maa** si-a-khadh **zowj**-a-**tee** li-nu-**Haa**-wil an **na**-ra ma-**kaan maa** ja-**deed***
4. A toothbrush and toothpaste are very important.
5. Answer "a" is correct: the receptionist. Otherwise, you would be asking b) an outside line or c) a hair dryer.

Chapter 18

1. ***an**-a bi-**Haaj**-a nu-**qood** li-**bint**-ee*
2. ***hee**-a **fee Haaj**-a (**taH**-taj)am-**waal** li-**kalb**-haa*
3. How many traffic lights are there before the tower?
4. I have an emergency situation. Is an exception possible?

Chapter 19

1. You don't really expect to find your answer here, do you?
2. ***ah**-lan wa **sah**-lan, is-mee **key wa an**-a **ak**-thar min tha-laa-**theen san**-na. u-**Hib** al-**lugh**-at al-'ar-a-**bee**-a li-'**han**-na-haa **lugh**-a ja-**meel**-a **jid**-dan. '**and**-ee **us**-ra ka-**beer**-a wa **hee**-a mu-**him**-a **jid**-dan **lee**.*

   Hello, and welcome. My name is K. I am more than 30 years old. I like the Arabic language because it (she) is a very beautiful language. I have a large family, and it (she) is very important to me.

Chapter 20

1. ***an**-a **zur**-tu us-**taadh** fee **jaa**-m'ia '**and**-maa **kun**-tu **fee** al-**qaa**-hir-a. **qaa**-la **hoo**-a **lee** an **hoo**-a **mu**-him-a **jid**-dan al-zi-**yaa**-ra **il**-a al-as-**waaq fee** al-ma-**dee**-na. dha-**hab**-naa sa-**wee**-an **wa kaa**-na mum-**taaz**. ash-ta-**rey**-tu ka-**theer min al**-ma-**laa**-bis wa **ai**-Daan ash-**yaa'h li-us**-ra-tee.*

I visited a professor in a university when I was in Cairo. He said to me that it is very important to visit the markets in the city. We went together, and it was wonderful (excellent). I bought many clothes (much clothing) and also things for my family.

Chapter 21

1. *u-**fat**-tish (investigate) 'an **Hal**-wa-**yaat** li-ow-**laad**-ee.*
2. What is the best restaurant in the area?
3. *ra-**jaa**-'han, **maa'h** wa na-**beedh***
4. What are the ingredients in the falafel (pepper balls)?

Chapter 22

1. *ta-waq-**q'aa**-naa* means "we expected." The "*–naa*" at the end shows that the verb "expect" is conjugated for the past tense and for the first-person plural (we).
2. We are still looking for deodorant.
3. ***idh**-hab. **if**-tash **'an**-haa.*
4. Are you (f) able to recommend a pharmacy?
5. We arrived in the morning, and we planned on traveling to the city.
6. I might talk with the doctor. (Note: ***qad*** plus present tense means "might," and ***qad*** plus past tense means "did.")

Chapter 23

1. This is not the shirt I want.
2. ***ukh**-ee **ya'a**-mil **fee magh**-sal*
3. It was nice but not the best.
4. Are you able to recommend a place for repairing a camera?
5. We are busy now, but we will not be present in the future.
6. ***qad** ur-sil **ha**-dhaa aS-**Sun**-dooq ka-ba-**reed jow**-wee?*

Chapter 24

1. This is my new number. Get in touch with (call) me tomorrow.
2. I heard that, and I believe the problem was the battery.
3. *yum-kin-**nee an ow**-Sa bi-**ak**-thar min **ha**-dhaa al-**maT**-'am **fuq**-T.*
4. ***keyf**-a **a'a**-rif **maa man ya**-jib an ta-ta-**kal**-lam **m'a**-hum?*
5. If you go there, you must know there is a dress code.
6. Can I help you? Breathe deeply, and stay here. I will search for your family.

Chapter 25

1. ***ah**-lan wa **sah**-lan **fee** ij-ti-**maa'a**-naa. al-**yoom sowf**-a **nad**-rus qa-**lee**-lan **'an** al-**aa**-la **Haa**-si-ba.*
2. ***'and**-ee mush-**kil**-a tak-nee-**kee**-ya. **an**-a **las**-tu mu-ta-**'ha**-kid **idh**-a-haa ash-**shaa**-sha **ow** al-**low**-Ha ma-**faa**-taH.*
3. *al-mu-**deer** mas-**'hool 'an ha-dha-hi** al-mush-**kil**-a. aS-**Saa**-Hib mas-**'hool 'an** as-**saf**-r **fuq**-T.*
4. Today, I had to go (it was upon me to go) to the market to buy some things from there.

Index

Numbers

A

B

C

D

E

F

G

H

I

J–K

L

O

P

Q

R

S

T

U

V

W-X-Y-Z